Central Sites, Peripheral Visions

HISTORY OF ANTHROPOLOGY

Central Sites, Peripheral Visions

CULTURAL AND INSTITUTIONAL CROSSINGS IN THE HISTORY OF ANTHROPOLOGY

Edited by

Richard Handler

HISTORY OF ANTHROPOLOGY
Volume 11

THE UNIVERSITY OF WISCONSIN PRESS

The University of Wisconsin Press
1930 Monroe Street
Madison, Wisconsin 53711

www.wisc.edu/wisconsinpress/

3 Henrietta Street
London WC2E 8LU, England

Library of Congress Cataloging-in-Publication Data
Central sites, peripheral visions : cultural and institutional crossings in the
history of anthropology / edited by Richard Handler.
p. cm. — (History of anthropology ; v. 11)
Includes bibliographical references and index.
ISBN 0-299-21920-8 (cloth : alk. paper)
1. Anthropology—History. 2. Anthropology—Philosophy. I. Handler, Richard, 1950–
II. Series.
GN17.C44 2006
301.09—dc22
2006008623

Information for Contributors

Normally, every volume of History of Anthropology will be organized around a particular theme of historical and contemporary anthropological significance, although each volume may also contain one or more "miscellaneous studies," and there may be occasional volumes devoted entirely to such studies. Since volume themes will be chosen and developed in the light of information available to the Editorial Board regarding research in progress, potential contributors from all areas in the history of anthropology are encouraged to communicate with the editor concerning their ongoing work.

Manuscripts submitted for consideration to HOA should be typed twenty-six lines to a page, with 1¼-inch margins and *all* material double-spaced. Documentation should be in anthropological style. For exemplification of stylistic details, consult the published volumes; for guidance on any problematic issues, write the editor. Unsolicited manuscripts will not be returned unless accompanied by adequate postage. All communications on editorial matters should be sent to the editor:

Richard Handler
Department of Anthropology
University of Virginia
P.O. Box 400120
Charlottesville, Virginia 22904-4120 U.S.A.

Contents

Central Sites, Peripheral Visions

ANTHROPOLOGY ON THE PERIPHERY OF THE CENTER

Practitioners of a peripheral discipline, anthropologists have long centered their efforts in the conceptual territory stretching between the terms "center" and "periphery." At the turn of the last century, anthropologists looked outward from their newly secured locations at central institutions (museums, universities, and government bureaus in a few globally dominant nation-states in Europe and North America) to the peripheral, "primitive" cultures the discipline had taken as its objects of study. Some anthropologists then (as today) took too literally the distinction between primitive others and civilized selves. Certainly, the racial ideology of those dominant nation-states had uses for (and continues to have use for) a science of primitive (or otherwise inferior) others. But anthropology's countervailing tendency, as articulated at that moment by Boas and his students—to locate the unity of the human species in the inevitably particular cultural experience that constitutes life for all people—reminded practitioners that there are no primitive human beings and that any periphery can be defined only relative to an arbitrarily demarcated center.

Anthropology was nonetheless, then (as now), a peripheral discipline compared to other human sciences that had constituted themselves in terms of objects of study that modern common sense considered central: economics, politics, history, even sociology. This disciplinary configuration is historically specific, of course, as is the conceptual division of reality into objects of study. That anthropology had constituted itself as a discipline was, as Boas suggested, an historical accident:

> The special task that is actually assigned at the present time to the anthropologist is the investigation of the primitive tribes of the world that have no written history, that of pre-historic remains and of the types of man inhabiting the world at present and in past times. It will be recognized that this limitation of the field of work of the anthropologist is more or less accidental, and originated because other sciences occupied part of the ground before the development of modern anthropology. (1908:269)

3

The emergence of those other sciences was also historically accidental. Anthropology's peripheral peoples had "dropped through the boundary spaces between the gradually separating disciplines" of the human sciences during the nineteenth century (Stocking 2001:311). Thus the "work" of studying them fell to anthropologists only because, as Boas put it, "no one else cares for it" (1904:35; cf. Bunzl 2004:437). Or, to put it another way, anthropology created itself as a discipline out of materials that fell into other disciplines' residual categories (if they were noticed at all).

Anthropologists have always been masters at generating intellectual capital from such unwanted raw materials. The discipline remains at once central and peripheral in the academy: central because the empirical knowledge it controls, and the theoretical play such knowledge enables, can be used to challenge many of the commonsense truths of other disciplines; but peripheral because, in the end, empowered natives in dominant nation-states have a way of ignoring any knowledge that does not allow them to rationalize their commonsense assumptions and practices. (As the Iraq war demonstrates, such natives do not pay attention even to their own history, let alone the history of others.) Anthropologists have made places for themselves, therefore, within hegemonic institutions, where they are respected but ignored. Centrally peripheral, we might say, or peripherally central.

The anthropological relativism that allows us to play conceptual games with terms like "center" and "periphery" has trouble, however, negotiating "power." We can, after all, count undergraduate enrollments, doctoral degrees, research dollars, and faculty positions; and when we do, we find that anthropology has "less" or "fewer" than other disciplines in the human sciences. To be institutionally peripheral in our society is to be "really" peripheral, and anthropologists' understanding that their marginality is a cultural phenomenon does not by itself allow them to effect economic and political change.

In any case, a good deal of the more recent theorizing about centers and peripheries has been grounded not in a relativizing project but in a generalizing one: to understand the "world system" that has developed in the last five hundred years. In these models there really are centers and peripheries, defined in terms of control over economic and political processes. The work of Frank (1967), Wallerstein (1974), and Wolf (1982), to name only the best known, took aim at spurious entities; it relativized the notion of "a" society or culture, objectively bounded. Their work saw "the local" enmeshed in a global system, and although localities, in all their cultural and social specificity, are not to be explained away (in these models) as merely a function of the centers that dominate them, their existence is nonetheless deeply conditioned by their place in a world order, more or less objectively given and objectively understood (Rowlands 1987; Champion 1989b).

The essays collected in this, the eleventh volume of History of Anthropology, reflect the play between relativizing and universalizing notions of center and periphery. David Koester's essay begins at the beginning (as it were) of the contemporary world system of nation-states. Icelandic elites responded to insulting ethnographic descriptions issuing from faraway centers of learning. Such descriptions not only marginalized Iceland, placing it on the edge of the known, civilized world, they also denigrated it. Koester shows us very clearly that the emergence of a global system of sociopolitical relationships was in part grounded in historically particular types of ethnogeographical knowledge, including knowledge that insulted those it described and that therefore often elicited passionate responses. Looking over the shoulders of geographers in Iceland, Germany, France, and England, Koester depicts emergent national identities that were at once central (one's view from, and of, one's country) and peripheral (one's awareness of others' denigrating judgments about one's country).

Fast-forward to the late nineteenth century. Well-institutionalized nation-states now dominate most portions of the globe, either as national homeland or colonial possession. The cosmographical-ethnographic tradition Koester describes has mutated into a scientific-anthropological discourse about human racial, linguistic, and cultural difference. Those theories of difference are not disconnected from politics, as they are used both to justify hegemonies and to critique injustice. The papers of Kath Weston and Brad Evans show two very different uses to which one type of anthropological knowledge, that concerning "diffusing" cultural materials, could be put. Focusing on British India's offshore penal colony, the Andaman Islands, Weston shows colonial officials tracking both escaped convicts and ethnological specimens. Such specimens fed into colonialist visions of wild people and yet-to-be-pacified areas. Those visions, in turn, helped constitute "the offshore" as at once part of the nation-state (its "back of beyond," in Weston's terms) and a no-man's-land where the laws of national justice and civilized behavior did not apply. In Evans's paper Boas puts diffusing cultural materials to very different use. Evans argues that in the late nineteenth century anthropologists and folklorists were much preoccupied with mounting evidence of the widespread diffusion of cultural materials (e.g., the motifs of myth and folklore) across any and all national, cultural, and racial boundaries. Boas seized upon the fact that different types of materials (cultural, linguistic, genetic) diffused in different directions and at different rates to attack the social-evolutionary synthesis, in which "race, language, and culture" moved through history together, carried by neatly demarcated, transhistorical human groups. It was Boas's attention to diffusion, to cultural motion from center to center or across peripheries (today's "hybridity" and "traveling culture" [Clifford 1992]), that ultimately led him and his students to the twentieth-century notion of culture.

Geographic or geopolitical location within a social system shapes the life chances of individuals; residence at, access to, or egress from centers and peripheries makes a difference for anthropologists and for the people they study. George Stocking's essay on Robert Gelston Armstrong is a paradigmatic tale of a person expelled from the center. A white, upper-middle-class, U.S. male citizen earning a Ph.D. in the Department of Anthropology at the University of Chicago, Armstrong was socially and educationally qualified to enter academia at the center. But his connections to the Communist Party made it impossible, in the early 1950s, to find satisfactory academic work in the United States. Moving off to Nigeria to conduct research, he came eventually to make a professional and personal home there. He became central to a local social and research scene, a fact that makes Stocking's historical evaluation of Armstrong's career an extended meditation on the relationship between anthropology's centers and its peripheries and on the workings of "influence" at and across such locations.

Finally, Arthur Ray follows Alfred Kroeber and his colleagues from one central institutional location, the university, into another, the courtroom. That movement "decenters" the anthropologists, who, as expert witnesses, at once retain the prestige of their university position while finding it subordinated to legal modes of truth making. The anthropologists find they are proxies for dueling lawyers, and both the lawyers and anthropologists are proxies for the Indian litigants, who had been truly marginalized, throughout most of U.S. history, vis-à-vis such central institutional sites as courts and universities.

Like much work in the history of anthropology, all of the essays gathered in History of Anthropology 11 move across the border between "presentism" and "historicism." All take us into various past worlds to study them for their own sake, but each also uses a particular history to reflect on the present-day hegemonic order (a transnational world system of nation-states, the wars and repressions it breeds, and anthropologists' varying stances toward it). Indeed, the tension historians experience between presentism and historicism (Stocking 1965; cf. Butterfield 1963) is similar to that anthropologists experience as they find that their studies of other cultures inevitably lead them to reflect on their own. It is no wonder, then, that the history of anthropology, as a peripheral subfield within anthropology, has stimulated some central debates among anthropologists who find lessons in disciplinary history for their present-day political and theoretical concerns.

Acknowledgments

As George Stocking's essay on Robert Armstrong grew far more substantial than its author had at first envisioned it, it seemed to me and to several colleagues and members of the editorial board (Ira Bashkow, Matti Bunzl, Daniel Segal, Pauline Turner Strong) that the Armstrong essay interacted with emergent work that was coming our way. I am indebted to Ira Bashkow for suggesting "center and periphery" as a theme, and I borrowed the notion of cultural and institutional crossings from a volume edited by Daniel Segal (1992). Combining the two as title and subtitle seemed to describe the essays collected here, all concerning human movements across various kinds of boundaries, and all contextualized in terms of cultural and institutional centers and peripheries, as these were understood by both participants and observers within the stories told by the contributors to History of Anthropology 11.

References Cited

AA   *American Anthropologist*
JHBS   *Journal of the History of Behavioral Sciences*

Boas, F. 1904. The History of Anthropology. In Stocking 1974:23–36.
———. 1908. Anthropology. In Stocking 1974:267–81.
Bunzl, M. 2004. Boas, Foucault, and the "Native Anthropologist": Notes toward a Neo-Boasian Anthropology. AA 106:435–42.
Butterfield, H. 1963. *The Whig Interpretation of History*. London.
Champion, T., ed. 1989a. *Centre and Periphery: Comparative Studies in Archaeology* Cambridge, Eng.
———. 1989b. Introduction. In Champion 1989a:1–21.
Clifford, J. 1992 [1997]. Traveling Culture. In *Routes: Routes: Travel and Translation in the Late Twentieth Century*. Ed. J. Clifford, 17–46. Cambridge, MA.
Frank, A. 1967. *Capitalism and Underdevelopment in Latin America*. New York.
Rowlands, M. 1987. Centre and Periphery: A Review of the Concept. In *Centre and Periphery in the Ancient World*. Ed. M. Rowlands et al., 1–11. Cambridge, Eng.
Segal, D., ed. 1992. *Crossing Cultures: Essays in the Displacement of Western Civilization*. Tucson, AZ.
Stocking, G. 1965. On the Limits of "Presentism" and "Historicism" in the Historiography of the Behavioral Sciences. *JHBS* 1:211–18.
———. 1974. *The Shaping of American Anthropology, 1883–1911: A Franz Boas Reader*. New York.
———. 2001. *Delimiting Anthropology*. Madison, WI.
Wallerstein, I. 1974. *The Modern World-System*. New York.
Wolf, E. 1982. *Europe and the People without History*. Berkeley, CA.

THE POWER OF INSULT

Ethnographic Publication and Emergent Nationalism in the Sixteenth Century

DAVID KOESTER

In 1599 readers of English geographer Richard Hakluyt's *Principal Navigations, Voyages, Traffiques and Discoveries of the English Nation* may well have been astonished to encounter a text in which an Icelandic bishop railed against the poetry of a "German pedlar" in language that was as vituperative as it was irate. Offended by what he took to be ethnic slurs, Bishop Guðbrandur Þorláksson criticized not only the author of the poetry, Gories Peerse, but equally the Hamburg-based publisher, Joachim Löw, for greed and irresponsibility.

> There came to light about the yeare of Christ 1561, a very deformed impe, begotten by a certain Pedlar of Germany: namely a booke of German rimes, of al that ever were read the most filthy and most slanderous against the nation of Island.[1] Neither did it suffice the base printer once to send abroad that base brat, but he must publish it also thrise or foure times over: that he might thereby, what lay in him, more deeply disgrace our innocent nation among the Germans & Danes, and other neighbour countries, with shamefull, and everlasting ignominie. So great was the malice of this printer, & his desire so greedy to get lucre, by a thing unlawfull. And this he did without controlment, even in that citie [Hamburg], which these many yeres hath trafficked with Island to the great gaine, and commodity of the citizens. His name is Joachimus Leo, a man worthy to become lions foode. (Jónsson 1904:93–94)

1. This spelling ("Island") for Iceland is taken directly from the Latin original, in which the Icelandic word *Ísland* ("ice-land") is not translated. About this time English was gaining an *s* in

---

David Koester is associate professor of anthropology at the University of Alaska Fairbanks. His doctoral research focused on historical consciousness in Iceland. He is currently working on a life history of Tatiana P. Lukashkina, an indigenous educator of Kamchatka, Russia.

Bishop Guðbrandur's comments appeared as preface to "A Briefe Commentarie," a critique of writings about Iceland that appeared first in Latin in 1593 and then in English in 1599. The author of the "Commentarie" was Arngrímur Jónsson, an Icelandic clergyman who later gained recognition as a historian and expert on Icelandic antiquities and became known as Arngrímur the Learned. He was not, however, the bishop's first choice for the task. Icelandic historian Jakob Benediktsson notes that Bishop Guðbrandur's interest in defending Iceland went back at least to 1588, when he recommended to the Icelandic national law assembly, the Alþing, that Oddur Einarsson be named bishop of Skálholt. Oddur had trained in Denmark and was for a time a student of Tycho Brahe. Guðbrandur recommended him in part because he wanted a man "who has the training and learning both to preach the word of God and also to answer the many libels which have been published, and which may be published, on our fatherland" (quoted in Benediktsson 1957:33). Oddur agreed to undertake this task, but his *Qualiscunque descriptio Islandiae*, written in 1589, was, for unknown reasons, not published until 1928 (Benediktsson 1968:vii). After Oddur, Guðbrandur turned to Arngrímur, who was a grandson of the bishop's aunt and who had been under the bishop's foster care for a number of years (Benediktsson 1957). Explaining in the introduction to the "Commentarie" that he was writing at the bishop's request, the young parson offered examples of ancient warriors who had given their lives to defend their country. He admitted that it was not his intention similarly to "undergoe voluntary death" but that he was prepared to accept any envy and criticism that might result from his efforts. He argued that readers should not find fault if he took up his pen to defend Iceland and Icelanders against the slanders of poets and correct the less-than-complimentary writings of cosmographers and historiographers.

Coming one hundred years after the printing of Columbus's journals and an intervening century of explosive growth in publications about the world at large, this event in the history of ethnopolitical critique provides us with an unusual window on nationalism, emerging in specific relation to the publishing of ethnographic and geographic (then cosmographic) writings. Positioned in time two hundred years before the romantic and modernist nationalisms of mainland Europe, Arngrímur's work displays a broad and colorful spectrum of patriotic sentiment intended for a discursive arena in which the manipulation and management of national status figured prominently. The analysis I present here takes a point of view different from those theories of nationalism that seek its origins in nation-internal institutional mechanisms such as mass education

---

"island" (from "iland"); this article about an island named Island, in the widely read *Principal Navigations*, surely added to the orthographic confusion. To make matters worse, the translation refers to other parts of the Danish realm as the king's "most ample territories and Islands." My full translation of Peerse's poem can be found at http://www.faculty.uaf.edu/ffdck/yslandt.pdf.

and industrialization (Gellner 1965:147–78, 1983:40) and that date its emergence to the end of the eighteenth century (Hobsbawm 1990; Eriksen 1993).
Their associated arguments concerning print capitalism and the fabrication or
elaboration of national languages, customs, and cultural symbols in the development of shared nationalist sentiments (Anderson 1983; Smith 1998) have
been important, but they are limited by depicting the formation of nationalism
primarily in terms of such internally codified concepts as ethnicity, language,
dynasty, territory, and law. My aim, in contrast, is to understand the formation
and effective power of the discourse that made these elements of "nation" compelling as a source of individual identity and group affiliation. This discourse
was political and ethnographic, and it increasingly brought the world into an
all-encompassing frame of distinctly populated territories.

It was perhaps the focus on shared internal mechanisms that encouraged
many theorists to date the origins of nationalism to the period of the Enlightenment. This was the period when, as Marcel Mauss wrote, "la Trinité des Con-
stituants—la Nation, la Loi, le Roi" [the Trinity of Constituents—Nation, Law,
and King] took its modern form (1920:575). The idea that nationalism was a
product of the Enlightenment has been widely repeated and accepted as common knowledge. For example, Eriksen (1993:15), following Handler (1988),
has argued that "nationalism and social science, including anthropology, grew
out of the same historical circumstances of modernisation, industrialisation
and the growth of individualism in the nineteenth century." Citing van Gen-
nep and Hobsbawm, Handler had, in his study of Quebec nationalism, actually
written, "it is well known that nationalist ideologies and social-scientific inquiry developed in the same historical context—that of the post-Renaissance
European world—and that the two have reacted upon one another from their
beginnings" (1988:8). We will see that this reactive process was taking place in
the Renaissance period itself, though it has been obscured in part by general
historiographic trends that ignore the period from the Middle Ages to the Enlightenment (Karant-Nunn 1994), particularly in tracing the roots of the social
sciences (with notable exceptions such as Stagl [1995] and, of course, Foucault). Recently, literary historians have recognized the development of national consciousness in sixteenth-century genres ranging from the Petrarchan
sonnet to the novel and the essay (Hampton 2001; Kennedy 2003). Hakluyt's
Principal Navigations, in which Arngrímur's "Commentarie" appeared, was an
effort to promote English national pride (Helgerson 1992; Rubiés 1993:175).
Some have argued that a term other than nationalism should be applied
(Roberts 1980:480–82), while others have maintained that nationalism can
at least be attested for England in this period (Greenfeld 1992; Llobera 1994).
By focusing on the internal dynamics of creating a national identity (e.g.,
Seton-Watson 1977; Llobera 1994; Pickett 1996), the predominant theories
have sought to explain nationalism by means of local mechanisms that enabled

peoples to share language, territory, laws, manners, and customs and recognize them as shared. Foster's review (1991) of over 150 studies of the formation of national identity shows the pervasiveness of this theoretical tendency, as does Smith's more recent review (1998).

Icelanders' responses to ethnographic writings suggest that in the history of expressions of ethnic pride and national sentiment, internally focused codifications of shared imaginings are at best only part of the story. Interestingly, Icelander Guðmundur Hálfdanarson's review of contemporary historical and political scientific literature on nationalism contrasts with Foster's, in that Guðmundur explicitly considers external, distinguishing-from perspectives ("how [a group] distinguishes itself from others") as well as internal, belonging-to aspects ("why a group would consider itself a people") (Hálfdanarson 1996:27). We need to consider what Sahlins refers to for a slightly later period as "an oppositional model of national identity" (1989:9), in which nations gain definition and apparent unity in contradistinction from each other. Ethnographic writings, from the early days of the print era, were informed by images of nations within the context of other nations. While nationalism may require a territorialized community, imagined or otherwise, it cannot exist as nationalism unless there is a world in which national groups mark themselves as distinct from one another (Ardener 1989:68; Williams 1990:128). Barth made this point many years ago in relation to ethnic groups (1969; see also Eidheim 1969), but the idea was largely ignored in theories of nationalism until recently (Hastings 1997; Smith 1998, 1999). Images of national groups promulgated for others as well as for the national community itself are the building blocks of political nationalism. For Bishop Guðbrandur, this world of nations perceiving other nations loomed ominously in the Icelandic imagination, and it is the ominousness, the power wielded in sixteenth-century discourses of otherness and national difference, that I will elucidate in this essay.

Ethnographic Insult and the Human Sciences

Such a perspective has implications for what Herzfeld has called the "suppressed link" (1987:16–18) between the history of the human sciences and the development of ideas of nations, peoples, and groups as acting agents. We see in the Icelandic defense how readers of ethnographic texts interpreted evaluative statements about "us" and "them." The concept of nationalism refers to a discourse of power among peoples and an integration of power within discourse. As ideas and characterizations of nations were published in catalogs of mundane, "immoral," and bizarre "manners and customs," these in turn served as the basis for the discursive development of nationalism in the rhetoric of a globalizing framework of value-laden difference. Studies of nationalism and colonialism have sought to understand the effects and effectiveness of European imperialism through analysis of various essentializing, objectifying, exoticizing discourses (Comaroff and Comaroff 1992; Mitchell 1992; Stoler 1992; Bhabha 1994; Thomas 1994; Herzfeld 1997), contextualized within the broad discursive parameters of "race," "ethnicity," and "culture" (Todorov 1993). But in all of this discussion, supported by much philosophical and rhetorical analysis of ethnographic authorship (Clifford 1983, 1986; Pratt 1986; Rosaldo 1986; Bhabha 1994), there has been relatively little recognition of the historical depth of the "ethno"-graphing of human difference and of an equally politicized and much more fundamental, timeworn feature of ethnographic writing—insult.

From the earliest days of its practice, descriptive writing about peoples has been political, that is, implicated in both the allocation of political standing and the development of political theory. Evans (1991) has argued that the fundamental impetus of Herodotus's ethnohistoriographic *History* was a desire to explain the Persian imperialist impulse. The connection is perhaps even clearer in Julius Caesar's account of the Gallic Wars, in which bald ethnographic description is placed squarely among his descriptions of how he succeeded in dominating distant peoples (Caesar 1982:88–89, 138–46). Ethnic denigration and praise was a strategic rhetorical feature of Ciceronian oratory (Vasaly 1993), and the practice continued as the European conception of barbarian others changed from "not Greek" or "un-Roman" in the Graeco-Roman tradition, to "morally inferior" in post-Roman Europe, and to "heathen" during the time when Christianity had spread both administratively and culturally through the former dominions of Rome (Jones 1971; Pagden 1982). At the same time, the exaggerated and exoticized revisions of Herodotus in the widely copied and later printed works of Pomponius Mela, Julius Solinus, and Pliny and increasing numbers of travelers' writings helped to create a readership and market eager for peculiar, miraculous, fabulous, and even satanic representations of difference (Helms 1988:211–36; Rubiés 2000:139–41). By the time Johann Boemus published his *Omnium gentium mores, leges, & ritus ex multis clarissimis rerum scriptoribus* (1520)—a compendium of customs and morals—the use of comparison in judging forms of social organization was well established. Aristotle's comparison of constitutions in the *Politics* had, for instance, been known both from Aquinas and more widely after Leonardo Bruni's Latin translation in 1437–38 (Copenhaver and Schmitt 1992:77), and the comparative framework came to play a role in the Spanish debate over the status of American Indians (Pagden 1982). In Boemus the wonders and varieties of social life that made for popular reading would, his seventeenth-century English translator pointed out, also allow readers "to form intelligent judgements as to what 'orders and institutions' were 'fittest to be ordayned' in their own lands for the establishment of perfect peace" (Aston 1611). Thus, it needs to be kept in mind that the description of human differences and similarities and the positioning of peoples in a morally evaluative political framework was an already well-established genre as it achieved new dispersal in print—as both Talal Asad (1973) and Edward Said (1979) have famously argued.

In sum, early ethnographic publication had powerful effects in the later development of an encompassing global discourse of ethnonational status differentials. Those who are accustomed to think of "ethnography" as specifically the empirical methodology of modern anthropology may find my use here anachronistic. Literary understandings of the time, however, justify the usage. In the literal sense of its Greek components, "writing about peoples," the genre was well established. Sixteenth-century geographic texts typically included peoples and their customs within one descriptive section of the work, often marked by a structural division in the text. Both Arngrímur and his chief antagonist, Peerse, divided their writings into geography and wonders, on the one hand, and "the inhabitants," on the other. Arngrímur's chief historiographic inspiration, Jean Bodin's *Method for the Easy Comprehension of History* (1566), had similarly followed Augustinian tradition in treating human history as distinct from divine and natural history (Bodin 1566:15–18). Though claims have been made that the term *ethnography* was coined in the 1770s (Vermeulen 1992, 1994; Stagl 1995:249–68), the word was known in Denmark in Arngrímur's time. Royal historian Anders Sørensen Vedel used it in the title of his planned history of Denmark, *Chorographia Regni Daniæ og Ethnographia Danica,* and defined it in his *Promus Condus* (1586) (Wegener 1851:135, 141; Jørgensen 1931), which confirms Mühlmann's dating to this period (Fischer 1970:174).[2]

My approach to discursive development differs from that of Foucault, who was interested in "the effects of power peculiar to the play of statements" (1980:55). I want to understand statements *as* power, effective not only in an isolated discursive field but also as part of the historical political apparatus in which nations and theories of nations were formed. In various genres—from derisive, rhyming travel accounts to scholarly cosmographies and historiographies—ethnographic writing, broadcast by print, not only described a social world of peoples and nations, it shaped and remade that world. My analysis here attempts to shed light on Herzfeld's "suppressed link" by coming to grips with the discursive efficacy of ethnographic publications in this period. It thus responds to the problems Foucault encountered as he faced the implications of

2. I am grateful to Karen Skovgaard-Petersen, Manuscript and Rare Book Department, the Royal Library, Copenhagen, for confirmation of this usage in Vedel's work. Wegener's biographical sketch of Vedel listed the first three volumes as *Chorographia Regni Daniæ, Ethnographia Danica,* and *Ethographia gentis Danicæ. . . .* Vedel had studied in Wittenberg under Caspar Peucer (Wegener 1851:39).

the politically weakened notion of discourse he had developed in *The Archae-ology of Knowledge*—a weakening that stems, I would argue, from his unwill-ingness to accept the performative power of language as true power.

As we shall see, social groupings alternately performable as "we" or "they" became shared identity as ethnographic insult drew taut otherwise loose bonds of common experience, history, or geographical location. The Icelandic reac-tion to sixteenth-century ethnographic writings exposes the development of this discursive political arena in the process of its formation and displays many of the discursive mechanisms by which ethnic evaluative assessment took place. Thus, the most salient aspect of this case—especially in terms of the na-tionalisms and colonialisms that were to come later—is the manner in which both the discourse on nations and the felt reality of national identity developed in the context of the power-laden, evaluative, hierarchical, ethnically differen-tiating discursive practice of ethnographic publication. As we follow the reac-tions and explore the intentions of readers and writers of this literature we open a window on the construction of the power relations that have come to reside in the beating heart of the nationalist idiom.

Genealogy of a Global Vision

Nationalism is not solely based in comparison of characteristics but entails as well a peculiar, geographically ordered politicization of peoples (Smith 1999:149–59). It suggests that all of humanity is divided into groups of people that constitute sociopolitical units attached to territories in a world frame. Al-though the word *nation* did not, in the sixteenth century, bring to mind the idea of a state apparatus essential to twentieth-century ideas of nationalism, there was a common idea of territory, language, religion, and political unity that tran-scended the immediate politics of actual sovereignty. Thus, Hakluyt's English edition of the "Commentarie" refers to Danish, German, Italian, and other na-tions, despite their internal political divisions. Iceland was at the time a colo-nial territory under the Danish monarchy, but it was also understood to be a nation. As used throughout the text, "nation" referred to Iceland's historical autonomy and geographical isolation, its distinct social and economic forms, and its linguistic uniqueness. To make sense of the formation of nationalist sen-timent of the kind in Arngrímur's "Commentarie," we need to examine how the human-inhabited world conceptually came to be imaged as a finite globe, di-vided into territorially distinctive groups of people.

The European orientation that Pratt calls "planetary consciousness" (1992:15ff.) has deep roots in European literary history and received a power-ful catalyst to sedimentation with the advent of printing. Along with the grow-ing boom in cartography and map printing in the sixteenth century (Eisenstein

1980), descriptions of peoples of the world had become popular and were published widely (Rubiés 2000). Compilations in the form of cosmographies contained royal genealogies and topographic descriptions of cities, towns, and routes of travel. They expanded in geographical scope, and accounts of daily life grew in number and size. Cosmographers gathered the information in large measure from prior published works and through correspondence with merchants, travelers, and officials. They purveyed stories and characterizations that ranged from judiciously tempered encomia pleasing to distant monarchs to slanderous or moralistically indignant accounts of putatively inferior others. With expanding trade and travel, a European worldview developed, one grounded in ethnographic description. Groups of people began systematically to be located and described in a global vision and "map-conditioned sense of the world" (Helgerson 1992:53).

The works that Arngrímur criticized, in addition to the travel poem, were scholarly histories and cosmographies. Three of them dealt specifically with the Scandinavian peoples within the world of nations: Jacob Ziegler's *Schondia*, the book of Scandinavia from his *Terræ sanctæ* (Ziegler and Weissenburg 1536), the *Chronica Regnorum Aquilonarium* of Albert Krantz (1546), and Olaus Magnus's *Historia de gentibus Septentrionalibus, earumque diversisis statibus, conditionibus* (1555). Two others were voluminous cosmographies that mentioned Iceland among the lands of the world described: the *Cosmographei* of Sebastian Münster (1537, 1544, 1550) and *Cosmographia Petri Apiani*, revised by Gemma Frisius (Apian 1550). Though I have designated these by their date of first publication, it is not known what editions of these works Arngrímur consulted, nor does he indicate any awareness of or concern for their relative age. Although historically organized when treating well-known parts of Europe, the cosmographic texts often collapsed ancient and contemporary reports as they portrayed exotic creatures and peoples inhabiting distant and unexplored zones of the globe. Cosmographers had at hand a well-established genre of compilations of ethnographic depiction originating most notably in Herodotus but overwhelmed in popularity by the derivative compilations of Pomponius Mela and Julius Solinus (Hodgen 1964). "The art of cosmography," as Münster called it (1550:iii), with the increasing production of maps and travelers' accounts, brought tremendous amounts of information from around the world into the form of published volumes, and it inspired the organized collection of such information until its decline (Bowen 1981:93). Especially in Münster's case but for most who published under the title of cosmography, Ptolemy's compendious *Cosmographia* (Geography) (Ptolemaeus 1475) helped to bring order to this massive project of accumulation. Ptolemy deserves our attention at the outset because his influence led to a global (geographic) vision essential to the (ethnogeographic) image of an encompassing world of peoples.

Although it is widely recognized that Ptolemy's work was based on numerous precedents (Sezgin 1987b:2), it is nevertheless clear that his system of organiz-ing human inhabitance around a mappable globe according to an inscribable geometrical structure had a profound influence. Written over seventeen hun-dred years ago, his *Cosmographia* contained the longitude and latitude of over eight thousand places with precision to five minutes (Sezgin 1987b). Ptolemy posed cosmography as a globalizing study. According to Sezgin, he (or at least the Ptolemaic text that has come down to us) described it as the "imitation in writing of all the known parts of the earth, including everything connected with it—open countryside and coastlines, as well as harbors and settlements—thus distinguishing it from *chorographía* which deals with particular parts of the inhabited earth as though they had no *connection with the whole*" (1987b:3, em-phasis added). What made cosmography a distinct form of scholarship was its system of geometrically relating the places of the world to a global schema.

Arab scholars kept alive the knowledge of Ptolemy through the Middle Ages and elaborated on the world-encompassing foundation that it laid out (Sezgin 1987a). Medieval Arab trade routes and lands stretched from West Africa and Spain to the Indian Ocean, and several travelers wrote accounts of the places within that vast span of territory. Works in the genre of *chorographia* such as Ya'qubi's *Book of Countries* (891) and al-Bakhi's (d. 934) *Routes and Kingdoms* were disseminated among Islamic centers of learning as early as the tenth cen-tury. In the span from Iraq to Delhi there were over sixteen observatories, and during the thirteenth century Cordova, Seville, Toledo, and Granada in Spain and Tangier and Ceuta Fez in Morocco became important centers for mathe-matical and astronomical learning (Ahmad 1980:20, 40, 45). Sezgin notes that it was Caliph al-Ma'mun's command early in the ninth century ordering Mus-lim scientists to create a map of the world that revived the knowledge of the text of the *Cosmographia* (Sezgin 1987b:12). The most influential of the great Arab geographer-historians, Ibn Khaldun, not only described places that he knew from travel, but in his *Muqaddimah* of 1377, he elaborated on Ptolemy's scheme, detailing the nature of the seven cultivated latitudinal zones, with ac-counts of their inhabitants and characteristics (Ibn Khaldun 1958:109–73). Thus, what emerged in Islamic scholarship, before it was widely appropriated by Europeans, was a global image of the world and a manner of theorizing the inhabitants in territorialized groups.

Medieval scholars in Europe may have been influenced by Ptolemy, at least indirectly, and understood the idea of encompassing the globe in a system of lon-gitude and latitude even before a full Latin translation was available. Bernard Silvester had written a *Cosmographia* or *De Mundi Universitate* in 1147 (Bartlett 1982). Excerpted parts of Ptolemy's *Cosmographia* appear in late manuscript copies of John Holywood's (Sacrobosco's) *De Sphæra Mundi* (ca. 1250), a global compendium that was widely known and used well into the print era (Sacro-bosco 1450; Parry 1963; Penrose 1955:8). Sacrobosco's world sphere depicted zones of inhabitance, discussed climatic theories, and included a table of places located by latitude and longitude that closely resembled the tables in Ptolemy's *Cosmographia* (Sacrobosco 1450).[3] Although a Greek monk discovered a copy of Ptolemy's *Cosmographia* in 1295 (Delano-Smith and Kain 1999:51), the first Latin translation did not appear in Europe until early in the fifteenth century, when Jakobus Angelus traveled with his mentor, Byzantine scholar Manuel Chrysoloras, from Constantinople to Rome to warn of what they saw as the impending threat posed by Turks (Sezgin 1987b). The medieval *mappamundi* tradition also contributed to the image of an encompassed world filled with ethnically and religiously distinct peoples and places. The spaces on the maps indicated both sacred and profane places, from individual cities and their famous buildings to the earthly paradise. Lacking a grid system, they show no direct influence of Ptolemaic cartography (Delano-Smith and Kain 1999), but they nevertheless contributed to a view of a world divided among distinct peoples.

With the translation of Ptolemy's *Cosmographia* in 1406 and the appearance of Cardinal Pierre d'Ailly's *Imago Mundi*, written in 1410, the groundwork had been laid in European scholarship for the explosion of geographical publication that was to take place when printing changed the way the world was known. Islamic science had created a vast network of observatories from which scholars compiled new cosmographic information to fill out the world picture. Some of this scholarship had filtered into European monastic circles through Portugal, Spain, and Turkey. Interest in studies of Greek, Hebrew, Arabic, and other languages associated with biblical times and biblical scholarship grew in the early sixteenth century, and, as we will see, these studies were closely associated with the development of Renaissance cosmography. When the first edition of Ptolemy went to print in 1475 (Ptolemaeus 1475) and came out with maps two years later (Parry 1963:13), a world-encompassing knowledge of a global humanity, infused with an imperial competitive will to know, already existed. What changed was the global extension that took place with the mechanical reproduction of this power-infused method for systematizing knowledge of the world and its peoples. Maps and globes spread rapidly across Europe. In 1530 the soon-to-be-renowned cosmographer and professor of Oriental languages Sebastian Münster described the Ptolemaic system in his local description of German lands (1530) and elaborated further on it in the introduction to his great and widely read *Cosmographei* (1550:21–40). Erasmus published the first Greek-language edition of Ptolemy's *Cosmographia* in Basel in 1533 (Berggren and Jones 2000:52). Wittenberg professor Doctor Caspar Peucer, of whom

---

3. The manuscript copies of *De Sphæra Mundi* that I have been able to examine were probably written after 1406 and may thus show late influence of Ptolemy. Delano-Smith and Kain maintain that the geographical tables were not in Sacrobosco's text, though they do not say which text they examined (1999:42).

more below, had fifteen volumes of Ptolemy's works in his library, including the *Cosmographia* (Kolb 1976:18). The system continued to be used as sixteenth-century voyages and "discoveries" were added to the world picture in works such as Corneille Wytfliet's *Descriptionis Ptolemaicae augmentum, sive Occidentis notitia brevis sic commentario* (Wytfliet and Skelton 1597).

At the same time, travel writing constituted a genre distinct from but contributing to cosmographic compilations. Known in written form as early as Herodotus, it continued in Europe in medieval pilgrimage writings and later in the accounts of merchants and emissaries (Campbell 1988; Rubiés 2000), although it did not immediately influence more academic cosmographic scholarship. Writings of the likes of Mandeville and Marco Polo fed the European imagination and created a literary arena for exotic descriptions backed up by the authenticating effect of having-been-witness. "Out of this," writes Said, "come a restricted number of typical encapsulations: the journey, the history, the fable, the stereotype, the polemical confrontation. These are the lenses through which the Orient is experienced, and they shape the language, perception, and form of the encounter between East and West" (1979:58). More than lenses, in fact, these genres represented discursive regimes that, as Said ultimately argues, articulated and performed differences in status between ethnic groups. It was not merely that ethnographic writings exoticized and in some cases clearly labeled groups as immoral idolaters or cannibals but that in both truth and fantasy ethnographic writing constituted a complex status-assessing discursive form.

The Dishonorifics of Ethnographic Discourse and the Performative Creation of the National Group

By the sixteenth century the popularity of and widespread familiarity with travel writing fed into the development of systematic observational and publishing practices. Standard categories of ethnographic description—diet, clothing, housing, laws, religious customs, marriage customs, and so on—made it possible to compare the accounts of diverse travelers going to the same destination and to compare customs from diverse places (Rubiés 2000:215–17). The systematic nature of both travel writings and cosmographic compilation was encouraged on several related fronts involving the development of printing and an enthusiasm for the establishment of new methods. In the 1540s Philipp Melanchthon (1497–1560) and Johannes Sturm (1507–89) facilitated the use of analytical categories by moving discussions of method from their traditional place in textbooks on rhetoric to treatises on logic. Similarly, Petrus Ramus (1515–72) promoted a method of organizing information into visually oriented schemata of bifurcating tables (Ong 1972). Jean Bodin's *Method for the Easy Comprehension of History* (1566) described the practice of historical study from the initial ordering of one's reading to the means by which to assess and make historical judgments. As travel for education, diplomacy, and trade replaced pilgrimages, the practice of traveling was routinized into a method and an art, the *ars apodemica*. More and more, explorers and travelers were studiously and purposefully recording their observations and reflections (Rubiés 1993:168–69, 1996, 2000:85; Stagl 1979, 1983:15, 1995). According to one early set of instructions, travelers were to describe "population, languages, names, diet, lifestyle, clothing of various regions, native talents, morals and evils, machines, money, alliances, taxes and tolls, war preparedness and weapons, holidays and free time" (Mejer and Rantzau quoted in Stagl 1979:613). They were admonished to devalue hearsay and fantastic tales and to substitute personal observation recorded in a journal. These "methods" combined with the new power of print to disseminate notions of ethnic descriptive frameworks. At the same time, the cross-checking critique of regularized observations important in the development of astronomy, cartography, and physics (Eisenstein 1980) contributed to the ordering of the ethnographic publication process as well. That process consisted of observers systematically inquiring and writing down what they had heard or seen and cosmographers compiling and annotating travelers' accounts and historical texts. For both, the potential threat of a published challenge by critical others contributed to the development of a consistent rhetoric of verisimilitude.

Thus, even in this early period, the power of scholarly discourse appeared to lie in the method and "the proved reliability of the writer" (Bodin 1566:336). Nevertheless, though truth and authority were important elements in the communicative efficacy of sixteenth-century ethnographic publication, another legacy of the ethnographic tradition maintained its place in the texts. The developing methodologies and critical feedback possibilities did not dampen the spirit of ethnic denigration or nationalistic self-praise in travel or even scholarly writing. In explaining his notion of author reliability, Bodin complained of some writers that they "wrote so vaingloriously about their own fellow countrymen, that they made no concession to others and thought that the gods themselves were not their equals" (1566:336). At the same time, some of the insulting statements were clearly intended to amuse: "Native born Icelanders do not think it unclean when dirty hair or occasionally a couple of lice pollute their butter; they are a 'licey' people" (my translation of Peerse from Seelman 1883:122). Thus, in this context, though many of the statements had the appearance of factual report, time and again in the "Commentarie" Arngrímur shifted the discussion from questions of truth, reliability, and accuracy to insult. If it were not for the mocking tone of the rhyme (coastal Low German original on the left), the following statement might seem to us a simple description of dietary facts:

Dartho harden vulen Visch ungesolten,
Darby veel Botter mit Hare
　ungeschmolten.
Ock solten se dar dat Flesch går nicht also.
Isset mager, so ethen se Tallich dartho.
. . .
Ane Solt und ock ane Brodt
Dûncket en de Spyse wesen gudt.
Van den Selhunden dat geile Speck
Ane Solt und Brodts yn eren Beck
Dat ethen se so gyrigen ungefaden
Alse werent Hôner und Hasenbraden.

Then they eat hard, rotten fish, unsalted,
And with it large amounts of unmelted
　butter with hair.
And neither do they salt meat.
If it is lean, they eat tallow with it.
. . .
Without salt and bread
They think food is good.
They greedily gulp seal fat
Without salt and bread in their bowl.
They eat it as greedily
As if it were a chicken or rabbit steak.
(Seelman 1883:122, my translation)

To Arngrímur this was not merely ethnographic description. He explicitly rejected the implied moral evaluation: "[W]e confesse it to be even so: namely that . . . victuals are used in most places without the seasoning of salt. But, whereas strangers boast that all their victuals are more pleasant and whole-some: yet we denie that to be a sufficient reason, why they should upbraid us in regard of ours. . . . God, in nourishing and susteining of us Islanders, is not tyed to bread and salt" (Jónsson 1904:188). Arngrímur did not dispute the truth or falsity of the claim. He did not deny that Icelanders ate hard, rotten fish or but-ter with hair, and he admitted that they had neither salt nor bread. Salt and bread were not just sustenance; they were marks of higher status that had been transferred into the realm of the discourse of national characteristics. His com-plaint was about being upbraided, about the social valuation in these state-ments that would make Icelanders objects of derision. Some statements may have been in some degree true, but when a "slanderous hogge hath drawen [a reproach] from the maner of living, and specially from the meate and drinke of the Islanders . . . in a large invective . . . with eloquent railing and wittie slaun-der" (Jónsson 1904:186), something beyond the power of truth was invoked. There was another force at work here, a source of power about which the Ice-landers seemed most concerned, the performative power of ethnographic dis-course in print. Status performatives are not just statements of evaluation, they are social acts of assessment that, like tax assessments, create social differenti-ation as they pronounce it. As Judith Irvine puts it, "such forms of speaking are not merely an index of some independently generated social differentiation." Rather, they "may indeed *effect* social differentiation" (Irvine 1989:255).

The effect of ethnographic insult was in part dependent on a semantics of categories of human achievement and activity and a status-marked "lexicon" of actions and deeds in those categories. The descriptive categories of travel writing and cosmography—diet, housing, language, child-rearing practices, and so on—constituted an axis of selection comprised of status-marked possibilities. Food descriptions ranged from fine and complex cuisines that included agricultural products, spices, and salt to the saltless, meatless diets of some and to the extreme insult of the cannibalism of others. The categories of ethnographic description worked to assess status in the discursive world of European readers much like honorific lexical choices in some languages in which alternate words for object referents (e.g., "house," "rice," "wife") establish status relations of speaker and hearer (Irvine 1998:54–55). Ethnographic status performance made use not of object referents but of what we might call ethnographic category equivalence ("type of housing," "diet," "marriage practices"). If, as Irvine argues, in most cases of verbal abuse "evaluative statements [are] grounded in specific cultural systems of moral judgment" (1993:109), in printed ethnographic description the systems of moral evaluation were both culturally specific and transcultural (though decidedly not pancultural). Rubiés has pointed out that it was in the articulation of these ethnographic discriminations that the evaluative scale of moral measurement swung from a transnational and transcultural grounding in Christian religiosity to an even broader, if no less discriminatory, ideal of civilization (1993:170). Each category had European standards that, unmarked or praiseworthy, expressed Christianity and/or civilization: houses were expected to be *built* and made of sturdy, durable materials; food included bread, salt, and meat; sexual relations were ordered as monogamous marriage. For each category there were dishonorable variants that established the low status of the people described: houses that were caves or tents; food that was breadless, saltless, and meatless, or the other extreme, that included human flesh; sexual activity that involved marriage in common or lascivious women. This was a semiotic system in which the categories were determined not simply by an objective set of European customs but by oppositional definitions created in ethnographic encounters (i.e., encounters that would be written about).

    In expressing social status, insult mobilizes all functions or features of the communicative event, including the participant framework—addressee, addresser, target/referent—and the social context and message (Irvine 1985, 1993; Brenneis 1988; Hanks 1996:145–54). Moreover, unlike the honorific lexicons of some languages, with their status-marked alternate words for object referents, ethnographic characterizations are ostensibly *about* the people whose status is being assessed. In this regard, ethnographic characterizations functioned more like directly addressed status performatives such as the well-known "t/v" distinctions ("you" familiar, "you" formal, higher, plural). To say *vous* in French or *vy* in Russian both marks the status of the addressee and creates a status relationship between speaker and addressee in the context of the utterance (Brown and Gilman 1960; Friedrich 1979). Ethnographic status utterances—"cave dweller" (troglodyte), "forest dweller" (savage), "non-Christian" (heathen, pagan, idolater)—similarly designated and created the status of their target. But they differed from second-person pronominals in that they were not addressed to (written for) the group whose status was affected. Peerse, writing in coastal dialect, Low German verse and publishing in Hamburg (Seelman 1883:111), did not address his text to Icelanders. In this regard, ethnographic writing is perhaps most akin to the status-assessing speech genre gossip, where the party discussed is intentionally not in the group among whom the gossip statements circulate (Gluckman 1963; Abrahams 1970; Brenneis 1984; Merry 1984).

Insult also took place in the form of oblique metonymic references to peoples via various aspects of geographical description. Physician-geographer Caspar Peucer made passing reference to Iceland in his *De dimensione terræ et geometrica numerandi* (1554) in the midst of a Ptolemaic description of the habitable world. Peucer's work was divided into two sections, a geographical description of the world, with explanation of the geometry by which it was constructed, and a portrait of sacred territories, "Locorum terræ sanctæ" (Peucer 1554:188). Brief mention of Iceland had similarly appeared in Jacob Ziegler's *Terræ sanctæ* (Ziegler and Weissenburg 1536), in which he enumerated the sacred lands as Syria, Palestina, Arabia, Aegyptus, and Schondia (Scandinavia). These descriptions of the world from an encompassing Christian frame of reference were grounded primarily on the distinction between Christians and others (McGrane 1989). Nevertheless, they also show that both the Christian and non-Christian worlds were significantly disarticulated into nations and peoples (indeed, Rubiés argues [2000] that travel writing contributed to developing secularization in Europe). But what is perhaps more significant for this discussion is the manner in which Christian attributions provided a brush for shading the world picture with positive and negative tones.

Arngrímur had criticized Peucer for writing that great moanings could be heard from the depths of Mount Hekla, which the inhabitants believed came up through an opening into hell. Münster's account had told of newly departed souls beckoning their friends from the fiery depths (1550:985). Arngrímur argued that behind these descriptions was an attempt to find in Iceland a diabolical wonder, to demonstrate a connection between Iceland's active volcanoes and the fires of hell. He did not deny that Hekla was an active volcano, but he insisted that there was no perpetual fire and, moreover, that the two other mountains the cosmographers described did not exist. Such erroneous contentions were unfortunate for Münster and Frisius, who, Arngrímur ironically noted, "being about to report the woonders of Island . . . [they] . . . doe presently stumble, as it were, upon the thresholde, to the great inconvenience of them both" (Jónsson 1904:105). He would "easily grant," he wrote, that "Frisius in writing these things did not entend to reproch any, but only to blaze abroad new & incredible matters" (Jónsson 1904:120). Nevertheless, he perceived the status-lowering effect among the readership. The danger was that others would see justifiable grounds for insult: "[F]rom hense also they say y^t reproches are justly used against our nation: namely, y^t there is nothing in all the world more base, & worthlesse then it, which conteineth hell within the bounds therof" (Jónsson 1904:122). If the world contained sacred locations, this distant, forbiddingly cold island with burning mountains was being portrayed as their profane opposite. In defense, he compiled a list of other volcanoes, from Pike on Tenerife to Vesuvius to Cophantrus in Bactria, and explained that they were considered natural phenomena and that there was no attribution of hell to their burning pits. The cosmographers would not make such a claim about them, he contended, because these places were well known and "men would yeeld no credite to those things," whereas "they thought the burning of Hecla (the rumor whereof came more slowly to their eares) to be fitter for the establishing of this fond fable" (Jónsson 1904:119). "But get ye packing," he blasted, "your fraud is found out: leave off for shame hereafter to perswade any simple man, y^t there is a hel in mount Hecla" (Jónsson 1904:119). Iceland's volcanoes had been unfairly singled out, and he concluded this refutation on precisely national grounds: "[W]e do also hold, y^t the Islanders are no whit nearer unto this extreame & darke prison, in regard of the situation of place, then the Germans, Danes, Frenchmen, Italians, or any other nation whatsoever" (Jónsson 1904:125).

Cosmographic descriptions were syntagmas made up of ethnographic and geographic semiotic units and organized by national chapter headings. Both authors and readers presupposed the tie of land and people. As the ground of insult, this filial bond between people and land became an axis for the emotional ties that came to be expressed as national. Whether one disputed the claims or accepted them, the implicit "we" corresponding to the ethnographic "they" created a social group of "we Icelanders." Insult drives the wedge that separates and distinguishes identities by forcing its object to deny the insult or be insulted. It is a repulsive and attractive force that draws each individual into or out of the national delimitation. With Ptolemaic geography, everyone on the sphere could be located and described and hence become—willing, agreeing, or not—participants in the status system.

Anthony Smith has said that in his early work he underestimated the importance of emotional attachment to language, customs, and cultural heritage in the development of nationalism (1998:188–89).[4] Yet, though groups may hold and be nostalgic about practices and beliefs, their attachment need not be through the nation. The attachment becomes national when practices and

---

4. Smith writes that he now finds it useful to think of nationalism as the political outgrowth of romantic historicism. The wider world of cosmographic dialogue, however, suggests that romantic historicism itself cannot be disentangled from the web of ethnographic status contestation.

beliefs enter into the comparative or disputatious realm of national status. As I
began to suggest above, the anthropological and linguistic study of insult can
help to make sense of this process. This research has increasingly turned its focus from patterns of language use and social context (Bricker 1971; Labov 1972;
Brenneis 1980; Abrahams 1992) to pragmatic contexts and consequences of
status-performative speech (Irvine 1993). Early on, Ruwet (1982:249) argued
that French "performatifs de l'insulte" were dependent on pragmatic conditions
and knowledge of the world in general. Ethnographic utterances were speech
acts, the effects of which were to pronounce both status and social group. By
virtue of sharing government, territory, laws, customs, religion, and so on, these
groups, across social strata from peasant to burger to aristocrat, were each made
to share the moral status of their national complex. Arngrímur's text demonstrates the power of this discourse to create—to make affectively meaningful in
a way that leads to action—a group along national lines. Though he recognized
that statements were ostensibly about the land or that they came from limited
experience or rumor, this high-status clergyman responded from the perspective of "our nation," "we Islanders" (Jónsson 1904:135). If some authors, "that
they may be accompted superiors, sometimes whette their stiles against the
person, name and fame of this or that particular man, sometimes . . . against a
whole countrey" (Jónsson 1904:96), then, by the new mode of "vicarious participation" made possible by printing (Eisenstein 1980:132), readers could simultaneously perceive their own national identifications and their status in
the global frame of nationally divided humanity.

   If, as was often the case, the insult to the nation triggered a patriotic response,
then the most important discursive development in the promulgation of nationalism by ethnographic descriptions in cosmographic tomes was not the
performance of status differentials but the creation of social groups. With printing, the insult is "blaze[d] abroad," as Arngrímur wrote (Jónsson 1904:120), and
unknown readers anywhere, of any status, could know of it. He feared that this
might be the whole world, "sithens it hath pleased some strangers by false rumours to deface, and by manifolde reproches to injurie my sayd countrey, making it a by-word, and a laughing-stocke to all other nations" (Jónsson 1904:96).
When print made depictions of nations "publike and perpetuall," it was possible
for some individuals to contest the status-creating effects of such depictions.
Yet, contested or not, the performatively created national groupings of "we's"
and "they's" remained in place, increasingly fixed with the hardening affect
of honor and dishonor and cemented with every act of rebuttal. Thus, Arngrímur's example points us to the location of the application of power, particularly in interethnic contexts, as it was becoming the doxic background to a
printed discourse of nations. Cosmographic discourse, purveying a Ptolemaic
vision of the world, ordered by methodical inscription practices and mechani-
cally reproduced in print, served to strengthen the notion of nation not only by

denoting peoples but most subtly and powerfully by the performance of group identification and difference tinged with the sting of ethnic valuation.

Cosmographic Nationalism

One could argue that Arngrímur and his countrymen may have had more reason to be nationally sensitive to the insults of the ethnographic literature than many other Europeans. Iceland was an island community with a known recorded history in which the concept of "we Icelanders" can be seen from an early date (Hastrup 1982). Moreover, status pronouncement and management were critical components of Iceland's ancient literature. The Icelandic sagas are statements of public opinion that established the status of heroic individuals and their descendant lineages. The sagas are, in a sense, metasagas, telling of verbal performances that positively and negatively established status in the early Icelandic community (Bauman 1986; Koester n.d.). Social roles and institutions in medieval Iceland reflected the place of status-performative speech in social life. Icelandic skalds were known for the praise poetry they composed in royal courts and for which they received monetary rewards (Bauman 1986). Conversely, insult poetry was controlled by the ancient legal codes, which stipulated fines for the creation or performance of status-lowering insult poetry (Finsen 1879:392–93; Arngrímur wrote about these laws in his national history of Iceland, *Crymogæa* (1609), and detailed the historic documents [Jónsson 1985]). There were recognized genres of status assessment recorded in the literature, including the quasi-ritualized forms "man-comparison" (*mannjafnaðr*) and "insult" (*senna*) (Swenson 1991). Less formally, status-assessing gossip was an important political dynamic in saga society (Kress 1991). All of these forms of status-conscious and status-performative speech were well known to Arngrímur and are part of the discursive and cultural background of his authorial stance.

Yet while it is important to keep this literary background in mind as part of the context of Arngrímur's writing, there is also ample evidence that over much of Europe nation-delineated status pronouncements were widely recognized and printed both in the national histories that proliferated beginning in the early sixteenth century and in the cosmographic dialogue that accompanied them. National historical writing emerged from various historical corners in this period: the town histories that derived from monastic chronicles became national when in the case of cities such as London the town was the focus of national life. Printers in Europe began to publish medieval "national histories" such as those by Geoffrey of Monmouth in 1508 and Gregory of Tours in 1512. National histories were also commissioned: Henry VII, for example, commissioned Polydore Vergil of Urbino to write a history of England (Thompson

1967:592–99). It was on the inspiration of King Henry's antiquarian, John Le-
land, that Danish royal historiographer Anders Sørensen Vedel (1542–1616)
traveled throughout Denmark and planned his twenty-two-volume *Chorographia regni Daniæ og Ethnographia Danica* (Jørgensen 1931). If Hakluyt, in
publishing his *Principal Navigations*, was promoting the nation by recording English success and encouraging future English maritime domination, his inclusion of an Icelander's defense of Iceland suggests that he was not merely patriotic but was sympathetic to nationalism as a value in itself. English nationalism
is often cited as a prototype or precursor of the nationalisms that were to come
later (Greenfeld 1992; Llobera 1994; Hastings 1997), and a good measure of
world-encompassing national valuation can be seen in English cosmographic
literature.

Unbeknownst to the Icelanders and perhaps to Hakluyt as well, many of the
slanders repeated in Peerse's poem were published earlier in *The Fyrst Boke of
the Introduction of Knowledge* (1547) by the English monk, Andrew Boorde. Not
only did he write that Icelanders ate tallow, lived in caves, and sold their dogs
while giving away their children, he also said, in a blatant insult, that "they be
beastly creatures unmanered and untaughte" (Boorde 1547:31). He described
his comparative method of ethnographic and geographic proclamation in the
chapter following his description of Norway and Iceland: "The vii Chapyter
sheweth howe the Auctor of thys boke how he had dwelt in Scotland and other
Ilands did go thorow and rounde about christendom, and out of christendome,
declarynge the properties of al the regyons, countreys and provynces the whiche
he did travel thorow" (Boorde 1547:32). With declarative act closely tied to
travel experience, Boorde divided the Christian and non-Christian worlds into
regions and countries. Boorde's decrees of difference according to distinct properties expressed status evaluation that both incorporated and superseded religious affiliation. His conclusion, with oblique reference to Ptolemaic geometry,
concerned not Christendom but one nation that stood out among the rest:

> Forasmoche as the most regall realme of Englande is cituated in an angle of the
> world, havyng no region in christendom nor out of christendom equivalent to it.
> The commodities, the qualite and the quantite, with other and many things
> considered within and about the sayd noble realme, wherof if I were a Jewe, a
> Turke, or a Sarasin, or any other infidele, I yet must praise and laud it, and so wold
> every man if thei dyd know of other countries as well as Englande. Wherfore all
> nacions espieng this realme to be so commodious and pleasant, they have a con-
> fluence to it more then to any other region. (Boorde 1547:33)

For Boorde, geographic positioning, ethnographic compilation, and religious
comparison led to nationalist conclusion. Boorde's crude work, however pre-
tentious the title, did not compare in writing style, carefulness of composition,
extensiveness, or organization with the cosmographic works to which Arn-

grímur responded. I present it here as an example of the less scholarly, perhaps more commonplace understanding of ethnographic speech acts. Boorde not only declares the properties of other lands but declares what others must say— "and so wold every man." His conclusion, coming on the heels of bald insults to Icelanders and Norwegians, demonstrated his intention to insult nationally, to announce the lower status of other countries while asserting the superiority of his own, all under the guise of universal knowledge.

At the other end of the scholarly spectrum, however, similar notions of ranked nations, of honor and dishonor, fame and disrepute, were at work in the development of historical writing about nations and peoples. In his *Method for the Easy Comprehension of History* Bodin identified praise and praiseworthiness as important criteria for focusing on peoples in a universal history.

> From the Greeks we come to the Italians, who are surrounded by the Alps and both seas. Since they excelled all peoples in the majesty of their empire and the glory of their deeds and through their great reputation for justice became so pre-eminent that they appear to eclipse all other nations not only in laws and institutions but also in the superiority of the language until the present, the entire antiquity of this people must be diligently investigated. (1566:23)

Other peoples fall in a lower rank of historical worthiness:

> Although the Spanish and the Britons are renowned on account of their past, yet their deeds have not been so famous as those mentioned earlier. In a similar cat-egory are the Arabs, who were noted for the antiquity of their race, but for a long time remained hidden away in slothfulness, until, bursting forth from the deserts, they drove the Persians and the Greeks from the control of Asia and Africa and won great victories in Europe. (Bodin 1566:23–34)

Finally, then, "when we shall have grasped the most important heads of the nar-rative, as it were, we may come gradually to the details. We shall investigate not only the great states but also certain mediocre and unimportant ones" (Bodin 1566:24).[5] For this French historiographer, national prowess was a means for the ordering of history. Knowledge of the status of nations and peoples would serve to guide one in developing a historical understanding of the world, show-ing the princes, nobles, jurists, and others for whom he wrote the way to virtu-ous and praiseworthy historical action.

Thus, though there may have been unintended or collateral effects of status-laden writings, there were intentional, practical aims as well. Stagl writes that Italian humanists, "being experts in the management of public opinion, . . . knew well that describing a human group as a self-contained unit can strengthen the distinctive consciousness of that group" (1995:103). He suggests that their

---

5. Jakob Benediktsson's introduction (1985) to Arngrímur's *Crymogæa* describes the heavy de-pendence of Arngrímur's later work on Bodin's *Method*.

more northerly humanist neighbors took up this perspective in their scholarship, combined with ancient rhetorical formulas for praise of places (Stagl 1995:80). One such humanist, the eminent cosmographer Sebastian Münster, is of interest here not only because he was one of Arngrímur's most frequent targets of rebuttal but because his career brings together ethnographic compilation, Ptolemaic cosmography, and practical humanistic scholarship. A brief examination of Münster's life and work will help us understand how the status-performative pronouncements of places and peoples across the Ptolemaic globe figured in the practice of humanist cosmography and the development of nationalist discourse.

Sebastian Münster, Cosmography, and Nationalism

Greenfeld (1992) has argued that German humanists of humble origins, whose status in society had been gained through academic achievement, were the protagonists of a nascent German nationalism. The career of Sebastian Münster may well present the archetype of this social category. Münster was born into a poor family, about which not much is known, in Nieder-Ingelheim in 1489 (Hantzsch 1898:6). He dedicated his life work to two lines of study, Hebrew literature and cosmography, with associated geographical, mathematical, and astronomical sciences. It is worth noting that many of Münster's teachers were specialists in "Oriental" languages and that the influence of Arab and Islamic science continued to flow into the German Renaissance through this connection.

Münster's scholarly work began in Tübingen, where he lectured in scholastic theology and mathematics at the Franciscan monastery. In Tübingen he studied Greek grammar and literature with Philipp Melanchthon and Latin rhetoric and history with Heinrich Bebel, and he was particularly influenced by mathematician and astronomer Johann Stöffler. With Stöffler he learned the theory and technology of cartography and cosmography based on the astronomical and geographic writings of Ptolemy. His first publication was a Hebrew text, published in Basel in 1516. He studied and worked in Tübingen from 1514 to 1524, but it is also likely that he spent time in Vienna in 1517–18. There he studied more geography and natural science with Johann Camers, publisher of Pliny, Pomponius Mela, and Julius Solinus, and with mathematician and astronomer Georg Tannstetter, who had edited and published Sacrobosco's *De Sphæra Mundi* (Hantzsch 1898:6, 10–13). In 1524 Münster took up a position in Hebrew studies at the University of Heidelberg, where he continued his study of cosmography. He converted to Protestantism before resettling in 1528 in Basel, where he published his *Erklerung des newen Instruments der Sůnnen* (Explanation of the New Solar Instruments) (1528). He became the first professor of Oriental languages in Basel in 1529 (Burckhardt 1945), published a trilingual dictionary of Latin, Greek, and Hebrew-Chaldean in three-column format in 1530 (Hantzsch 1898:23), and published a book on lunar instruments in 1531. At the same time, he edited and published a full Hebrew Bible with Latin translations. We might apply to Münster Said's comment that for the romantic Orientalist, "anyone who, like Schlegel or Franz Bopp, mastered an Oriental language was a spiritual hero, a knight-errant bringing back to Europe a sense of holy mission it had now lost" (1979:115). This role was established in the Renaissance with precisely this heroic Christian mission of locating and publishing important religious texts. These scholars found practical use for their linguistic abilities, which gave them access not only to the biblical world but also to the mathematical and geometrical writings of Arabic and Hebrew scholarship. And as Said continued, "what mattered was not Asia so much as Asia's *use to* . . . Europe" (1979:115).

At this point in his life Münster had acquired both skill and reputation in publishing popular types of printed works: religious texts, maps, and practical informational compendia. In 1528, with patriotic intentions he had sought to compile information about German lands and appended to his book on solar instruments an "exhortation and request to geography enthusiasts to help in the correct description of the German Nation." In 1530, at the urging of a Basel printer, he published an eighty-page educational text about German geography in which he presented a brief accounting of Tacitus's Germania and raised the question of Germany's borders (Hantzsch 1898:36–37). Münster thought it was the obligation of scholars to serve the "gemeinen Mann" [common man] and the "gemeinen Nutzen teutscher Nation" [public well-being of the German nation].[6] In 1537 he published a German translation of his Horologiographia, on the functioning of time-telling devices (1533), intended for artisans such as painters, builders, and metal craftsmen. He also made use of practical, geometrical knowledge himself—his career included the publication of 142 maps, many of which were of individual nations, both past and then existing.

One could speculate that such pleas for political unity that would mirror the unity of the German-speaking scholarly world contributed to the conceptual and political unification processes that characterized emerging European nationalisms. From the early use of the term *nation* in monastic scholarly communities (Kemiläinen 1964), scholars were identified with their ethnic-national origins. Münster's career took him to Tübingen, Heidelberg, Vienna, and Basel and put him in contact with German-writing correspondents all over the German-speaking countries. His call for help and his dedication to serving the

6. Hantzsch quotes Münster here but does not give a clear reference to the source. Shortly before his death Münster published a geometry text that explained in common terms the mathematics and techniques of geometric reckoning (Hantzsch 1898:129).

interests of the *teutscher Nation* suggest a conception of national unity. He expressed a similar idea of unity in his introduction to the chapter on Italy in the *Cosmographei*. Explicitly framing map consciousness in the text, he instructed the reader to take in the depiction of Italy as a whole and "have a good sense of how it is separated from all other lands" (Münster 1550:clxvi). It should be noted, however, that even within Germany the exercise of group status differentiation in publication was a developing trend. Greenfeld (1992:284) argues that pan-German nationalism did not take hold in part because of the territorial rivalries of German princes. This corresponded to regionalized status pronouncement in ethnographic and geographic writing. Stagl writes that "while Rhetoric was moving in the opposite direction, the praise and scorn of regions had become a developed descriptive scheme" (1979:616). Münster's *Cosmographei* contributed to this discursive divisiveness by separating the regions of Germany into princedoms, just as nations were divided throughout the rest of the world. The principle that the nearer and better known could be more finely divided and described created smaller groupings antithetical to the pan-German unity Münster advocated. He may have been indifferent to status divisiveness because his characterizations were primarily in the form of praise.

Princely wrangling aside, all of Münster's career suggests that, with international vision, he had national concerns himself and that his scholarship was dedicated to developing geopolitical, national self-awareness. Out of the 1,234 pages of text, book 3 of the *Cosmographei* on the German nation filled 656 pages. Rubiés mentions that Münster's French translator, François de Belleforest, expanded the French section, commenting that Münster was "'in love with his country (as reason demands)'" (1993:180). Münster explained that he would describe "*our* German lands" (emphasis added), and he does not, of course, use this possessive pronoun for other countries. The *Cosmographei* was not organized purely into national chapters, nor was every national characterization filled with praise or insult. At the same time, though inconsistent in the amount of space given and the nature of the characterizations, national organization—for example, Hyspania, Gallia, Engelland, Italia—figured prominently in the book, chapter, and section headings, and page headers maintained national identifications as internal regions were described.

We still might ask whether status differentiation played into his understanding of national interests and the construction of Münster's 1544 *Cosmographia*. Some descriptions were clearly denigrating or insulting. In his first cosmography of 1537 he described the land of Tartaria as barren and the inhabitants as "a rude and bloodthirsty people" who lived in tents. The 1544 edition showed an image in the Tartar section of roasting humans on a spit (Münster 1544:625). Closer to home, he wrote in the *Cosmographei* of 1550, "The Spaniard has a clever mind. . . . When they have half studied they act as if they are very learned and show it with their gabble." He continued, "You can hardly find anyone who speaks Latin well. . . . [T]hey are always mixing it up" (Münster 1550:lxxvi). If nations, in their scope and unity, are imagined, such quips can create the affective reality of the national imaginary.

Münster's letters provide insight into how national descriptions were managed. In August 1545, shortly after finishing the second edition, Münster wrote to the chief counsel of the Swedish court, Georg Normann, in Stockholm: "I am glad that the King is pleased with my work. What I wrote about the remote tribes of your country and about the gold mine I did not make up out of my head, rather either Olaus Magnus or Ziegler had said this before me. I will cut it in the third edition" (Burmeister 1988:54). Here it is clear that Münster was aware of the valuations implicit in national depictions. In this case, his correspondence was concerned with the image management of a foreign monarch's realm. It is important to note that each foreign language edition was edited for its target audience (Strauss 1965:146). Münster asked that Normann send any corrections and commented, "Whenever we receive strange or foreign news we tend to believe that it is right, indeed we have had the opinion of Scandinavia that cosmographers had toward Africa for many years, as they say, Africa always brings something new" (Burmeister 1988:54). Though it is possible that both King Gustav and Münster were interested in accuracy rather than appearance, national bias seems to be present in Münster's chapter on Denmark, in which he told how Swedish prisoners were mistreated under the rule of King Erik.

Effects of speech acts can be hard to gauge in material terms, but status-performative utterances can have material, economic consequences (Irvine 1989). Similarly, as I mentioned above, medieval Icelandic skalds received patron rewards for praise poetry, while insult poetry bore the risk of statutory fine. Münster's correspondence reveals that printed accounts of nations in cosmographic discourse were not entirely removed from such a political economy of speech acts. In 1550, writing on the occasion of the publication of the immense fourth edition, Münster wrote to Normann's liege lord, King Gustav Vasa: "Illustrious and powerful King, it is now four years since Your Majesty sent me, because of the dedication of the German edition of my Cosmography[,] . . . a letter and with noble and royal kindness and generosity, a gift" (Burmeister 1988:23). He went on to say that ties had been maintained by a visit from Normann in intervening years. The gift suggests that the king, at least, was concerned with how his country would be portrayed—that he perceived the literature as affecting his nation's status and sought to reward a positive depiction. The discourse of cosmographic national descriptions was not just a reflection or chronicling of the international political world of the time; it was also a manifestation of it.

Münster died in 1552, but the publication of his cosmography continued, expanding to over a thousand pages until its final edition in 1628 (Strauss 1965). Forty years after Münster's death readers from a distant island, who had not been given the opportunity to manage their image, would complain of mistreatment.

Power, Publishing, and Discourse

In this discussion it may seem that I have outlined a historical progression—that what I have tried to describe is the emergence of nationalism as consequence or effect of ethnographic publication. First, there were traditions of ethnographic writing that expressed political interests in peoples around the known world. Then, the tradition of mapping the globe as it had been codified by Ptolemy and elaborated in Arab science spread widely with the advent of printing. People were mapped onto this geometrical locating system, and increasingly ordered methods for recording and organizing ethnogeographic information allowed Ptolemaically plotted peoples to be portrayed as having locally distinguishing characteristics. In Hegelian fashion this discursive system posed external others whose antithetical images served to define nations as (collective) selves. The characterizations attached to these selves, however, were not neutral. Following venerable ethnographic tradition, they invoked politically conscious, power-imbued insult (and praise). In this system the other-image made possible the apparent unity of one's national self, but it did so by reflecting back a dialogically constituted self ennobled or besmirched by value-laden categories of diet, clothing, housing construction, religion, and the like. The writings thereby performed a world of "we's" and "they's" that rankled as they ranked. As the divisions of the mapped world became more uniform and the everyday presence of maps brought border consciousness to administrations (and to border populations), nations came to be known as territorially bounded units made up of individuated citizenries, each with its own character and characteristics, each bound by a sense of national honor and status.

While such an explanation might have some appeal (e.g., Mignolo 1995:315), it was not my intention to oversimplify so profoundly. This historical progression ignores the fact that Roman and medieval European scholars spoke of nations in the absence of Ptolemaic geometry and that Ptolemaic geometry was used to place individual cities and sacred and Christian territories as much as to locate peoples in politically unified realms. Neither does such a narrative take into consideration the contributions of urbanization processes (Armstrong 1982); the rivalrous politics of history in the Italian city-states (Cassirer 1946; Struever 1970); the historical projects of dynastic monarchies; the later development of political economic theory among German Cameralists, who defined nations in terms of population and economic potential (Small 1909); and the Europe-wide dissemination of pamphlets theorizing nation-focused, "reason of state" politics (Tuck 1989). It leaves out individual incentives such as the social mobility of merchants and businessmen within nations (Greenfeld 1992). It does not consider nation-based ideas of international relations from the Spanish jurists to Grotius (Carro 1971; Losada 1971). Finally, it ignores the profound effect that wars had on territorial group formation and group relations and fails to weigh the long-term effects of various forms of domination through taxation, administration, and delimitations of rights, especially on developing citizenries in the print-conscious world. All of these are important lineages in the genealogy of nationalism and need to be considered in understanding its relationship to changing theorizations of the social world. My aim here was, rather, to understand the embedding of power in the discourse on nations and to see "nationalism" emerging as a focus on, sensitivity toward, and adherence to the gravitational force of this power. Nationalism is and descends from a status-performative, globally circumscribed discourse that has roots in the globalizing vision of Ptolemaically inspired cosmography and the history of ethnographic writing.

It is also important to note that power relations in the discourse cannot be seen as merely a function of the powerfulness of any "speaking nation," even if that could be clearly identified in each case. Bourdieu (1991:107–16) criticized Austin's analysis of speech performatives for failing to recognize the significance of the social position of the performing speaker. He argued that in order to create through speaking, to name people or their deeds, the speaker must be located in a position of power, that is, higher than those of whom he or she speaks. This positioning then became important in his discussion of regional identity, when he argued that struggles of regional and ethnic identity were "struggles over the monopoly of the power to make people see and believe, to get them to know and to recognize, to impose the legitimate divisions of the social world and, thereby, to *make and unmake groups*" (Bourdieu 1991:221). While it is clear that what I have said agrees with Bourdieu's position that "regionalist discourse is a *performative discourse*" and that at issue is the power to make and unmake groups, it is important to see that this making and unmaking is more complex than a reflex of domination (Butler 1997). Social position is only one aspect of the context that makes the exercise of power possible and that power creates. What I hope to have shown as well is that from the early days of ethnographic publishing the status indexes and insults created participant frames as they performed status marking. The social position of the author mattered not because of a presupposed nation-internal social status but because the author was an ethnic-national voice and referent point around which groups of "us" and "them" could be performatively created. Arngrímur's "we Icelanders" was arguably just as powerful in creating the social reality of Iceland-versus-other-nations as Münster's pronouncement of "they," the Icelanders, even though Münster's scholarly authority was vastly greater in the European audience frame. Ethnographic publications created "we's" and "they's" that were identified and experienced as nations, and it is in this felt reality translated into personal honor and status that we should seek a powerful source of the discursive makings of nationalism.

Thus the study of ethnographic publications offers us an alternative to those theories of nationalism that seek to understand it purely as a result of nation-internal mechanisms. From the perspective of such theories, we may wonder at such phenomena as how "Englishness could stand for everybody in the British Isles" and how this national consciousness "always had to absorb all the differences of class, of region, of gender, in order to present itself as a homogenous entity" (Hall 1991:22). "The power of a hegemonizing nationalism to take in its stride a whole range of dissenting voices" (Chatterjee 1993:151) becomes less perplexing if we see the larger framework of the international, the cosmographic, globalized articulation of status relations that made it possible to insult or mark as better or worse flatly across the lines of class, region, gender, and ethnicity.

Recent discussions of globalization and transnational social movements have pointed to the theoretical significance of an image of a world of nations. As Liisa Malkki put it, "one way of studying the naturalization of nationness is to pursue the international; for underlying all the competing nationalisms of the modern era lies a fundamental vision of global order itself, a vision of the international" (1994:42). One might presume from current discussions that this global perspective is a distinctly modern phenomenon. But the contemporary global vision, however much it has changed, has long been an essential component in the formulation of concepts of "nation" and the felt reality of national identity. Nationness was naturalized when creative indexes of national "we's" and "they's" were made simultaneously individually and nationally compelling by a widely disseminated discourse of peoples in the world. It absorbed the differences of class, region, and gender as it performed social hierarchy of a different sort, the repercussions of which are still being felt today.

Acknowledgments

This essay has been a long time in the works and has taken me to a number of rich library collections. I would like to thank librarians at the Regenstein Library, University of Chicago, the Fiske Icelandic Collection, Cornell University, the John Carter Brown Library, Brown University, the Rare Book and Manuscript Library, Columbia University, and the Manuscript Division of the Öffentliche Bibliothek, Universität Basel. I would like also to thank two anonymous reviewers for helpful criticism. Special thanks to Rosalind Morris, George Stocking, Jr., and Richard Handler for critical readings and numerous helpful comments and suggestions.

References Cited

AE   *American Ethnologist*
ARA   *Annual Review of Anthropology*
HA   *History and Anthropology*

Abrahams, R. D. 1970. A Performance-Centred Approach to Gossip. *Man* 5:290–301.
———. 1992. Insult. In *Folklore, Cultural Performances, and Popular Entertainments: A Communications-Centered Handbook*. Ed. R. Bauman, 145–49. New York.
Ahmad, N. 1980. *Muslims and the Science of Geography*. Dacca.
Anderson, B. 1983. *Imagined Communities: Reflections on the Origin and Spread of Nationalism*. London.
Apian, P. 1550. *Cosmographia Petri Apiani*. Ed. Gemma Frisius. Antwerp.
Ardener, E. 1989. Language, Ethnicity and Population. In *The Voice of Prophecy and Other Essays*, 65–71. Oxford.
Armstrong, J. A. 1982. *Nations before Nationalism*. Chapel Hill, NC.
Asad, T. 1973. Two European Images of Non-European Rule. In *Anthropology and the Colonial Encounter*. Ed. T. Asad, 103–18. Atlantic Highlands, NJ.
Aston, E. 1611. To the friendly Reader. In *The manners, lawes, and customes of all nations*. London.
Barth, F. 1969. *Ethnic Groups and Boundaries*. Oslo.
Bartlett, R. 1982. *Gerald of Wales, 1146–1223*. Oxford.
Bauman, R. 1986. Performance and Honor in 13th-Century Iceland. *Journal of American Folklore* 99:131–50.
Benediktsson, J. 1957. Introduction and Notes. In *Arngrimi Jonae Opera Latine Conscripta*, vol. 4, *Bibliotheca Arnamagnœana*, vol. 12. Copenhagen.
———. 1968. Formáli. In *Brevis Commentarius de Islandia 1593*. *Íslenzk rit í frumgerð*, vol. 2. Reykjavík.
———. 1985. Inngangur. *Crymogæa*. In *Safn Sögufélags*. Ed. J. Benedktsson. Reykjavík.
Berggren, J. L., and A. Jones. 2000. *Ptolemy's Geography: An Annotated Translation of the Theoretical Chapters*. Princeton, NJ.
Bhabha, H. 1994. *The Location of Culture*. London.
Bodin, J. 1566 [1945]. *Method for the Easy Comprehension of History*. Trans. B. Reynolds. New York.
Boorde, A. 1547. *The Fyrst Boke of the Introduction of Knowledge*. Institut für Anglistik und Amerikanistik (Salzburg), 92:2.
Bourdieu, P. 1991. *Language and Symbolic Power*. Trans. G. Raymond and M. Adamson, ed. J. B. Thompson. Cambridge, MA.
Bowen, M. 1981. *Empiricism and Geographical Thought: From Francis Bacon to Alexander von Humboldt*. Cambridge, Eng.
Brenneis, D. 1980. Fighting Words. In *Not Work Alone*. Ed. J. Cherfas and R. Lewin, 166–80. Beverly Hills, CA.
———. 1984. Grog and Gossip in Bhatgaon: Style and Substance in Fiji Indian Conversation. *AE* 11:487–506.
———. 1988. Language and Disputing. *ARA* 17:221–37.

Bricker, V. 1971. Three Genres of Tzotzil Insult. *Janua Linguarum, Series Practica* 158:183–203.

Brown, R., and A. Gilman. 1960. The Pronouns of Power and Solidarity. In *Style in Language*. Ed. T. Sebeok, 253–76. Cambridge, MA.

Burckhardt, P. 1945. *Basler Chroniken*. Basel.

Burmeister, K. 1988. *Sebastian Münster in Wort und Bild 1488–1988*, vol. 37. Ingelheim.

Butler, J. 1997. *Excitable Speech: A Politics of the Performative*. New York.

Caesar, G. J. 1982. *The Conquest of Gaul*. Trans. S. A. Handford. London.

Campbell, M. 1988. *The Witness and the Other World: Exotic European Travel Writing, 400–1600*. Ithaca, NY.

Carro, V. 1971. The Spanish Theological-Juridical Renaissance and the Ideology of Bartolomé de Las Casas. In Friede and Keen 1971:67–125.

Cassirer, E. 1946. *The Myth of the State*. New Haven, CT.

Chatterjee, P. 1993. *The Nation and Its Fragments: Colonial and Postcolonial Histories*. Princeton, NJ.

Clifford, J. 1983. On Ethnographic Authority. *Representations* 1:118–46.

———. 1986. On Ethnographic Allegory. In Clifford and Marcus 1986:98–121.

Clifford, J., and G. Marcus, eds. 1986. *Writing Culture: The Poetics and Politics of Ethnography*. Berkeley, CA.

Comaroff, J., and J. Comaroff. 1992. *Ethnography and the Historical Imagination*. Boulder, CO.

Copenhaver, B., and C. Schmitt. 1992. *Renaissance Philosophy*, vol. 3. New York.

Delano-Smith, C., and R. Kain. 1999. *English Maps: A History*. Toronto.

Dirks, N., ed. 1992. *Colonialism and Culture*. Ann Arbor, MI.

Eidheim, H. 1969. When Ethnic Identity Is a Social Stigma. In Barth 1969:39–57.

Eisenstein, E. 1980. *The Printing Press as an Agent of Change*. Cambridge, Eng.

Eriksen, T. 1993. *Ethnicity and Nationalism: Anthropological Perspectives*. Boulder, CO.

Evans, J. 1991. *Herodotus, Explorer of the Past*. Princeton, NJ.

Finsen, V., ed. 1879. Grágás (efter det Arnamagnæanske Haandskrift Nr. 334 fol., Staðarhólsbok). Copenhagen.

Fischer, H. 1970. "Völkerkunde," "Ethnographie," "Ethnologie": Kritische Kontrolle der frühesten Belege. *Zeitschrift für Ethnologie* 95:169–82.

Foster, R. 1991. Making National Cultures in the Global Ecumene. *ARA* 20:235–60.

Foucault, M. 1980. *Power/Knowledge: Selected Interviews & Other Writings 1972–1977*. New York.

Friede, J., and B. Keen, eds. 1971. *Bartolomé de Las Casas in History: Toward an Understanding of the Man and His Work*. DeKalb, IL.

Friedrich, P. 1979. Structural Implications of Russian Pronominal Usage. In *Language, Context and the Imagination*, 63–125. Stanford, CA.

Gellner, E. 1965 [1978]. *Thought and Change*. Chicago.

———. 1983. *Nations and Nationalism*. Ithaca, NY.

Gluckman, M. 1963. Gossip and Scandal. *Current Anthropology* 4:307–16.

Greenfeld, L. 1992. *Nationalism: Five Roads to Modernity*. Cambridge, MA.

Hálfdanarson, G. 1996. Hvað gerir Íslendinga að þjóð. *Skírnir* 170 (vor):7–31.

Hall, S. 1991. The Local and the Global: Globalization and Ethnicity. In *Culture, Globalization and the World-System*. Ed A. D. King, 19–39. Binghamton, NY.

Hampton, T. 2001. *Literature and Nation in the Sixteenth Century: Inventing Renaissance France*. Ithaca, NY.

Handler, R. 1988. *Nationalism and the Politics of Culture in Quebec*. Madison, WI.

Hanks, W. 1996. *Language and Communicative Practices*. Boulder, CO.

Hantzsch, V. 1898. Sebastian Münster, Leben, Werk, wissenschaftliche Bedeutung. *Abhandlungen der philologisch-historischen Classe der Königlichen Sächsischen Gesellschaft der Wissenschaften* 18(3).

Hastings, A. 1997. *The Construction of Nationhood: Ethnicity, Religion and Nationalism*. Cambridge, Eng.

Hastrup, K. 1982. Establishing an Ethnicity: The Emergence of the "Icelanders" in the Early Middle Ages. In *Semantic Anthropology*. Ed. D. Parkin, 145–60. London.

Helgerson, R. 1992. Camões, Hakluyt, and the Voyages of Two Nations. In Dirks 1992:27–63.

Helms, M. 1988. *Ulysses' Sail: An Ethnnographic Odyssey of Power, Knowledge, and Geographical Distance*. Princeton, NJ.

Herzfeld, M. 1987. *Anthropology through the Looking Glass: Critical Ethnography in the Margins of Europe*. New York.

———. 1997. *Cultural Intimacy: Social Poetics in the Nation-State*. New York.

Hobsbawm, E. 1990. *Nations and Nationalism since 1780*. Cambridge, Eng.

Hodgen, M. 1964. *Early Anthropology in the Sixteenth and Seventeenth Centuries*. Philadelphia.

Ibn Khaldun. 1958. *The Muqaddimah (An Introduction to History)*, vol. 43. New York.

Irvine, J. 1985. Status and Style in Language. *ARA* 14:557–81.

———. 1989. When Talk Isn't Cheap: Language and Political Economy. *AE* 16:248–67.

———. 1993. Insult and Responsibility: Verbal Abuse in a Wolof Village. In *Responsibility and Evidence in Oral Discourse*. Ed. J. Hill and J. Irvine, 105–34. Cambridge, Eng.

———. 1998. Ideologies of Honorific Language. In *Language Ideologies: Practice and Theory*. Ed. B. Schieffelin et al., 51–67. New York.

Jones, W. 1971. The Image of the Barbarian in Medieval Europe. *Comparative Studies in Society and History* 13:376–407.

Jónsson, A. 1904. A Briefe Commentarie. In *The Principal Navigations, Voyages, Traffiques and Discoveries of the English Nation*, vol. 4. Ed. R. Hakluyt, 88–197. Glasgow.

———. 1985. *Crymogæa*. Reykjavík.

Jørgensen, E. 1931. *Historieforskning og Historieskrivning i Danmark indtil aar 1800*. Copenhagen.

Karant-Nunn, S. 1994. Humanism to the Fore: Renaissance Studies in Germany Today. *Renaissance Quarterly* 47:930–41.

Kemiläinen, A. 1964. *Nationalism: Problems Concerning the Word, the Concept and Classification*, vol. 3. Jyväskylän.

Kennedy, W. 2003. *The Site of Petrarchism: Early Modern National Sentiment in Italy, France, and England*. Baltimore, MD.

Koester, D. N.d. Reputation and Deliberate History in Saga Iceland.

Kolb, R. 1976. *Caspar Peucer's Library: Portrait of a Wittenberg Professor of the Mid-Sixteenth Century*. St. Louis, MO.

Krantz, A. 1546. *Chronica Regnorum Aquilonarium Daniæ Suetiæ Noruagiæ*. Argent.

Kress, H. 1991. Staðlausir stafir: Um slúður sem uppsprettu frásagnar í Íslendingasögum. *Skírnir* 165:130–56.

Labov, W. 1972. Rules for Ritual Insults. In *Rappin' and Stylin' Out: Communication in Urban Black America*. Ed. T. Kochman, 265–314. Urbana, IL.

Llobera, J. 1994. *The God of Modernity: The Development of Nationalism in Western Europe*. Oxford.

Losada, Á. 1971. The Controversy between Sepúlveda in the Junta of Valladolid. In Friede and Keen 1971:279–307.

Malkki, L. 1994. Citizens of Humanity: Internationalism and the Imagined Community of Nations. *Diaspora* 3:41–68.

Mauss, M. 1920 [1969]. La nation. In *Oeuvres*, 3:573–625. Paris.

McGrane, B. 1989. *Beyond Anthropology: Society and the Other*. New York.

Merry, S. 1984. Rethinking Gossip and Scandal. In *Toward a General Theory of Social Control*. Ed. D. Black, 1:261–85. New York.

Mignolo, W. 1995. *The Darker Side of the Renaissance: Literacy, Territoriality, and Colonization*. Ann Arbor, MI.

Mitchell, T. 1992. Orientalism and the Exhibitionary Order. In Dirks 1992:289–317.

Münster, S. 1528. *Erklerung des newen Instruments der Sůnnen/ nach allen seinen Scheyben und Circkeln. Item eyn vermanung Sebastiani Münnster an alle liebhaber der künstenn/ im hilff zů thun zů warer unnd rechter beschreybung Teütscher Nation*. Oppenheym.

———. 1530. *Germaniae atque aliarum regionum, quae ad imperium usque Constantinopolitanu protenduntur, descriptio*. Basel.

———. 1537. *Horologiographia post priorem aeditionem*. Basel.

———. 1544. *Cosmographia. Beschreibung aller Lender durch Sebastianum Munsterum in welcher begriffen aller voelcker, herschafften, Stetten und namhafftiger flecken herkomen: Sitten, gebreüch, ordnung glauben, secten, und hantierung, durch die ganze welt, und fürnemlich Teütscher nation. Was auch besunders in iedem landt gefunden, unnd darin beschehen sey. Alles mit figuren und schoenen landt taflen erklert, und für augen gestelt*. Basel.

———. 1550. *Cosmographei oder beschreibung aller länder, herschafften, fürnemsten stetten, geschichten, gebrauchen, hantierungen etc. jetz zum dritten mal trefflich sere . . . gemeret vnd gebessert*. Basel.

Olaus Magnus. 1555. *Historia de gentibus Septentrionalibus: Earumque diuersis statibus, conditionibus, moribus, ritibus, superstitionibus, disciplinis, exercitiis, regimine, victu, bellis, structuris, instrumentis, ac mineris metallicis, et rebus mirabilibus, necnon vniuersis penè animalibus in Septentrione degentibus, eorumque natura*. Rome.

Ong, W. 1972. Ramus, Peter. In *The Encyclopedia of Philosophy*. Ed. P. Edwards, 7:66–68. New York.

Pagden, A. 1982. *The Fall of Natural Man: The American Indian and the Origins of Comparative Ethnology*. Cambridge, Eng.

Parry, J. H. 1963. *The Age of Reconnaissance*. London.

Penrose, B. 1955. *Travel and Discovery in the Renaissance, 1420–1620*. Cambridge, MA.

Peucer, C. 1554. *De dimensione terræ et geometrica numerandi*. Wittenberg.

Pickett, T. 1996. *Inventing Nations: Justifications of Authority in the Modern World*. Westport, CT.

Pratt, M. 1986. Fieldwork in Common Places. In Clifford and Marcus 1986:27–50.

————. 1992. *Imperial Eyes: Studies in Travel Writing and Transculturation*. New York.

Ptolemaeus, C. 1475. *Cosmographia*. Trans. J. Angelus. Vicenza.

Roberts, J. 1980. *The Pelican History of the World*. London.

Rosaldo, R. 1986. From the Door of His Tent: The Fieldworker and the Inquisitor. In Clifford and Marcus 1986:77–97.

Rubiés, J.-P. 1993. New Worlds and Renaissance Ethnology. *HA* 6:157–97.

————. 1996. Instructions for Travelers: Teaching the Eye to See. *HA* 9:139–90.

————. 2000. *Travel and Ethnology in the Renaissance: South India through European Eyes, 1250–1625*. Cambridge, Eng.

Ruwet, N. 1982. *Grammaire des insultes et autres études*. Paris.

Sacrobosco (John Holywood). 1450. *De Sphæra Mundi*. Ms. 183, Rare Book and Manuscript Library, Columbia University.

Sahlins, P. 1989. *Boundaries: The Making of France and Spain in the Pyrenees*. Berkeley, CA.

Said, E. 1979. *Orientalism*. New York.

Seelman, W. 1883. Gories Peerse's Gedicht van Island. *Jahrbuch des Vereins für niederdeutsche Sprachforschung* 9:110–25.

Seton-Watson, H. 1977. *Nations and States*. Boulder, CO.

Sezgin, F. 1987a. *The Contribution of the Arabic-Islamic Geographers to the Formation of the World Map*. Frankfurt.

————, ed. 1987b. *Klaudios Ptolemaios Geography, Arabic Translation*. Frankfurt.

Small, A. 1909. *The Cameralists*. Chicago.

Smith, A. D. 1998. *Nationalism and Modernism*. London.

————. 1999. *Myths and Memories of the Nation*. Oxford.

Stagl, J. 1979. Vom dialog zum Fragebogen, Miszellen zur Geschichte der Ethnologie. *Kölner Zeitschrift für Soziologie und Socialpsychologie* 31:611–38.

————. 1983. Das Reisen als Kunst und als Wissenschaft (16.–18. Jahrhundert). *Zeitschrift für Ethnologie* 108:15–33.

————. 1995. *A History of Curiosity: The Theory of Travel, 1550–1800*. Chur, Switzerland.

Stoler, A. 1992. Rethinking Colonial Categories: European Communities and the Boundaries of Rule. In Dirks 1992:319–52.

Strauss, G. 1965. A Sixteenth-Century Encyclopedia: Sebastian Münster's Cosmography and Its Editions. In *From the Renaissance to the Counter-Reformation*. Ed. C. Carter, 145–63. New York.

Struever, N. 1970. *The Language of History in the Renaissance: Rhetoric and Historical Consciousness in Florentine Humanism*. Princeton, NJ.

Swenson, K. 1991. *Performing Definitions: Two Genres of Insult in Old Norse Literature*, vol. 3. Columbia, SC.

Thomas, N. 1994. *Colonialism's Culture: Anthropology, Travel and Government*. Princeton, NJ.

Thompson, J. W. 1967. *A History of Historical Writing*. Gloucester, MA.

Todorov, T. 1993. *On Human Diversity: Nationalism, Racism, and Exoticism in French Thought*. Trans. C. Porter. Cambridge, MA.

Tuck, R. 1989. *Hobbes*. Oxford.

Vasaly, A. 1993. *Representation: Images of the World in Ciceronian Oratory*. Berkeley, CA.

Vermeulen, H. F. 1992. The Emergence of "Ethnography" ca. 1770 in Göttingen. *History of Anthropology Newsletter* 19(2):6–9.

————. 1994. Proiskhozhdenie i institutsionalizatsiia poniatiia Völkerkunde (1771–1843). *Etnograficheskoe obozrenie* 4:101–9.

Wegener, C. 1851. Historiske Efterretninger om Anders Sørensen Vedel. In *Den danske krønike af Saxo Grammaticus oversat af Anders Sørensen Vedel*. Ed. C. Wegener. Copenhagen.

Williams, B. 1990. Nationalism, Traditionalism, and the Problem of Cultural Inauthenticity. In *Nationalist Ideologies and the Production of National Cultures*. Ed. R. G. Fox, 112–29. Washington, D.C.

Wytfliet, C., and R. A. Skelton. 1597 [1964]. *Descriptionis Ptolemaicae augmentum, sive Occidentis notitia brevis sic commentario*. Amsterdam.

Ziegler, J., and W. Weissenburg. 1536. *Terræ sanctæ, quam Palæstinam nominant, Syriæ, Arabiæ, Ægypti & Schondiæ doctissima descriptio*. Strasbourg.

ESCAPE FROM THE ANDAMANS

Tracking, Offshore Incarceration, and Ethnology in the Back of Beyond

KATH WESTON

They had great hopes for the boy. With his intelligence he might have become a teacher, a translator, a diplomatic envoy. Put differently, in the language of those who sought to colonize him, he might have served as an important source of knowledge about the Jarawas, the last "hostile tribe" of "marauders" in the Andaman Islands, and, upon his release, a lesson in the power and benevolence of the British administration for "his friends" back in the forest. Transported to the penal colony of Port Blair in late February 1902 as a captive taken during a government-organized moonlit raid on a suspected Jarawa encampment, the unnamed boy succumbed to dysentery and fever less than three months hence. His fellow detainees, also children, a baby and an older youth "who could not be induced to speak," perished within the year. "All three Jarawa captives are dead, and nothing has been learnt of their language," noted the chief commissioner, the highest colonial official on the islands, in his annual administration report (RAA 1902–3:44). Which loss he regretted most—life or linguistics— the attenuated prose of government documents does not reveal.

In the British penal colony at Port Blair in the Andaman Islands, popularly known as Kala Pani, or Black Water, prison discipline and the emerging discipline of anthropology lived on intimate terms. Kala Pani was nicknamed for the

---

Kath Weston directs the Women, Gender, and Sexuality Program at Harvard University. Her books include *Gender in Real Time: Power and Transience in a Visual Age*; *Families We Choose: Lesbians, Gays, Kinship*; and *Long Slow Burn: Sexuality and Social Science*. Her current research focuses on offshore incarceration, surveillance regimes, and configurations of identity under different forms of the state.

vast expanse of ocean that separated it from the Indian subcontinent, where most early detainees had come of age. This colony's settlement in the Bay of Bengal, founded in 1858, originally provided a place for the relocation of prisoners taken during the 1857 War of Independence (or Indian Mutiny, depending on one's perspective). Almost from the first, however, "mutineers" (and later "freedom fighters" cum "terrorists") were incarcerated under grueling conditions alongside people criminalized for ostensibly apolitical offenses. In colonial India there was no clear separation between political and apolitical crimes. Train robberies yielded spoils that sometimes financed nationalist struggle, while apparently straightforward charges of manslaughter correlated with a rise in violent disputes over money and land when the colonial government raised taxes. Even the most avowedly apolitical of prisoners could have their escapes celebrated retrospectively as a sacrifice (*balidan*) for freedom in nationalist tellings of Andamanese history (Pandya 1997).

After occupying the islands in 1942, Japanese authorities shut down the colony's Cellular Jail, only to reopen it to house local residents accused of espionage. Former convicts were forced to labor on the construction of an airstrip and other projects associated with the war. Then in December 1943 Japan invited Netaji Subhas Chandra Bose, commander of the Indian National Army (Azaad Hind Fauj), to raise the flag of independence in Port Blair, effectively refiguring the Andamans as a transnational site caught within the net of shifting political jurisdictions and a moving border.

Following World War II the archipelago reverted to British control until India gained independence in 1947. The government of India now maintains the remains of the British Cellular Jail as a national memorial, complete with sound and light shows in Hindi and English that commemorate the struggle for freedom from colonization (Aggarwal 1995:46, 229). At the Aberdeen bazaar in Port Blair the descendents of convicts mingle with naval officers, staff from the Anthropological Survey of India, couples from Bengal on honeymoon packages, and servers-in-training from the tourist hotels who eagerly await their next posting.

Back in the nineteenth century the convict ships that set out for the Andamans from Calcutta, Burma, and Madras packed journalists accused of sedition, men convicted of murder or theft, and "hereditary female poisoners" together with the authors of conspiracies (organized or imagined) directed at the colonial state. Magistrates tended to sentence prisoners to transportation to the Andamans for offenses they considered grave. In addition to life convicts the islands at various points housed thousands of term convicts, including women remanded to the Andamans after 1862 in an effort to encourage marriage for privileged categories of male prisoners. With the rise of a nationalist movement directed against British rule and, more recently, Hindutva politics, stories of political prisoners cast in a heroic mode drew attention away from the fate of the

1. The view from one wing of the British Cellular Jail in Port Blair, overlooking seating for the sound and light show. (Photo credit: Kath Weston)

vast majority of prisoners, as the Andamans became "thoroughly colonized by the hegemonic memory of Indian nationalism" (Sen 2000:v).

These same islands have gained renown among anthropologists and non-governmental organizations for a rather differently fetishized reason, their first inhabitants: *adivasis*, or "tribals," to subcontinent-based human rights groups; "savages," "primitives," "aborigines," and "junglies" (a pejorative even in the nineteenth century) to penal colony officials; and "indigenous peoples" to A. R. Radcliffe-Brown's intellectual heirs. For indigenous rights activists, the very notion of a sound and light show commemorating freedom from colonization in this multiply colonized space evokes no little irony. Anthropologists remember the Andamans primarily for the contribution that Radcliffe-Brown's research there made to the history of the discipline and the standardization of fieldwork as an investigative method. Ask them about the Andaman Islanders and they tend to recall page after page of rituals, myths, and analysis of "social function," not the passages that Radcliffe-Brown used to mark the impact of the penal colony at Port Blair on everyday life among everyday Andamanese.

In this essay I want to bring these different sides of the Andaman archipelago's troubled histories together, as they were bound up together, from the time that the penal settlement was authorized by one of the East India Company's last official acts. This rereading links anthropology to incarceration, incarceration to indigeneity, ethnologists to penal colony officials (for in the beginning, they were one and the same), Andamanese trackers to prisoners still in their fetters, scientifically delineated tortures in the prison to carefully annotated descriptions of Aka-Bea peacemaking ceremonies, Andamanese children carried off to be raised in the settlement nursery to rumors of Jarawas attempting to escape into the forest and convicts attempting to escape to the mainland by raft. The essay is part of a larger project that focuses on the interplay between ethnographic investigation and penal colony administration, on the links between the birth of anthropology and the elaboration of the prison in the context of different sorts of states. What follows, then, is a disciplinary history in which ethnology remains on close if often fractious terms not only with missionary enterprise and colonial administration but also with prison operations, internment, and a host of other measures that found their justification in the eradication of perceived threats to the prevailing institutions of government.

Ethnology, ethnography, and detention intersected in the Andamans in some remarkable ways. Long before Radcliffe-Brown set foot on the islands, penal colony officials routinely integrated descriptions of encounters with Andamanese together with documentation of prisoner escapes and tallies of manufactures in their monthly reports (Man 1932; Portman 1990). The Cellular Jail constructed in Port Blair incorporated many of the architectural features of scrutiny built into Jeremy Bentham's Panopticon design. Some of the surveillance techniques used in contemporary detention centers were rehearsed on convicts in the Andamans, even as photographic records and anthropometric measurements of Andamanese assembled by prison administrators found their way into the collections of the British Museum.

Indigenous Andamanese were seldom formally incarcerated, but they were encouraged to take up residence in the system of Andaman Homes established by prison authorities. Penal settlement officers disagreed about the degree of autonomy and freedom of movement that residents of the homes should enjoy. Barnet Ford, superintendent of Port Blair from 1864 to 1868, believed that residents should be free to come and go as they pleased. When forty residents of the Ross Island Home fled to South Andaman by log, boat, and raft during the night, he opposed a proposal to send a military detachment to retrieve them (Roy and Choudhury 2002:51). In later periods, however, residents of the homes lived under guard by convicts and in turn became objects of study (Pandya 1991; Tomas 1991). Well into the early twentieth century, the Andaman Homes provided a convenient site for recruiting the teams of Andamanese trackers assigned to bring back escapees as well as artifacts of ethnographic interest "discovered" in the course of their pursuits.

By moving across disciplines in this way (anthropology and history, chain gangs and resettlement policies, jail cells and government records), I also want

2. Inside the Panopticon of the British Cellular Jail, completed in 1906 using convict labor. Note the work shed in the yard, designed to shelter convict manufactures from the twice-yearly monsoons. (Photo credit: Kath Weston)

to begin to map the contours of offshore incarceration as a form of imprisonment with a distinctive relationship to the surveillance of prisoners, the invention of fieldwork, the formation of social science, and the security apparatus of the modern state. I use the term *offshore incarceration* to refer to a type of detention that locates prisoners at a remove from the imprisoning state, outside its territorial borders (at least initially) yet within the claims of its political jurisdiction. In the Andamans medical officers sought to account for radical weight loss in newly arrived prisoners not by pointing to the effects of harsh physical labor and scanty rations but by calling attention to "the extreme depression caused by transportation across the seas to a distant and lonely place, where a prisoner realises that he is entirely cut off from all communication with the outer world and friends and where, in the majority of cases, the climate is wholly strange and uncongenial" (RAA 1906–7:40). This geographic elsewhere doubles as a fantasy elsewhere to the extent that detention in a place signified as the back of beyond is often designed to discourage detainees from imagining the possibility of return or release.

At a time when offshore incarceration has become a globally proliferating, increasingly familiar form of imprisonment (witness the camp set up by the

U.S. government to house so-called enemy combatants on its naval base at Guantánamo Bay, Cuba, or the detention centers for asylum-seekers that the United Kingdom has proposed to locate abroad), the debts that such facilities owe to colonial forms of incarceration have scarcely been studied (Risen and Shanker 2003). Neither David Arnold's (1994) classic account of the "new penology" in the colonial prisons of British India nor Peter Zinoman's (2001) insightful reading of "the ill-disciplined prison" in Vietnamese colonial history addresses the means by which certain penal institutions came to be imaginatively located in the back of beyond, whether for the prisoners incarcerated there, for their relatives and compatriots, for organizers who used prison conditions to mobilize nationalist sentiment, or for agents of the state.

One of the key practices that joined offshore incarceration in this sense to a nascent anthropology on the Andaman Islands was the codification of tracking by search parties as a government-sponsored punitive yet simultaneously investigative practice. Tracking escaped prisoners, tracking bodies that had dodged the government census, tracking the children of "friendly" Andamanese for relocation to boarding facilities, tracking sick islanders for removal to settlement hospitals, tracking "undiscovered tribes": in these tales of pursuit, of mythical peoples and vestiges of inhabitation, of abandoned villages, of smoldering campfires left behind by runaway prisoners, of coconut saplings planted in the course of raids, of pig skulls carried back by settlement officials as trophies, lies material for a theorization of the offshore. On the other side of the metaphorical waters called Kala Pani dwells a better understanding of the significance of the state's administrative elsewheres for anchoring discourses of terror and offshore detention that have experienced an unsettling revival of late.

The Tracking and the Trace

Tracking expeditions such as the one that netted the three promising young Jarawa captives described at the opening of this essay were a regular feature of life in the Andamans from the time that the first complement of prisoners, military guards, and administrative overseers landed on the islands. "The only way to catch the wild Jarawas is by sending out armed police and convicts, using the friendly Andamanese as trackers," wrote the chief commissioner of the Andaman and Nicobar Islands late in the nineteenth century. "The latter are too much afraid of the Jarawas to catch them alone and unsupported by firearms. Arrangements have accordingly been made to make paths through the jungle, in and behind the Jarawa country, along which parties of police or convicts and Andamanese can move rapidly" (RAA 1894–95:19).

Even as the penal settlement at Port Blair boasted of the civilizing and restorative effects of its forest clearing, agriculture, and manufactures, administrators secured a daily discipline by tracking down fleeing convicts and ethno-logical subjects, a practice of hunting, raiding, and capture that officials would have identified in a subject people as distressingly nomadic. Search parties fea-tured a variable mix of Andamanese, penal colony administrators, military police (sepoys, including officers, or *jemadars*), trusted convicts, and servants. The men assigned to these details might number anywhere from two to more than a hundred, depending upon the length of the journey, its goals, the rough-ness of the terrain, seasonal changes in the weather, and the level of adminis-trative embarrassment involved. Jarawa attacks on settlement work parties, es-cape attempts by convicts of notoriety, and incidents in which prisoners fled en masse provoked a proportionately more vigorous response. An unusually large search party of one hundred Andamanese, for example, was dispatched under the command of Nga Ya Nyun, a prisoner promoted to jemadar, in December 1905 after "convict Jan, one of the ringleaders of the once notorious 'Gumatti' gang of outlaws and ruffians," escaped with several of his former associates (RAA 1905–6:13). Some of these expeditions followed creeks and trails in-land; others required piling into the station steamer *Enterprise* or *Kwangtung* and stopping at various points along the coast.

While the British officials included in these parties sometimes reported the findings generated en route as their own, Andamanese performed almost all the actual tracking. Whenever possible, the colonial administrators who consti-tuted the search parties preferred to recruit trackers from among those Anda-manese who had "come in" from the forest to settle at one of the government-sponsored, prison-run settlement stations known as the Andaman Homes. Trackers' services were obtained, as J. N. Homfray put it during his tenure as officer in charge of the homes, through "a judicious mixture of coaxing and compulsion" (RAA 1872–73:20). In 1905 the administration regularized track-ing with the formation of an Andamanese company of "Bush Police" formally charged with the duty of pursuing runaway convicts and conducting reprisals against Jarawas. "The men had practice [with bows and arrows] twice a week, on Thursday 4 P.M. on the Gymkhana Ground and on Sundays at Haddo. Four men, Bira, Balia, Daniel and Mathew, were also trained to use a 12 bore gun and have already learnt to shoot fairly well" (PSP 9/05:93). As the Andamanese population was decimated, due in part to a syphilis epidemic exacerbated by rape and sexual contact in the homes ideologically dedicated to Andamanese protection, Burmese prisoners eventually took over much of the tracking. By 1939, when four Kachin sepoys from the Burma Frontier Force arrived in Port Blair to train men in the art of tracking for use in operations against Jarawas, this form of indigenous knowledge had been reconstituted as a teachable, sale-able, transferable skill.

Not all the tracking, of course, set out to pinpoint the location of Jarawa hunting camps, to kidnap children from the forest for relocation in the settlement orphanage, or to bring back human captives for further study. More regular still were the search parties sent out after convicts who attempted to run away from the scurvy and the gangrene, the bloody chain gangs and fetid accommodations, the hours that prisoners worked lashed to grinding mills like bullocks, the capricious punishments, the medical experiments with quinine (carried out on female prisoners) and the carceral experiments with solitary confinement, the prohibitions against talking to fellow prisoners, and the mounting death toll that officials blamed on an unhealthy, malarial environment but that undoubtedly was magnified by an inadequate diet and the practice of working the incarcerated past the powers of human endurance (Aggarwal 1995; Sen 2000). By the early twentieth century administrative reports listed "over work" as a common motive for escapes (e.g., RAA 1907–8:4). With a convict population of more than fourteen thousand in the settlement's heyday, fugitive prisoners could well exceed one hundred in any given year.

When authorities were not chasing after runaway prisoners and what they called "wild aboriginals," they sometimes dispatched tracking parties for other purposes, such as to assist with the census of 1901, the first ever to enumerate Nicobaris and Andamanese, in which the government of India demanded an impossible accounting for every last inhabitant of the islands. More routinely, during the annual administrative tour of the islands, settlement officials undertook to find, detain, and scrutinize Andamanese for signs of advanced syphilis (PSP 9/05:134). Suspected syphilitics, like convict escapees, orphanage runaways, and representatives of "tribes" new to the administration, were carried, willingly or forcibly, to government stations, in this case for medical attention. "Among the first sufferers [of syphilis] were two or three head-men who resisted every attempt that was made to confine them to Viper for treatment. On their *escaping* from that Island and returning to their homes fresh cases naturally occurred, most of which have it is believed, been discovered and placed under treatment at Viper" (PSP 10/78:29, emphasis added). Yet the hospitals and other settlement institutions touted for making medical care available fostered the spread of diseases such as measles, which devastated indigenous communities, by bringing people from far-flung parts of the islands into close contact.

As the trails hewn by tracker and tracked crisscrossed the hills and meandered through coastal waters, incarceration effectively expanded its reach beyond the walls of the Cellular Jail, the Female Jail, and the old prison barracks on Viper Island, until the whole of the Andamans began to figure as a prison. It was not only convicts caged in cells who found themselves in a specifically offshore kind of camp but most other inhabitants of the islands as well, in ways that differed according to the lines drawn by privilege, tracking, and coercion. Even two free men brought from Behea to teach Port Blair convicts how to make sugar were reported to the secretary to the government of India as having "absconded" shortly after their arrival (PSP 3/82:203).

Work on the Cellular Jail that has come to symbolize the penal colony was not completed until 1906, relatively late in settlement history. Before convict labor could erect barracks and administrative buildings, the islands had assumed the contours of an open-air prison where inmates had no place to bathe but the sea, no roof but a bit of thatch or the trees, fetters perhaps, but no walls to hold them in at night except the walls that fear erected after the guards were dismissed, leaving convicts with stories of the depredations of "wild" Andamanese. Ironically, given these representations, in the early skirmishes that Andamanese fought with the invaders setting up the penal colony, such as the 1859 Battle of Aberdeen, they often made careful distinctions among their opponents, targeting European officers, military police, and convict trusties with their arrows while drawing shackled prisoners to the side to safety. Centuries of experience with the slave ships that ventured into Andamanese waters in search of prey may have made the circumstances of people in fetters all too recognizable.

In the nineteenth century, as now, the rhetorical classification of prisoners deemed a threat to the state was politicized and historically rather fluid. Over the years the "mutineers" of 1857 were joined in colonial government documents by "conspirators" in bomb cases and "terrorists" sentenced to transportation. By 1901 administrators had grouped men who, after independence, would be celebrated as heroes and "political prisoners" together with another class of convicts, *dacoits*, "the Government of India having ruled that the crime of waging war against the Queen should be treated on the same footing as the crime of dacoity" (RAA 1900–1901:14). Four decades later, under the Defence of India Rules, "security prisoner" became the preferred term, the government having considered and discarded "state prisoner" and "*détenu*" (Singh 1998:160).

As the convict-built Cellular Jail neared completion, newly arrived prisoners spent at least six months confined within its walls, subject to experiments in isolation and in new forms of work discipline carried out within factory sheds arrayed in the yard. Political prisoners and (after 1906) prisoners determined by medical officers to be "recipients in unnatural crime" generally never left the confines of the Cellular Jail. Other male convicts were permitted outside, after an initial period of "accommodation," on work details and eventually to farm and engage in petty trade. They quickly learned that more than bars could make a cage. The very sky opened up by the convict gangs assigned to take down the forest incongruously served to restrain ticket-of-leave prisoners, also known as self-supporters. Self-supporters were usually life convicts charged with apolitical offenses who breathed a bit more freely, to be sure, once they were allowed to marry female term convicts, bring their families from overseas, grow crops, and engage in commerce after demonstrating years of good behavior. But they were convicts, nonetheless, who would be remanded to fetters if they aided escaping prisoners and hunted down if they ventured outside their villages without a pass.

More surprisingly, the islands sometimes figured rhetorically as a site of off-shore incarceration for settlement officials and their families. While differently positioned than their charges, to be sure, many nevertheless experienced themselves as exiles and the islands as something akin to a punishment posting. Certainly, it was theirs to punish and theirs to inflict the lash, not to suffer it; they had the privilege of shopping at the government godown rather than being forced to turn over a portion of already meager rations to unscrupulous guards. But, like term convicts, these "trusted agents" of the colonial government experienced themselves as waiting upon the pleasures of government, restrained from assuming a more desirable life on the subcontinent, biding their time until retirement or an invalid pension should set them at liberty. "You are called upon to labour in a by-path of life and therefore the more conspicuous rewards of public service are not for you," R. C. Temple, then chief commissioner of the Andamans and Nicobars, superintendent of the penal settlement, and author of *Legends of the Panjab*, admonished an audience that had gathered at the Volunteer Drill Hall to celebrate the sixtieth year of Victoria's reign. "Well," Temple continued, "let that be: for this must content you, though it is no small contentment. That when the long day of your service in this remote corner of the Empire is past, yours will be the consciousness that you have been able to bear an honourable part in building up a far-reaching organization for the reform of the criminal, in pushing forward a great work of practical philanthropy[,] . . . that you helped to set a bright jewel in the noble crown of charity that rests upon the Queen" (ANG 7/97:68). Caught up in government service, all but the highest functionaries had to secure passes and permissions to travel not only off-island but to different jurisdictions within the islands themselves. Should they have departed without authorization, they too would have been pursued, and by more than ignominy or dismissal.

Perhaps most paradoxically, more and more locations in the islands began to signify as an offshore kind of incarceration for indigenous Andamanese—"paradoxically," since indigeneity would seem to contradict or at least mitigate the movement implicit in the concept of the offshore. Yet indigeneity is something of an anachronism here, since the colonial government relocated Andamanese to unfamiliar parts of the islands where they expected to fall sick and often did. Over the years a smaller number of Andamanese experienced a doubling of offshore transport, being removed first to Port Blair, then off-island to places like Rangoon for further "cultivation," study, and display.

The coercive aspects of government-run institutions established for the "benefit" of Andamanese were painfully obvious to the children removed to the nursery and the orphanage, where English was the only language permitted and contact with Andamanese adults forbidden. (On this policy there was some disagreement. The Port Blair Church Mission, which took the view that relocating children away from their "tribes" would jeopardize their ability to live as adults among their own people, made an unsuccessful bid in 1870 to take charge of the Andaman Home on Ross Island and integrate it with mission schools to be established at locations closer to the forest [Roy and Choudhury 2002:63].) Orphanage children who attempted to rejoin their families or to escape retraining for service occupations within the settlement were pursued by trackers sent as far into the jungle as necessary. In this the orphanage mirrored the boarding schools established in the nineteenth and early twentieth centuries by colonial regimes from Australia to North America for the specific purpose of seizing and detaining new generations of indigenous peoples, the better to civilize them (Lomawaima 1994; Beckett 1997; Child 1998; Archuleta et al. 2000; Sen 2000:230–34).

Meanwhile, in the self-styled system of refuges called the Andaman Homes, so-called friendly Andamanese, including trackers, were placed under supervision by prison authorities and guarded by prisoners. While the men went out on tracking expeditions or collected edible birds' nests, Andamanese women labored without pay to produce tens of blankets, hundreds of *morahs* (stools), and thousands of thatching leaves for use in the provisioning of settlement buildings, all tabulated for the chief commissioner's perusal on a monthly basis. Along with the blankets, the Andaman Homes and the orphanage produced a version of the sentimental colonialism described for the Philippines by Vicente Rafael (2000), in which the violence of colonialism assumed the trappings of domesticity, recasting a master-slave relationship into the idiom of parent and child. Uncompensated labor figured in government accounts as useful instruction in a home setting, living under guard as a benevolent gesture on the part of the administration to protect, as they put it, "our" Andamanese from the depredations of "wild savages."

Convicts, on the other hand, qualified as natives of another sort, the object of improvement schemes that had their sentimental aspects yet were forever subject to the whims of undisguised mastery. As chief commissioner, Temple did not shirk from applying the language of slavery to describe the life of the newly arrived prisoner: "For the next three years he is a slave, as that word is ordinarily understood, locked up with other slaves in barracks at night," eligible with time and good conduct for "less slave-like forms of labour, and . . . a little—a very little—allowance to buy a few small luxuries or to place in the Savings Bank." Regular deposits in the bank were supposed to ensure that the term convict, upon release, would emerge as "no pauper, no mere jail-bird, no unwelcome burden upon his relatives, but a self-respecting citizen with a little capital of his own earning, for years habituated to provide for himself in an orderly way and thoroughly broken to harness, as it were" (ANG 7/97:66–68).

This manufacture of sentiment, whether or not allied with a discourse of slavery, helps explain some of the apparent disconnects in settlement records, particularly regarding the often ludicrous expectations placed upon

3. Aberdeen Bazaar, Port Blair, where self-supporter (ticket-of-leave) convicts originally established many of the shops. (Photo credit: Geeta H. Patel)

Andamanese captives, who officials hoped would emerge from captivity to cultivate a détente. The administration report for 1872–73, for example, undermines within the space of two pages its own argument for the sentimental attachment fostered by the "care" the government provided to Andamanese children. After tendering the claim that "the care bestowed upon the children of the islanders brought up at the Ross Orphanage and in the Nursery at Viper [Island], has quite won their [Andamanese] hearts, and established a bond of friendship which ought never be severed," the report observes that children raised in the nursery "do not readily take to their own people again, and one of the little orphans who have been entirely brought up by natives of India will not go near one of its own people, though it will go readily to natives of India or Europeans" (RAA 1873:45–46).

A similar sense of non sequitur pervades the repeated accounts of Andamanese who, after being dragged to Port Blair against their will and subjected to demonstrations of weaponry at the rifle range, were sent back to the forest "loaded with presents" in the hope that they would testify to the good treatment they had received during their imprisonment, thus bringing about amicable relations. M. V. Portman, a settlement officer who donated many of his photographs and other records to the British Museum, outlined in 1880 a strategy for cultivating friendship and knowledge through capture:

By lying in wait at the South Brother Island for a turtling party, by establishing a small settlement on the Little Andaman itself; or else, by surrounding one of their huts at night, capturing the inhabitants (the surrounding party being thoroughly armed and instructed to resist with force, any attack on the part of the savages) and to keep those we captured, long enough with us at Port Blair for them to appreciate our kindness, and for us to learn their language, appear to me to be the only methods by which the establishment of friendly relations with the Little Andamanese can be effected. (PSP 10/80:82)

He continued to echo this hope in the face of all evidence to the contrary, even upon the occasion of the release of a "surly and evil tempered" Jarawa captive taken during one of the tours of the islands who "kept begging my Andamanese to kill him by throttling him or cutting his throat, and rejected all overtures of friendship" (ANG 5/95:6). A world away from the eighteenth-century European understanding of the sympathy proper to sentiment, in which, as Adam Smith (1997:2) had it, "we conceive ourselves enduring all the same torments, we enter as it were into his body, and become in some measure the same person with him."

The detention-like qualities of the Andaman Homes system may at times have eluded the perceptions of their administrators, but they were not lost on the many Andamanese who elected to return to the forest after making their own inspections of the homes during the 1870s, when settlement officials still preferred to organize relocation through persuasion and presents for those who agreed to "come in" from the jungle. (Note the recourse to a language of policing in the recurrent phrase "come in": the same phrase was routinely applied to dacoits and other criminals who surrendered to authorities.) "So wedded are these people to a nomadic life," wrote the superintendent of Port Blair, "that the numerous advantages which they obtain at the Homes are at times not sufficiently attractive to induce them to take up their residence with us permanently. They seem to think that in doing so they must forfeit their liberty for good and all" (RAA 1875–76:45).

The trackers themselves, well aware of the increasingly carceral space established on the islands by the regimen of pursuit, often preferred to bring their captives back to jail or orphanage, as the case might be, without resorting to beatings or weapons. They also developed a habit of inexplicably losing their grip on captives in some of the later raids on Jarawa villages organized by the settlement authorities.

In an extended sense, tracking did as much as chains or iron gratings to establish the Andamans as the dreaded Kala Pani, the iconic offshore site for punishment and torture of nationalist prisoners whose sufferings have come to represent the whole of captive experience on the islands in popular accounts. For it was the pursuit of human prey that brought the islands' very differently situated inhabitants together in a commerce by definition unwanted. And it was tracking that supplied the material traces—arrows, skulls, fire rings, twigs bent by footsteps, shipwrecked rafts—that lent credence to the rhetoric settlement officials enlisted to discourage unauthorized movement around the islands.

Put simply, the message of penal colony officers to prisoners was this: venture forth unguarded and you shall perish. Your prospects are few and all of them grim: murder at the hands of undomesticated savages, fatal hunger, disease, drowning. "The convicts are alive to the fact that without a boat of some sort there is no escape from the islands, and that the only alternatives are a miserable lingering death from exposure and starvation, and recapture," wrote Superintendent D. M. Stewart in his administration report for 1872–73. Runaway convicts trailed without success were listed in official reports as likely, if not undoubtedly, having perished from shipwreck, want of food, or attack by Jarawas.

How effectively the administration had conveyed the threat of death to prisoners more than a decade after the settlement's founding can be gauged from the figures for escape attempts in the year that Stewart made his report. Out of a total of 160 fugitive prisoners, only 93 were recaptured. Stewart, of course, preferred to dwell on the positive: 44 taken by land and 49 by sea. All of them had been tracked, some as far as Sumatra, including one Jemadar Khoda Buksh, a senior petty officer who had long played by the rules, going so far as to apply for a ticket-of-leave to open a shop at Trinkut in which he had already invested the better portion of his painfully acquired savings. Someone made a complaint about him to the superintendent that threatened him with demotion to hard labor, thus prompting his flight (RAA 1872–73:6–9).

While the discourse of imminent demise upon escape superficially addressed convicts who might be tempted to take their chances with ocean or forest, its hidden audience was composed of bureaucratic superiors in the Home Department who required persuading that a competent administration had done all it could to deter and punish escape. The difficulties of defining escape in a space made increasingly carceral were quite evident to officials who had to render an accounting. According to Temple, acting chief commissioner in 1895, "the whole question of recording escapes in Port Blair and comparing them with those from ordinary jails is a difficult one, e.g., it does not follow that because an escaped convict is not recovered in Port Blair that he is at large" (RAA 1894–95:5). Temple reiterated for the benefit of the government of India the standard litany of fates supposed to lie in store for a runaway in the islands: he might have drowned, starved, or died at the hands of Jarawas, with penal colony officials none the wiser. What's more, because gangs of convicts were often assigned to fish the seas or work in the forest far from the settlement, the location of a living body in space at any given point in time could not serve as a reliable indicator of incarceration. Other markers were tried. Iron leg rings, once used to identify runaways who had not been hanged immediately upon apprehension, eventually gave way to chain gang sentences and blue checked clothing for third-class convicts with a record of flight. Wire fencing intended to secure convicts who labored outside the settlement at mealtimes (a common occasion for escape) failed to produce the expected control through enclosure. Nor could such measures address the other sort of escape for which officials were frequently called to account: the way that Jarawas repeatedly managed to elude pursuit while continuing to live on the outskirts of the settlement.

Administrators who claimed to have diligently pursued antagonistic Jarawas and discouraged flight by recalcitrant convicts did whatever convincing they could manage by marshalling tactile forms of evidence as well as enlisting the arts of rhetoric. For this penal colony officials drew upon the bounty of the hunt, brought back by search parties as ethnological artifacts and soon-to-be-archived stories.

Cutting for Sign

Like the Shadow Wolves, the all-Native tracking unit employed since 1972 by the U.S. government to interdict smugglers and narcotics on the Tohono O'odham reservation, which spans the U.S.-Mexican border, Andamanese trackers of earlier centuries went about their work by "cutting for sign" (Shively 2003; Wheeler 2003). Cutting for sign involves attending to burnt leaves, matted ground cover, drops of blood, bits of twine or fabric threads caught on a bush, flies buzzing about a pile of fish bones, a length of bamboo abandoned in a nineteenth-century hunting lodge, or a plastic drinking bottle left behind in a twenty-first-century desert, that is to say, a host of small disturbances revealing the passage of someone along the way. But that is only the beginning. The warmth of a doused fire tells of time since the passing. The amount of sap flowing from a broken branch yields similar testimony. The impression made by a foot or a shoe speaks of adults moving swiftly or heavily laden, women versus men, a characteristic shuffling mark created when someone turns around to check for pursuit. Identification and interpretation become thoroughly intertwined.

For Andamanese trackers such as Iragud and Henry, who informally led the 1902 expedition that brought back the three young Jarawa captives, the record of the process by which they went about detecting sign is a bit sketchy, mediated as it was by government officials who tended to naturalize their skills. The report on the expedition written by Percy Vaux, the officer in charge (less than a month before he would die in a raid on a Jarawa village), noted that the trackers ("our Janglis") had explained to him the purpose and positioning of lookout huts that he would never have recognized as such as well as a "dozen well made vessels which the Andamanese said were honey pots" (SUP 3/02:26, 29). Cutting for sign in the course of a search could require hours, often days, of work. When this expedition first set out, "on either bank, signs of Jarawa were visible

in the shape of felled saplings and leaves. . . . About 10 O'clock we came on the
fresh traces of a Jarawa. There was only one man, and he was evidently hunting, but after following his tracks for a considerable distance we gave it up, as he
was obviously after game, and his tracks led nowhere." Later in the afternoon,
though, things picked up.

> As the signs of Jarawas increased, so did our excitement. At last about 2 PM, the
> Andamanese seemed nonplused but after searching here and there went up a
> beaten track without hesitation, which ascended a hill, and there was the Jarawa
> camp. We approached it with the utmost caution, only to find it empty. It was a
> six hut camp, arranged with the usual two look-out huts at the sides; it had been
> left about a week, and there were only pig skulls and an old basket in it. . . .
> Thinking all was over we proceeded quite carelessly, when suddenly the An-
> damanese spread themselves out with every sign of excitement and a column of
> smoke could be discerned and afterwards huts. With the utmost caution again we
> approached and again found the huts empty. The occupants could only have left
> six hours before at earliest. The logs were smouldering, boiled prawn heads were
> strewn about, water vessels made of leaves with water in them were in the huts,
> and everything betokened recent habitation. But no cooking pots or bows were
> in the huts, some baskets, arrows, and a child's bow were all that we could find.
> The Andamanese were doubtful whether the Jarawas would return, saying no
> property of value had been left. Still I determined to wait and we lay in ambush
> round the camp. (SUP 3/02:26–27)

After an hour and a half, at the trackers' urging the party gave up and began
the long journey back to the shore. There they discovered that a few Jarawa—
two or three men, a woman and a child, in full view of those left behind on the
penal colony launch—had doubled back upon the search party's tracks. The
outnumbered Jarawas had set out ahead of the search party, departing from the
"abandoned" huts the trackers would spend the afternoon exploring, then following the search party's trail in reverse until they reached the coast, where
they "looted" one of the boats. This looting seems to have consisted primarily
of the sensible precaution of removing two of the boat's oarlocks, which effectively hampered their pursuers' progress. "While they were following my
tracks," wrote Vaux, "Mr. Bonig and his party had come on theirs, and were
hurrying after them as fast as possible, arriving an hour too late, and it was too
late to hunt them farther so they had had the narrowest escape" (SUP 3/02:28).
Recounting the oarlock incident, Vaux noted that only two of four were taken,
"thoughtfully leaving . . . two to pull the boat back with, the only considerate
thing I have ever heard of Jarawas doing." In future, members of search parties
learned to hide their oarlocks before setting out for the day.

Few tracking expeditions embarked without ethnology in at least rudimen-
tary attendance. Forestry Department officials brought back any arrows they
found along with their timber samples; police wallahs handed in net bags and

water vessels seized from forest huts. Andamanese buildings were dutifully sketched and photographed. One runaway convict, Dudhnath Tewari (aka Tewary, Tiwary), who lived with a group of Andamanese in the forest following his 1858 escape, eventually returning to warn the settlement of an imminent attack, became a sort of ethnologist in his own right, reporting on what he had learned of Andamanese life during his time at large (Pandya 1991).

Settlement officials often referred to objects they captured as specimens. Wrote Vaux, for example, "I took one specimen of everything to take back to Port Blair, and left everything else in its place so as not to frighten the Jarawas" (SUP 3/02). The practice of retrieving what Radcliffe-Brown would later call household utensils became so customary that during periods when the penal colony administration sent out parties for the deliberate purpose of establishing contact and cultivating alliances with heretofore undiscovered "tribes," trackers received specific instructions to leave such items in situ, lest their confiscation be misunderstood (PSP 06/77:47).

These captive implements, reborn as artifacts, were studied with care by the fortuitously named E. H. Man, deputy superintendent of the settlement, and by Portman, Man's successor as officer in charge of the Andaman Homes, both of whom went on to write monographs about Andamanese life (*On the Aboriginal Inhabitants of the Andaman Islands* [1885] and *A History of Our Relations with the Andamanese* [1899], respectively). When in 1914 Radcliffe-Brown (1964) wrote up the fieldwork he conducted in the Andamans from 1906 to 1908, he situated Man's and Portman's researches at the beginning of an intellectual lineage by using them as a baseline for his own investigations, however vociferously he might have disagreed with the details of Portman's observations and the Christian eschatological cast of Man's interpretations of Andamanese rituals and myths.

Then as now, the line between artifacts and collectibles was never clearly drawn. Once the residents of the Andaman Homes began to produce for retail fish arrows, baskets, models of Andamanese canoes, and copies of Chowra Island (Nicobari) pots, the distinction between disciplinary contribution and fiscal contribution began to blur in earnest. By the early twentieth century all sorts of "Andamanese curiosities" were available for sale, including wreaths of bones for 1 rupee, a "skull ornament" for 50 rupees, and "belts, as worn by Andamanese men and women" for 2–4 annas, obtainable either at the Andaman Homes godown at Haddo or by ordering from one of the salesmen who made the round of the islands (ANG 1/03:20). Human remains began circulating in a way they had never been meant to be exchanged.

Some things, of course, could not be brought back from the forest or the shore by tracking parties, except in reports and diaries. Among these more tenuous traces were footprints, which repeatedly inserted themselves into records in ways that echoed the impressions made by naked feet in travel and adventure stories. Consider the following passages. First: "Footmarks of adults and children were also observed near the hut, but none of the people were met with." Next: "They were unfortunate in experiencing very bad weather while absent and accordingly returned sooner than they had intended. They discovered some tracks . . . but nothing more." And finally: "Going towards my boat, I was exceedingly surprised with the print of a man's naked foot on the shore, which was very plain to be seen in the sand." The first observation appears in a government report from the Andamans dated 1877, the second in a published diary excerpt from the 1902 reconnaissance parties sent out to look for Jarawa. The third, of course, marks the famous (non)appearance of Friday in Daniel Defoe's *Robinson Crusoe* in the days before Friday received his name from the man he learned to call Master (PSP 6/77:22; SUP 3/02; Defoe 1994:152). Penal colony officials drew upon travel stories quite consciously, sometimes with a malicious sort of playfulness that figured at Andamanese expense. In 1861, very early in the history of the settlement, three Andamanese men were captured, detained, and assigned new names before being shipped off to Rangoon by steamer to impress upon them the superior resources possessed by the British. Their names of record? Friday Blair, Crusoe Blair, and Jumbo Blair (Tomas 1991:78).

In these different types of sources the reactions of the narrators upon finding footprints diverge sharply. Settlement officials expected to inspire apprehension in Andamanese, attempting to foster "friendship" but willing to settle for "a more satisfactory state of feeling towards us, viz., one of fear rather than animosity" (PSP 8/76:70). In contrast, Defoe's narrator, possessing European presumptions of advancement but no arms, moved swiftly from the assumption that the discovered footprint belongs to "savages" to a trepidation of his own, marked by immediate regret that he had dug quite so large and indefensible an entrance for his cave (Defoe 1994:158–59).

All of which begs the question of who was the hunter and who the hunted, which inhabitants gatherers and which ones gathered, which islanders the more authentic residents of a hunting camp, not to mention what strange fruit might be brought back from the chase for distribution. Some insightful accounts have explored the manufacture of ethnographic evidence in the Andamans through photography and other activities undertaken in the constrained environment of the Andaman Homes (Pinney 1997; Tomas 1991). Tracking, an expansive activity that collapsed distinctions between free and incarcerated space, played an equally important part in establishing an economy of hunting (captives), gathering (captives), and gifting (released Jarawa captives), an economy that filtered back as observations into the ethnological descriptions generated by settlement administrators. What matter that the officer-ethnologist's prey was not turtle or wild boar, the gathering concerned less with beeswax than with prisoners, the gifting a traffic not in jawbones but looking glasses and red cloth left behind in deserted huts as signs of "friendship."

4. The forest takes back buildings on Ross Island, the penal colony's administrative center. The Andaman Administration allotted Ross Island to the Indian Navy in 1967, retaining title to its colonial-era buildings. (Photo credit: Kath Weston)

A practice of cutting for sign of the wild and the nomadic painted a rustic backdrop for a carceral regime in which settlement officials set convicts to the brutal work of building a naval yard, tea plantations, an oil mill, and a brick factory en route to state-planned self-sufficiency, a goal that would prove more elusive than any fleeing captive. All of which may be of some assistance in interpreting the cryptic comment that appeared in the local gazette when, in 1895, a tracking party dispatched to Rutland Island "succeeded in capturing a couple of Jarawas, but not of the kind wanted" (ANG 5/95:5).

Finding Nothing but What Must Have Been: The Politics of Surmise

What is perhaps most striking about the written accounts of tracking expeditions that set forth to restore residents of various sorts to their allotted places in the Andaman Islands is how often these expeditions came up with nothing— or, rather, how often they came up with nothing but the sign, the track, and the trace of fleeing subjects rather than the bodies that were the putative object of the search. Time after time, tracking parties returned to file reports that worked minor variations on the theme of absence and its confirming signifiers: "The other two runaways are believed to have lost themselves in the jungle. Parties are however searching for them, although it is probable that they have fallen into the hands of the Jarawas or perished from hunger" (PSP 12/78:71). Or this: "Moonshee Beola's expedition in search of some members of the 'Jarawada' tribe only resulted in his bringing me some more bows and arrows, cooking vessels, baskets, &c., belonging to those people" (PSP 2/76:24). A practice such as tracking that produces the trace of flight effectively augments escape, in the sense that a trace can be considered "the surplus that escapes even multiple meanings" (Buck-Morss 2002:12).

While settlement officials regularly listed and numbered convicts, who became spectral only upon running away, some officers were prone to doubt the very existence of the people whom other Andamanese called Jarawa. Radcliffe-Brown, writing at the beginning of the twentieth century, cautioned against facile applications of the term:

> The word Jarawa is apparently derived from the Aka-Bea language, but is now used by all the friendly natives (i.e. the natives of the Great Andaman Group) to denote those of the Little Andaman Group. In the official publications dealing with the Andamans, however, the term Jarawa has come to be applied solely to the hostile natives of the Great Andaman. . . . It must be remembered, however, that the so-called Jarawa probably call themselves Önge, while the Önge of the Little Andaman are called Jarawa by the natives of the friendly tribes of the Great Andaman. (1914:12)

He also maintained that in earlier times some indigenous residents of the islands had applied the term to Europeans, the implication being that Jarawa may long have figured as an "othering" term with multiple potential applications.

E. H. Man, whose father had claimed the islands for Queen Victoria in 1858, wanted very much to confirm his belief in "the Jarawada" as a bounded group subject to discovery. During his tenure as officer in charge of the Andaman Homes he periodically sent out special tracking details in hopes of settling, once and for all, the question of whether Jarawa really existed and, if so, what manner of "men" they might be. When convicts assigned to build roads and take down the forest became the targets of Jarawa resistance, administrators ordered "friendly" Andamanese from the homes to guard work files but continued to cast Jarawa as spectral figures, their existence eventually affirmed but their "haunts" still acknowledged as extremely difficult to ferret out. "Beyond recent footmarks in the vicinity of the canoes no further signs of the proximity of some members of this remarkable [sic] exclusive tribe were met with," reads yet another fairly typical report (PSP 10/78:54). For officials such as Man who repeatedly sent out trackers on a fruitless hunt for Jarawa, Robinson Crusoe's lament would have seemed apt: "All this labour I was at the expense of, purely from my apprehensions on the account of the print of a man's foot which I had seen"

(Defoe 1994:161). With the exception of a few figures glimpsed and a few captives brought back from the forest, for the better part of settlement history the Jarawa apprehended by the colonists were their utensils and their tracks.

This constant reiteration of the trace in lieu of the quarry might be considered a mark of failure if it were not that it doubled as an accomplishment of another sort. For there was a sense in which the sign cut from the islands by trackers yielded prey every bit as important as any bodies retrieved, burned, or buried. The traces of movement and flight recovered by tracking expeditions in turn set the stage for a kind of politics that by the late nineteenth century had become intimately associated with state-sponsored forms of surveillance: what might be called a politics of surmise, set up by the sign that trackers hacked from the beaches and the forest. In the process, tracking helped mark the islands as a specifically offshore location, tethered through longing and narration to the Indian subcontinent rather than other possible sites.

To explain the part played by tracking in transforming the Andamans into the kind of offshore establishment that has become notorious in the annals of state custody requires a brief excursion into the physics and metaphysics of the offshore. Islands no doubt offer certain pragmatic advantages when it comes to restricting the movements of bodies. There is also a long history of using islands to house exiles and convicts, especially "hardened" criminals and prisoners constituted as a threat to the state (Saint Helena, Devil's Island, Alcatraz, Sado Island, Robben Island, Buru Island, and Guantánamo numbering only among the most famous). Yet offshore incarceration facilities need not be physically located on islands, nor would an island location automatically mark a prison or penal colony as the kind of offshore institution that has helped establish the beyond-a-border as increasingly central to the state.

With incarceration, as with high finance, the offshore is a relative, moving location that might as easily encompass a Swiss bank encircled by mountains or a landlocked military base as an Internet gambling venture run out of the Caribbean. The cages at Guantánamo, Cuba, might overlook the waters of an ocean bay, but Guantánamo does not represent an offshore site for residents of Cuba in the sense that it does for prisoners from Afghanistan or warders from the United States. The Andaman archipelago comprises nothing but islands, yet Burmese prisoners transported there later in the colony's history knew very well the islands' closer proximity to Burmese shores vis-à-vis the much more distant shores of the Indian subcontinent. Thus they were able to resignify this group of islands from the far-off back of beyond it represented to many Hindustani convicts, an imaginative location that rendered flight a fool's errand, to incarceration at only a slight remove from "home" with ample opportunities for flight. Small wonder that escape attempts by Burmese convicts multiplied in ways that frustrated their British captors.

As a social location constituted as an elsewhere to the more practiced jurisdictions of a colonial state or nation-state, the offshore describes less a transnational or global relationship than a relationship that exceeds a given state's borders. And this excess is a directed excess, of the sort that moves from here to there rather than simply "abroad." When the chief commissioner of the Andamans and Nicobars in 1882 sent arrest warrants to the inspector general of police of British Burma for several Burmese convicts who had put out to sea on a raft, he tacitly acknowledged the possibility of escape from the islands and the failure of back-of-beyond rhetoric to have the expected deterrent effect on many convicts who took Burma as their point of mainland reference. No site is, in and of itself, an offshore site. A place for incarceration can only figure as offshore vis-à-vis a location that, taken as originary, constitutes its onshore: in the case of the Andamans, through reiterated references back to the Indian subcontinent.

In terms of sheer distance, the Andamans are not even as far away from the subcontinent as some of the other penal colonies in the British Empire to which convicts from colonial India were transported, such as Tenasserim in Burma or the Straits Settlements on the Malay Peninsula. Yet it was the penal colony at Port Blair that came to be construed most distinctively as a back of beyond, becoming the most iconic site of imprisonment for prisoners detained by the colonial government, its remove symbolized by the water, Kala Pani, that simultaneously joined it to and separated it from a mainland. And not just any mainland: although the islands are, as noted, geographically much closer to Burma than India and received shipments of political prisoners at the end of several high-profile cases tried in Rangoon, the mainland for which Kala Pani provided an imaginative elsewhere, especially in nationalist discourse, was British India.

The ambiguity that marked the relationship of the Andaman archipelago with successive governments is characteristic of locations figured as offshore sites. Popular histories mark the Andamans as the first spot in a newly independent nation over which an Indian flag flew; geography lessons in Indian schools cite the Andamans as the southernmost point in the country (e.g., Tamta 1992; Aggarwal 1995). Yet the same books that celebrate the Andamans as the Ur-site for the raising of the flag also chronicle struggles for the "repatriation" of prisoners from the islands. This English word featured prominently in the campaigns associated with the hunger strikes by political prisoners that culminated in the relocation of political prisoners to "the mainland" in 1938. Repatriation: a move back to the patria that presumably cannot originate from within the patria without introducing certain ambiguities about the status of the ground in question. Those ambiguities can be glimpsed as well in the overtones of surprise that accompany the answer to the question about the southernmost point in India (i.e., it's not what you'd think). Nor can the association of the Andamans with the first raising of the flag do much to resolve these ambiguities, occurring as it did in 1942 under the auspices of Japanese occupation. (The independent nation: it's not what you'd think!)

Similarly troubled and contested affiliations prevailed in the case of the offshore incarceration facility established by the United States at its naval base in Guantánamo, Cuba, following its military incursion into Afghanistan. "Guantánamo, Cuba": there is the crux of the dispute. The website of the Directorio Turístico de Cuba (www.dtcuba.com) in 2004 described Guantánamo as a territory of 900 kilometers, "part of which is illegally occupied by an American aero naval base." The U.S. government countered with the claim that it legally leases the land from Cuba, though admittedly for a pittance. The *Guantánamo Bay Gazette*, published by and for personnel at the base, adopted the byline "the only U.S. Naval Base on Communist soil" (www.gtmo.net), while the nickname "Gitmo" (from the military acronym GTMO) refigured the site as American. Meanwhile, a state that had long argued that its military bases abroad constituted U.S. territory (to prevent its citizens from becoming subject to the laws of the countries in which the bases were situated) contended that Guantánamo detainees should not come under the jurisdiction of its own federal courts due to its offshore location.

However betwixt or between, the constitution of the offshore as an elsewhere defined vis-à-vis a state (and thus tethered to it) guarantees that the offshore will shadow, anchor, and enable the state with its every evasion, even when the state (or the institutional investor) seeks a haven from media coverage, the better to conduct its interrogations. Even when the state (or the institutional investor) seeks to escape taxation by directing capital flows to and through a place imagined as outside more regular channels of commerce. Even when the state (or the institutional investor) supports policies that render offshore labor practices integral to economic relations in the jurisdictions to which they refer back, be this in the form of penal colony plantations, privatized prison labor, or sweatshops dressed up as special export zones. Even, perhaps especially, when a colonial state or a nation-state seeks to shield the products of its surveillance from surveillance in their own right.

Before the Andaman Islands could become Kala Pani, Black Water, the back room of beyond that figured in popular imagination by the nationalist period as the place from which there might be no return, something more had to happen than the occupation of a set of islands. Before Port Blair could become the administrative center for the kind of prison operation where the colonial state could pursue its vendettas in relative seclusion, at times coming close to abolishing communication between convicts and people left behind, something more complex had to happen than a directive establishing the islands as the simpler space of imprisonment or exile.

For this the practice of tracking supplied a crucial technique because it drew a boundary around the islands that established them as an offshore location in a way very different from the crash of the ocean's waves. For this the traces brought back from the hunt of fleeing not-quite-captives, traces that had to stand in for bodies not (yet) found, provided something tangible on which to hang presumptions of a fate always accounted for, if not controlled, by the state. The sea was already there, but it was the bits of driftwood from jerry-rigged rafts that officials held up to say that prison breaks must come to no good. The people grouped together under the rubric "Jarawa" were already there, but the arrows brought back from expeditions and the sketches of hunting lodges published in the gazette helped to establish them as a savage and looming sort of threat. When patrols generated so much of the "evidence," who was to say where ethnology left off and the work of incarceration began?

A politics of surmise describes a politics that advances traces of the sought not as evidence of what has happened but as evidence of what most likely has happened. When Andamanese trackers recaptured all but one of a group of twelve escaped convicts in 1876, rather than reporting the remaining prisoner as unaccounted for, Man proposed to account for his absence with conjecture: "He has probably ere this met his death either from want or at the hands of the 'Jarawas' into whose territory the runaways had unwittingly wandered when pursued" (PSP 08/76:76). A quarter of a century later, much the same sort of discourse continued to shape official summaries of escapes: "No doubt a number of runaway convicts of whom all trace is lost have been killed by Jarawas Iragol" (PSP 2/05:185).

With a politics of surmise, conjecture and conviction pass for verities, even as probability begins a slippery descent into certainties. The ashes of a fire pit become a sign that escaped convicts might or must have been waylaid rather than a sign that they could have made alliances with Jarawa (as some did) or still roamed about the islands. There had indeed been sightings of prisoners who survived in the forest for months or years after escape: a party of Bush Police encountered "runaway convict No. 27,832, Kalia . . . in the Bamboo Flat jungle sitting over a rock with a dah (sword-knife) in his hand"; a road crew of convicts attacked by Jarawas described one of the attackers as "a bigman [sic] with long straight hair and beard who was smeared with red mud and who they conclude was an escaped convict who had joined the Jarawas and was living with them" (PSP 11/06:127, 4/82:8). A careful reading of colonial records also turns up cases in which runaways hung about the villages outside Port Blair, making it "almost impossible for the Junglies [sic] to capture them, as they invariably pass themselves off as Ticket-of-leave men" (PSP 1/81:130). By narrating such episodes sparingly and separately from the passages in which they enlisted surmise to "document" the failure of attempts at flight, penal colony officials used notfinding and the lost trace to establish the Andamans rhetorically as a place not only impossible to escape but also impossibly far away from the more desirable space to which, as an offshore location, it constantly referred back.

The kind of politics in which cutting for sign asserts the "fact" of the presumed is with us still and may be gathering momentum. In the lead-up to the 2003 U.S. invasion of Iraq, the display of satellite photographs at speeches and press briefings, to take but one example, set the stage for the affirmation that what the photograph did not reveal—underground caves, biochemical manufacturing facilities—must be there, undetected. The photograph, construed as evidence, becomes but a trace of unseen objects of the hunt, objects that have yet to be produced and may never be.

Whatever the historical period, as Veena Talwar Oldenburg (2002) so eloquently points out, it is dangerous to succumb to a rhetoric that evades responsibility for the effects of government policies by culturalizing their effects, just as it is dangerous to underestimate the ability of a state to produce that which it claims to seek. The ill-fated Percy Vaux returned from the first 1902 expedition with numerous Jarawa artifacts and nothing but praise for the "marvellous" tracking abilities possessed by Andamanese who could find their way home "without a compass and with hardly a glimpse of the sun to guide them" (SUP 3/02:31). C. G. Rogers, deputy conservator of forests who commanded another party on the same expedition, came away with a rather different impression. After "moving in circuits," running short of rations, losing all "traces" of Jarawa, and trudging twice up what turned out to be the same hill, Rogers resolved to take matters in hand. "I stopped them [the trackers] about 9–15 A.M., and we had a talk. They then confessed that they knew nothing about finding their way in the forest and had (so they said) never had to find their way in one" (SUP 3/02:34). That this should have come as a shock to penal colony officials who had spent more than a generation relocating people from the forest to the Andaman Homes is revealing indeed.

Incarceration off (Other) Shores

At Guantánamo Bay, on another island where the legacies of colonization continue to run their course, there are only the ghosts of indigenous Taino trackers. When the United States established a prison camp there early in the twenty-first century, indefinite detention became the order of the day. In this case a corporate nation-state charged its military with the duty of tracking, a practice now associated more with "stress and duress" techniques of sensory overload and sleep deprivation than the threat of escape. By 2004 only one escape route from Guantánamo had opened up, and that was suicide, a road that prisoners traveled with increasing regularity.

Although both the penal colony in the Andamans and the detention camp at Guantánamo (GTMO) can be considered instances of offshore incarceration (in the sense I have used the term here), they are not analogous. One could certainly draw parallels by calling attention to the respective incarcerating states' investment in compiling lists of belongings issued to prisoners (a dhoti and an earthen pot for "necessaries" in the Andamans, plastic flip-flops and an extra towel to serve as a prayer mat at Guantánamo), the recourse to manacles to enforce discipline (cross-bar fetters in the Andamans, restraints that bind prisoners to wheeled tables en route to questioning in Cuba), the humanitarian claims associated with the appointment of on-staff medical officers in each case, or the prosaic advertisements in the back of each colony's gazette (the going rate in nineteenth-century rupees for servants, a 1990 Ford Ranger with new paint). But such parallels would obscure as much as they reveal. Guantánamo, unlike Port Blair, was a military base before it ever was a prison, its cells built not by prison labor but under contract with a private company closely associated with the government. An economy of incarceration that offers prisoners hamburgers from fast food outlets run by multinational corporations as incentives for cooperation cannot compare with the economic self-sufficiency prized in the Andamans, where officers hoped to grow enough *subzis* (vegetables) and produce enough oil to supply everyone in the penal colony at a time when the perceived failures of the East India Company during the 1857 war had brought corporate governance into disrepute. At Guantánamo, where return entails moving prisoners who hold citizenship in many parts of the world back across a multiplicity of borders, there would be a clamor for repatriation but not to a single patria, much less to the land to which the acronym GTMO refers back. The offshore can signify very differently for a capturing state seeking to evade its own courts and for captives in whom the state seeks to cultivate a sense that there may be no coming back from beyond.

If offshore incarceration at Guantánamo and offshore incarceration in the Andamans are not analogues, they do, however, exist in a historical relationship. Practices such as tracking bolstered imaginative appeals to the back of beyond that established the Andaman archipelago as more than just another island prison. Practices such as tracking also helped produce the Andamans as a site for the incitement of fear: the fear of death that authorities vainly hoped would deter convicts from flight; the fear of military might and the inevitability of encroachment that authorities hoped (equally vainly) to inculcate among Jarawa; and the conqueror's fear of all that might escape his control. In so doing, tracking became integral to the historical formation of not only ethnology but also an offshore type of incarceration specific to the modern state. Considered this way, the Andamans represent a trace just discernible in contemporary offshore incarceration facilities whose operations tend to be debated under the sign of international law, human rights, and civil liberties rather than history.

While the form assumed by tracking in the Andamans may have gone the way of time, the searches to which offshore incarceration today becomes party can still assume the disciplinary stance of colonialism in its most classical, ethnologically enhanced form. Paul Johnson (2003), a historian and columnist for

Forbes magazine, has written about the offshore prison at Guantánamo, where prisoners at the time of writing had had no access to judicial review, with unabashed praise as "the psychological/legal solution to the captured-terrorist problem" that "strikes a chill into the darkest of fundamentalist minds." An article posted on the website of the Joint Task Force at Guantánamo pledged that "grizzled GTMO veterans" going "home for the holidays" would always "remember how they felt the first time they looked a detainee in the eye and instantly realized just why they were here" (Pellegrini 2002). In the face of the arrogance required to read the complexities of history from a gaze, to wrest fact from surmise, to find the justification for state policy in bodies destined for a cage, it is worth remembering the history of the Andamans long enough to ask who represents the hunter in this civilization story. Only this time the forest assumes a terrifying and vast interiority. For what is interrogation, what is torture, but a practice in which the prisoner's body is cut for sign?

Acknowledgments

This essay has benefited greatly from the thoughtful comments of John Comaroff, Eng-seng Ho, Neni Panourgiá, Anindyo Roy, and Kumkum Sangari, each of whom read an earlier draft of the manuscript. Max Carocci at the British Museum generously provided assistance in locating some of the more elusive sources. I would also like to thank the staff of the Oriental and India Office Collections (OIOC) at the British Library for directing me to specific holdings on the Andaman Islands. Richard Handler has been an inspiration throughout. This project owes its inception to my partner, Geeta Patel, who offered encouragement, food, leads, and unsurpassed critique over the course of my work on the manuscript.

References Cited

Aggarwal, S. N. 1995. *The Heroes of Cellular Jail*. Patiala (Punjabi, India).
Archuleta, M., et al., eds. 2000. *Away from Home: American Indian Boarding School Experiences, 1879–2000*. Phoenix, AZ.
Arnold, D. 1994. The Colonial Prison: Power, Knowledge and Penology in Nineteenth-Century India. *Subaltern Studies* 8:148–87.
Beckett, S., ed. 1997. *The Stolen Generation: A Legal Issues Paper for Lawyers and Other Advisors*. Sydney.
Buck-Morss, S. 2002. A Global Public Sphere? *Situation Analysis* 1:10–19.
Child, B. 1998. *Boarding School Seasons: American Indian Families, 1900–1940*. Lincoln, NE.
Defoe, D. 1719 [1994]. *Robinson Crusoe*. London.
Johnson, P. 2003. The Long Haul in Iraq. *Forbes*, September 29:35.
Lomawaima, K. 1994. *They Called It Prairie Light: The Story of Chilocco Indian School*. Lincoln, NE.

Man, E. 1885 [1932]. *On the Aboriginal Inhabitants of the Andaman Islands*. London.

Oldenburg, V. 2002. *Dowry Murder: The Imperial Origins of a Cultural Crime*. New York.

Pandya, V. 1991. From Photography to Ethnography: Andamanese Documents and Documentation. *Visual Anthropology* 14:379–413.

———. 1997. Sacrifice and Escape as Counter-Hegemonic Rituals: A Structural Essay on an Aspect of Andamanese History. *Social Analysis* 41 (2):66–98.

Pellegrini, F. 2002. Goings and Comings: 'Tis the Season for Rotation as Units across GTMO Get Ready to Head Home for the Holidays. www.nsgtmo.navy.mil/JTFgtmo/News/nov22.htm.

Pinney, C. 1997. *Camera Indica: The Social Life of Indian Photographs*. Chicago.

Portman, M. 1899 [1990]. *A History of Our Relations with the Andamanese*. New Delhi.

Radcliffe-Brown, A. 1914 [1964]. *The Andaman Islanders*. New York.

Rafael, V. 2000. *White Love and Other Events in Filipino History*. Durham, NC.

Risen, J., and T. Shanker. 2003. Hussein Enters Post-9/11 Web of U.S. Prisons. *New York Times*, December 18.

Roy, P., and S. Choudhury. 2002. *The Lost Horizon: A Tale of Ross, the Deserted Island Citadel*. New Delhi.

Sen, S. 2000. *Disciplining Punishment: Colonialism and Convict Society in the Andaman Islands*. New Delhi.

Shively, L. 2003. Controversy Surrounds Transfer of "Shadow Wolves." *Indian Country Today*, June 11:A1–A2.

Singh, U. 1998. *Political Prisoners in India*. New Delhi.

Smith, A. 1759 [1997]. *The Theory of Moral Sentiments*. Washington, D.C.

Tamta, B. 1992. *Andaman and Nicobar Islands*. New Delhi.

Tomas, D. 1991. Tools of the Trade: The Production of Ethnographic Observations on the Andaman Islands, 1858–1922. *History of Anthropology* 7:75–108.

Wheeler, M. 2003. Shadow Wolves: An All-Indian Customs Unit—Possibly the World's Best Trackers—Uses Time-Honored Techniques to Pursue Smugglers along a Remote Stretch of the U.S.-Mexico Border. *Smithsonian* (January):40–47.

Zinoman, P. 2001. *The Colonial Bastille: A History of Imprisonment in Vietnam, 1862–1940*. Berkeley, CA.

Archival Sources

The following documents (identified in parenthetical citations by the acronyms listed here) were consulted at the Oriental and India Office Collection of the British Library, London.

ANG   *Andaman and Nicobar Gazette*. 1895–1903.

PSP   Proceedings of the Superintendent of Port Blair and the Nicobars. 1876–1906.

RAA   Report on the Administration of the Andaman and Nicobar Islands, and the Penal Settlements of Port Blair and the Nicobars. 1872–1908.

SUP   Supplement, ANG. Extracts from Reports and Diaries of Two Reconnaissances of the Country Supposed to be Occupied by the Jarawas. 3/1/02:25–49 (OIOC V/11/3698).

WHERE WAS BOAS DURING THE RENAISSANCE IN HARLEM?

Diffusion, Race, and the Culture Paradigm in the History of Anthropology

BRAD EVANS

It is something of a reversal of the relationship customarily imagined to exist between anthropology and modernism to find the anthropologist Franz Boas exhibited as an exotic in the culture of the Harlem Renaissance. And yet there can be no question that Boas has become an important point of reference for understanding the vogue for Harlem art and artists in the 1920s and 1930s. Boas's work on the relationship between race and culture has been seen with increasing frequency as setting in motion a reformulation of the culture concept central to the aesthetics and politics of modernism (see Posnock 1998; Hegeman 1999; Menand 2001; Elliott 2002; Manganaro 2002; Brown 2003; Pierpont 2004; Evans 2005). But it is Harlem that seems to provide the paradigmatic instance of Boas's crossover into a more widely public and aesthetic realm (Baker 1994; Hutchinson 1995; Williams 1996; Liss 1998; Helbling 1999). One moves easily from his association with W. E. B. Du Bois and tutelage of Zora Neale Hurston when she studied anthropology at Barnard, for example, to the idea that the cultural civil rights project of the Harlem art movement emanated from his research; one recognizes in his early interest in African art

Brad Evans is associate professor of English at Rutgers University and is the author of *Before Cultures: The Ethnographic Imagination in American Literature, 1865–1920*. He is currently working on the aesthetics of transnational regionalism at the fin de siècle in Europe, Japan, and America and the historical relationship between anthropology and pragmatism.

and civilization, including his advocacy in 1907 for a museum of African and African American culture, a genial complement to Albert C. Barnes's famous collection of African sculpture and textiles; and one readily understands that the seminal work of Boas's student, Melville Herskovits, on "the myth of the Negro past" was itself heavily influenced by the pan-Africanism of the Harlem Renaissance poets and writers. Boas's work on race and culture might be said to have authorized many of the social scientific forays of Harlem Renaissance writers. But more interestingly, I think, putting Boas into the Harlem mix elicits its own pleasing strangeness, making the bohemianism of both the Harlem vogue and American anthropology more visible.[1]

This move to recuperate Boas in literary and historical criticism and, in particular, for Harlem has often suffered, however, from an overdependence on a paradigmatic history of the emergence of a "Boasian" concept of culture. The assumption has been that Boas's culture concept was directly consonant with his antiracism and that as such the Harlem Renaissance was able to emerge along lines pioneered by Boasian anthropology that posited culture over race as the causal element in social productions. This account is flawed for at least three reasons. First, it places too much importance on the culture concept, which was far from the dominant motif in Boas's work until well into the 1920s. Second, it misreads the logic of Boas's arguments against race in such a way as to confuse them with the positions of more widely publicized advocates of cultural pluralism of the same period, like Randolph Bourne and Horace Kallen. The effect of such a conflation of Boas with pluralism trivializes his empirical research, making it sound as if his arguments stemmed merely from an admirable but suspect ethical stance, when in fact they followed from decades of fieldwork in ethnology, linguistics, and physical anthropology. Finally, it fails to give us a Boas who has much to say in the context of our own critical preoccupations. The overstatement of Boas's move to posit the stability and integrity of cultural wholes occludes his extensive and sophisticated work on what now goes by the name "hybridity"—the hybridity of both peoples and cultural artifacts. Boas's purchase for Harlem, as for the humanities more generally, stems first and foremost from an appreciation that artistic style was culturally expressive; but Boas wouldn't have gotten to that point had he not passed through what registers to-

---

1. On black internationalism see Posnock 1998 and, especially, Edwards 2003. Throughout this essay I will be using the term "Harlem Renaissance," although it should be noted that this nomenclature is itself disputed. Many during the period tried to avoid defining the movement by its association to any one place, preferring the nomenclature of the "New Negro." Edwards makes an entirely convincing case that both of these solutions fail to mark the intense translation of ideas and texts between the United States, Europe, Africa, and the Caribbean, including, quite literally, the personal contacts between black intellectuals traveling between these places. As such, it is crucial to note with Edwards that the "'New Negro' movement was at the same time a 'new' black internationalism" (2003:3, 322 n. 8).

day as a distinctly "postmodern" phase of analyzing what goes by such names as "transcultural flow" and "travelling cultures" (Appadurai 1996; Clifford 1997). Boas, notably, called it "dissemination"—his word, not Homi Bhabha's—and it was a central, if overlooked, tool used to call into question the use of racial categories in the description of cultural characteristics (Boas 1891; Bhabha 1994). To rethink Boas's work along these lines clarifies the lines of transit between his work and the cultural politics of Harlem, just as it joins a broader move to reposition Boas in the history of anthropology (e.g., Bashkow et al. 2004; Silverstein 2004).

The Culture Concept and the History of Anthropology

Ironically, part of the problem in locating Boas in the Harlem Renaissance, as in the genealogy of cultural pluralism more generally, comes from the success of the history of anthropology as an emergent subdiscipline in both the social sciences and the humanities and particularly from the way the field built on George Stocking's (1968, 1974a) revitalization of Boas in two volumes from anthropology's "crisis years" in the late sixties and early seventies. Stocking's early work, in particular, focused attention on Boas's intellectual and institutional centrality to the emergence of a distinctly anthropological sense of culture. However, an overreliance on this story of Boas's work on the culture concept and a tendency to neglect Stocking's many qualifications has occluded the significance of much of Boas's comparative work on diffusion, which presently holds more potential to address a rather different set of "enduring epistemological antinomies that characterize anthropological inquiry generally" than those Stocking had in mind in 1974 (Stocking 1974a:1). It may well be time to historicize Stocking's initial interventions on the subject of Boas so as to reposition and revitalize, once again, the genealogy of Boasian anthropology.

Stocking would surely not contest the argument that his initial recovery of Boas was of its time (i.e., "presentist," to use Stocking's word [1968:1–12]), and so one might understand the enthusiastic tone of his 1974 piece, "The Basic Assumptions of Boasian Anthropology," in relation to its own historical context (notwithstanding its deeply "historicist" thrust to understand the history of Boasian anthropology in its own terms). At the center of the essay—and particularly in its crucial first six pages—is the argument for Boas's early, temperamental preference for the study of "the integration of elements in a single culture," culture being defined along recognizably Herderian lines as "an integrated spiritual totality that somehow conditioned the form of its elements" (Stocking 1974a:5, 6). Such an argument was explicitly geared to undermine an eclipse of Boas in anthropology dating to the 1950s and 1960s (Stocking 1974a:18–20). This eclipse was made famous in Kroeber and Kluckhohn's (1952) seminal attempt at the definition of culture for anthropology, in which they argued that Boas provided scant theoretical elaboration for the project of anthropology, which, for them, had come to be defined as the study of "culture." In their exhaustive definition of the term, the two go directly back to E. B. Tylor's 1871 definition, writing of Boas that he was not interested in "systematically theorizing" culture and that, as such, he "contributed little to Tylor's attempt to isolate and clarify the concept[,] . . . [and] indirectly he hindered its progress by diverting attention to other problems" (Kroeber and Kluckhohn 1952:296–97).

Stocking's main line of argument responded directly to Kroeber and Kluckhohn by tracing the outline of the culture concept back to the "basic assumptions" made by Boas in even his earliest work. Although somewhat out of step with the Parsonian move toward systems analysis that was becoming dominant in the field, Stocking was nonetheless able to situate Boas at the head of an Americanist anthropological tradition that took culture as its central term (a genealogy most recently elaborated by Regna Darnell [1998, 2001]). Moreover, Stocking's emphasis on Boas's incipient recognition of an "integrated spiritual totality" played well outside anthropological circles. In sync with the civil rights movement generally, it also had a direct appeal to such developments as the "Native American Renaissance" in literature, in which writers like Simon Ortiz and Leslie Marmon Silko emphasized the same attributes, thereby offering critics the opportunity to reconcile at least one line of cultural anthropology with an emergent multiculturalism (e.g., Krupat 1992). Indeed, Boas's antiracism and good intentions with the culture concept lent to the recuperation of his basic assumptions something of a "salvage" quality, to use a term frequently used to describe Boas's own project in the late nineteenth century. Anthropology could be read as being rotten on both sides of Boas historically (with evolutionists on one side, cold war collusionists on the other), but Boas came out not only relatively clean but also with an undeniable relevance to cultural movements in both the humanities and the social sciences. (For examples of the use of Boas in recent humanities scholarship see Krupat 1992; Sundquist 1993; Hegeman 1999; Elliott 2002; and Brown 2003.)

Despite my great debt to Stocking's work, I want to return to Kroeber and Kluckhohn's judgment of Boas and particularly to its reference to his attention to "other problems." Indeed, one of my goals here is to suggest how these other problems resonate more provocatively today than do many of Kroeber and Kluckhohn's concerns about culture. Though not as prone to say "adieu" to culture as Michel-Rolph Trouillot (isn't that just a way to say "bonjour" to some new word?), I agree with him, at least provisionally, that "without culture, we may even revitalize the Boasian conceptual kernel" (Trouillot 2002:58).

For the culture concept, after three decades of critique, is not what it used to be. Stocking had defined Boas's culture concept as "a relativistic, pluralistic, holistic, integrated, and historically conditioned framework for the study of the determination of human behavior" (1974a:19). While it may have played well in the 1970s and 1980s, this definition's emphasis on holism and integration faces trouble along two axes of contemporary critique. First, as Trouillot and others have argued, a persistent problem with "culture" is that it suffers from the paradox of being an antirace concept "on the essentialist track with a racialist bent" (Trouillot 2002:40; see, similarly, Clifford 1988 on the "predicament" of culture; Herbert 1991; and especially Michaels 1992; for influential reviews see Brightman 1995; Darnell 1997; and Kuper 1999). In effect, the claim goes, culture never got over the Herderian romantic racialism that defined it in the nineteenth century as it made its way out of Germany, inscribing instead new, race-based boundaries on social structures that were, moreover, often implicitly nationalist (cf. Balibar and Wallerstein 1991). The second axis of critique is that of globalism, which, like the racialist line, brings into question the artificiality of culture's imagined boundaries, its reductive claims to "wholeness" in a world defined not by stability but by the flow of peoples and goods (e.g., Appadurai 1996; Clifford 1997). In this respect, some critics have begun to argue for a more "sociological approach" to conceptualizations of culture, which might include shifting "from generalizing about culture to giving a reasoned account of people[,] . . . show[ing] how cultural images, knowledge, and representations are deployed, and sometimes created, by situated persons with purposes, acting in complex life situations" (Barth 2002:32; also Bonnell and Hunt 1999).

That Boas has been so closely associated with the culture concept thus opens his work up to critique, for he is liable to be either marginalized in accounts of the emergence of modernist pluralism or depicted as a racist despite himself. In several major studies of modernist aesthetics and American history, for example, Boas has simply not played the role that he seemingly ought to play. Posnock, Bramen, and Menand, for example, all trace the emergence of cultural pluralism not through Boas but through the pragmatist philosophy of William James. Posnock, for whom Boas would seem to be an obvious choice in discussions of race and modernist intellectuals, barely mentions the anthropologist; relying entirely on Stocking's 1974 essay, he motions at various times toward the way Boas's reluctance to frame general laws might have been analogous to the Jamesian compunction to dismiss "all the single word answers to the world's riddle" and in particular to dismiss race (William James quoted in Posnock 1998:57). Bramen (2001:205–6) mentions him only in passing, and then mainly to accuse him of relying on racialism. Menand (2001:383–87) notes his importance to the history of the culture concept but focuses on the inefficacy of his anthropometric studies in calming the racist hysteria of the 1910s and 1920s over immigration policy. Interestingly, although Michaels has been more persistent than anyone in the humanities in pushing the critique of the culture concept along the lines suggested by Trouillot, he specifically—and uncharacteristically—exonerates Boas of the charge of racism. He quotes Stocking to the effect that Boas was not a cultural pluralist "in a consistent sense" (Stocking 1968:231) and then goes on to suggest that "although admirers of Boas' antiracism . . . often identify that antiracism with his presumed pluralism, it is, in fact, the racists Boas meant to oppose whose conception of culture was more purely pluralist" (Michaels 1995:173). Although I agree with Michaels on this point (but not on many others), it proves disappointing to the historian of anthropology to find Boas, thus exonerated, reduced to a footnote, which is the only place he appears in Michaels's book. Even if he comes off as having been relatively enlightened, Boas is returned to the position of irrelevancy assigned him by Kroeber and Kluckhohn.

Though taking exception to Michaels's desire to do away with the culture concept because of its inherent racism, Hegeman implicitly agrees with his characterization of Boas's relationship to early-twentieth-century pluralism. She describes the story of Boas as the creator of the culture concept as a "modernist fable," noting, like Michaels, that Boas's relativism was not free from value judgments (Hegeman 1999:32). But she then goes on to argue that the significance of Boas's work on culture was to reconceive of it "in spatial terms," such that anthropological significance resides in "the physical site of origin of an artifact" and "discrete cultural contexts" (Hegeman 1999:37, 40). This move, suggested to Hegeman in the first instance by the museum debate with Otis T. Mason over the classification of ethnological objects, a debate that Stocking had first cited (1968:205, 1974a:1–6) as one of the key harbingers of Boas's "holistic approach" to culture, inadvertently opens the anthropologist up to the second critique, a failure to take sufficient account of cultural flow.[2] Hegeman convincingly historicizes the emergence of Boas's "spatialized culture concept" in the context of positions the anthropologist took during World War I (1999:41). But in so doing she leaves little room for using Boas to think through our own theoretical engagements, such as the anthropological theorization of "the field" and "borders" (Gupta and Ferguson 1997; Bashkow 2004) or how one might, in the historian Thomas Bender's words, "frame the narrative of American history in the context of a self-consciously global age" (2002:vii). For Hegeman, Boas's culture concept took shape precisely as a result of its delimitation of groups of people in particular spaces. To get to that "full-blown" spatial understanding of culture, what had "largely to be abandoned" was the extensive comparative work on the diffusion of cultural elements that Boas had done up to then. Tantalizingly, Hegeman notes that the

2. I take it that the frequency with which this debate is cited is paradigmatic of the influence of Stocking's recovery of Boas as well as of the problems with that influence (see, e.g., Hinsley 1981:98–100; Jacknis 1985:77–83; Hyatt 1990:18–21; Baker 1994:201; Elliott 2002:1–8; Manganaro 2002:9; Brown 2003:88–89). As I will discuss later in this essay, the centrality of diffusion to the article is rarely cited.

previous studies of diffusion would have emphasized "contact, exchange, migration, conquest" and "contextual porosity and exchange" (1999:41), precisely those things, in other words, for which theories of globalization have recently attempted to account.

What both lines of this critique of culture take for granted is an emphasis on its definition, in Stocking's words, as an "integrated spiritual totality," an emphasis that renders the concept bounded by both race and geography. But what if, keeping in mind the validity of Kroeber and Kluckhohn's complaint that Boas did not formally define the culture concept until very late in his career, we were to reemphasize the supposedly abandoned line of Boasian diffusion? Justification for such a move is found in Stocking's own work, which has always been clear to note a tension in Boas between a particularist approach that concentrated on integration and a comparative one that attempted to trace the historical and geographical distribution of cultural elements (1968:213–14, 1974a:6; see also Bunzl 1996). Rather than focus on Boas's documentation of "integrated" cultures, we might choose to emphasize his repeated assertion that cultures were complexly interwoven entities that anthropologists needed to "unravel" (e.g., Boas 1910a:340, 1920:213). Given Boas's reluctance to put the culture concept down on paper, it seems more than reasonable to suggest that he kept diffusion much more in play and to a much greater purpose than has been previously acknowledged. Indeed, I would argue, the emphasis on diffusion made Boas's particular line on the culture concept different from other nineteenth- and twentieth-century versions of cultural pluralism. Diffusion not only provided Boas with his best argument against racism but also assured that aesthetic style would come to hold a privileged spot in the interpretation of culture.

Accounting for the Persistence of Race in Boasian Thought

Before moving on, however, I think it important to note the single most common mistake in the critique of Boas and the culture concept. It is frequently assumed that as culture emerged as a key word in early-twentieth-century thought it came to occupy the same space as had the nineteenth-century concept of race, thus enabling a diachronic "race into culture," and that, as such, culture inherited the essentialist problems of race (Michaels 1992). Starting from such an assumption, critics have tended to argue that the development of culture into an anthropological word in the early twentieth century was a way to get around a preexisting notion of race without really replacing it (Appiah 1992; Liss 1998). There is no doubt that what Boas meant by culture could be used to argue against the adequacy of race as a categorical marker of distinction. Michaels, moreover, has broadly documented the slippage between race and culture in the writing of American pluralists in the twenties. But "race" and "culture" were *both* given new connotations in the early twentieth century. If there was a "race into culture," it happened synchronically, with culture coming to inhabit a definition held earlier in the nineteenth century by a concept of race that had been itself inflected by what in the twentieth century was going to be called culture.

In romantic discourse about the "genius of the nation" race was typically not a strictly biological entity. Rather, it was an umbrella term that conflated nature and nurture, or what we would call "race" and "culture." It was a general notion related to the Herderian *Volksgeist*, or folk spirit, found to be at the core of modern nations. As Stocking (1968, 2001) points out in an essay that has received significantly less attention than his work on the culture concept, there was also a Lamarckian evolutionary conception, holding that race was capable of transmitting acquired characteristics, which persisted in American social scientific thought well into the late nineteenth century. It was with something of a combination of these notions that, for example, the French literary historian Hippolyte Taine (1863) could speak of an English literary tradition that began not in England but along the coast of "Anglo-Saxon" Denmark and the American author Sarah Orne Jewett (1887) could write of the legacy of the Normans in the social life of small villages in coastal Maine. For each, traits that were socially acquired and that were made visible in the organization of literary art or rural communities could be carried by bloodlines. Self-cultivation within groups could reshape the biological contours of their race. Conceived of as such, race not only failed to denote a purely biological essentialism throughout much of the nineteenth century, it could also be used to suggest something very much like cultural pluralism.

Moreover, the bifurcation of race and culture in the early twentieth century was not just Boas's idea. In a very real sense it had been insisted upon by the Supreme Court in its 1896 decision in *Plessy v. Ferguson* when it upheld the states' right to segregate based not on culture but only on skin color (Lofgren 1990). No amount of "culture" counted in the ensuing Jim Crow legislation, for which "one drop" of blood was determinative. Nowhere do we get a better sense of the psychic effects of this shift in categorical meaning of race than in the writing of Du Bois. The first chapter of *The Souls of Black Folk* (1903a), originally published in 1897 in the *Atlantic Monthly*, reads as a direct response to the Plessy decision of the previous year. The situation for Du Bois, which he famously described as a feeling of "two-ness,—an American, a Negro; two souls, two thoughts, two unreconciled strivings" (1903a:364), most likely had its genesis in this decision. As Du Bois explained, his two-ness sprang from his situation as a black intellectual and an American, where his cultural aims failed to correlate with the limits imposed upon his biological race. This bifurcation was fundamentally contradictory to Du Bois, temperamentally a romantic in both his thought and his personal life. His education became an element that the Jim Crow legislation could no longer see because of his blackness. No amount of cultivation or any anthropologically defined cultural affiliation would permit Du Bois to ride in the train with Boas or his other peers. There is nothing anthropological about this move to separate race and culture; rather, it occurred in the post-Reconstruction environment when the United States became a segregationist state, at which point the biological component of the race concept became ascendant and culture began to surface as a way to theorize that which was not biological (see also Roediger 1991; Haney-Lopez 1996; Jacobson 1998).

Thus if we take the history of the culture concept seriously, the distinction Boas made could not have marked a transition between a nineteenth-century biological conception of race and a twentieth-century culture concept that deemphasized biological essentialism. Rather, both the essentialist definition of race and the nonessentialist concept of culture developed at the same time. They developed, moreover, at a moment when an entire range of categories that had previously been deployed to mark social difference became functionally disabled by developments in U.S. history. The end of slavery, the figurative closing of the frontier, the end of the Indian Wars, urban migration, upswings in immigration, the beginnings of U.S. imperialism, and the development of the culture industry all contributed to an enormous flux in the hierarchies by which difference could be defined. "National character" would be increasingly difficult to locate when the nation included territories overseas, sectional differences between the states, differences in custom and language between regions, and immigrant bearers of unassimilated nationalities within the nation. In literature regional dialect became a constitutive component of novels published in New York and Boston. Japanese screens and Negro minstrelsy made their way into the "cultivated" salons and drawing rooms of Gilded Age capitalists. A history of anthropology that focuses on Boas's drive to replace the category of race with that of culture vastly oversimplifies the widespread matter of finding a new vocabulary for difference that preoccupied both scientists and artists at the turn of the century.

Nowhere is this oversimplification more problematic than when considering the persistence of racial thought in Boas's own attempts to address the race problem in his adopted country. Boas made several different kinds of arguments against the usefulness of race in ethnographic description, but the category remained oddly legitimated throughout his career. His most well known position was that stemming from racial measurement, which I will not take up here except to note with some bemusement that the accuracy of Boas's numbers remains in dispute (Gravlee et al. 2003; Sparks and Jantz 2003; cf. Williams 1996). More remarkable was his second, which he took when addressing the graduates of Atlanta University—at the request of Du Bois—in 1906 and the American Association of Science in 1908 (reprinted the next year in *Science*) and when writing in the first volume of the NAACP journal, the *Crisis* (Boas 1906, 1908, 1910b). Here we clearly see something like the emergence of the culture concept. The Atlanta commencement address is particularly interesting because of Boas's telltale pluralization of culture, as when he argued that "there have been cultures different from ours and . . . the qualities that are to-day dominant and most highly esteemed . . . have not always had the same value" (1906:310). This intervention and particularly Du Bois's enthusiastic recollection at a much later date of the address (1939:vii) have been much heralded for presaging, more broadly, the social implications of Boas's particularist interest in studying integrated cultures. Both Hutchinson (1995:63) and Helbling (1999:22–23), for example, quote Du Bois enthusiastically to the effect of his being "too astonished to speak" at the end of Boas's talk by way of making the case that the anthropologist's development of the culture concept was central to the intellectual and cultural spirit of the Harlem Renaissance (but see Baker 1994; Williams 1996; and Liss 1998 for somewhat more reserved assessments).

However, to go back to those pieces proves not a little disappointing, for Boas readily admitted not only the legitimacy of a category of race but also the current state of inferiority of the Negro race in America. He did so explicitly in his AAS address: "I do not believe that the negro is, in his physical and mental make-up, the same as the European. The anatomical differences are so great that corresponding mental differences are plausible. There may exist differences in character and in the direction of specific aptitudes" (Boas 1908:328–29). His point, of course, was to argue that, notwithstanding the existence of race, it was no limit to potential. But to make that point he was willing to concede, albeit conditionally, that the brain of "the negro" may, in fact, have a "slightly inferior size, and perhaps lesser complexity of structure," although he additionally, and somewhat paradoxically, insisted that the "range of variation" within the races was greater than that between them (Boas 1908:329).[3]

Though not commenting so directly on anthropometric studies, Boas's rhetorical gesture in Atlanta two years earlier had been similarly confounding. Boas began his commencement address to the overwhelmingly black audience by noting "the present weakness of the American Negro, his uncontrolled emotions, his lack of energy," this by way of arguing only that such traits were not racially inherent, as demonstrated by the achievements, vaguely demarcated in history, of Africans (1906:311). Even though most critics have located Boas's significance to the Harlem Renaissance in terms of his separation of the culture concept from that of race, we see here the extent to which his progressive po-

---

3. This point about variation would seem to challenge the viability of the category of race, as it did for Boas in 1921, when he published on the topic in the *Yale Review* (1921:387). In 1908, however, the existence of race was something that Boas seemed willing to concede as a matter of course.

litical stance in fact depended on the racial category. Having granted the current state of the race's degradation in the United States, Boas encouraged the Atlanta University graduates to look "confidently . . . to the home of your ancestors" and recover "what has been lost in transplanting the Negro race from its native soil to this continent" (1906:313). He used the historical achievements of blacks in Africa—in smelting iron, in sculpture—to show that there were no limits to their potential in America. But the "predicament" such an argument poses for the anthropological concept of culture in the plural should by now be familiar. How could the Atlanta University students look "home" to Africa if the line of the "cultural" inheritance had been "lost"? The answer was by way of turning to their "ancestors," which was to say by way of the blood ties of race, without which Boas's argument would have lacked coherence.

This line of Boas's antiracist strategy in the United States might best be understood in terms of his engagement with a Jewish racial strategy in Germany. As provocatively argued by Bunzl, Boas was influenced by the *Bildung*, or education, ideal espoused during the period of the Jewish enlightenment in Germany, especially as it was filtered through the *Völkerpsychologie* ethnological work of Heyman Steinthal and Moritz Lazarus (Bunzl 2003; also Kalmar 1987). Emphasizing the plasticity of *Geist*, or group spirit, and the infinite possibility of improvement, the argument from *Bildung* conceded that the Jewish race had undergone centuries of deprivation but asserted that there were no natural limits on its ability to regenerate itself, to grow on a moral and cultural level, and to contribute to the brotherhood of man. As manifest in the work of Steinthal and Lazarus, this move was committed to universalism, which goes far in explaining why Boas was also an assimilationist. In his Atlanta University speech Boas replicated this strategy, suggesting that the situation of "Jews of Europe . . . illustrates the conditions that characterize your own position" (1906:315). Just as forced separation and lingering racism had debilitated the Jewish "people" in Europe, so too had forced migration and slavery debilitated the Negro race in the United States. The solution, Boas suggested, was to come to the "arduous work" of "improvement" and "adaptation" with an optimistic belief in the race's capability of doing so, an optimism firmly supported by the "teachings of history" (1906:315).

Helbling's and Hutchinson's notion of Du Bois being particularly taken with Boas's commencement address also makes perfect sense in the context of German-Jewish *Bildung*, though whether Du Bois got it from Boas or from his own period of study in Germany is difficult to know (Evans 2005). Already in 1897 Du Bois had argued in similar, pluralist-universalist terms for the "conservation of races," writing in terms of *Bildung* that for "the development of Negro genius, of Negro literature and art, of Negro spirit, only Negroes bound and welded together, Negroes inspired by one vast ideal, can work out in its fullness the great message we have for humanity" (1897:820). Boas's emphasis on Africa enhanced and expanded this vision, but it would be wrong to over-look the historical context and simply assume that Du Bois's enthusiasm was for the pluralization of culture—wrong in the first instance because Du Bois, in a professional career spanning seventy years, never pluralized the word. Most fa-mously, in *The Souls of Black Folk* he pictured the Negro striving to be a "co-worker in the kingdom of culture, to escape both death and isolation, to hus-band and use his best powers and his latent genius" (1903a:365). It was in much this same sense that Du Bois used the term when he gave it his most direct def-inition thirty years later. Writing on the theme of "cultural equality," he ex-plained, "by equality, I do not mean absolute identity or similarity of gift, but gifts of essentially equal values to human culture. By culture, I mean that or-ganized tide which men call civilization" (Du Bois 1929:394). In this formula-tion it was the plural "gifts" that were relativized, while "culture" maintained its singular attachment to ideas about human development and civilization across the globe. Similarly, in his autobiography of 1968, written at the end of his long life, Du Bois maintained culture's transnational, developmental asso-ciation with civilization, speaking repeatedly of "human culture" and "modern culture" as that to which the striving of humankind should aspire (1968:236, 349, 358, 363, 388, 392).[4] Divided from Boas on the culture concept, Du Bois was united with him in the continued use of race as a category of distinction and particularly in the deployment of race in conjunction with a profound eth-ical commitment to universalism.

They were, moreover, united in this line of thought by personal contacts in New York having little direct connection to anthropological work, as suggested by both men's association with Felix Adler's "ethical culture" movement. Of Jewish-German background like Boas, Adler established the Ethical Culture Society along lines similar to those set out in the *Bildung* model as a radically assimilationist and secular movement espousing a broadly antidiscriminatory message of universal brotherhood through self-cultivation. Adler was familiar to the Boas family in Germany, and when Boas moved to New York the two be-came correspondents. The Ethical Culture Society ran a school in the city that Boas supported both by being on its board and by enrolling his children there. In letters to Adler from the period Boas also shared with him his political phi-losophy and discomfort with the nationalism surrounding World War I (see correspondence in FBP; also Hegeman 1999:48; Cole 1999:109; Boas 2005). Adler was also a personal acquaintance of Du Bois, who, like Boas, was sending his daughter to Adler's school during this period (Du Bois 1928:1003). Du Bois

4. For additional details concerning Du Bois's use of "culture" see Evans 2005. On race see, for example, Du Bois's discussion of the concept in *Dusk of Dawn* (1940), especially chapter 5. For the attempts of critics to determine what he meant by race see Appiah 1992; Reed 1992; and Holt 1990.

and Adler knew each other well, as suggested by the fact that they were elected cosecretaries of the Universal Races Congress of 1911, held in London (Lewis 1993:440). The similarity of their philosophies is documented by the epigraph Du Bois used for his 1914 Atlanta University publication, *Morals and Manners among Negro Americans*, where he quotes Adler: "We must depend for the peace and progress of the world upon the formation of a horizontal upper layer of cultured persons among all the more civilized peoples—a cross-section, as it were, of the nations, whose convictions and sentiments shall supply the moral force on which international arbitration courts and similar agencies will have to depend." Du Bois (1903b) had famously called the same "upper layer" the "talented tenth."

In short, the persistence of race in the political strategies of both Boas and Du Bois can be traced, at least in part, to this nineteenth-century Jewish response to racism in Germany. The two men were much further apart intellectually and (as we will see) personally than has generally been assumed; however, when holding on to race and channeling it through a *Bildung* model of ethical culture, they were pursuing a similar tactic that retained the idea of self-cultivation as a process for racial harmonization. The shortcoming of this strategy, of course, was that it did little to move beyond the basic problem of race, which remained a biologically delimited concept even when its plasticity and historicity were acknowledged. The point, however, is not that either man failed to "complete the argument," as Appiah (1985) has put it when suggesting that Du Bois should have moved beyond race and toward something like an anthropological definition of culture. Rather, it is simply that the category of culture as it developed in Boasian circles neither depended upon nor premised the demise of the category of race. Race and culture both continued to play central roles in Boasian anthropology; they were, however, separate and uncorrelated categories, each one deployed to explain different sets of data and address different methodological, substantive, and, at times, political problems.

Recovering Boasian Diffusion

Noting the persistence of race in Boasian thought already relieves a major burden on the culture concept, for there is no need to argue that one supplants the other. The theory by which Boas imagined an anthropological relationship between these two categories was diffusion; at the same time, however, diffusion had the fundamental effect of exposing the seams that had linked biology and social characteristics in the popular imagination. In particular, it was diffusion that showed that the correlation of biological and intellectual potential being used to underwrite the establishment of segregation in the country was false. It did so not by intervening along the axis of a debate about nature versus nurture—races versus cultures—but by gesturing toward something strikingly like a postmodern appreciation for the movement of people, material culture, and language across the hierarchical distinctions of difference. Instead of arguing that race was insignificant when compared to culture, it added language as a third variable and argued for a lack of correlation between them all. Race, language, and culture moved—all across the map—at different rates and in different directions.

Here the Kroeber and Kluckhohn argument against which Stocking was writing clarifies Boas's significance. Even though they underestimated his influence and miscalculated his contribution to American anthropology, Kroeber and Kluckhohn were correct to argue that "Boas was interested in the complex interactions of culture, language, race and environment; he was much less interested in the nature and specific properties of culture" (1952:297). It would be easy to misread this passage and take it to mean that Boas was not interested in "specific cultures." Clearly, he was; he had a strong disposition not only to the "tribal arrangement" of museums but also to particularist approaches to anthropological problems generally (Bunzl 1996:18). That is not to say, however, that culture was necessarily the conceptual category around which he organized the bulk of his research, including the critique of race and social evolutionary theories.

Diffusion was a topic on which Boas published repeatedly, both explicitly and implicitly. Stocking (1974b:130) notes at least six publications by Boas on the topic between 1891 and 1914, most of which were reprinted in *Race, Language, and Culture* (Boas 1940). I would go further and suggest that the topic was implied in some form in almost everything Boas published during this period. Indeed, even that key citation in contemporary rehearsals of Boas's early development of the culture concept, the debate with Mason on the classification of ethnological exhibits (Boas 1887a, 1887b), was framed in terms of—and not against—the study of diffusion. The first of the museum debate articles, published in the journal *Science*, was titled "The Occurrence of Similar Inventions in Areas Widely Apart" (1887b). This problem of similarity was precisely the one propelling the widespread interest in origins—the origins of language, folklore, races—characterizing the incredible range of social scientific and humanistic research into diffusion during the period. In the museum debate Boas challenged conventional classificatory methods dependent upon comparative analogy and insisted instead on the inductive study of particular cases for which "the tribal arrangement of museum specimens is the only satisfactory one" (1887a:64). It is important to remember, however, that this critique of the comparative method was aimed at the social-evolutionary uses of it, not at the study of diffusion generally. In the same essay Boas cited three answers to the problem of similar occurrences in areas widely apart: the migration of peoples, the migration of ideas, and the idea that "like causes produce like effects" (1887a:61).

He objected only to the last one, which lent itself to evolutionary interpretations. Like effects spring from unlike causes, he argued, such that a rattle may be a children's toy in one place but a religious symbol or a work of art in another. By contrast, he did not critique the other two explanations, and they came to play a regular part in his ethnological repertoire. Unfortunately, less attention has been given to them as well as to what he might have meant in concluding the article with the qualification that the comparative method remained "the most effective method of finding problems" and played "an active part . . . in the origin of philosophical systems and grand ideas which sometimes burst upon scientists" (1887a:65).

Although predominantly drawing attention to the "like effects from unlike causes" argument, Stocking has noted the significance of this concluding line. Not only was the study of dissemination always the other half of Boas's particularist inclinations, it was, singularly, "the medium of his critique of evolutionary ethnology in the period between 1887 and 1896" (Stocking 1974a:5)—a periodization that I would be inclined to extend well into the 1900s. Of course, as Stocking points out, there is a need to qualify this claim. Diffusion was not necessarily antithetical to an evolutionary position; but as an explanatory factor, "independent invention was much more central to [the evolutionists'] nomothetic purpose" than it was to a historical particularist like Boas (Stocking 1968:205). Still, in Boas's hands diffusion fundamentally disproved independent invention and, in turn, the notion of social evolution itself. The greater part of the antievolutionary purchase of Boas's work came not from its particularist call for the culture concept in museum classification but from its emphasis on the transcultural flow of material culture. Moreover, Boas's ideas about museum classification had little effect on the "philosophical systems and grand ideas" of evolutionary theories that clearly perturbed him. As Jacknis has noted (1985:80–81), Mason and others at the Bureau of American Ethnology ended up following Boas's exhibit methods just a few years later at the World's Columbian Exposition in 1893. This methodological overlap with Boas did not, however, force most BAE scholars to reconsider their theoretical framework, which remained staunchly evolutionary.

The study of diffusion, by contrast, challenged not only evolutionary but also romantic nationalist and racialist interpretations. It did so by refusing to collapse the categories of race, language, and material culture—elements seen to be disseminating across the hierarchical boundaries imagined to demarcate social difference. In 1890 William Wells Newell, the first editor of the *Journal of American Folklore* (*JAF*), described the "rude shock" he experienced at discovering that folklore was radically discontinuous with the categories taken to constitute the nation and specifically with race and language. Contrary to the Herderian conceptualization of folklore as a sign of national character, it was increasingly realized that folklore traveled widely across those categories and at much greater rates, leaving Newell to conclude that "differences of race and language are not necessarily an indication of differences in tradition" (1890:26). As an example, we might consider the folklore recorded by Joel Chandler Harris from ex-slaves in Georgia, popularly reproduced as the "Uncle Remus" stories, which became a touchstone in arguments about the origins of folklore in the *JAF* throughout the 1890s. Variants of Harris's tales were located not only in the black South but also in the West among Native Americans, in South America, in Western Europe, and even in Asia. In the introduction to his first volume of Remus tales, *Uncle Remus, His Songs and His Sayings*, Harris not only makes the case for the tales' global diffusion but goes so far as to claim that the tales had "become a part of the domestic history of every Southern family" (1880:vii), which, perhaps inadvertently, goes to confirm the ability of folktales to jump over racial boundaries. If folklore and other cultural elements did not match up with race, then race would have little explanatory power in ethnological studies.

It is important to understand the mechanics of this argument because it is one that shows up throughout Boas's work in the first decade of the 1900s. For example, he used exactly the same structure of argument in his introduction to the *Handbook of American Indian Languages* (1911a). The organizing problem remained the similarity of occurrences in peoples widely apart, but Boas took the step of including an extended theoretical overview of the subject. He did so in order to demonstrate the artificial nature of classification itself:

> An attempt to correlate the numerous classifications that have been proposed shows clearly a condition of utter confusion and contradiction. If it were true that anatomical form, language, and culture are all closely associated, and that each subdivision of mankind is characterized by a certain bodily form, a certain culture, and a certain language, which can never become separated, we might expect that the results of various investigations would show better agreement. If, on the other hand, the various phenomena which were made the leading points in the attempt at classification are not closely associated, then we may naturally expect such contradictions and lack of agreement as are actually found. (Boas 1911a:7–8)

Here Boas got at the separation of race and culture by a route much different from that of the 1906 Atlanta University speech. Rather than an ethical problem it was one of empirical necessity. One could not collapse race into culture or race into language because the fundamental discovery of the ethnographic work Boas commissioned for the *Handbook* was that the categories themselves intersected and diverged at irregular angles. The point, in other words, was not that culture should replace race as an analytical category but that a whole array of cultural elements—language, material culture, traditions, folktales, and songs—simply did not match up with race or each other. Race failed to describe the anthropological problems at hand.

Work on diffusion has frequently been misconstrued by critics looking to bring a Boasian cultural pluralism to bear on the artistic movement in Harlem. Hutchinson, for example, is right to place the Harlem Renaissance within the multiracial intellectual context of American anthropology and philosophy. But his use of Boas is not only problematic, it is typical in its overemphasis of Stocking's history of the paradigm shift toward the culture concept. For example, Hutchinson cites Herskovits's biography of Boas to the effect that a 1903 essay, "The Decorative Art of the Indians of the East Coast," published first in *Popular Science*, "represents a pioneer analysis of the symbolisms of a nonrepresentational art form in terms of its own canons of interpretation" (Hutchinson 1995:66). But one need only turn to Boas's last paragraph for fundamental qualifications: "The historical explanation of customs given by the native is generally a result of speculation, not by any means a true historical explanation" (1903:563). In other words, what Boas recognized here was not culture on "its own" terms but the old bugaboo of what he elsewhere calls the problem of "secondary explanations"—explanations by primary informants of their own beliefs and customs that misrepresent the historical diffusion of cultural elements (1898:96). Indeed, had Hutchinson gone to the article instead of to Herskovits's myth-making account of it he would have seen that it was almost entirely given over to a description of the dissemination of decorative art, such that a "uniform type" of native art can be discovered across large expanses of North America, "notwithstanding local peculiarities" (Boas 1903:554). Boas stated expressly that his purpose in writing was to show that dissemination was as widespread "among the primitive tribes of North America" as "in the art of the civilized peoples of the Old World" (1903:547).

It is, of course, possible to get from that intent to a more general "assault" on racist intellectual paradigms, but the route was different from the "ethical imperative" that Hutchinson invokes (1995:66). Indeed, I would argue that Boas's position is most provocative when he is seen to have avoided falling back upon the question of ethics. And he did avoid such a move when, as in the 1903 article, he challenged the position, staked out at once by romantic nationalists and social evolutionists, that "the decorative designs used by primitive man do not serve purely esthetic ends, but that they suggest to his mind certain definitive concepts" drawn directly from nature (Boas 1903:546). Boas's more complex argument was that decorative forms traveled easily across even remote cultural areas and were often symbolic of nothing but pleasing aesthetic techniques. Indeed, the article reads as detailed art history when describing how to distinguish Arapaho from Shoshone parfleches (rawhide bags or envelopes) by whether the colors are laid on delicately or in large areas; but the point was that "despite many minor differences of this sort, . . . the general type is very uniform" (Boas 1903:555). Following the lead of Frank Hamilton Cushing and William Henry Holmes, Boas stressed the dependence of changes in decorative art on material and technique and the "transfer of designs developed in one technique to another" (1903:546). In this instance he did so by pointing out that basic techniques represented in material culture were diffused across the boundaries of language and geography without respect to internalized belief systems—by emphasizing, in other words, the hybridity and flow of cultural forms. One could make neither romantic-nationalist nor evolutionary claims from the decorative arts if they were not indigenous to the peoples who were supposedly developing them.

This argument was important for at least two reasons. First, Boas's change in emphasis in this article, away from organic explanations of the decorative arts as reflections of systems of belief and toward explanations of transcultural borrowing and exchange, reflected a move he made repeatedly to disrupt the accepted categories by which social difference had been understood up to that time. This emphasis remained constant in all of Boas's work, right up to the 1930s. Although anthropometric techniques received primary place in the most influential of Boas's early works, *The Mind of Primitive Man* (1911b), diffusion was the clinching argument against the adequacy of race from chapter 8, "Race, Language and Culture" (note that the chapter title anticipated that of Boas's 1940 retrospective compendium), on to the end of the book. Similarly, in his popularization of anthropological theory, *Anthropology and Modern Life* (1928), Boas began his critique of race with an anthropometric argument but closed with the "geographical and historical distribution" of similar traits: "They convince us of the independence of race and culture because their distribution does not follow racial lines" (1928:60, 61). Again, race did not disappear in this argument. It did not give way to culture. Rather, race became an inadequate category of description because things like language, folklore, and art did not correlate with it. As such, dissemination remained significant throughout Boas's career for the way it offered what was probably his most provocative challenge to both evolutionary and romantic epistemologies of Native American and African American racial differences.

Second, the argument from diffusion was important because it led to a humanistic concept of culture that took aesthetic style as a central component. As the culture concept became more important for Boas and his students in the 1910s and 1920s, diffusion regularly became the first part of a two-step process that finished with a study of what Boas frequently called "literary style" (1914:466, 479). Since things like folklore and decorative techniques were widely disseminated, one was left with understanding variation with the artistry with which they were redeployed. Style, the "artistic finishing touch required for the tale wherever the art of story-telling demands it," thus became the "explanatory element" in Boas's thinking because it was the one thing that marked real difference between cultures that otherwise exchanged traits indiscriminately (1914:480). As this emphasis emerged, the study of diffusion, which depended on an analysis of content dominant in what Conn has described as the "object-based epistemology" of museum anthropology (1998:4–9), ceded its importance to the study of patterns of style within individual cultures. It is this version of a strikingly humanistic, post–natural sciences version of culture that is now primarily identified with Boas and his students, particularly with Hurston, Edward Sapir, and Ruth Benedict. Moreover, this shift in anthropological concerns not only made anthropology more palatable to authors and artists in the 1920s but also demonstrated that anthropologists were themselves animated by stylistic developments in modernist literature and art (Hegeman 1999; Manganaro 2002).

A quick example can be found in Boas's writing on Native American folklore. In 1914 Boas argued that "the explanatory element" would come not "as an expression of native philosophy, but rather as an artistic finishing touch required for the tale wherever the art of story-telling demanded it" (1914:480–81). His first step, based on diffusion, was to contravene the possible influence of race when he noted, "there is no tribe in North America whose tales can be considered as purely local products uninfluenced by foreign elements. We have found that some tales are distributed over almost the whole continent, others over more or less extended parts of the country" (Boas 1914:479). Writing in a modernist mode and attuned to the visual arts, Boas noted that "everything appears . . . in flux," leaving him to think of folklore as "a constant play with old themes" and as "mosaics of different style" (1914:480). Boas concluded, however, that "the tales of each particular area have developed a peculiar literary style, which is an expression of the mode of life and of the form of thought of the people . . . and that the associated explanatory elements depend entirely upon the different styles of thought" (1914:479–80). This dual finding of hybridity and artistic invention became key to the argument for culture as a category of anthropological significance. Folklore could not be thought of in terms of race because of diffusion; it had to be thought of in terms of culture because of the peculiarity of aesthetic styles.

The particularist argument in Boas's work is almost always accompanied by this diffusionist two-step: first, clear away race by noting diffusion; second, understand particularity through an analysis of style. Such was explicitly the case in another article he wrote as Harlem blossomed in 1925, "Stylistic Aspects of Primitive Literature." In the analytical section of the article Boas explained at length the significant difference between the widespread distribution of literary "form" and the peculiar development of literary "style." That similar forms—the riddle, the proverb, the epic—were widespread across large areas containing many different races was proof for Boas of the irrelevance of race: "The distribution of . . . forms among Europeans, Mongols, Malay and Negro," he writes, "proves the independence of literary development from racial descent" (Boas 1925:498). Moreover, that this distribution was limited to areas circumscribed by a history of contact showed that there was not an evolutionary development in form. He noted, for example, that the riddle was common throughout Europe, Africa, and Asia but that it had developed in the Americas only along the Yukon River and among the Eskimo of Labrador, where one could trace its routes through Asiatic contact.

The concept of style, by contrast, allowed Boas to consider cultural differentiation. Discussing the stylistic aspects of primitive literature, Boas chose for consideration stories disseminated among many different North American tribes or even stories that had been taken from European sources. An extraordinary example comes with his consideration of the transformation of a biblical story recorded by Benedict and Elsie Clews Parsons: a "nativity story of the Zuni in which Jesus appears as a girl, the daughter of the sun" (Boas 1925:499). The story was transformed to account for the fertility of domestic animals (all the animals lick the baby except the mule, which is punished with sterility), a change that Boas explained by noting that the increase of fertility was "a thought uppermost in the minds of the pueblos" (1925:499–500). The point was that such stylistic elements, which elsewhere included "poetic metaphor" and "descriptive terms," gave to common forms "a local coloring that [could] be understood only in relation to the whole culture" (Boas 1925:500, 498).

As noted earlier, a kind of pluralism had been in place in the nineteenth century, and so Boas's development of it in terms of a "whole culture" drew on an established tradition coming out of Germany (Bunzl 1996). But his emphasis on the reception and redeployment of disseminated elements marked a significant advance. Whereas previous studies of diffusion in folklore emphasized plot elements that were shared between cultures, the study of style emphasized performance as a marker of what was unique to particular cultures. The move, in other words, was from the study of something like *langue* to that of *parole*, from stories to storytelling, from content analysis to literary analysis. With this emphasis on style, the Boasian study of diffusion made way for an ethnographic understanding of Harlem writing not in terms of its essentialist content but in terms of its production of a particular style that would quickly move beyond Harlem's perceived racial and geographical borders.

Boas in and around Harlem

With a renewed sense of Boas's investment in dissemination, it becomes possible to relocate his place in the thought of the Harlem Renaissance. An overemphasis of the culture concept has led to a number of crucial misreadings of Boasian anthropology and its influence on the Renaissance, misreadings that risk keeping Boasian thought on the sidelines of an exciting reevaluation of that movement in terms of its transracial and internationalist contexts (see

Posnock 1998 and, especially, Edwards 2003). Boas's connection to Harlem has generally been made by noting, in the first instance, his relationship with Du Bois, who announced many of the principles taken up by the movement at roughly the same time Boas is said to have made his definitive move toward the culture concept (see Williams 1996; Baker 1998; Hutchinson 1995; Helbling 1999). As I have already tried to suggest, the manner in which this relationship has been construed is paradigmatic of a serious problem with the now conventional history of Boas's development of the culture concept because Du Bois was no "Boasian" in the strict sense of the term.

Even on a personal level, the line from Boas to Harlem does not run through Du Bois. While it is true that the two crossed paths and influenced one another, one might more readily claim that their association was characterized by missed opportunities than by what Baker has called a "lifelong friendship" (1998:125; also Williams 1996:41). Hutchinson argues that Boas was "virtually the house anthropologist for *Crisis* magazine," (1995:63) but he only published in it once, when his address to the Second National Negro Conference of May 1910 was reprinted in the first edition (Boas 1910b). The correspondence between the two was terse and surprisingly limited. Although Boas came to give the commencement address at Atlanta University at Du Bois's request, it would be difficult to make much out of their compact letters on the subject. Du Bois had to write to him twice before receiving a reply, and then Boas responded with an equivocal two-sentence letter that read simply, "Dear Sir,—I have your kindly invitation to attend the conference at Atlanta at the end of May. I shall be very glad to accept unless prevented by unforeseen circumstances" (FBP:4/25/06). There is record of only six other occasions of correspondence, and each is characterized by a failure to find meaningful avenues for cooperation. Du Bois, for example, wrote in 1929 to ask for an article for the *Crisis* and in 1935 for *The Encyclopedia of the Negro*, both of which Boas declined to submit. Boas wrote in 1936 to ask Du Bois to join in founding the American Committee for Anti-Nazi Literature, but Du Bois responded in the negative because he had been offered a fellowship by the Oberlaender Trust to do research in Germany for six months. Along the same lines, Liss notes that Boas declined a request from the *New York Evening Post* to review Du Bois's 1920 autobiography, *Darkwater*, on the grounds that the "book is so much an emotional literary product" (quoted in Liss 1998:152). And neither man receives a mention in the other's recent biographies, with the exception in Lewis of a passing reference to Boas's Atlanta University address and a short treatment of Du Bois's refusal of the 1936 offer to join the anti-Nazi committee (Lewis 1993:351–52, 2000:396, passim; Cole 1999).

My point, however, is not that the connections between Boas and Harlem are made tenuous by a more demanding investigation of the anthropologist's relations with key figures like Du Bois. Rather, it is that the assumption that these connections developed along an axis with the culture concept fundamentally misreads the Harlem Renaissance and reduces the wide range of Boas's work in the early 1900s to what amounts to an ethical choice for a pluralism he never adopted. For example, citing Boas by way of Stocking's work (1974b), Hutchinson makes much of what he calls Boas's "revolutionary contention that race and culture are independent of each other" (1995:65). He makes the strong case for Boas's influence on Du Bois and Harlem by arguing for his "devastating" and "relentless assault upon racist intellectual paradigms and social policies" (Hutchinson 1995:62, 64). Notwithstanding the hyperbole, it is, of course, the case that Boas, beginning in the late nineteenth century, argued for a relativist—not pluralist—position, writing that "civilization is not something absolute, but that it is relative, and that our ideas and conceptions are true only so far as our civilization goes" (1887a:66). It is a problem, however, to see him establishing merely "an ethical imperative to respect . . . individuality" that presages not only the cultural pluralism of the 1920s but also the "multiculturalism" of the 1980s, this latter pluralism having led, it is worth noting, to the current renaissance of the Harlem Renaissance (Hutchinson 1995:66). Boas's antiracism was certainly ethical, but, as we have seen, it was also grounded in a range of studies having little immediate relationship to the emergence of the culture concept.

Without the Boasian two-step from diffusion to style we are prone to end up with something like a reactionary recollapse of the categories of race and culture. To be sure, a kind of romantic racialism characterized some but, importantly, not all of the work associated with Harlem. Throughout the seminal anthology of the movement, *The New Negro* (1925), one frequently comes across authors who emphasize race psychology or instinct in their explanations of what distinguished the art of Harlem. In most instances this emphasis did not demonstrate the lack of a relativist ethical stance but the failure to consider the diffusion of cultural elements across racial boundaries. Nowhere was this clearer than in the piece contributed by the influential white collector of modernist art, Albert Barnes, who attributed the strength of Harlem art to the "psychological complexion of the Negro as he inherited it from his primitive ancestors" (1925:19). Not only did Barnes have unreformed ideas about the inheritance of acquired characteristics along the lines of race, he also exhibited an odd sense that black and white races had somehow failed to interact over four centuries of living side by side in the United States. Barnes wrote of the Negro as "a primitive race . . . held in subjection to a fundamentally alien influence," of his "primitive art," and of his being an "exotic, a thing apart" from "the white man"—and this despite Barnes's own incorporation of African art into his collection, not to mention, say, Picasso's use of it (1925:19, 20). What kept the races so "apart" in Barnes's mind was not segregation but racial inheritance—precisely the old nineteenth-century conflation of race and culture that the diffusionist project rendered obsolete. That Barnes could get away with such remarks in the 1920s depended on a fundamental misunderstanding of cultural flow, on either not knowing or not understanding the significance of the empirical work Boas and others had been doing on diffusion. Despite his pluralist intentions, Barnes did not clear the racial hurdle; to the extent that his work was typical of the popular reception of Harlem art in the 1920s, it ought to be important to us to recognize that Boas was not there to be found.

By contrast, there were authors much more attentive to the Boasian strategy, primary among them the movement's key anthologist, Alain Locke. A Harvard Ph.D. who for most of his career taught philosophy at Howard University, Locke emerged in the late 1920s as one of the key intellectual rivals to Du Bois. As Posnock (1998), Anderson (2001), and Edwards (2003) have pointed out, Locke's position on the cultural politics of the renaissance turned crucially on the notion that Harlem was producing a cosmopolitan aesthetics, one drawing on the rich cross-racial and internationalist influence of its urban setting. This "cosmopolitanism," a word that has, of course, gained a certain following in postmodern and postcolonial theory, ran on lines similar to those made by Boas in his work on diffusion. In his introduction Locke called a "fiction" the notion that the "life of the races is separate" before going on in a chapter on the legacy of African art forms to note that "the American Negro, even when he confronts the various forms of African art expression with a sense of its ethnic claims upon him, meets them in as alienated and misunderstanding an attitude as the average European Westerner" (1925:9, 255). Locke's point, in each case, was to make the argument that what was happening in Harlem was not caused by racial inheritance or psychology but by environmental factors in Harlem that gave the global flow of aesthetic forms a peculiar "local coloring." Like Boas, Locke deployed a two-step argument that began with the permeability of racial boundaries, which is to say their descriptive inefficacy, before moving on to the particularity of Harlem style. In this respect the particular formulation Locke used to describe the racial component of Harlem's cultural politics was quite subtle. For him, Harlem's "forced attempt to build . . . Americanism on race values" was "a unique experiment": "The racialism of the Negro is no limitation or reservation with respect to American life; it is only a constructive effort to build the obstructions in the stream of his progress [i.e., segregation] into an efficient dam of social energy and power" (Locke 1925:12). There was, to be sure, nothing inherently natural in the resulting dam; it was man-made.

One can imagine Boas agreeing with Locke, in this instance, that Harlem's style was marked racially only to the extent of the segregation forced upon it—a point at least theoretically consonant with the position taken by Boas's student, Melville Herskovits, in a contribution to the anthology. Going against the Africanist grain of the volume as a whole, Herskovits argued, "What there is to-day in Harlem distinct from the white culture which surrounds it, is . . .

merely a remnant from the peasant days in the South. Of the African culture, not a trace" (1925:359). Famously, he went on to argue almost entirely against his own point twenty years later in *The Myth of the Negro Past* (1945). Locke, however, would have been sympathetic to Herskovits's earlier point, for Locke was at pains in the anthology to argue that racial bounds did not delimit cultural influence. In principle if not in actual findings, Herskovits's point in the article was in keeping with both Locke's position and the position of Boasian diffusionism.[5]

Beginning in the late 1930s and continuing into the early 1950s, after the Harlem Renaissance had largely run its course, Locke found himself having to defend *The New Negro* against the charge that its cultural pluralism was isolationist. This defense took the shape not only of insisting that he had always promoted an understanding of the New Negro movement in terms of the "reciprocal cultural interchange and influence, of Negro on white, and white on Negro" but in fending off "the culture-mongers who thrive on fashionable exoticism and bad anthropology" (1942:317, 1938:265). By "culture mongers" Locke clearly did not have Boas and his students in mind but more vehement nativist pluralists who go unnamed except by way of association with "Nordicism." Locke was a supporter of what he called "the militant but unquestionably scientific school of anthropologists captained by Professor Boas," whom he credited for having "dared, in season and out, to challenge false doctrine and conventional myths" (1935:232). For Locke, however, Boas's militancy was not associated with the culture paradigm—nor, for that matter, was *The New Negro*. Rather, Locke writes that Boasian thought implied a "comparative technique" deployed in the study of "race and culture contacts" (1935:232–33). These contacts, as he is at pains to show, were assiduously documented in *The New Negro*, in which he had explicitly written not only that the movement was not "separatist" but also that it would be impossible to "encyst the Negro as a benign foreign body in the body politic . . . even if it were desirable" (Locke 1925:12).

In this context it is not surprising that when Locke reviewed *The Myth of the Negro Past* in 1942 he was far from satisfied with what he considered to be its "overemphasis" on the hypothesis of African culture survivals. Locke worried that this approach might lead to conceptualizing races as if they were isolated entities, whereas he believed it essential to consider them in terms of the interplay of the forces of cultural survival and assimilation (1942:314). Although he appreciated Herskovits's book for its emphasis on the linkages between the survival of African cultural elements and the slave trade that had initially forced their dispersion, he was unhappy with its "moralistic departure from

---

5. Locke and Herskovits were, moreover, on friendly terms. Herskovits joined Locke at Howard in the 1920s to collect anthropometric measurements at the predominantly black university (Helbling 1999:52).

scientific objectivity." Locke complained that this tactic threatened to spoil the anthropologist's "liberal conclusions" and "damn the Negro as more basically peculiar and unassimilable than he actually is or has proved himself to be" (1942:318). Indeed, he contrasted Herskovits's work with another anthology he himself had recently coedited, *When Peoples Meet: A Study in Race and Culture Contacts* (1942, revised 1946). Locke described this anthology as a "sourcebook" that attempted to "show what characteristically happens when peoples meet, and what interests, attitudes and policies condition their subsequent relations" (Locke and Stern 1942:4). Tellingly, the Boas excerpt he included was not about the culture concept. Rather, he chose a section of *The Mind of Primitive Man* that argued that the advances of any race or civilization are predicated upon the exchange of ideas with others, such that "none of these civilizations was the product of the genius of a single people" (Boas 1911b:22). Similarly, he selected from Benedict's *Patterns of Culture* (1934) a section making the point that the diffusion of cultural material and people has been the constant norm across the globe—"the great spread of white civilization is not an isolated historical circumstance" (quoted in Locke and Stern 1942:12–13)—despite the Western sense that other societies lived in relative isolation.

Locke provides but a limited example of thought from the Harlem Renaissance, and yet his work suggests the force an alternate trajectory of Boasian influence might have. A theory that articulates the descriptive categories of race and culture without merely debunking them and that also finds a way to work through the dialectic of dispersion and integration ought to prove useful to the effort now under way to expand thinking about both Harlem and the methodologies of anthropology in the contexts of globalization. Boas's work on diffusion has, in this light, at least three things to recommend it. First, to recover Boas's early-twentieth-century interest in uncorrelated circulation allows us to conceptualize in a fuller historical sense both the Boasian project for anthropology and the Harlem Renaissance's project for culture, a reconceptualization that has the added benefit of presentist relevance. To note, with Boas, that "everything is in flux" allows us to admit the slippage between race and culture in contexts like that of Harlem, thereby accentuating, from within both the historical and theoretical contexts of anthropology, the open-ended and diffuse configurations that generated the Harlem vogue.

Second, the emphasis on diffusion should remind us to avoid a "multiculturalist" (and romanticist) tendency to recollapse races and cultures into cultural productions, a move evident in Boas's time with the first round of cultural pluralism exemplified by Kallen and Barnes. A parallel move may occur, as Brodhead has noted in a slightly different context, when the academy reflects ethnic and cultural diversity by expanding the canon of literary works that are taught (1993:107–8; cf. Guillory 1993). This practice presupposes a conceptual equivalency between literature and social populations, between texts and cultures, such that canonical inclusiveness can be imagined as social inclusiveness. But as Locke might easily have countered, this move has often failed to account for the significant circulation of art across various racial, cultural, linguistic, national, temporal, and other geographies. Who, for example, is to say that Hurston's *Their Eyes Were Watching God* (1937) is more representative of black folk and folklore, Harlem, the 1930s, or Haiti (where she wrote the novel) than of students who read it at large state universities like Rutgers in the early 2000s? Working from Boas, one might start with the point that there is never a one-to-one correlation between particular arts and discrete cultures and go from there.

Finally, and admittedly somewhat ironically, putting a Boasian version of diffusion back into play might generate a useful revaluation of the Boasian culture concept. As I have suggested, in its time diffusion led to an understanding of aesthetic style in cultural terms—or, one might say, following Benedict, an interest in patterns of culture. If culture today often seems inadequate to the task of conceptualizing circulation and hybridity, and if literature appears prone to be reduced to a commodity in sociological models emphasizing the flow of texts, then the Boasian two-step from diffusion to style might remind us of the interest to be found in following through from flow to reception, from systemwide formulations of hybridity to the particularity of hybrid forms. To suggest as much is, to some extent, only to recognize the continual ebb and flow of academic orientations, the cycling through of interest from particular phenomena to their synthesis (and back again). As has frequently been noted, this dialectic animated Boas's understanding of the relationship of anthropology to the project of the sciences generally (especially in Boas 1887c; for discussion see Stocking 1996). But to note that diffusion was an indispensable component of the way Boas came to conceptualize culture does more than reiterate that cycle. Attention to diffusion helps us to understand that the structures of affiliation and dissonance that culture came to describe only became visible after attention was drawn to the interplay between the particular and the diffuse. Or, to put the matter a bit differently, what was significant in Boas's paradigmatic orientation was not his choice to be, in his own somewhat cryptic words, a "cosmographer" instead of a "physicist" (1887c:642)—a particularist instead of a synthesizer—but the fact that, in practice, his work depended upon the articulation of them both.

Acknowledgments

I would like to thank Matti Bunzl, Ira Bashkow, and Richard Handler for their provocative and extremely useful critiques of this essay at early and late stages in its development. My debt to the scholarship of George W. Stocking, Jr., whose stimulating seminars at the University of Chicago started my thinking on these subjects, should be obvious to all.

References Cited

AA   American Anthropologist
HOA History of Anthropology

Anderson, P. A. 2001. *Deep River: Music and Memory in Harlem Renaissance Thought.* Durham, NC.

Appadurai, A. 1996. *Modernity at Large: Cultural Dimensions of Globalization.* Minneapolis, MN.

Appiah, K. A. 1985. The Uncompleted Argument: Du Bois and the Illusion of Race. *Critical Inquiry* 12:21–37.

———. 1992. *In My Father's House: Africa in the Philosophy of Culture.* New York.

Baker, L. 1994. Franz Boas within the Struggle for Racial Equality. *Critique of Anthropology* 14:199–217.

———. 1998. *From Savage to Negro: Anthropology and the Construction of Race, 1896–1954.* Berkeley, CA.

Balibar, E., and I. Wallerstein. 1991. *Race, Nation, Class: Ambiguous Identities.* New York.

Barnes, A. C. 1925 [1992]. Negro Art in America. In Locke 1992:19–25.

Barth, F. 2002. Toward a Richer Description and Analysis of Cultural Phenomena. In Fox and King 2002:23–37.

Bashkow, I. 2004. A Neo-Boasian Conception of Cultural Boundaries. *AA* 106:443–58.

Bashkow, I., et al. 2004. A New Boasian Anthropology: Theory for the 21st Century. *AA* 106:433–94.

Bender, T., ed. 2002. *Rethinking American History in a Global Age.* Berkeley, CA.

Bhabha, H. 1994. *The Location of Culture.* New York.

Boas, F. 1887a. Museums of Ethnology and Their Classification. In Stocking 1974b: 63–67.

———. 1887b. The Occurrence of Similar Inventions in Areas Widely Apart. In Stocking 1974b:61–63.

———. 1887c. The Study of Geography. In Boas 1940:639–47.

———. 1898. Summary of the Work for the Committee in British Columbia. In Stocking 1974b:88–107.

———. 1891. Dissemination of Tales among the Natives of North America. In Boas 1940:437–45.

———. 1903. The Decorative Art of the Indians of the East Coast. In Boas 1940:546–63.

———. 1906. Commencement Address at Atlanta University, May 31, 1906. In Stocking 1974b:310–16.

———. 1908. Race Problems in America. In Stocking 1974b:318–30.

———. 1910a. Ethnological Problems in Canada. In Boas 1940:331–43.

———. 1910b. The Real Race Problem. *Crisis* 1:22–25.

———. 1911a. Introduction to *Handbook of American Indian Languages, Part I.* Bulletin no. 40, Bureau of American Ethnology. Washington, D.C.

———. 1911b. *The Mind of Primitive Man.* New York.

———. 1914. Mythology and Folk-Tales of the North American Indian. In Boas 1940:451–90.

———. 1920. The Classification of American Languages. In Boas 1940:211–18.

————. 1921. The Problem of the American Negro. *Yale Review* 10:384–95.

————. 1925. Stylistic Aspects of Primitive Literature. In Boas 1940:491–502.

————. 1928. *Anthropology and Modern Life*. New York.

————. 1940. *Race, Language, and Culture*. New York.

Boas, N. 2005. *Franz Boas, 1858–1942: An Illustrated Biography*. Philadelphia.

Bonnell, V., and L. Hunt, eds. 1999. *Beyond the Cultural Turn: New Directions in the Study of Society and Culture*. Berkeley, CA.

Bramen, C. T. 2001. *The Uses of Variety: Modern Americanism and the Quest for National Distinctiveness*. Cambridge, MA.

Brightman, R. 1995. Forget Culture: Replacement, Transcendence, and Relexification. *Cultural Anthropology* 10:509–46.

Brodhead, R. 1993. *Cultures of Letters: Scenes of Reading and Writing in Nineteenth-Century America*. Chicago.

Brown, B. 2003. *A Sense of Things: The Object Matter of American Literature*. Chicago.

Bunzl, M. 1996. Franz Boas and the Humboldtian Tradition: From *Volksgeist* and *Nationalcharakter* to an Anthropological Concept of Culture. HOA 8:17–78.

————. 2003. Völkerpsychologie and German-Jewish Emancipation. In *Worldly Provincialism: German Anthropology in the Age of Empire*. Ed. M. Bunzl and G. Penny, 47–86. Ann Arbor, MI.

Clifford, J. 1988. *The Predicament of Culture: Twentieth-Century Ethnography, Literature, and Art*. Cambridge, MA.

————. 1997. *Routes: Travel and Translation in the Late Twentieth Century*. Cambridge, MA.

Cole, D. 1999. *Franz Boas: The Early Years, 1859–1906*. Seattle, WA.

Conn, S. 1998. *Museums and American Intellectual Life, 1876–1926*. Chicago.

Darnell, R. 1997. The Anthropological Concept of Culture at the End of the Boasian Century. *Social Analysis* 41:42–54.

————. 1998. *And along Came Boas: Continuity and Revolution in Americanist Anthropology*. Philadelphia.

————. 2001. *Invisible Genealogies: A History of Americanist Anthropology*. Lincoln, NE.

Du Bois, W. E. B. 1897. The Conservation of Races. In Du Bois 1986:815–26.

————. 1903a. *The Souls of Black Folk*. In Du Bois 1986:359–547.

————. 1903b. The Talented Tenth. In Du Bois 1986:842–61.

————. 1914. *Manners and Morals Among Negro Americans*. Atlanta, GA.

————. 1928. So the Girl Marries. In Du Bois 1986:1003–9.

————. 1929. Cultural Equality. In *The Oxford W. E. B. Du Bois Reader*. Ed. E. J. Sundquist, 394–400. New York.

————. 1939. *Black Folk Then and Now*. New York.

————. 1940. *Dusk of Dawn: An Essay Toward an Autobiography of a Race Concept*. New York.

————. 1968. *The Autobiography of W. E. B. Du Bois: A Soliloquy on Viewing My Life from the Last Decade of Its First Century*. New York.

————. 1986. *Writings*. Ed. N. Huggins. New York.

Edwards, B. 2003. *The Practice of Diaspora: Literature, Translation, and the Rise of Black Internationalism*. Cambridge, MA.

Elliott, M. A. 2002. *The Culture Concept: Writing and Difference in the Age of Realism*. Minneapolis, MN.

Evans, B. 2005. *Before Cultures: The Ethnographic Imagination and American Literature, 1865–1920.* Chicago.

Fox, R. G., and B. King, eds. 2002. *Anthropology beyond Culture.* New York.

Gravlee, C., et al. 2003. Boas's Changes in Bodily Form: The Immigrant Study, Cranial Plasticity, and Boas's Physical Anthropology. *AA* 105:326–32.

Guillory, J. 1993. *Cultural Capital: The Problem of Literary Canon Formation.* Chicago.

Gupta, A., and J. Ferguson, eds. 1997. *Anthropological Locations: Boundaries and Grounds of a Field Science.* Berkeley, CA.

Haney-Lopez, I. 1996. *White by Law: The Legal Construction of Race.* New York.

Harris, J. C. 1880 [1921]. *Uncle Remus, His Songs and His Sayings.* New York.

Hegeman, S. 1999. *Patterns for America: Modernism and the Concept of Culture.* Princeton, NJ.

Helbling, M. 1999. *The Harlem Renaissance: The One and the Many.* Westport, CT.

Herbert, C. 1991. *Culture and Anomie: Ethnographic Imagination in the Nineteenth Century.* Chicago.

Herskovits, M. 1925. The Negro's Americanism. In Locke 1925:353–61.

Hinsley, C. 1981. *The Smithsonian and the American Indian.* Washington, D.C.

Holt, T. 1990. The Political Uses of Alienation: Du Bois on Politics, Race, and Culture. *American Quarterly* 42:301–23.

Hutchinson, G. 1995. *The Harlem Renaissance in Black and White.* Cambridge, MA.

Hyatt, M. 1990. *Franz Boas, Social Activist.* Westport, CT.

Jacknis, I. 1985. Franz Boas and Exhibits: On the Limitations of the Museum Method of Anthropology. *HOA* 3:75–111.

Jacobson, M. F. 1998. *Whiteness of a Different Color: European Immigrants and the Alchemy of Race.* Cambridge, MA.

Jewett, S. O. 1887. *The Story of the Normans, Told Chiefly in Relation to Their Conquest of England.* New York.

Kalmar, I. 1987. The *Völkerpsychologie* of Lazarus and Steinthal and the Modern Concept of Culture. *Journal of the History of Ideas* 48:671–90.

Kroeber, A. L., and C. Kluckhohn. 1952. *Culture: A Critical Review of Concepts and Definitions.* New York.

Krupat, A. 1992. *Ethnocriticism: Ethnography, History, Literature.* Berkeley, CA.

Kuper, A. 1999. *Culture: The Anthropologist's Account.* Cambridge, MA.

Lewis, D. L. 1993. *W. E. B. Du Bois: Biography of a Race.* New York.

———. 2000. *W. E. B. Du Bois: The Fight for Equality and the American Century, 1919–1963.* New York.

Liss, J. 1998. Diasporic Identities: The Science and Politics of Race in the Work of Franz Boas and W. E. B. Du Bois, 1894–1919. *Cultural Anthropology* 13:127–66.

Locke, A. 1935. The Eleventh Hour of Nordicism: Retrospective Review of the Literature of the Negro for 1934. In Stewart 1983:227–35.

———. 1938. Jingo, Counter-Jingo and Us: Retrospective Review of the Literature of the Negro for 1937. In Stewart 1983:257–66.

———. 1942. Who and What Is 'Negro'? In Stewart 1983:309–18.

———, ed. 1925 [1992]. *The New Negro: Voices of the Harlem Renaissance.* New York.

Locke, A., and B. J. Stern, eds. 1942 [1946]. *When Peoples Meet: A Study in Race and Culture Contacts.* New York.

Lofgren, C. A. 1990. *The Plessy Case: A Legal-Historical Interpretation*. New York.

Manganaro, M. 2002. *Culture, 1922: The Emergence of a Concept*. Princeton, NJ.

Menand, L. 2001. *The Metaphysical Club*. New York.

Michaels, W. B. 1992. Race into Culture: A Critical Genealogy of Cultural Identity. *Critical Inquiry* 18:655–85.

———. 1995. *Our America: Nativism, Modernism, and Pluralism*. Durham, NC.

Newell, W. W. 1890. Additional Collection Essential to Correct Theory. *Journal of American Folklore* 3:23–32.

Pierpont, C. R. 2004. The Measure of America: How a Rebel Anthropologist Waged War on Racism. *New Yorker*, March 8:48–63.

Posnock, R. 1998. *Color and Culture: Black Writers and the Making of the Modern Intellectual*. Cambridge, MA.

Reed, A. 1992. Du Bois's "Double Consciousness": Race and Gender in Progressive Era American Thought. *Studies in American Political Development* 6:93–139.

Roediger, D. 1991. *The Wages of Whiteness: Race and the Making of the American Working Class*. New York.

Silverstein, M. 2004. Boasian Cosmographic Anthropology and the Sociocentric Component of Mind. *HOA* 10:131–57.

Sparks, C., and R. Jantz. 2003. Changing Times, Changing Faces: Franz Boas's Immigrant Study in Modern Perspective. *AA* 105:333–37.

Stewart, J. C., ed. 1983. *The Critical Temper of Alain Locke: A Selection of His Essays on Art and Culture*. New York.

Stocking, G. W. 1968. *Race, Culture, and Evolution: Essays in the History of Anthropology*. New York.

———. 1974a. The Basic Assumptions of Boasian Anthropology. In Stocking 1974b:1–20.

———. 1974b. *A Franz Boas Reader: The Shaping of American Anthropology, 1883–1911*. Chicago.

———. 1996. Boasian Ethnography and the German Anthropological Tradition. *HOA* 8:3–8.

———. 2001. The Turn-of-the-Century Concept of Race. In *Delimiting Anthropology: Occasional Essays and Reflections*, 3–23. Madison, WI.

Sundquist, E. 1993. *To Wake the Nations: Race in the Making of American Literature*. Cambridge, MA.

Taine, H. 1863. *Histoire de la littérature anglaise*. Paris.

Trouillot, M.-R. 2002. Adieu, Culture: A New Duty Arises. In Fox and King 2002:37–60.

Williams, V. J. 1996. *Rethinking Race: Franz Boas and His Contemporaries*. Lexington, KY.

Manuscript Source

FBP   Franz Boas Papers. Microfilm collection of the professional papers of Franz Boas. Scholarly Resources, Inc., Wilmington, DE.

UNFINISHED BUSINESS

Robert Gelston Armstrong, the Federal Bureau of Investigation, and the History of Anthropology at Chicago and in Nigeria

GEORGE W. STOCKING, JR.

"Unfinished Business" as Personal History, 1953–1979

In October 1977, in preparation for the fiftieth anniversary of the establish-ment of a separate Department of Anthropology at the University of Chicago, I arranged (while on leave at Harvard) to have a questionnaire sent to all those then listed in our department records as having received either the M.A. or Ph.D. degree in order to collect information for an historical account of the de-partment. In addition to fairly standard biobibliographic facts, the one-page document asked respondents to comment on their "intellectual orientation." Of the two hundred–plus responses elicited, the most dramatic and provocative was that of Robert Gelston Armstrong, who in 1952 had received his Ph.D. for a dissertation entitled "State Formation in Negro Africa" (1950b). Writing from the University of Ibadan in Nigeria, Armstrong sent back the completed questionnaire and an accompanying vita, along with a page-and-a-half intel-lectual autobiography covering his three periods in the department—for two years in the early stages of World War II, again for two years in the immediate postwar period, and for another eight months from July 1949 to March 1950. Along with this material he also sent a single-spaced seven-legal-page letter

---

George W. Stocking, Jr., the founding editor of History of Anthropology, is Stein-Freiler Distinguished Service Professor Emeritus in the Department of Anthropology and the Committee on Conceptual and Historical Studies of Science at the University of Chicago. He is currently at work on a series of essays on anthropology in the United States in the post–World War II period.

expanding on various aspects of his Chicago experience, both positive and negative. The latter focused on what he called his "unfinished business" with the department: the withdrawal of a promised "very junior appointment" in the fall of 1953 after the Federal Bureau of Investigation "approached the University" with news that Armstrong had been a Communist. Called to Chicago from his parental home in Cincinnati early that September, Armstrong had a long interview with Fred Eggan and Sol Tax, at the end of which they told him "they were prepared to continue with the appointment." Shortly thereafter, however, "a different member of the Department," returning to take over as chair, "raised a big row," and the appointment never got beyond Dean Ralph Tyler's desk. "You may deduce my attitude towards this aspect of my Chicago experience from my subsequent history": two years out of academia, four years at a segregated university in the south, and (at the time Armstrong wrote to me) seventeen years attached to the University of Ibadan, where he had for a decade been director of the Institute of African Studies (GSP:RA/GS 11/28/77).

Returning in January 1978 from a semester at Harvard (after what had been an absence of eighteen months from the department), I devoted the winter quarter to a seminar on the history of the Chicago department, in the course of which I drafted two chapters on its prehistory, from 1892 to 1929, when it was the lesser part of a combined Department of Sociology and Anthropology. But as I wrote to Armstrong in mid-March 1978, my delay in answering his earlier communication reflected not only this busy-ness but also the fact that his letter had forced me to confront "difficult problems" I had not faced in my previous historical work: how to write the history of an "institution of which one is still a member" and of an event whose enactors were my colleagues and about which I had no evidence other than the reminiscence of the aggrieved party. Seeking collaborating information of the sort that historians usually rely on, I asked Armstrong if he could provide documentary materials. In response he sent me a copy of a brief political autobiography he had prepared prior to his 1953 meeting with Tax and Eggan along with copies of two contemporary letters, one from Robert Redfield, the other from Sherwood Washburn, whom I had surmised was the vetoing chair, both letters confirming critical details of Armstrong's account (Armstrong 1953; GSP:RR/RA 10/14/53, SW/RA 9/21/53). In the meantime, however, I had also been in touch with Tax and Washburn, both of whom professed not to recall the events Armstrong had recounted. Washburn in fact offered as a parting thought an anecdote he attributed to Redfield: "All that would have been necessary to stop McCarthy was for *one* person to stand up and say 'stop!'" (as reported to Armstrong in GSP:6/29/78). Although I recall Armstrong spending an evening in my apartment in the summer of 1978, when he passed through Chicago during a trip to the United States, there seem to have been no more letters between us, and over the next year the departmental history languished. In the event, the three chapters I had drafted (covering the period down to 1938) were put away in a file drawer. The only published work I was able to manage was an historical brochure for the fiftieth anniversary library exhibit, with six hundred words of text for each of twenty-four display cases, none of which mentioned "the Armstrong affair" (Stocking 1979; cf. Stocking 2004b).

In retrospect, it is clear that my abandonment of the departmental history was, as an analyst might say, "overdetermined." Painful memories of other extended blockages in my work, which have left several sets of notes and drafts gathering dust in filing cabinets, suggest that there are enduring character qualities or psychodynamic processes at work. In each case, however, these underlying factors were reinforced by situationally specific ones. In the case of the aborted departmental history it seems clear to me in retrospect that a powerful inhibition was the history of my own political involvement, which in a number of ways paralleled Armstrong's, although at a slightly later historical moment and with a different outcome. Joining the Communist Party in the year that Armstrong left it, I had quit in 1956, severely disillusioned by the Khrushchev revelations. When I was offered my first academic job at Berkeley in 1960 I had to undergo a higher level academic interview before the case could go forward, although not because of FBI intervention but because in signing the California loyalty oath I had volunteered, as a footnote, the fact of my prior party membership during the specified five-year period of political purity. By that time, however, the flames of McCarthyism had died down, my appointment went through, and in the four decades since I have enjoyed the perquisites and privileges of membership in two elite academic departments, first at Berkeley and then at Chicago.

Not, however, without a recurring sense of moral unease. Although I did not cooperate with the FBI on the three occasions when they interviewed me (nor with any government investigative or legislative agency at any time), I have sometimes felt my privileged position as a relativizing liberal academic tinged, if not tainted, by betrayal. Betrayal not of "the party" but of the ideals that had motivated my membership, for which comrades close to me had suffered not simply loss of employment but in some cases terms in jail—and in one case, lifelong exile (Grossman 2003). Where others, including Armstrong, were victimized, I had been lucky enough to survive unscathed—"walking between the raindrops," as a friend of mine recently put it. But in 1977, feeling still marginal to anthropology and to the department, I was reluctant to risk carrying its history forward into the postwar era where I would feel obligated to treat "the Armstrong affair." Instead, I retreated for the next two decades into the past of a previously stalled project on British anthropology, in which all of the major actors were long dead and I was free to interpret their actions without meeting them in the hallway (Stocking n.d.)

By the early 1990s, when *Victorian Anthropology* had been in print for five years and the second volume of my British project was nearing completion (Stocking 1987, 1995), the anthropology of the post–World War II period in the United States had begun to reengage my interest, both from an historical and a personal point of view. On the one hand, it stood in a generatively contrastive relationship to the very different, if not "reinvented," anthropology of the most recent fin de siècle; on the other, it was a critically formative period in my own intellectual career, which by 1990 was moving toward a close. With the latter terminus in mind I envisioned a final research project tentatively entitled "Anthropology Yesterday: From the Science of Man in World Crisis to the Reinvention of Anthropology, 1945–1972." Motivated in part because I was in a mood to think of "a life" (my own included) as having a certain integration of narrative and meaning and in part because I did not want to leave another book unfinished, I conceived the project as a series of biographically focused essays, each of which would stand on its own but a number of which, should I manage to complete them, might make a book with an implicit thematic unity. Armstrong was not originally one of the figures I had in mind. However, there was a point when it dawned on me that, although little remembered, his life was in fact emblematic of important tendencies in mid-twentieth-century anthropology in the United States and that in making his "unfinished business" part of the historical record of that period I could also fulfill a moral obligation implied in our interchange a quarter century ago, when he recounted for me experiences that still caused him pain.

From Melville to Marxism and Chicago Anthropology, 1917–1942

Robert Gelston Armstrong was born in Danville, Indiana, on June 29, 1917, the eldest son of upper-middle-class parents who were "very religious and orthodox Methodists" and who "preferred a quiet life-style with a small set of friends and rather narrow cultural interests."[1] His paternal grandfather, however, "had spent nine years at sea on whaling ships in the Pacific" in the "precise period" of the novels of Herman Melville, including Melville's "narrative of a four months' residence among the natives of a valley of the Marquesas Islands; or, A peep at Polynesian life" (1847). Armstrong never met his grandfather, who had died before he was born. But he knew of his adventures through his diaries, which Armstrong discussed with an aunt who had known him

---

1. Unless otherwise indicated, the quotations in this section come from Armstrong's questionnaire response and our subsequent correspondence in 1977–78, including a copy of the political autobiography he prepared for the interview with Tax and Eggan (Armstrong 1953), and in a few cases from the responses of other students to the 1977 questionnaire.

well—auguries, one suspects, of Armstrong's later turn to anthropology. There were auguries also of his later wide-ranging intellectual interests: from an early age he was "something of a polymath" and over time a polyglot as well. While attending high school in Cincinnati he got "a solid grounding in Latin, French, and German," subsequently adding Italian, Spanish, Portuguese, Russian, Yoruba, and Idoma. It was also during high school, in the early years of the Great Depression, that he had a series of "adolescent brushes" with idea systems that were "brand new" to him and to which he responded with "a certain enthusiasm"—Italian Fascism, Roman Catholicism, and Rochdale Consumer Cooperation, "in that order"—to the considerable consternation of his mother, who "tearfully predicted" that he "would become a priest."

Upon his graduation from Western Hills High School in 1934 Armstrong entered Miami University in Oxford, Ohio, an institution with historical ties to the antislavery movement. It was there that he had his first encounters with Marxism and with anthropology, the two intellectual forces that were to shape his later life. He subsequently recalled "first becoming acquainted with Marxian economic ideas through two books by John Strachey"—presumably, *The Coming Struggle for Power* (1933) and *The Nature of Capitalist Crisis*, a comparison of "the principal existing explanations of the occurrence of economic crisis," with "reasons for rejecting all except one" (Marxism) (1935:2). Testing his new ideas "against professional work," Armstrong majored in economics but was never able to get his instructors to meet "head on" such central issues as value theory. Concluding that there were "mountains of books and articles which dismiss Marx in a sarcastic paragraph or two, but precious few attempts to understand or refute his whole system," he abandoned economics. It was "in this mood," he later recalled, that he joined the Communist Party in 1939.

Armstrong's first encounter with the "polyglot literature" of anthropology came while he was pursuing a minor in sociology at Miami and took a course given by Asael Hansen, a Chicago Ph.D. who had worked with Redfield in Yucatan. Almost immediately he perceived the discipline as a "chance to go into the wide world and turn every talent I had to good advantage." After spending a year at home in Cincinnati following his graduation from Miami he visited Chicago in the summer of 1939, where he talked with Eggan, a fledgling faculty member who combined Radcliffe-Brownian social organization interests with a more traditional Boasian historicism. Armstrong was not put off when Eggan, having mentioned "an aspect of anthropology" in which he had little interest (kinship?), "mildly suggested" that perhaps he "should consider a different field." Rather, he was "indignant": "I had already made up my mind." Earlier that day he had talked with the head of the campus branch of the Young Communist League, who told him that Chicago was "a University where the winds of controversy blow" (cf. Coven 1992). Committed to the idea of racial equality, "both personally and politically," Armstrong was "therefore interested

1. Robert Gelston Armstrong, c. 1940. From his student file in the Department of Anthropology Papers. (Courtesy of the Special Collections Research Center, University of Chicago Library.)

in the discipline that had developed its scientific rationale." Moreover, "the intellectual life of Chicago had an unmistakable magisterial tone" that he found "an attractive complement to its reputation for controversy and innovation."

In the fall of 1939 Armstrong entered the University of Chicago Department of Anthropology, where the program offered "a whole new dimension of life": "I felt that I had come home." Fay-Cooper ("Papa") Cole, the longtime chair who later recalled to Armstrong that he had once cautioned Radcliffe-Brown "against making disciples of students," taught him "much about life in universities." Although "his shadow was still there," Radcliffe-Brown himself had left for Oxford after the 1937 seminar series in which he had systematized his "natural science of society" (1937), and Armstrong's courses were in the more traditional "four field" mode. During his first quarter he took General Ethnology with Eggan, North American Archaeology with Cole, and Old World Prehistory, taught "none too willingly" by the linguist Harry Hoijer. During the third quarter he took Physical Anthropology with Wilton Krogman and Archaeological Methods with Cole, and he was "privileged" to have his introduction to linguistics from Manuel Andrade—and before his sudden death "to know something of [Andrade's] gentle, elegant wit and wisdom." But it was Redfield, with whom he took courses on "The Folk Society" and "Mayan Cultures" during his second quarter, who was to become his primary mentor and counselor. Like some other students who spoke of Redfield in Olympian terms, Armstrong later recalled him as "a god" who "indulged no one": "Debating him was like sharpening your knife on a big, fast-turning very abrasive grindstone. You could only hope that your steel was good enough that you would still have a knife and not just an empty handle after the exercise."

Aside from the formal curriculum, the vibrant student life of the department was an important part of Armstrong's education, "both personally and intellectually." The departmental secretary, Ernestine Bingham, a "motherly-sisterly hostess of all occasions" (as another student recalled her), "did a lot to loosen up and broaden the self-indulgent, narrow puritanism" that Armstrong had brought with him "from home." The frequent parties at Bingham's house and the lunchtime meetings around the anthropology table at International House were "full of intense discussion," and there was an Anthropology Club that was "seeking to spread straight-thinking in regard to racial and minority groups" (DAP:Cole/Biehle 2/10/41). And beyond the department there was hot debate on the Chicago campus about the issue of preparedness and American participation in the European War, which broke out just as Armstrong arrived on campus (Coven 1992). As late as January 1941 a majority of students polled supported the position taken by Chancellor Robert Hutchins, who although dissociating himself from "all Nazis, Fascists, Communists and appeasers" nevertheless felt that the United States could "better serve suffering humanity" by staying out of the war in Europe (University of Chicago *Maroon* 1/27/41).

For Armstrong, the strongest influence among the student cohort was his best friend, John Murra, who in the fall of 1939 "had just returned from the Spanish Civil War." Four decades later he recalled that what Murra reported to him "of his experiences [in Spain] helped me later in my Army days and politically taught me to qualify my naïve enthusiasm for 'the party line.'" However, in the political autobiography Armstrong prepared in 1953 his account still echoed prewar Communist orthodoxy: Marx and Lenin had shown that "the capitalist system operates to produce wars, and World War II was arriving right on schedule" (cf. Howe and Coser 1962). When the British prime minister, Neville Chamberlain, and others "prevented the making of an [anti-Hitler] alliance," Armstrong concluded that Chamberlain hoped Hitler would attack

2. John Murra was born in 1916 in Odessa, where he learned to speak both Russian and Roman-ian; schooled in Bucharest, Romania, he later learned German and French and a bit of English. In 1934 he immigrated to the United States, where he received a bachelor's degree in sociology at the University of Chicago in 1936 and began graduate studies in anthropology. Shortly thereafter, how-ever, he left to serve in the Spanish Civil War in the International Brigades, in which he held offi-cer's rank as a translator in the central political command. In February 1938 he managed a transfer to the artillery and subsequently on the Ebro front suffered a wound that paralyzed him for two months. Early in 1939 he crossed the border into France but was interned for some months before returning in June to Chicago. He met Armstrong upon reentering the anthropology department that fall. (Castro et al. 2000:26–32; photo reproduced courtesy of the National Anthropological Archives.)

Russia. And when the Russians "arranged to avoid the blow" by signing a non-aggression pact with Germany in August 1939 he "saw no call to be disillu-sioned." Although he later remembered having become "thoroughly alarmed at the decay of the whole moral position [of the party] during the next two years," at the time he continued to play an active role in the lively campus antiwar movement. Late in April 1941 he chaired the Peace Action Committee, which was sponsoring the last prewar "peace strike"—only two months before the Nazi invasion of the Soviet Union precipitated a second major alteration in the Communist "party line" and eight months before the Japanese attacked Pearl Harbor.

By then Armstrong had achieved a "high pass" in each of the five subfields of his master's exam ("ethnology" and "social anthropology" having been separated under the influence of Radcliffe-Brown) and in the fall of 1941 had taken up an exchange research fellowship at the University of Oklahoma for fieldwork among the Cheyenne and Arapaho Indians (DAP:Cole/Dean of Graduate School 3/12/41). The original plan had been for him to spend a year doing research for a doctoral dissertation on acculturation, but two months after Pearl Harbor his fieldwork was cut short by the reclassification of his draft status. It was only by special appeal that his induction was deferred for six weeks to enable him to write a master's thesis based on his first three and a half months of fieldwork (DAP:Cole/Selective Service Board #9 2/2/42; Armstrong 1942:1). In the time available, all Armstrong could manage were three substantive chapters: a seventy-page review of the history of the Cheyenne (and the closely related Arapaho) derived from monographic and primary sources and another sixty pages on their contemporary economic life and the new developments in their religion. His thesis, "The Acculturation of the Cheyenne and Arapaho Indians of Oklahoma," is nevertheless illustrative of important tendencies in prewar American anthropology in its Chicago recension, as manifest in the work of a radically oriented graduate student (of whom there were a number at Chicago).

Armstrong was "guided throughout" by the "Memorandum for the Study of Acculturation," published in 1936 by a three-man committee of the Social Science Research Council and a primary document in the shift of Boasian historical ethnology toward the study of present processes, of which Redfield was the primary author (Redfield et al. 1936; Stocking 1976:144; cf. Madden 1999). Redfield's influence is evident also in Armstrong's characterization of Cheyenne society as a "folk society" (1942:7, 20, 98, 126). In principle, however, Armstrong saw society "as a dynamic, interacting whole," the various parts of which were "constantly producing mutual changes" and in which the most dynamic force was "the productive activity of mankind"—in contrast to the "reproductive activity" of the procreation and rearing of children, which was under most circumstances "rather resistant to change" (1942:5). Since the mid-nineteenth century, however, the Cheyenne had been subjected to two great shocks: their military defeat by General Custer in 1869 and subsequent removal to the Oklahoma reservation; and the implementation of land allotments in severalty following the passage of the Dawes Act in 1887. The former had destroyed their traditional economic dependence on buffalo hunting; the latter had enabled an aggressively invasive "land run" by "a people who heavily outnumbered them and who had a much more advanced technology" (Armstrong 1942:60). As a result the Cheyenne, rather than following the officially prescribed path to "civilization" through nuclear family farming, were reduced to impoverished dependency on the income from the individual leasing and sale of their once communal lands.

However, despite the seventy-year effort of government and missionaries to eradicate the "old communal economy," certain of its values and attitudes were still functioning, "with little diminished strength," most strikingly in the "astonishing" role of "gift-giving" at funerals, weddings, births, holidays, and religious occasions (Armstrong 1942:93–103). And although the deculturating efforts of Mennonite missionaries had achieved a limited success, the most striking new development, the Peyote cult (which by 1940 involved "approximately seventy-five percent of the Cheyenne"), fitted easily into the traditional religious ideology and had a "profoundly functional" role in maintaining a distinctively Cheyenne identity (Armstrong 1942:70, 109–15).

If Armstrong's stay on the Cheyenne reservation was by present standards brief, his fieldwork seems in retrospect strikingly participatory in style and empathic in attitude. In describing the "conscious methodology" of "informal participation" he employed while "assembling and classifying his data," he emphasized his avoidance of questionnaires, direct interviews, and (except at the end to fill in gaps) paid "informants" (a term he used only twice, both times in quotation marks). Instead, he depended primarily on "informal conversations" (in English, since he learned only fifteen words of the language of the elder Cheyenne). This, to an extent that it was "almost impossible" to convince the Indians that he was "doing any work," since the best material came from "people who were just loafing around," and he simply joined in (Armstrong 1942:1–3).

Armstrong felt that the anthropologist's first concern "must be the vigorous pursuit of all the relevant data." But he rejected the idea that this could be done with "absolute, detached, dispassionate objectivity." Every investigator brought with him into the field "a collection of preconceived ideas," and if he got close enough to the group to see how they "live and move and have their being," he would inevitably be "emotionally affected by them." The ethnographer's "principal ideas" and his "emotional reactions" should therefore be stated so that the reader could, if necessary, discount them "in judging his work." For Armstrong, the former (his ideas about society, social change, and acculturation) were easily and succinctly stated. In contrast, his initial statement of his emotional reactions to the "personal experience" of his first "direct contact with a folk society" scarcely went beyond the thought that there was "much in their character" that was "intrinsically lovable" and that "it hurt when one of his Indian friends was not making a success of things" (Armstrong 1942:4–8). Along the way, however, there were clues to a greater involvement: his "immense" enjoyment of joining in the War Dance; the impact of the Cheyenne's intense "religious fervor" on one who "had his fill of Gospel Hymns at a very tender age"; his appreciation of the "irresistible" (and physiologically based) "feeling of brotherhood" engendered in the peyote ritual, derived from his own participation in four peyote meetings (Armstrong 1942:4, 107, 116, 3–5, 112; cf. FEP:RA/FE 1/7/42).

Somewhere between "preconceived idea" and "emotional reaction" were the ideas about civilization that Armstrong evoked throughout the thesis. He explicitly accepted the notion of "civilization" as "a vast and utterly complex and ever changing social mechanism—like a machine in its complexity, in the great number of its specialized parts and in its constant motion" (Armstrong 1942:79). There had in fact been promising starts toward such a civilization in the early reservation period, when the Cheyenne were allowed to work together on a "collective project" such as a cattle herd for the local school or the "Cheyenne and Arapaho Transportation Company" (Armstrong 1942:44–47). But these starts had been cut short by the systematic identification of "civilization" with "the American pattern of agriculture" and by the policy of "most of those who have dealt with Indian affairs," which "openly aimed at breaking up all the old culture of the Indians." For adherents of this "cult" of civilization, "White civilization" was a "ritualistic or fetishistic" ideology, something that could be taught by taking young people away to the "seminary" in Carlisle, Pennsylvania, and the acceptance of which would be "marked by certain stigmata," including the clothes one wore and the way one wore one's hair (Armstrong 1942:74–79).

It was in this context of preconceived idea and experienced emotion that Armstrong ended his thesis with a rousing affirmation of cultural resistance, which ran strikingly counter to the general thrust of "acculturationist" anthropology in this period (and which, it is worth noting, anticipated the similar position taken by Tax a decade later [Stocking 2000:194]). Despite "every effort of the government to smash their culture" and the "more pervasive influence of contact with the White community," the Cheyenne had maintained their "cohesiveness" as a "true folk community." After watching "at first hand the workings of White culture for fifty years" they not only had an "understanding of the culture of their White neighbors," they had "rejected it" (Armstrong 1942:126, 129). And with his foreshortened master's thesis thus completed, Armstrong was inducted into the U.S. Army in early April 1942.

Cryptanalysis, Battle Stars, and Denazification, 1942–1945

For the next three and a half years Armstrong served as an enlisted man and noncommissioned officer, specializing in cryptanalysis and "the teaching of codes and ciphers" (DAP:RA curriculum vitae, c. 1946). Assigned at first to the Military Police, he soon applied to Infantry Officer Candidate School for training in military intelligence, in which he was ranked as one of the two or three best in his section before he was "relieved" for "lack of sufficient technical training" and reclassified as an "M.P." Writing to John Murra in August 1943, he was still unsure "whether I got fucked or simply fucked up." Although at first inclined to suspect that his reclassification was merely military bureaucratic inefficiency, he later had grounds for believing that it had been for political reasons. At the time, however, a friend from Chicago in the classification section got him reassigned to the Signal Corps "with a good classification." Initially stationed in Panama, where Americans were "at great pains to insulate themselves" from contact with the "contaminating influence" of the native population and of GIs (who were "white" but socially unacceptable), Armstrong led a "sort of monastic life." However, his work as a cryptanalyst in the message center left him free time for reading anthropology, and with the connivance of contacts among the MPs he was able to enter "off-limits" areas of Panama City to observe the "contrast of culture" (JMP:8/28/43).

By May 1944 Armstrong was back in the United States, serving as code clerk at Camp Shelby, Mississippi, while waiting out a six-month period required by army regulations between periods of "overseas" service, as Panama was regarded (JMP:RA/JM 5/7/44). After several months, however, it began to seem "more and more incongruous that I should be sitting back and twirling cipher divides while there was a war going on," and he decided to risk another application to the Infantry Officer Candidate School. Despite high ratings from his company commander, however, the application "sort of blew up in [his] face" when it stirred up old political issues that had lain "dormant in the office files." Suddenly transferred to a line company, where he served as squad leader, he discovered that he rather liked training exercises with live ammunition and found the intellectual level "many notches higher" than in headquarters, which was full of "neurotic little goldbricks." In his spare time he read Karl Wittfogel on Chinese society, Karl Kautsky on slavery, and (approvingly) Earl Browder on Communist Party cooperation in national unity during the war and into the postwar world (JMP:RA/JM 7/3, 9/1, 10/23/44; cf. Browder 1944).

By early 1945 Armstrong was in Belgium as staff sergeant in charge of the intelligence section of a battalion of the Ninety-ninth Infantry Division, first in the Ardennes Forest battle, then at the Remagen Bridge, and finally in the Ruhr Pocket operation (SSD:RA/ST 9/3/53). Writing to Murra some months later about the "business of not taking prisoners," he recalled that "a certain amount of that went on in our battalion," depending on "how tired or mad or in a hurry our fellows were." Keeping track of one prisoner in a "pitch dark forest" during a cold night in February had been "very near more trouble than he was worth," and "our fellows often shot at Jerries attempting to surrender, especially if there had been a hard fight shortly before." But after the breakthrough over the Remagen Bridge, "taking prisoners became one of the main preoccupations of the battalion." Ten casualties and a hundred prisoners were a normal day's work—although the "wounds hurt just as much and the KIA's [killed in action] were just as dead as when the going was tougher" (JMP:4/10, 10/11/45).

Early June 1945 found Armstrong on his way back to his unit by train after a month in Paris "convalescing from an attack of measles [*sic*]." While there he had read the letter published under the name of Jacques Duclos, a leading French Communist (but emanating in fact from Moscow), in which Earl Browder was attacked for abandoning the class struggle (Howe and Coser 1962:437). Despite his earlier approval of Browder's policies, Armstrong now concluded that Browder (who was removed from party leadership) had "unfortunately . . . strayed much further from a Marxist position than we realized" (JMP:RA/JM 6/3, 9/3/45). Although he later recalled that he had "become practically inactive [in the Communist Party] for professional reasons after June 1941" and that after his induction the following year his connection was "automatically severed" (Armstrong 1953), it seems clear that his identity as a Communist was still intact and that his experience in occupied Germany was a major factor in his later return to active party membership.

Initially, the "only stiff-necked Nazis" Armstrong met were German staff officers, and he held out hope for the German youth; later, however, he was disturbed by a pervasive German arrogance, especially regarding the "slaves in their midst," and by their failure to display the "slightest sympathy for anyone but themselves." In contrast, the Russians were "wonderful, vigorous folk" who removed "tremendous quantities of heavy machinery" as well as the "whole Kaiser Wilhelm Institute, . . . complete with scientists!" While "we" were still debating whether Göring was a "war criminal," the Nazis captured by the Russians "have been hard at work these many months rebuilding Minsk, Kiev, and points east" (JMP:8/30/45). By that time, too, Armstrong had concluded that there were "some things about the American conduct of the war that stink to high heaven"—specifically, that the strategic bombing attacks were directed not against the German war machine "but against the German people." Citing an article in the *Stars and Stripes*, the newspaper voice of American servicemen, and with references to his own personal experience, he listed ten cases in which industrial facilities like I. G. Farben had been preserved, sometimes even by the verbal countermanding of target orders while bombers were warming up for takeoff. And there was the case of the official of a major steelworks who bragged to Armstrong of his connections with Dillon Reed and Co. in the United States (JMP:RA/JM 6/10, 8/30/45).

By the fall of 1945 Armstrong had been transferred to the Office of Military Government in Berlin, where he served briefly as a Russian translator (a language in which he was "largely self-taught") and then in the Office of Monuments, Fine Arts, and Archives surveying the condition of scientific museums and museum collections in the American zone. In this role he was concerned

not only with the implementation of denazification but with the neglect of anthropological materials relative to those of the "fine arts" and with the looting
of museum materials generally as well as pervasive bureaucratic inefficiency
(DAP:RA/Cole 12/1/45). In 1953 he put the matter rather more categorically
to Redfield: "I had only a soldier's eye view, but my pretty first-hand information is that really fantastic corruption extended right into his [Eisenhower's]
personal staff." Generalizing, he felt his postwar experience in Germany was
"one of the crucial pivot-points of my political thinking for a long time"
(RRP:10/30/53). Back in the United States early in 1946 Armstrong "rejoined"
the Communist Party, and in the spring of that year he reentered the University of Chicago Department of Anthropology.

Scouting a Dissertation Topic and
Teaching at Atlanta University, 1946–1948

After taking courses in research methods and linguistic analysis Armstrong devoted his efforts primarily to the preparation of a dissertation project. As if to
mark its genesis in the early moment of the global expansion of U.S. anthropology in the postwar period at a time when research support in some areas
lagged behind topical vision, there was an evident disjunction between his
topic (African economic and social organization) and its methodology (library
research). As originally sketched, it was to be a study of the "historical and
functional relationships of the cattle-keeping and tillage complexes in Africa"
based on a "comprehensive survey" of the existing literature, including the reports of medieval Arab geographers and the evidence of archaeology. But despite
the implied reference to British "functionalist" social anthropology, the specific
"hypothesis" it sought to test was one previously put forward by the Vienna diffusionist Wilhelm Schmidt: that there was "close correlation between horti-
culture and matriliny on the one hand and between herding and patriliny on
the other." The unstated relationship to Armstrong's Marxist interests was indicated by the further suggestion that "the entire work would be a test" of what
he now chose to specify as "the overall hypothesis" of his master's thesis: that
"changes in the economy and technology of a culture are highly productive of
change in the rest of the culture" and that "while the economy and technology
are themselves subject to influences from the rest of the culture," they were
"even more subject to influences resulting both from internal technological development and from diffusion of traits from foreign countries." Annotations in
the handwriting of Eggan and Redfield suggest a concern with the brevity of
Armstrong's proposal: "ask student to enlarge"; "need restatement giving detail"; "rewrite and give title [and] table of contents" (DAP: "Proposed Problem
for PhD. Dissertation").

Late in November 1946 the department approved a longer version of the project, now entitled "The Economic, Political, and Social Organization of Native Africa, a Functional and Historical Survey." What is striking is less that it was to be a library dissertation than that, in a department where Radcliffe-Brown had spent seven years, the ethnographic literature it proposed to analyze did not include recent work in British social anthropology. Instead, it took as its base point three prior attempts "to bring order into the African materials": the Boasian culture area approach of Melville Herskovits (and of the English physical anthropologist Wilfrid Hambly); the culture circle approach of Schmidt's culture historical school; and C. G. Seligman's prefunctionalist attempt "to elucidate the origins and genetic relationships of the various peoples and culture types of Africa by means of linguistic, physical-anthropological and culture-comparison techniques." Rejecting in general the attempt to investigate "cultural origins" without reference to "social processes," Armstrong was particularly critical of the attempt to "derive all cultural manifestations of importance from outside Negro Africa" on the basis of an assumption that was "entirely unproved and a priori unacceptable": the implied or stated denial that "the Negroes of Africa could [themselves] originate culture traits or complexes." Foreshadowing much of his later work, he had "the feeling" that "one day we shall come to see in the African tropical rain forests one of the great regions of culture climax and invention of the most ancient world" (DAP:thesis project).

Armstrong's hypothesis was now recast: assuming that "from most ancient times, the getting of animal food has been man's work, and the getting of vegetable food women's work," he suggested that "a notable increase in the relative weight of the one or the other has led to a strengthening of the economic position of the particular sex concerned, and hence to matriliny or patriliny, as the case may be." As carried on by writers going back "at least to [Christoph] Meiners" in the late eighteenth century, the argument had been "largely deductive," with "no systematic attempt to present empirical data either for or against the theory" and no "weighting of the relative importance" of the culture traits observed or their "relevance to the problem at hand." In contrast, his study would be based on a systematic "cartographic survey" of sub-Saharan Africa, focusing on culture elements relevant to "economic process" and "political process" (as components of a totalizing "social process"). By charting their distribution on a large-scale "political and economic map," it should be possible to discuss their "interrelations and internal workings" and to determine which groups "fit the hypothesis and which do not." Anticipating the importance of "large political states even into Eastern and Southeastern Africa," Armstrong suggested that such a map would emphasize "peak phenomena of African culture" that had been obscured by the culture area and culture circle approaches. But he also regarded the whole venture as "an experiment in method," procedurally reminiscent on the one hand of "the basic philosophy of Gestalt Psychology" and on the other of cryptanalysis, insofar as it proceeded by a "carefully inductive study of texts" in order to determine their basic structure as a prerequisite to approaching "the problem of meaning" (DAP:thesis project).

In the event, it was several years before Armstrong was able to begin serious work on the dissertation. In November 1946 Redfield received an inquiry from Rushton Coulborn, a medievalist and student of civilizations then teaching at Atlanta University, asking him to recommend someone for an assistant professorship. Redfield approached Armstrong, who knew little about the school but expressed an interest "on the assumption that one has at least a reasonable degree of academic freedom there." But he also pursued other avenues during the winter quarter while taking reading courses in linguistics, ethnology, and social anthropology. Late in February he wrote to Robert Lowie at the University of California, Berkeley, inquiring about possibilities in German institutions, citing his postwar experience and the positive role that American anthropologists with an appreciation of German scholarship might play there: "There are some Augean stables that still need cleaning" (RLP:2/25/47). Although Lowie had nothing immediate to suggest, the Atlanta option was apparently still in process. Responding to Coulborn's inquiry late in April, Alfred Kroeber wrote: "I don't recall Robert Armstrong, but you are lucky to get anyone at all the way things are at the moment, and doubly so to get someone from Chicago" (AKP:4/23/47).[2]

Thus it was that in the fall of 1947 Armstrong began an appointment as assistant professor in the "newly organized department of anthropology" at the nation's oldest graduate institution with a predominantly African American student body, where W. E. B. Du Bois had taught until three years before (AUA:AUB [12/47]:4). Except for his acquaintance with fellow graduate student St. Clair Drake at Chicago, it was the first time in all Armstrong's prior "experience and thinking" that "Negroes and Negro life" had "come alive" for

---

2. An interesting option that never developed was the field of "Russian Research" that was being encouraged in the early cold war period by foundations with ties to the federal government. In July 1947 John Gardner of the Carnegie Corporation, then in the early stages of establishing the Russian Research Center at Harvard, asked Louis Wirth of the University of Chicago Department of Sociology to offer comments and personnel suggestions. After expressing some doubt about foreign area programs in general (as too frequently "concocted ad hoc") and Russian research in particular (as an "area of 'dangerous thought' to a lot of people," in which the barriers to "effective contact and free access" were great), Wirth suggested several candidates, including Murra and Armstrong, as "deeply interested in Russia" and likely to be available to spend time there in "actual field work" (RRC:LW/JG 7/15/47). The possibility was still alive that October when Gardner met with Redfield, who suggested Armstrong as "in the top 10 percent of graduate students" and as aspiring to be "a specialist in Eastern Europe" (RRC:JG memo 10/20/47). The fact that Murra and Armstrong, whose radical connections were locally well known, should have been proposed for the Russian Research Center suggests that retrospective views of the center as a locus of government-sponsored anti-Soviet research might require some modification, at least in regard to the perceptions of some potential participants in the early stages of its formation (cf. Diamond 1992:55–110).

3. Armstrong explicating a kinship diagram for the students in his class on folk society in the Social Science Seminar Room of the then-new classroom building at Atlanta University, from the *Atlanta University Bulletin* of December 1947. (Courtesy of Archives and Special Collections, Robert Woodruff Library, Atlanta University Center.)

him. And from the beginning he was involved in attempts to "make and keep contacts in the White as well as the Negro community." In November he persuaded the dean of the Episcopal Cathedral (where he sang in the choir) to allow Negroes to attend services. That same month he was active in organizing a rally for Secretary of Commerce Henry Wallace (whose opposition to President Truman's foreign policy already foreshadowed the Progressive Party presidential campaign of 1948) and was able to report to Murra that the three thousand people present were almost equally divided between "White and Negro," with "absolutely no segregation in seating." In February he attended the state "Wallace-for-President" convention (JMP:11/30/47, 2/17/48) and that same month was involved in a conference on the report of President Truman's Committee on Civil Rights ("To Secure These Rights"), the recommendations of which had just been sent to Congress (Patterson 1996:150). On this occasion, however, his attempt through a well-known faculty liberal at Georgia Tech to get the cooperation of students in the American Veterans Committee ran up against its Board of Regents' formal prohibition of faculty or student participation in "interracial conferences" (DAP:RA/FE 1/25/48, RA/RR 2/6/48; JMP:RA/JM 10/10, 11/30/47).

Most of Armstrong's energies at Atlanta, however, were devoted to "trying to appear brilliant three hours a day five days a week" for "inadequately

prepared" students, some of whom, coming "from little cross-roads denominational colleges, were barely literate." More positively, he reported to Murra that
he enjoyed an "academic freedom . . . as complete as at Chicago." Ira Reid, the
department chair, had given him "*carte blanche* to experiment and to make mis-
takes," and he "never felt the need to pull my punches on any question that has
come up in the classes," in which the students in general were "alive" and asked
"a lot of questions." But in practice his four courses were all versions of introductory anthropology, "served up with various sugar coatings," each with a
"more or less extended dose of evolution" (a concept "completely new to about
half the class"). In a large introductory course for undergraduates he tried to
teach "a sense of problem" by assigning a term paper in which the culture described in an anthropological monograph was "to be compared with some other
culture or cultures known to the student." Because the "experimental exercise"
proved too "new and complex" for most of the students, he "ignored it for grad-
ing purposes" except in the few cases where students did "especially well." His
graduate course Early Man and His Culture was a disappointment, in part because the texts by W. W. Howells and Earnest Hooton used "objectionable
racial material and slurring comments": "What really finished Hooton so far as
my students were concerned was plate 9, where a Negro man is chosen for comparison with the great apes" (Hooton 1946). Scanting a course entitled New
World Prehistory that had only four students, Armstrong gave his maximum
energies to a graduate course on Redfield's "Folk Society" that attracted some
of the best students in the department and was, on his recommendation, extended from one semester to a full year (JMP:10/10/47; DAP:RA/FE 1/25/48,
RA/RR 2/6/48).

    Despite the generally favorable situation and the fact that Atlanta Univer-
sity had so many faculty members from the University of Chicago that it took
on "the aspect of a colony of that august institution," Armstrong had difficulty
setting up "an entirely satisfactory routine" that would allow time not only
for work but also for "extracurricular activities" and "love life" (JMP:10/10,
11/30/47). Most of all, he was "intellectually lonesome" and had "yet to meet
a person—except maybe Coulborn, in part—who actually gets excited over
theoretical questions." While this had been just "as true of the University of
Oklahoma as of Atlanta University or the city of Atlanta generally," it was
nevertheless a "fairly serious" disadvantage, and by late January he was considering other possibilities for the following year. One thing he felt fairly certain
of: it was pointless to "piddle around" about completing his dissertation, since
"no school, not even A.U., is in a position to treat me as I should like to become
accustomed to being treated" until he had a doctoral degree. One possibility
was to take advantage of the fact that "they let me know in a lot of ways that
they like me here" and simply to let his classes "slip enough to find the time to
do the writing," as several colleagues did. But Armstrong doubted he "could

bring myself to do this until I had taught for three or four years and could teach a fairly decent course without much preparation." Another possibility was to get time off, and in fact he had asked for and been promised leave for the summer and the fall semester of the following year, probably with a locally available Carnegie Foundation grant to support faculty research on a project that "will improve the teaching ability of the faculty member" (DAP:RA/FE 1/25/48). But even then, there was the question of what project.

Although his dissertation proposal on African social organization had been conceived as library research, Armstrong had also explored funding possibilities for fieldwork in Africa, including financing by the British Colonial Social Science Research Council. Having heard nothing from them, he thought of applying for a grant from the Julius Rosenwald Fund, which had a special interest in African American topics. However, he put the matter aside because he did not have enough materials in Atlanta to "work up an intelligent problem in a specific area—say the Gold Coast, or the Plateau Province of Nigeria." Concluding that "the Africa deal seems to be on ice for the present," he reported to Eggan that another possibility had recently developed: the study of Puerto Rico directed by the neo-evolutionary cultural ecologist Julian Steward—one of the landmark anthropological projects of the postwar period (DAP:RA/FE 1/25/48; Steward et al. 1956; cf. Wolf 1978).

Teaching and Researching Social Change in Puerto Rico, 1948–1949

The initiative for the Steward project had come from Clarence Senior, a social democratic economist who was director of the Centro de Investigaciones Sociales established at the University of Puerto Rico in the early 1940s during the administration of the development-oriented liberal colonial governor, Rexford Guy Tugwell (Steward et al. 1956:v; Lauria-Perricelli 1989:32, passim; Kerns 2003). In part because of his fluency in Spanish at a time when education in the vernacular was an important political issue, Armstrong's friend and mentor Murra was invited in 1947 to join the social science faculty as temporary visiting professor and at an early stage of the Steward project was made its "resident field director"—or, as Murra put the matter to Armstrong, he "had it dumped into his lap" (Castro et al. 2000:76; Lauria-Perricelli 1989:103, 114). Late in 1947 Murra wrote to Armstrong suggesting (independently of the project) that if he wanted to teach at the University of Puerto Rico for a year ("at a salary increase") Murra was "pretty sure" that he "could swing it." Armstrong responded by proposing that he might also "tack on" to the Steward venture and "do a project of my own," supported in part by the Carnegie Foundation grant for faculty research. Although he was concerned that this might "involve a change of thesis subject" and would take "a little longer than a purely library thesis on Africa," it had the advantage of "making possible a piece of fieldwork under good conditions." After consulting with Redfield and Eggan and receiving assurance of leave and research support from Atlanta, he accepted the Puerto Rico offer and joined the Steward project (JMP:JM/RA 11/30/47; DAP:RA/FE 1/25/48, RA/RR 2/6/48; JMP:RA/JM 3/16/48).

Arrangements for Armstrong's Puerto Rican venture were worked out in correspondence with Murra over the spring of 1948. In addition to such practical matters as what clothing to bring and what car to buy and the more personal one of whether a position might be found for an African American colleague of Armstrong at Atlanta University, there were three major areas of concern, each of them in some sense "political": the situation at the University of Puerto Rico; the courses and texts that Armstrong would be teaching; and the specific focus of his research for the Steward project. Writing to Murra on the day he wired his acceptance of the Puerto Rico offer, Armstrong commented on the "pounding of tom toms" in the American media (which were "scared shitless" by the strength of the Communists in the impending Italian elections) and wondered how Puerto Rico was "taking the war scare" (JMP:3/16/48). For Murra, however, the focus of political issues was more local: on April 14 there was a major student strike at the university, sparked by the expulsion of five students who had organized demonstrations on behalf of the nationalist leader, Pedro Albizu Campos. Murra glossed the situation in terms of the "queer aspects" assumed by fascism and social democracy in a colonial situation, with the "fascist" Albizu and "his storm troopers in black shirts" taking advantage of real student grievances to gain control of the student movement, while the social democratic rector, rejecting Murra's all-night effort to temper with "sociological understanding" his speech to the faculty, railed against "outside agitators," with the result that the school was closed for a month (JMP:4/20, 5/18/48).

"Politics" was also at issue in the planning of Armstrong's courses: Introductory Anthropology and Social Change. For both men "social change" was a relatively noncontroversial rubric within which a Marxist perspective might be offered to give the students "a notion of what imperialism is really like." By assigning Redfield's *Folk Culture of Yucatan* (1941) Armstrong could "go from it to a consideration of change in general" (JMP:JM/RA 4/8/48). Armstrong proposed to go even further: "If we are going to talk about change at all . . . why not give them something in Dialectics?" Fortunately, a text published at the Leningrad Institute of Philosophy (Shirokov 1938) was available in Spanish translation as *Tratado sistemático de filosofía marxista*, and parts of it might be reproduced, "minus the last word" in the title (JMP:4/28, 5/20/48). Murra, however, felt that the Shirokov text had best "remain undistributed," though Armstrong could "freely talk and use ideas from it" (JMP:5/10/48). In the end, Armstrong settled for Redfield's *Yucatan* and (despite his distaste for the author)

Carleton Coon's *Reader in General Anthropology* (1948) for the Social Change course as well as Ralph Linton's *Study of Man* (1936) and Margaret Mead's *From the South Seas* (1939) for Introductory Anthropology (JMP:5/28/48).

In asking for leave from Atlanta Armstrong had proposed a study in the tradition of Chicago anthropology and sociology, with resonances extending back from Redfield and Cole to W. I. Thomas: "the impact of American culture on Puerto Rican immigrants to the United States through an analysis of letters and other documents written to their families in Puerto Rico" (AUA:Presidential Records 6/1/48). But while the Puerto Rico project had, in its initial stages, an acculturationist agenda (Lauria-Perricelli 1989:123–24), by the time Armstrong was involved it had been defined in Stewardian terms as a series of community studies representing "the adaptations of productive complexes . . . to different local environments," each regional "subculture" representing a different "level of sociocultural integration" within a "national sociocultural system" (Steward 1950:134; Steward et al. 1956:1–27). To carry out the community studies Steward chose a group of Columbia graduate students who shared a background of "progressive politics and socialist beliefs" and who found his "matter-of-fact materialism" and tolerant liberalism a congenial framework in which to pursue their own more radical agenda for "stretching anthropological paradigms" (Lauria-Perricelli 1989:140; Wolf 2001:39; Murphy 1981:180–81). After a seminar at Columbia and a month of orienting discussions at the University of Puerto Rico, the field staff dispersed to their respective sites: Eric Wolf to the "traditional" coffee municipality of San José; Robert Manners to the "tobacco and mixed crop municipality" of Tabara; Sidney Mintz to the corporate sugar plantation of Cañamelar; Raymond Scheele to San Juan, where he studied families prominent at the national level; and Elena Padilla, one of Steward's few female students, chosen by Murra as a replacement for Stanley Diamond, who left the project after six weeks (Steward et al. 1956:1–28; Lauria-Perricelli 1989:98–205; Kerns 2003:242, 250).

Steward himself then returned to Columbia, leaving the administration of the project largely in Murra's hands, with important issues thrashed out at the lively periodic project conferences, when the "Columbia gang," as Murra called them, gathered at the University of Puerto Rico. Initially, Murra suggested to Armstrong three possible fieldwork sites "in order of their [increasing] urgency": an all-Negro community, an industrial community, and one of the new regional urban centers such as Caguas, in which a new way of life, "bustling with a variety of commercial and industrial activities," was emerging—an "autochthonous growth" with important political and social consequences. But although the last was Murra's personal choice, "the guys" were not much interested in it. While their thinking was "clear in large, world-scale matters," their understanding of how to study a national culture in a modern society was "extremely dim" (JMP:3/24/48). Armstrong favored Caguas but, being "a great believer in eating my cake and having it too," hoped it might be combined with an all-Negro community, which was the preference of his department chair, Ira Reid, although Reid did not insist (JMP:4/2/48). After some negotiation "the guys" agreed on Caguas but without much enthusiasm for Murra's favored topical focus ("fifty years of U.S. control and occupation"), from which he felt "a nice acculturation thesis could be fabricated" that would appeal to Eggan. But given the general framework of a "community study" within "a modern, multiclass society," emphasizing "the community's relations to insular structure and extra-insular power," Murra felt the "damn thing is anything we wanna make it." It was important, however, for Armstrong to arrive in Puerto Rico before Steward came down from New York on June 21 so that he could "meet the guys in their native habitat": if there was to be any more "packing of the staff . . . we better do the packing" (JMP:JM/RA 4/28, 4/29, 5/10, 5/18/48).

After a period of orientation Armstrong settled in Caguas, where he carried on fieldwork with the assistance of Delia Ortega Pabón, who had completed a master's degree in social psychology at the University of Chicago and was later for many years attached to the University of Puerto Rico in several research capacities. From Caguas he commuted the seventeen miles to his classes at the university, where he participated in several of the periodic conferences of his fellow researchers, who continued to debate the problem of how to study a national culture. By December Murra had concluded that "doing a national culture" was a "will-o'-the-wisp" of Steward. Writing to Armstrong, then on a holiday trip to the United States, he worried that it distracted from the "very interesting 4-way discussion of compadrazgo" that "the boys" had developed in the course of their rural agricultural community studies (JMP:12/27/48). In retrospective evaluations the ethnographic material on those communities has been seen as one of the strengths of the Steward project; its major weakness, the failure to deal adequately with the problem of national culture, which has been attributed in part to the fact that the study of Caguas was never completed (Lauria-Perricelli 1989:175–200, 324–28; Wolf 2001). Armstrong's fieldwork was apparently not a great success, and he himself later commented on his difficulty in conceptualizing Caguas as a "socio-cultural phenomenon" (cf. Stocking 2002d). In January 1949, when the pressure of "doing two full-time jobs, seventeen miles apart" became too great and when his appointment as a research fellow of the British Colonial Social Science Research Council finally "came through," Armstrong decided to withdraw from the Steward project (JSP:RA/JS 6/25/54).

As a result, Armstrong's "partial study of Caguas" is mentioned only once in the collective volume *The People of Puerto Rico* (Steward et al. 1956:vii), and the only piece he himself published from his Puerto Rican experience was a brief article in the Atlanta University publication *Phylon* in 1949. Entitled "Intergroup Relations in Puerto Rico," it was a frankly "impressionistic" description of the situation of Negroes in Puerto Rico as "roughly comparable to that of the Jewish population of the United States." Although race prejudice was far from absent, given "intelligence, good looks, good manners, initiative, hard work, money or 'pull,' a Negro [could] rise very high," and people would say of a light-skinned achiever without "bad hair": "He used to be a Negro, but he isn't any more" (Armstrong 1949:221–22). By the time the article appeared, Armstrong had returned to Chicago in order to resume work on his doctoral dissertation project, which he hoped to complete before undertaking fieldwork in Africa (JMP:7/5, 7/21/49).

The Aspiring Marxist Anthropologist as Universal Dialectical Materialist, 1949–1950

Armstrong later recalled that he and the Communist Party had "parted company—as friends" after he realized that the party was "unhappy about any real discussion of dialectical materialism that went beyond intoning the sacred texts" (GSP:RA/GS 11/28/77). Closer to the moment, in the political autobiography he wrote for Tax and Eggan he suggested that there had been no "serious advance in Marxist thought since the publication of Lenin's *Imperialism*," and "the whole intellectual structure" was now "obsolescent" (Armstrong 1953). It took no account of "the development of world economy during and after two world wars" and "almost no account of 20th century science, which has deeply changed our notion of matter—a basic point for materialist philosophy." Though Marxists might have Marx's books on their shelves, they no longer read him. The "great majority of active communists" had a "religious rather than a scientific attitude towards the Communist movement generally and towards Russia in particular," and the same religious attitude "had deeply permeated Russian thinking." As a result, Armstrong had decided that "neither the Soviet State nor the Communist Party represented a sufficiently glorious ideal to warrant taking the punishment that continued membership entailed" and that his "best contribution to the hopes of mankind" lay in his "continued scientific work, the results of which I can, of course, not guarantee to anybody." In this context Armstrong later recalled having embarked "on a theoretical study that still interests me"—presumably, the unfinished draft that survives in his student file entitled "Society and Matter" (1950a).

Contemporary correspondence indicates that Armstrong began writing "Society and Matter" in the fall of 1949, when he was "about ready" to start writing his dissertation but found that, after two years away, his Africa project "looked very cold indeed." In the meantime he had become "real interested" in a "lot of theoretical sidelines," which he had to "get off my chest," apparently because he felt that his "basic right to a materialist point of view had been called into

question" (JMP:10/4/49, 1/6/52; DAP:RA/RR 2/15/2l, RA/FE 4/30/51). But after a "five-months excursion into theoretical green pastures" he put "Society
and Matter" aside unfinished at a time when his interest in the Africa project
had been revived (JMP:10/4/49, 1/6/52). Although the draft that survives in his
student file is unmarked, one can easily imagine that it might not have been
well received. Politically, the timing was, to say the least, unpropitious, and,
quite aside from its Marxist orientation, its boundary-stretching content would
likely have been regarded as "not anthropology." But as an unusual if not unique
effort to move beyond Steward's "matter-of-fact materialism" and the Marxish
orientations of the "Columbia gang" toward an explicitly (if idiosyncratically
conceived) Marxist theoretical framework for anthropological research in a
political moment of burgeoning McCarthyism, "Society and Matter" seems
worthy of serious historical consideration (cf. Stocking 2002d).

Armstrong's typescript opens with a twenty-four-page prologue in which he
recounted how, in the course of collecting "data" from the monographic literature for "a thesis about African kingdom or state structures," he had run into un-
specified problems that took him "far into the physical and biological sciences."
Recalling a conversation with the polymathic Scottish physicist/philoso-
pher/politician Lancelot Law Whyte on the necessity of considering any phenomenon in the widest possible context, he proposed therefore to start "at the
outermost limits of the orbit I have traveled and then gradually to approach the
specific subject matter that occasioned the whole effort." With that, he took a
sudden turn back to his own military experience and began "by considering a
simple problem in cryptanalysis." Imagining that a message from a "well known
anthropologist," known to be an Americanist interested in "the general aspects
of this field," was intercepted and "brought to our code room" for analysis, he
reproduced fifteen lines of jumbled letters in groups of five. With occasional references to Percy Bridgman's *Logic of Modern Physics* and to seven appended
pages of alphabetical frequency tables, Armstrong proceeded to decode the first
two lines of the cipher: "south ameri cancu lture sanin terpr etati vesum maryb
yjuli anhst eward itist hepur poseo fthep resen tarti cleto provi," which might
be rephrased (although Armstrong did not do so) as "South American Cultures: An Interpretative Summary by Julian H. Steward. It is the purpose of the
present article to provi[de]" (Steward 1949:669). Having broken the code,
Armstrong asked his readers to note five facts: the cipher as a whole was very
much greater than the sum of its parts; each part reflected the whole by implication; to "understand thoroughly any given part we had to understand the
whole"; at no point did we have "an absolute QED proof of the various hypotheses we have used"; and the "crucial question" at every point was "the fit of
patterns to each other" (1950a:14–16).

In this context Armstrong suggested that his "simple cryptanalytic problem"—"the nearest thing to a problem in the physical sciences I am able to

handle"—shed "considerable light on certain problems that recur many times in the use of hypotheses in Anthropology." But he also granted the limitations of his analogy. Whereas there came a point in cryptanalysis "when one knows he has finished and [the] solution is complete because one has discovered all of the encoding or enciphering processes," this was seldom true elsewhere in physical and organic nature, where problems "seem at least to interlock endlessly with neighboring problems, and 'solution' is never complete." In compensation, however, there was "the advantage that we [anthropologists?] have much more by way of obvious clues than is the case with a good cryptogram" (Armstrong 1950a:16).

His cryptanalytic prologue out of the way, Armstrong turned to the substance of his argument, developed in a thirty-eight-page preface, followed by three chapters, before the manuscript broke off on page 107. What is immediately striking is the number and variety of thinkers whom Armstrong engaged in the attempt to define his dialectical materialist standpoint. There were philosophers, ranging from Heraclitus, Zeno, Plato, and Aristotle, through Aquinas, Kant, Hegel, down to Bertrand Russell, John Dewey, Alfred North Whitehead, Sidney Hook, and Mortimer Adler. There were political theorists, from Machiavelli to Ludwig Gumplowicz to Franz Oppenheimer and Robert MacIver. There were psychologists, from Freud to the Gestaltists Wolfgang Köhler and Kurt Koffka, down to Edna Heidbreder's (1935) summary of seven contemporary psychologies. There were natural scientists from Newton to Einstein down to E. H. Hubble, Norbert Wiener, and Leopold Infeld, as well as science writers like Joseph Needham and George Gamow. And of course there were Marxists, from Marx and Engels, through Plekhanov and Lenin, to those included in a translation of Shirokov's authorized Stalinist *Textbook of Marxist Philosophy* (1938). And there were even several anthropological writers and others less easily grouped, including Kenneth Burke, George Herbert Mead, Robert Redfield, C. F. von Weizäcker, and Benjamin Whorf. Strikingly, for someone trained at Chicago, there was no reference to Radcliffe-Brown or to Durkheim; even more strikingly, Armstrong's primary anthropological reference point was the *Methodik der Völkerkunde* of Wilhelm Mühlmann, a "German neo-Hegelian, a sinner," that is, a Nazi sympathizer, selections of which Armstrong had translated for Eggan and later sought, unsuccessfully, Lowie's help in publishing in the United States (RLP:RA/RL 10/15/47, RL/RA 10/20/47; Armstrong 1950a:57).

In style "Society and Matter" was conversational, with extended quotations from numerous interlocutors, some of them in Armstrong's own translations from the French, German, Italian, and Russian originals. But there were several whom he had in fact engaged face-to-face, including his first sociology teacher, Fred Cottrell, who "called my attention to the limitations of a two-sided interpretation of dialectical contradiction" (Armstrong 1950a:45). More recently, there was the dean of U.S. anthropologists, Alfred Kroeber, who when Armstrong had shown him some of his material on cultural integration had "complimented me as following on what one might call 'the great tradition' in Anthropology: the attempt to see man as a part of nature" and who suggested that insects, although more complicated structurally than vertebrates, "on the whole clearly represent a lower level of integration" (1950a:27, 104). The most important of his interlocutors, however, was Whyte, whose comment on context had authorized Armstrong's far-reaching venture and who, like Cottrell, cautioned him against taking "the wave-corpuscle nature of light as an example of contradiction" (1950a:45, 55). Indeed, at one point Armstrong suggested that "this whole argument" was an answer to an issue Whyte had raised "in conversation": that the "attempt to characterize a society as a material thing" had been "rendered obsolete by the discovery of the equivalence of matter and energy, one of the foundation blocks of modern physics" (1950a:76; cf. Whyte 1948:68–69).[3]

It was to meet this challenge—to show that "dialectical materialism" was not only a viable but a necessary standpoint for the understanding of society— that Armstrong formulated his argument in terms of "hypotheses," "corollaries," "empirical observations," and "criteria." Hypothesis I asserted that "the universe and everything in it" was one "material system, whose parts are organically interrelated," with the corollaries that the study of societies can be of direct help in the explanation of "merely biological, chemical atomic and sub-atomic structures"; that "quite a number of the observable regularities among biological, social, and cultural systems" were due to their "common materiality"; and that description and explanation of phenomena at each level required that "they first be isolated or distinguished conceptually from the purely material phenomena with which they are inseparably connected" (Armstrong 1950a:27–32).

Armstrong had been led to the formulation of these corollaries by thoughts on the problem of a holistic-aesthetic approach to "human nature" and the study of "social forms and types generally" that he had formulated while attending Redfield's seminar on human nature. To illustrate them he offered an

3. The circumstances of the conversation are not clear. Although Whyte visited the United States on a number of occasions, the only trip to Chicago specifically mentioned in his autobiography (1963:202) took place in March 1957, when he served with Mies van der Rohe on the jury for an international architectural competition; perhaps he lectured at Chicago on some occasion in the late 1940s, when Armstrong might have introduced himself afterward. The same question arises in the case of Kroeber, who was a visiting professor at the University of Chicago in the spring of 1938 and the fall of 1959 but who may have come for a lecture or a meeting sometime in the late 1940s (Kroeber 1970:212; PC:AC 2/15/02). The relevant point is that Armstrong was not shy when it came to engaging the attention of distinguished visitors whose interests were as wide-ranging as his.

extensive single-spaced insertion on the topic "Human Nature," which was to "serve analogically as a 'scenario' for this thesis generally," since he intended to "deal in similar fashion with the problem of kingdoms in Africa." Human nature was to be understood by "the contradictions that constitute it": a human being was a "material object" but also a "living, organic" object through which material objects passed and at the same time a "highly—if not perfectly—integrated whole." Human nature must therefore be conceived "thetically," in terms of the physical attributes that "distinguish man from the rest of the universe of phenomena," "antithetically," in terms of "the societies in which people (like many other biological organisms) live," and "synthetically," as "an exceedingly complex integration of the general and the particular-human" (Armstrong 1950a:32a–d; cf. Stocking 2002d:5–7, which contains slight errors, corrected here, in the transcription of Armstrong's first proposition about "human nature").

Armstrong's preface then continued with Hypothesis II, "taken of course, from Engels," that "motion is the manner of existence of matter," followed by the corollary that "the main form of motion of matter is its self-motion." Armstrong went on to devote twenty pages to Hypothesis III: "The basic manner of motion and therefore the basic category of the universe is contradiction" (1950a:39). It was here, after extensive quotations from Plekhanov, Zeno, Aristotle, and Engels, that he turned to topics specifically related to his anthropological research: the theoretical problem of state formation and the empirical problem of the boundaries of the community of Caguas in Puerto Rico. In regard to the former, the issue was how to integrate German and American theories as to the nature of the state. On the one hand, Gumplowicz and others advanced the "conquest theory" in which a conquered group was systematically exploited by an invading group; on the other, MacIver saw the state as an association within a territorially delimited area serving "the common interests of all its members" (Armstrong 1950a:42). Although these alternatives might seem logically opposed, Armstrong argued that by "the dialectic logic propounded by Plekhanov and Marx" it might be possible to accept both of them as "true." Appealing both to Machiavelli and to his own experience "in an army of occupation," Armstrong suggested that the state might be defined "by the following contradiction: that it functions to maintain an exploitative system . . . while at the same time with respect to other social and cultural aspects of the society it fosters and expresses a very real community of interest" (1950a:42, 44–45).

Acknowledging the difficulty of defining the idea of "contradiction," Armstrong offered the "empirical observation" that "the motion of material things is both directionally irreversible and cyclically repetitive," with illustrations from the popular literature of contemporary astrophysics. "Being in these matters a child with no respect for angel etiquette," he "rushed in" with an idea of his own: that the Einsteinian curvature of space might allow all the galaxies that were "fragments of the original explosion" eventually to "approach once again the place of their origin," followed by a hypothesis of his own for the origin of cosmic rays, "the major mystery of modern physics" (Armstrong 1950a:48).

As a further qualification of Hypothesis III, Armstrong offered the corollary that "the characteristic relation of opposites to each other is the dual, contra-dictory one of unity and conflict." It was in this context that he referred specif-ically to his Puerto Rican ethnographic work as an instance of the problem of the definition or identification of "opposites," which he acknowledged could only be done by "a more or less aesthetic or intuitional judgment." He had found it "extremely difficult to arrive at a fruitful definition of the socio-cultural phenomenon called the town of Caguas," despite the fact that one could "very easily" see the entire town of 25,000 people "by climbing one of the nearby mountains." It was "typically Spanish" in architecture and town plan, and "there was complete unanimity of informants and documentary sources that the name of this collection of houses and streets around a plaza was 'Caguas.'" But as the meeting place of five highways and a narrow-gage railway, Caguas was also "the communications center for the east-central part of the island." A "large majority" of the population "made their living" outside of the town, and even businesses whose physical plants were in it "had their decisive economic connections outside," with "various insular government offices and institu-tions" as well as extraterritorial ones: the Eastern Sugar Associates of Balti-more, Maryland, and the Chase National Bank (the mayor himself was an agent for General Electric). In addition to the cane-cutters living in the slums who worked in nearby fields, there was a "very large group of persons who com-muted to work in the San Juan area." And yet, despite the fact that "the people who made their living mainly in the town itself were a relatively unimportant group that was mainly performing services for those whose main connections were outside," Caguas was "known all over the island as a town with strong lo-cal feeling and pride."

> What then does this socio-cultural phenomenon consist of? From one point of view it is a nexus or vortex of contradictory or "opposite" relationships each of which is characterized by the fact that at least one of its terms is in some physical sense located in the town of Caguas. . . . The town's internal definition might be seen to lie in the fact of the conflict between common residence and external in-terest of its citizens. (Armstrong 1950a:53)

Armstrong felt his formulation (implicitly contrasted, one suspects, with that of Redfield) seemed "fruitful and good" in suggesting "a host of particular lines of investigation" and providing "a live framework for ordering the facts which we collect." But he was "far from satisfied with the concepts of 'opposites' and 'contradiction' in this situation," and, after noting several possible lines of crit-icism, he ended with a quotation from Mühlmann on "the danger points which lie in the dialectical method" and with the acknowledgment that Hypothesis III had been "the most important and the weakest part of the whole argument" (Armstrong 1950a:57–58).

After this lengthy prologue and preface the rest of "Society and Matter" consisted of three chapters. The first, entitled "Direction, Trajectory and Networks of Trajectories," argued, with reference to Heisenberg's uncertainty principle, that "the main conclusions of the quantum theory are in principle deducible from dialectics." This, despite the fact that physicists, "suffering from the shock of trying to use metaphysical concepts and Indo-European grammar to express their results," were inclined to resort to "theological and other mystical explanations for a situation that to a dialectician seems rather obvious" (Armstrong 1950a:60–61). Arguing from the path of a bullet and the pattern of paths across the University of Chicago Midway, Armstrong offered as Empirical Observation IV that "all the trajectories in the universe are formally interrelated," insofar as they occurred within "material media," and that "a trajectory as an organized thing is that [particular] body of material that in the main directs and channelizes the motion of the object in question." Trajectories were organized in networks Whyte called "structures," although Armstrong, reflecting dominant Boasian usage, preferred to call them "patterns" and suggested that a "structure was a special kind of pattern" (1950a:67).

The second chapter, "Material Things," opened with a hypothesis defining a material thing as the "synthesis" of "one or more material things moving in a trajectory or system of trajectories." From there Armstrong went on to argue that a society was not simply a "mental or emotional complex" but as much a material thing as was a uranium atom—with many quotations from contemporary physics and Gestalt psychology but without reference to Radcliffe-Brown or Durkheim. After correcting (by reference to the original Russian) the translation of a passage from Lenin's *Materialism and Empirico-Criticism*, Armstrong closed the second chapter by offering his sixth and final hypothesis: "The fundamental dialectic opposition is between matter in particular (thesis) and matter in general (trajectory, antithesis)" (1950a:69, 82).

In the third chapter, "Criteria of Organization and Integration," Armstrong moved from thesis and antithesis to the principles of synthesis, attempting to define a series of "criteria" that would apply to every "level" of organization from "the hydrogen atom to the modern super-state or to the United Nations" (1950a:83). Specifying three dimensions of organization and integration ("relative scope, relative intensity and relative efficiency") and offering the "proposition" that a "unit on any given level of integration" was formed by the integration of two or more previously existing units, Armstrong went on, with frequent references to Gestalt psychology, to formulate twelve "criteria of integration." Each of them enabled him to distinguish "more highly organized" units from others presumably "less highly organized": warm-blooded animals were more highly organized than cold-blooded ones; "a state with an army adequate to keep invaders out is more highly organized than a state too weak to do this" (Armstrong 1950a:92). And in several cases where levels of organization clashed with personal conviction, he offered a qualification; thus, in a passage resonant of Edward Sapir, he introduced a criterion of independence, in terms of which a "hermit or a frontiersman would show a higher degree of organization than a stenographer in a big city, since the stenographer is more or less swept away by the great social forces from which she cannot protect herself" (Armstrong 1950a:93; cf. Sapir 1924). Similarly, the "crude pattern" ("brute conquest and naked exploitation") by which Nazi Germany had succeeded in "restructuring" all of Europe to "suit German interests" had in fact revealed "certain crucial weaknesses" in its apparently "very high level of organization." In the end, he granted that "many of the senses [of organization and integration] are contradictory" and that he could not deal with the problem "except impressionistically." And yet, when he insisted that "all of these formulations are correct in various particular ways," he was not "merely trying in Pollyanna fashion to see some good in everything." It was rather that "in particular, definable situations" they formed "useful tools of analysis of real phenomena." That they should "turn out to have contradictory aspects should surprise no dialectician" (Armstrong 1950a:106).

The table of contents of "Society and Matter" listed two more chapters as "proposed." Chapter 4, on "patterns," would have dealt with "information, entropy and evolutionary development" and with "culture as a system of patterns conditioned by the human mind." Chapter 5, on "society," would have argued that although "a human society" was at once "a material thing" and a "biological thing," it differed "profoundly" from and synthesized "all the previous levels." Why these two chapters, which should have been the work's culmination, were never completed is not clear. Armstrong later recalled spending "a lot of energy on the application of the theory of dialectical materialism to anthropology and in the end found I was talking only to myself." According to another recollection, the abandonment came after he received his appointment "from the Colonial Office to study in Africa" and decided "to finish my PhD thesis before going." Contemporary evidence suggests the situation was a bit more complicated.

In January 1950, responding to Murra's suggestion that he might be able to connect with the Columbia Russian Research Center, Armstrong said that his thesis was "becoming more Marxian and theoretical and less specifically African ethnographic by the day." Weighing against this, however, was the belated information from England that he could probably get his first choice of field site in Africa ("the Pagan Tribes of Nigeria") along with at least six months in England, with "total freedom" to do whatever he liked (JMP:1/2/50). A month later he was debating whether to propose to the "Russian Institute [sic]" "some study in Soviet anthropology" in order to pursue his "interest in dialectical materialism"—or possibly to "combine the whole business with the

African study by making it a study of primitive communism, based on a fairly extensive survey of Soviet theories." Inasmuch as the Russians were carrying on "a considerable discussion of communism as such," the "African angle should catch their eye if decently done"; furthermore, "my naked pagans might hit them an interesting implicit blow below the belt on the puritanism question." If the British or the Russians objected, "I could simply go off on my own, on the R.I. [Russian Institute] salary," moving the project to Brazil, if necessary. Armstrong encouraged Murra to consult with "the boys" and let him know if the plan sounded practical "or was just a pipe dream" (JMP:2/3/50). Although no response was preserved, Senator Joseph McCarthy's announcement two weeks later that he had a list of 205 Communists in the State Department might have helped swing the balance.

The Aspiring Marxist Anthropologist as Ethnographic Comparativist, 1950–1952

The African option, although still at that point open, was soon threatened by a backdoor anti-Communist attack. At the beginning of January Armstrong had been given a one-quarter appointment as half-time instructor to fill in for his mentor, Redfield. At the same time, Edward Evans-Pritchard, Radcliffe-Brown's successor at Oxford, arrived in the department as visiting professor as part of a more general postwar transatlantic flow of established British social anthropologists westward and fledgling American anthropologists eastward. "As the junior member of the department" Armstrong was detailed to meet Evans-Pritchard's train when it arrived at 5:30 AM on a January morning. Although Redfield and Evans-Pritchard "did not hit it off" and the latter's reception by the department faculty was "chilly," he "went over big with the students," and he and Armstrong seem to have become fairly close. Despite being "a pretty complete tory," Evans-Pritchard managed to get Armstrong "a bit more steamed up on Africa," and by early February he had decided to do fieldwork there (JMP:RA/JM 2/13/50). Toward the end of February, however, Evans-Pritchard told Armstrong that the British Consul had contacted him in connection with his African research grant "to ask about my politics," and "E-P, who was not afraid of Marxists, had given a good report and said I was harmless." At the end of the quarter Armstrong went home to Cincinnati for several weeks, and "E-P went to Washington to see what was happening." By Armstrong's recollection of Evans-Pritchard's rather remarkable account, he "had a busy time of it":

> He found that the Colonial Office, on the instigation of the FBI, had cancelled my appointment "irrevocably," [but] the British ambassador in Washington had refused to accept or to transmit the cancellation "because it was improper

procedure." E-P then bearded the FBI in its den and likewise the State Department. He managed to persuade the FBI not to interfere in a British appointment.
Bill Brown, then head of the Africa Desk of the State Department, later head
of the African Studies Program at Boston University, after considering the whole
matter decided that the State Department had no objections. And so the whole
deal went through with no hitches.

There was, however, a brief coda. Having told Armstrong of his efforts on his
behalf, Evans-Pritchard looked him in the eye and said: "Now I have been frank
with you, [and] I want you to be frank with me. Have you ever been a member
of the Communist Party?" Armstrong replied that he had and "gave him the
dates," after which Evans-Pritchard said "he was ready to go on with the project; and that ended the matter" (GSP:RA/GS 11/28/77).

It was another half year, however, before Armstrong actually began his
African fieldwork, and in the interim he had a much more direct experience of
British social anthropology. He traveled to England on the Cunard *Parthia*,
along with Evans-Prichard and Lloyd Warner, who during the past two decades,
first at Harvard and then at Chicago, had pursued Radcliffe-Brown's "comparative sociology" project in various communities in the United States (Warner
1988:163). The otherwise "uneventful" transatlantic voyage was enlivened by
competition between Evans-Pritchard and Warner to "see who was closer to
the Radcliffe-Brown throne," with Warner's "Rex" trumping Evans-Pritchard's
"R-B" as index of intimate familiarity. Several weeks after their arrival, however, it was Evans-Pritchard who took Armstrong from Oxford to London to
meet Radcliffe-Brown, "who backed Warner up very solidly" in his dispute with
George Murdock on Murngin kinship (JMP:RA/JM 5/21/50).

Although Armstrong was troubled by the "international situation" (notably,
"the Korean business," on which he felt that North Korea, the U.S.S.R., and
China were on "pretty firm legal ground"), he spent the next six months working hard on his dissertation, save for three weeks in August traveling on the
Continent, where he witnessed a major Communist demonstration in Munich
and was given a glowing report of the progress of "the People's Democracies"
in Vienna (JMP:5/21, 8/26/50). At Oxford he was apparently close to Franz
Steiner, the poet and Semitic scholar who had just been awarded his second
Ph.D. and a lectureship in social anthropology (Evans-Pritchard 1956); Armstrong subsequently recalled that it was Steiner who gave "Society and Matter"
the only "real response" it ever received. But in his finished dissertation, "State
Formation in Negro Africa," the important social anthropological influences
were those of a trio of contributors to *African Political Systems* (Fortes and
Evans-Pritchard 1940), a major landmark in the Radcliffe-Brownian comparative project. Armstrong's "key" chapter on the Ashanti—a society "madden-
ingly difficult for an American or European mind to grasp"—owed whatever
"coherence" it had to the advice of Meyer Fortes. His chapter on the Barotse

Office Memorandum • UNITED STATES GOVERNMENT

TO : Director, FBI   DATE: October 20, 1950

FROM : SAC, Chicago   **SECRET**

SUBJECT: ROBERT GELSTON ARMSTRONG
SECURITY MATTER - C   4.4.2000
(Bufile 100-39986)   CLASSIFIED BY 60367 NLS/EP/00
           DECLASSIFY ON: 25X 6
           915570

Reurlet March 13, 1950, with enclosure.

On September 18, 1950, ██████████
██████ University of Chicago, was interviewed by SA ██████ in
connection with an LGE case. ██████████ stated that he had some
information concerning the subject which he felt might be of interest
to the F.B.I. and which he would furnish for whatever value it might
have.

██████████ has requested that his identity remain confidential in any
further investigation conducted concerning information furnished.

██████████ stated that ROBERT ARMSTRONG had formerly been a student
at the University of Chicago, where he had known him for possibly
██████ He stated that he believes ARMSTRONG is definitely a Communist
Party member and completely in favor of Communist activities.

██████████ stated that ARMSTRONG had recently been affiliated
with Atlanta University, Atlanta, Georgia,
that ARMSTRONG was involved in Communist Party activity in Atlanta.
██████ stated that he also believed that ARMSTRONG had been doing work
at the Maxwell Field Air Base near Atlanta and, therefore, he was curi-
ous why a person of ARMSTRONG's views should be allowed to do confidential Government work.

██████████ stated that to the best of his knowledge ARMSTRONG is
presently at Oxford University in England. He explained that ████████
██
██████████████ explained that he was not friendly
with ARMSTRONG and was very displeased that ARMSTRONG had been assigned
to the same cabin during the ocean voyage.

██████████ advised that ██████████
██████ whom he identified ██████████

RECORDED - 46
INDEXED - 46

ENF:ms
100-4662

OCT 23 1950
24

5 - NOV 1 1950   **SECRET**

4. The first page of an FBI report regarding Armstrong's activities during the summer and fall of
1950. On the second page (not reproduced here) the informant speculates about the motives for
Armstrong's trip to Africa, suggesting the possibility that it had "more serious implications than
were indicated on its face," specifically, that Armstrong might be involved in "espionage activities"
as a "foreign agent" (see below). (Courtesy of Jennifer Lewis, who obtained the file under the Freedom of Information Act.)

was read and criticized by Max Gluckman, who also made available "still un-published material." And those who knew his work would recognize "at many points" the influence of Evans-Pritchard, the de facto director of the disserta-tion whom Armstrong thanked for help "during a period of quite considerable personal problems" (1950b:ii–iii). By the time he embarked for Nigeria early in November the basic text of the dissertation was complete. Writing to Red-field from Ibadan, Armstrong apologized for sending him only a carbon (at a "king's ransom" in airmail expense) because Evans-Pritchard had not yet re-turned the ribbon copy Armstrong had given him for comments before sailing (DAP:11/10/50).

In terms of its central interpretive categories ("exploitation" and "contra-diction"), "State Formation in Negro Africa" was clearly a continuation of the larger anthropological project for which "Society and Matter" was to have pro-vided the epistemological groundwork. But in terms of its methodological, empirical, and comparative agenda it was an attempt to engage recent ethno-graphic work in British colonial Africa in a systematic and rigorously compar-ative manner, focusing on problems of political and social organization in order to investigate "the nature of state formation and development" within a Marx-ist framework. As Armstrong emphasized at several points, it was an "experi-ment" in anthropological method, broadly conceived (1950b:1)—and a re-markably ambitious one, the more so when one considers the external political environment in which it was undertaken.

At the empirical level of "data" collection and analysis it was carried on in a manner echoing the *Outline of Cultural Materials* of the Human Relations Area Files (Murdock et al. 1950), Kroeber's California culture element survey (Stocking 1991), and the *Notes and Queries* of the British Association and the Royal Anthropological Institute—not to mention its Ur-source in the works of E. B. Tylor (Stocking 1995:3–14, 2002c). With the assistance of Grace Gredys (Harris) and Patricia Copeland (Reining), two of the postwar cohort of gradu-ate students who had felt the influence of Armstrong's intellectual charisma, he had collected "extensive abstracts" from the African ethnographic literature that were then "classified according to a simple decimal system" (e.g., "122. Ways in which capital can be accumulated and used; 1221. Land; 1222. Gold; 1223. Cattle"). This system enabled him to "make a systematic judgment as to the degree of organization a particular kingdom represented": "It seemed to me that if we could know how much of a 'thing' a kingdom in Africa is, we have gone a long way towards getting a definitive answer to questions as to its origin: by diffusion, conquest, growth and development on the spot, etc." (Armstrong 1950b:35–41).

Conceptually, Armstrong's project was based on hypotheses about "the na-ture of the state" that he had developed or encountered in the course of his work on "Society and Matter" and in his prior preliminary research on "the relation of African pastoralism to African agriculture" (1950b:1, 8). In pursuing the latter he had "become impressed with the tendency, implicit in most of the scientific work on African cultures, to assume that any culture trait of interest to a European cannot have originated in Africa, but must have come from some other place"—a reference to the widely influential "Hamitic hypothesis." In its classic expression in the work of C. G. Seligman (1939), the Hamitic hypothesis assumed that the "great civilizing force of black Africa" was the "permeation" of sub-Saharan Africa by a light-skinned population carrying "Hamitic blood and culture" to "the Negro and Bushman aborigines" (Armstrong 1950b:9). In this context, one of the tasks Armstrong set himself and felt that he had accomplished was to "give the *coup de grace*" to this "moribund old war-horse" (1950b:284).

A second task Armstrong set himself was a critique of the "conquest theory of the state," with which the Hamitic hypothesis was "usually combined" (1950b:288). Here his results were less clear-cut. Granting that "in the course of history a number of states have been formed by conquest," Armstrong suggested that "the African materials indicate that even where conquest can be shown to have occurred, this fact may not be the most important of the processes involved in state and class formation" (1950b:19). And in the end, after the analysis of six ethnographic cases, the most he would grant was that conquest was simply one of a number of "causal factors" at work in state formation, the most important of which was "exploitation" (Armstrong 1950b:295).

With a glance back to Marx, Armstrong defined exploitation as "an interchange of economic goods characterized by the relationship $xL \neq L$ $(x - n)$, where L equals the labor which the economic goods have cost, and x and n are variables"—or, more simply, as "the failure of a reciprocity system to close completely" (1950b:319, cf. 23). Initially, he postulated that states originated "with the development of exploitative systems in society" and functioned "to maintain and expand these systems—'horizontally' (by conquest) and 'vertically' through the improvement of the economy and of the organization of the exploitative system itself: a) by increased administrative efficiency, and b) by development of a consensus system" (Armstrong 1950b:21–22, cf. 319). At several points in the dissertation, however, he indicated that his first formulation was inadequate and that his "early work" was marred by the idea that the state was "a manipulative plot on the part of an elite," with a "more or less elaborate consensus mechanism to sugar the pill" (Armstrong 1950b:311–12). At the outset he had included MacIver's theory of the state as "an association representing, defending and assisting the common interests of all of its members" among the "old hypotheses" he intended to critique (Armstrong 1950b:31, 319). But as he proceeded with his case analysis he was increasingly impressed by the importance of "consensus" mechanisms (e.g., the idea of "moral order") of a sort he associated with MacIver's hypothesis but that might perhaps be glossed in terms of tendencies within mainstream anthropological thought about the idea of "culture" (Armstrong 1950b:32). Toward the end of his investigation Armstrong elaborated at some length a "master hypothesis" in which he discussed "exploitation" in terms of "capital accumulation," "economic classes," and "social class structure." However, he gave much greater emphasis to "consensus mechanisms," including "common religion, common dress, a unified system of courts of justice, common history, common enemies, an easily conceptualized 'country' that is affect-laden, and certain subconscious psychological processes like placing the king in the father position." Furthermore, these consensus mechanisms had functionally adaptive benefits: "Most important of all, the state really does express and defend important common interests in the economy, internal peace and order, and external security from attack," making possible "large-scale technological and economic complexes" upon which "huge sections of the population become dependent" (Armstrong 1950b:42–43). While exploitation was "a powerful motive force for societal development," in the process it created "tensions" that must be "contained and channelized by appropriate social and cultural devices, or they will destroy the system in short order." And a "really good consensus system" would "conserve large bodies of traditional culture traits, bent and adapted to their new functions" (Armstrong 1950b:27–28).

It was in this context that Armstrong reintroduced the idea of "contradiction" that had figured centrally in "Society and Matter," now as a means of overcoming the tension between the idea that the state arose originally "to protect a condition in which there is no community of interest between the exploited and the exploiting classes" and the idea that it was also "the common way which serves us all." In language little modified from its earlier statement he suggested that if one accepted "the basic method of dialectic logic, as expounded by Marx and Plekhanov, it is possible to accept both of these propositions as true because we will define the state as expressing an essential contradiction": "The state is an association which is defined by the following contradiction: that it functions to maintain an exploitative system, thereby expressing a situation where there is no community of interest, while at the same time, with respect to other social and cultural aspects of the society, it fosters and expresses a real community of interest" (Armstrong 1950b:32, 319–20).

To test (or to document) his "master hypothesis" Armstrong presented six case studies, each based on sources ranging from early contact accounts through preacademic ethnographies up to the latest monographs of British social (and in one instance American cultural) anthropology, augmented by conversations with Evans-Pritchard, Fortes, and Gluckman. Basing himself "almost entirely" on the recent monograph by Eileen and J. D. Krige, *The Realm of a Rain Queen* (1943), Armstrong found among the South African Lovedu "a feudal kingdom of the earliest type: the 'storybook' situation where one really did exchange service and loyalty for security," founded upon the "magical power of the Queen" rather than on "military force" (1950b:63–64). The "genius" of the Lovedu political system was "its network of reciprocities" and of the legal system, "its procedure of reconciliations and compromises." But if there was little basis for capital accumulation, Armstrong argued that the queen and the district chiefs did form "an economic class" with a monopoly of land for the use of which they received payments in labor and kind (1950b:52). He went on to suggest that, as in the American Southwest, "the Apollonian pattern for handling overt interpersonal relations" exacted a price in terms of "covert aggressions and insecurities," which, as was "frequently" the case in "primitive societies," was expressed in "a strong witchcraft pattern" (Armstrong 1950b:64). In short, although exploitation was "minimal," it was present, and with consequences.

From the point of view of his "master hypothesis," Armstrong's second case was somewhat anomalous. Basing himself largely on an account by the German missionary Wilhelm Hofmayr (1925) and on Evans-Pritchard's "excellent" summary statement in *The Divine Kingship of the Shilluk of the Nilotic Sudan* (1948a), Armstrong had to strain to satisfy the criteria of his minimal definition of a state. Although there was "nothing in Shillukland that one could dignify with terms like 'administration' or 'government,'" he argued that it was an ideological, economic, and sociological "whole," which he classified as a "tribute state"—this, despite the fact that there was "little by way of a regularized taxation system," no "organized system of feudal relations," and "sharp limits" on the accumulation of capital (Armstrong 1950b:86–87). In short, the Shilluk case offered hardly any evidence of exploitation, and he used it largely to argue against the Hamitic conquest hypothesis. In the end, he could only call for further study "from the point of view of the theory of social class elaborated by Lloyd Warner and his associates," which might illuminate "the detailed workings of an exploiting, economically superordinate social class which is at the same time a systematically exogamous clan" (Armstrong 1950b:91).

Acknowledging that the Lovedu and the Shilluk were both "borderline cases," requiring "some pains" to fit within his definition of a state (1950b:101), Armstrong felt no such qualms in presenting his third case study: the Barotse group of what was then called Northern Rhodesia whose dominant tribe, the Lozi, had been Gluckman's special ethnographic preserve. Here "the problem of classification" did not arise: "The Barotse kingdom [was] a clear-cut example of a conquest state" (Armstrong 1950b:101, 92). The problem was rather how to explain why "a highly organized state" arose in Barotseland when it did not among the Nuer, the Dinka, and the Anuak, who also inhabited "flood-plain regions." Whether Armstrong was aware at this point of Gluckman's Marxist sympathies is unclear; but there is no doubt that he found congenial his Stewardian emphasis on the specifics of ecological adaptation in relation to technological development. After a lengthy discussion in which he reproduced a chart of Gluckman's on "differential tribal and regional production" (Armstrong 1950b:98–100), he insisted (against Oppenheim on the origin of the state) that "our main category of explanation must be the way in which the given system fits the ecological situation and the general technological situation of the people concerned"—the "origins of the ideas" that people had used to "solve their problems" being a different, "and I believe secondary, matter" (Armstrong 1950b:109). In the Barotse case the economy manifested a considerable development of "exploitative" features, as evidenced in the tribute system. But while this in turn permitted the "development of the technology through division of labor and specialization," the impossibility of storing food for longer periods "put sharp limits on the development of economic exploitation," and the chiefs found better use for food surpluses by "giving them away" to gain prestige (Armstrong 1950b:112–13). While there was only limited accumulation of capital, the "systematically exploitative aspect" of the economy created a system of "economic classes," and on that basis, too, a social class system could also be defined, "although not without some ambiguity" (Armstrong 1950b:118–19, 121).

Also problematic was Armstrong's discussion of the Ashanti in the region then known as the Gold Coast (now Ghana). Based on Edward Bowditch's 1819 account, the ethnographic monographs of the government anthropologist Robert Rattray (1923, 1927), the unpublished 1947 Oxford dissertation of Kofi Busia (later prime minister of Ghana), and "lectures by and conversations with Professor Meyer Fortes" (Armstrong 1950b:145), it was by far the most extensive of Armstrong's cases, occupying over a third of his dissertation. In terms of his "master hypothesis," the contradiction between exploitation and consensus was here the sharpest, and it took extensive argument to bring the two closer together. Armstrong found considerable evidence of capital accumulation and exploitation, based largely on the slave system and the frequent external wars; but if there were economic classes, there was little in the way of class conflict. Indeed, in the end he concluded that "the whole society was substantially a consensus society" in which "the various conflicts of interest are sufficiently slight that they can be overborne by the influence of the national religious cult, chiefly and kingly largesse, etc." (Armstrong 1950b:242). To resolve the contradiction he proposed a contrast between "dictatorial exterior versus democratic interior." Internally, Ashanti political life was "vigorously democratic because of the continued strength of the matrilineal kinship system, despite the growth of a powerful state on a developed economy" (Armstrong 1950b:244). Since in general Armstrong saw the state and the kinship system as inversely correlated, he was forced to explain "how so elaborate a state could arise without interfering with the kinship system." His answer was that the Ashanti state was "essentially predatory in its relation to West African and world economy" and that its "main exploitative relationships were external to the kingdom." The "constitutional pattern" was "an effective if tacit, and probably unconscious compromise" between the chiefly group "and the rest of society based on the principle that a democratically organised commonality made a very effective soldiery" who accepted a modicum of exploitation and the risk of death in war in return for "a 'pay-off' in slaves and booty which made them partners in the enterprise" (Armstrong 1950b:247). The upper class, in turn, stood "at the head of a moral system strong enough that, although decentralization was the foundation of state policy, they were able to dominate their part of the world for two centuries and fight seven wars with the British Empire" (Armstrong 1950b:250).

After this ringing peroration affirming the resistance of an imperial African state to the most powerful imperial state of modern Europe, Armstrong's last two case studies on two other West African groups, both presented in a single chapter, seem anticlimactic. The first was based on the work of Melville and Francis Herskovits among the Dahomey (1938), another slave-based kingdom against which Armstrong posed the Ashanti as a comparative reference point. By this time familiar with Evans-Pritchard's recension of the British social anthropological standard of fieldwork (two one-year stays around an academic break for collation and analysis of ethnographic material [1948b:76]), Armstrong was quite critical, albeit in an apologetic way, of the Herskovitses' ethnography, which had been done in six months, largely among elite groups in the capital city, "without anything like 'participant observation'" (1950b:251–52). Even so, Armstrong relied heavily on information that Melville Herskovits got on the last day of his fieldwork from a single (and uncorroborated) informant regarding a "secret census system" that Armstrong felt was "intimately linked up to the extremely elaborate taxation system" of the centralized Dahomean state. Even assuming "the procedures were never actually put into practice," the account showed "political thinking of a very high order" and helped to sustain his own argument that "the Dahomean state was more highly developed" than any of the states he had examined. In terms of his "master hypothesis" it should have been associated with "increased exploitation" (Armstrong 1950b:264), and indeed, Armstrong felt that it was by virtue of the transformation of the original system of communal labor into "an exploitative instrument" that continued to "preserve the outward forms of reciprocity," thus demonstrating again "the imaginative sophistication that seems to be the hallmark of Negro kingdoms" (1950b:269–70).

Armstrong's final case, the Nupe of Nigeria, required only the briefest treatment, since they were the subject of what was "far and away the best" extant study of an African kingdom: Siegfried Nadel's *Black Byzantium* (1942), a book that "should be known to any anthropologist," regardless of his or her "particular field of specialization" (1950b:270–71). The rise of the Nupe kingdom, a "clear-cut example" of a conquest state, had produced a "sharply stratified class society, with ethnic barriers reinforcing the effects of a strongly exploitative economy" and a correspondingly pronounced weakening of kinship institutions, in sharp contrast to their continuing strength among the Ashanti and the Dahomey (Armstrong 1950b:272). But in contrast to the latter, one looked "in vain" for "carefully considered policies and institutions of political and financial control" (Armstrong 1950b:273). The "unified state" depended instead on the "extremely atomized character of the classes and echelons" beneath the ruling group and upon the "magical powers" attributed to the king and "his entourage" (Armstrong 1950b:274, 280–81). The belief in the king's magic led Armstrong to a comparison of the Nupe state and the concealed exploitative structures of modern Western European society.

During the last hundred years the European "ruling classes" had "suddenly abandoned pomp and special costume." Businessmen, tycoons, presidents, cabinet ministers, kings, members of the Council of People's Commissars, and "even the Mikado" were more often seen in "ordinary 'business suits,'" and the "showy town houses of the Vanderbilts and Astors" were already being torn down. But the power these groups wielded was nevertheless "thousands of times greater than that of the older royalties." Granting some potency to the "obvious explanation" that modern class struggles and revolutions made it "more advisable to camouflage wealth and power," Armstrong felt that a more important factor was the "different structure of cohesiveness of modern nation-states," in which "power over people" was replaced by "power over things" and "the state itself becomes an intensely organized, impersonal 'thing.'" Leaders were still important, but the leader no longer represented "in his person the only integrative principle at work to hold the state together." That said, the "cruder" political techniques of the Nupe (and the fact that the "general level of exploitation" was only midway between that of Ashanti and Dahomey) required some explanation, which Armstrong felt might reflect the fact that they were "a fairly recent conquest state." On this basis, his results were "not out of line with what we might expect" (1950b:283).

Armstrong's more general remarks on the tension between expectations or hypotheses and results were offered under three headings in a final chapter of conclusions: "R.I.P. the Hamitic Hypothesis," "The Conquest Theory Cut Down to Size," and "The State as a Contradictory Activity," considered here in order of their relation to an argument that in retrospect seems to be the central point of the whole dissertation. First, the conquest theory: as Armstrong granted, "in actual fact, some element of conquest was seen to be present in the formation of every one of the states studied except Lovedu," a "special island of refuge in a sea of conquest and counter-conquest." But although the Lovedu had, as one might expect, the lowest "degree of exploitation," its "astonishingly heterogeneous population" had been "united without conquest into one of the most highly integrated states in Africa," an anomalous result Armstrong could account for only by the fact that it was "the smallest of the states studied"

(1950b:292). In contrast, two of the states, the Nupe and the Shilluk, were classic examples of the conquest situation, in which "a foreign nomadic, cattleherding tribe" conquered "an indigenous agricultural people" and formed a ruling aristocracy. Among the three remaining kingdoms (the Barotse, Ashanti, and Dahomey) conquest played "at best a partial role," less in their origin than in their subsequent development, in which "the slave trade" and the warfare associated with it sustained "exploitative systems involving social groups" that "were not themselves enslaved" (Armstrong 1950b:293). Considered along with the Nupe, the evidence of these four indicated that "in our sample kingdoms the greater exploitation exists where conquest played a lesser role," which he took as "demonstration that the origin and development of exploitation in state societies cannot be attributed solely to conquest in the sense that Gumplowicz, Oppenheimer and others use the word" (Armstrong 1950b:295).

In regard to "the central problem of the thesis"—the hypothesis that the state was defined by the contradiction of exploitation and consensus—Armstrong was in the end cautious. Reprising two of its briefer formulations, he began by stating that he did not regard the hypothesis as "capable of final proof or disproof at this time" (Armstrong 1950b:305). And in offering its longer statement he had in fact acknowledged that "to a considerable degree" his hypothesis was "also my conclusion, since it was formulated late in the study" (Armstrong 1950b:43–44). Its appeal was "mainly aesthetic and affective," and although it looked "imposing and complete," its "dialectical quality" was manifest primarily in that "the later parts [of his research] build upon the earlier ones"; if it was thereby persuasive, it was "often deceptively persuasive" (Armstrong 1950b:45).

There are passages in Armstrong's dissertation in which the wording ("primitive," "progress," "higher," etc.) or the treatment of topics ("capital accumulation" and "class formation") suggests that he not only began with a cruder view of state formation (which at several points he granted) but that he continued to anticipate a generally evolutionary development of the state in which there was a direct correlation of the degree of exploitation and the complexity of organization and an inverse correlation of these processes with the declining role of kinship organization and reciprocity. When such expectations were disappointed, the notion of "contradiction" served to accommodate various anomalies not only in the relationship of exploitation and consensus mechanisms but also in the departures from a residually implicit evolutionary sequence—or, if you will, the ethnographic variety that he actually found in pursuing his "field work in the monograph."

That variety functioned positively, however, in relation to the third of his hypotheses—the first, in order of actual presentation: the laying to rest of the Hamitic hypothesis (Armstrong 1950b:284–91). Armstrong offered his critique almost apologetically, as if it was necessary to beat the dead horse one more time in order to convince people still trying to ride it that it was in fact dead, and he dealt with the matter only incidentally in the body of the dissertation. But there was a sense in which the Hamitic critique functioned as the telos of the whole project. To reject the notion that state formation in Africa was the contribution of a conquering light-skinned Hamitic people was both to attack racial assumption and to assert the cultural creativity of dark-skinned African peoples, and if the state forms they created presented anomalies for Armstrong's prior hypotheses, the variety thus manifested was itself further illustration of their generative cultural power. From this perspective Armstrong, who reflected so many of the tendencies of the postwar period (acculturation, Stewardian ecology, neo-evolutionism, Marxism, British social anthropology, as well as the pervading scientism), was quite traditionally Boasian.

The retreat from vaulting Marxist ambition to a more modest ethnographically focused and multiform comparativism is manifest in other ways in Armstrong's conclusions: in the apology for not pursuing consensus mechanisms more systematically, or in the thought that states are "'tailor-made' to particular landscapes," or in the various suggestions for "many other studies that should be done," including the relation between social and economic class, or between kinship structure and the state, or the "florescence of decadent or moribund institutions." In this spirit, his final paragraph acknowledged the inadequacy of monographic research to the focal problems of his study: "exploitation and capital formation." Although it had produced "results of some validity and interest," Armstrong was "morally certain" that, given "six months residence in a couple of the kingdoms described here," he might have written a significantly different book: "I consider this thesis a necessary preparation for such field work" (1950b:305–14).

From Fieldwork in the Monograph
to Fieldwork in Nigeria, 1950–1953

After arriving in Ibadan, Nigeria, in early November 1950 Armstrong put the finishing touches on his dissertation at the new Nigerian Institute of Social and Economic Research of the University College (later the University of Ibadan), to which he was attached administratively during his fellowship period. Awaiting the arrival of his baggage by sea before going into the field, Armstrong wrote a letter to Redfield in which he acknowledged reservations that Evans-Pritchard and Fortes had about the exploitation concept. Neither of them, however, had attempted to suggest a "better word": "They are just uncomfortable"—or perhaps it was that "the subject was uncomfortable" (DAP:11/20/50). In response, Redfield reported that he had read the manuscript "from beginning to end" and liked it because "it is in some respects not so easy to like" as some other theses:

"You take some considerations and argue them out, publicly, which isn't done, you know." Redfield, however, was sympathetic to this kind of "public exposure of one's efforts to find general meaning in some facts" because it was a "weakness" he shared. Nevertheless, he thought there were "real troubles" with the idea of exploitation not so much because of "uncomfortableness" due to its "background in Marxism" but because "the concept is not so clearly defined as it sounds" (DAP:12/27/50). Armstrong acknowledged that his treatment of exploitation had been "unsatisfactory" and suggested that his discussions of the Hamitic and conquest hypotheses were more "solid" contributions to knowledge. Both of them implied exploitation as "the motive of state formation," but neither of them provided "enough intellectual stimulation" to sustain him through a whole thesis: "Like race relations, their interest is more political than theoretical." All of which was "merely to say that I will be studying exploitation and related problems for a long time to come" (DAP:2/15/51). In the shorter run, however, Armstrong was notified by Eggan that "we like your thesis and have accepted it as is for the thesis requirements for your Ph.D.," although the oral defense would have to be delayed until Armstrong was back in Chicago, unless it could be arranged in England during a visit there (DAP:FE/RA 4/11/51).

In the event, Armstrong did not return to England until January 1952 and for much of that time seems to have been out of touch with his Chicago mentors. His first year of fieldwork in Nigeria is much more fully treated in a series of lengthy letters to Murra, who during this period was working on problems of land reform in the research section of the United Nations Trusteeship Department. As in their Puerto Rico correspondence, political concerns, both global and local, were a striking feature. Commenting on the "international situation" shortly before the Communist Chinese launched their counterattack in Korea, Armstrong worried that in the event of full-scale war a friend of theirs who was a major in army intelligence might simply "do his 'duty,' and be all the more useful to them for all you and I have ever taught him." In contrast, his own summer holiday in Vienna had convinced him that "I don't just *have* to put up with this shit." If there really was to be a war, he intended "to play an honorable part in it"—this without explication other than to suggest he was "damned if I can see sitting it out at Tule Lake" (one of the Japanese relocation camps of World War II). That he still thought of himself as a Communist (and therefore liable to be interned) is suggested by his report that the new editor of the University of Chicago student newspaper (one of "our boys") had visited Poland "and maybe points east" after attending a peace congress in Berlin; that other Chicago friends were returning from France "full of determination to join up" after "watching the French C.P."; that he had just read and liked William Z. Foster's *Outline Political History of the Americas* (1951); that he was reading a Soviet novel in which "punches were pulled at the end" (political regeneration being accomplished by "productive labor" rather than "having people killed off"); and by his admiration of Mao Tse Tung's "wisdom in pulling away from the cities in his long period of illegality." By the end of the year he had concluded that the "whole peace or war issue" now hung on "a production race between east and west" in which, "if German re-armament spurs the Poles and the Czechs into really great efforts . . . I can see no reason why the Soviet Union could not sit the whole thing out, and leave the onus of attack on the west" (JMP:11/15/50, 5/6, 9/26/51, 1/6/52).

Feeling "isolated" from world events, Armstrong had much more to say about colonialism in Nigeria. He had left London with "bitter condemnation" of the British "ringing" in his ears. It came from Maj. Roy C. Abraham, who had for several years been the district officer among the Idoma (the group with which Armstrong was to work) and who was at that time the leading specialist on a number of West African languages. Abraham had described the Nigerian colonial government as "ignorant, selfish, and cruel," and, since arriving, Armstrong had heard the "same story over and over again and in different ways from all kinds of people." The new University College, a part of the postwar Colonial Development program initiated in London (Mellanby 1958), was in various ways being sabotaged by the local colonial government under the influence of Lever Brothers through its subsidiary, the United Africa Company, which maintained "an absolute monopoly in retail and wholesale trading activities" (Mohammed 1995:283). One "favorite trick" of the Nigerian colonial customs service was "to conceal the arrival of important materials and equipment, to hold it past the legal limit and then sell it at public auction." The chief of customs was reported to have remarked to one University College official: "What do you people want to go educating all those black bastards for?" But the arrogance of the university faculty was equally "spine-chilling," "actually worse in many respects than most of what one sees in the American South." On Armstrong's first night in the college dining hall the "whole company" of "masters"—the general term for white staff members—joined in "bawling out the cook over the meat, with such savage ferocity" that Armstrong went back the next day and apologized "for being a White man" (JMP:RA/JM 11/15/50; cf. DAP:RA/RR 11/10/50). The new University College reflected the "general British approach": "Set some fantastic 'standard,' [then] promote yourself to the position of arbiter and teacher, at a nice salary, during the many generations it will take for the bulk of the people to achieve that 'standard.'" And when someone like Kenneth Dike, who had an office upstairs from Armstrong (and who was a friend of Paul Robeson, the African American athlete, performer, and activist), managed by dint of sixteen years' residence abroad to "achieve a higher standard than nine-tenths of the staff," the "old Ramsey MacDonald act is used, with all the organ-stops pulled out," to "co-opt him into the system and separate him from his countrymen." And through it all "nobody even stops to ask why it is a good thing for Nigerians to learn to write Latin poetry" (JMP:11/15/50).

As for conditions beyond the University College, Armstrong argued they were "like most other colonies in the world." The Pax Britannica had no doubt brought changes "few people would like to see undone": feuds and head-hunting had ended, population had grown, and "there really is a quite re-spectable amount of literacy." Although the transportation of goods was still largely by "head-loading," there were roads, dispensaries, and schools as "con-crete returns" for the native taxes collected. But the "whole elaborate structure of peace and social services" was basically to "defend the interests of the U.A.C.": "Lever Bros. make big profits; dollars [sic] are earned (quite a lot of them); but the [native] taxpayers as a whole foot the bill, and the colony is left gutted, too." It all added up to "the total lack of any provision for the growth of the kind of capital or capital equipment that can mobilize productive labor on anything bigger than a yam patch." The Berom tribe, which had done "quite a bit of mining before the Europeans came," had derived "no particle of benefit from forty years of tin mining on its lands"; although the Berom provided the labor, all the profits "had gone elsewhere." And to make matters worse, the British really took "this Hamitic shit" seriously, teaching the Muslim Fulani in the north that they "are not Negroes at all" but "much superior" to the other people of West Africa and importing the administrative models of the north into southern areas to which they were ill adapted, requiring the imposition of "chiefs" where none had existed (JMP:5/6, 9/20/50).

But if Armstrong rejected ideas of racial superiority, he had definite no-tions of developmental differences within and between major Nigerian ethnic groups. Thus the Ibo included "in one teeming volcano" both "the most em-phatically advanced and the most emphatically backward peoples of Nigeria." And if Armstrong qualified "backward" (adding, "in the stereotypical sense of most naked, most atomized political organization, most surrounded by rumours of sale of human meat in the markets, etc."), he suggested, in the same para-graph, "you can see ten thousand years of cultural evolution in an hour's walk." In other contexts, early Russian history provided the comparative temporal touchstone: thus the Idoma center of Oturkpo reminded him of "a medium sized market town in Russia of the tenth century." The most striking compara-tive comments, in regard to the "lower middle class" character and attitudes of the more "advanced" groups in Nigeria, seem to reflect the influence of George Bernard Shaw, of whom Armstrong had been "reading a lot." The "stereotype" of backwardness had become "important in the thinking of Ibo," who were busily "turning themselves into lower-middle-class, sociological Protestants": the postmaster who refused to serve bare-breasted Idoma women, "telling them they were a bunch of primitives and should put some clothes on," or the loinclothed old woman in a mud hut who told him proudly that her son was in-spector of docks in Lagos but whose son would have been "humiliated beyond words" if Armstrong told him he "had met his mother" (JMP:11/15/50, 5/6 [cf. Stocking 2002a], 9/20/51).

The issue of lower-middle-class attitudes was the main theme of Armstrong's comments on the Hope Rising Movement, the Nigerian nationalist movement led by Nnamdi "Zik" Azikiwe, with whom Armstrong had an hour-long con-versation in July 1951. In general, Armstrong felt that at the "heart of the na-tionalist movement" were "teachers and scribes" whose "worship of the English [language]" was "abject." Like the "colonial lower-middle-classes all over the world," the "nationalist literates" had no "respect for their own culture and none for their more 'primitive' brethren." Thus it was that "the Zik Press calls in English for liberation from the English." Granting that these "petty-bourgeois folk" and others who were "trying with all their might" to become so were "forced by modern imperialism into a revolutionary position that is not at all of their own choosing," Armstrong predicted they would nevertheless "cheerfully set themselves up in business as an exploiting group at the first op-portunity." Without a strong "proletarian flywheel to the engine" of revolution, Nigeria would not be "a particularly nice place when its revolution gets under-way." Zik himself anticipated independence "within five years" and "possible" civil war in the aftermath. Armstrong, who believed that "revolution" was a "necessary thing" if there was to be any "chance of real economic develop-ment," felt that "even a civil war here would have the general effect of weaken-ing the British-American empire" (JMP:9/20/51).

In the meantime, however, Armstrong immersed himself in fieldwork among the Idoma, a "pagan" people 300 miles east of Ibadan, beyond the confluence of the Niger and Benue rivers, who had had a "bad reputation for being obstreper-ous" ever since they were "pacified" by British troops in 1917 (JMP:5/6/51). Under the absentee academic supervision of Evans-Pritchard, who "never bothers to bother about anything," Armstrong had effective carte blanche in defining his research (FEP:RA/FE 11/11/50). For the first several months he made a survey of the region, traveling in the "kit car" provided by his fellowship from the border of Ibo land in the south as far up into the Muslim north as Jos. In a letter to Eggan he described the Idoma in general as having been a "kind of absolute, headhunterish democrats" upon whom the British had been trying to impose an "emirate-type government" to facilitate tax collection, to which the Idoma reacted "none too kindly." He himself, however, had been welcomed "royally," which he attributed in part to his "being an American": "Idoma is chock full of veterans of the Burma campaign, and they all say 'Americans love Africans.' " He worried that his "royal reception" might be a "methodological problem analogous to that of measuring the electron," in which "the measure-ment process radically perturbs the object": "Are we studying these communities as they really are, or are we studying their reaction to the investigator?" However, he assumed that this problem could be dealt with when he actually settled in the field (FEP:4/30/51; JMP:5/20/51).

By mid-February 1951 Armstrong had chosen as his field site the village of Igumale, "a kind of Shangri-La" in the southwest corner of the Idoma district— this, over the opposition of the local district officer, who felt he should go to "some more 'typical' place." Once a point of European influence, Igumale had been "slumbering for twenty years" since the road to it had been "allowed to die." That respite, however, would end in a year after the opening of several nearby mines, when "the outside world" would descend on the town "like a ton of bricks." It was Armstrong's luck to have found it during its "last year of peace as a 'folk society,'" with "girls still go[ing] quite naked until marriage" and a "bitter dispute over the chieftaincy currently in process" (DAP:RA/RR 2/15/51). It was here that he first participated in the dancing at a feast, in which the young female dancers wore nothing but camwood body paint. When the Methodist Igumale schoolteacher objected to his "encouraging old customs," Armstrong responded that this was "his precise intention": he saw no reason why "the kids could not both dance and go to school." Reporting later to Murra that "every muscle I learned to loosen up at Ernestine's before the War" had "paid off big" in "rapport," he suggested that "dancing should be part of the training of every anthropologist" (JMP:5/20/51; cf. Stocking 2002a).

In the event, however, Armstrong did not settle down to intensive fieldwork in Igumale but became preoccupied, in the spirit of cryptanalysis, with cracking the code of the Idoma language—"a real running encipherment of what is being said": "Just identifying the common words in the midst of all the tone-perturbation and vowel substitution" was "a bitch" (JMP:5/20/51). Offering a more upbeat report to Eggan at the end of April, he said that he had the system "pretty well licked" and was building a card-file dictionary. Able already to "get simple business done in Idoma," he hoped in another month to go "on to kinship" (FEP:4/30/51). But at the end of September he was still in the district center, Oturkpo, still "mainly concerned with language." Writing to Murra at length about his latest "scrap" in a long-running fight with Methodist missionaries over the appropriate orthography for an Idoma reader (which had been "couched in a strange mixture of dialects that nobody speaks"), he planned now within a month to "set up shop in a bush compound near here." Once again, however, in October there was a delay when he suffered his fourth bout of fever since July, this one serious enough to require hospitalization in Enugu for ten days (JMP:9/20/51, 1/6/52).

By early January 1952 Armstrong was in Ibadan on his way back to England for a four- or five-month break. Instead of settling in a single bush field site he had spent the last several months digging through a "mountain" of "paper work" unavailable in England: the "huge mass of amateur reports in the files" as well as the "truly brilliant briar patch" of linguistic materials that Major Abraham ("a real 'bush' Sapir") had collected. It was not that he had "met no Idomas really": he had "hiked with them, danced with them, slept with them, loved them, hated them, dug and eaten yams with them, visited every damn Idoma district, discovered three new ones, and in many ways had a hell of a good time." But he felt "terribly diffuse about the whole project" and realized now that retiring into "the minutiae" of "writing a dictionary" had been a mode of escape. He had for a long time "systematically dodged kinship in anthropological literature" but could no longer because "in Idoma, kinship is what you've got." And on a "grand tour of outlying districts to check up on some hints in the old intelligence reports" he had found "a complete graded series [of political forms] from divine kingdom to most primitive anarchy with lots of degrees in between, . . . groups with varying amounts of Hausa, Ibo, Igala, or European influence, a couple of very primitive districts right next to Oturkpo that show little outside influence of any kind." What he hoped to find in England was a chance to "think about what the hell I am up to in Idoma country" (JMP:RA/JM 1/6/52).

Armstrong did a lot of thinking during his five months in England, but more to the end of formulating issues in correspondence and conversation with various anthropological interlocutors, representing various tendencies in midcentury anthropology, than to resolving them. Most of these issues can be posed in terms of oppositions (internal/external, intensive/extensive, psychological/developmental, linguistic/sociological, scholarly/activist) between which there could be either choice or resolution. Basically, there were two "problem alternatives." His predeparture "grand tour" suggested a "far flung study, with much use of the kit-car," of the "range of political structures in one ethnic group." But this would mean forgoing a "concern with the soul of the people," which implied "intensive study" in the Oxford tradition, at a single site, either Igumale or Iyala ("the anarchists, [and] the best dancers of the lot"). Elizabeth Bott, a student colleague at Chicago who was in London working at the psychoanalytically oriented Tavistock Institute, cautioned that he lacked the technical training for the study of the soul; Murra felt there was no "serious difference" between the study of the "soul" of a group (in the sense of "immersion in the culture" rather than "psychological sophistication") and the "developmental [political/sociological] approach" that Murra favored (JMP:RA/JM 1/29/52, JM/RA 2/24/52).

Hanging out with British social anthropologists, Armstrong was pulled in both directions. When asked by Isaac Schapera to give a paper on "American Contributions to Kinship," he had to bone up on a subject that, as he told Eggan apologetically, he had "rather avoided" in favor of language. In the process, however, he had finally begun to get "through my head what these British anthropologists mean by a 'lineage' (as opposed to a kinship system) and to appreciate its importance as a 'political institution.'" Although "most of the real social analysis" lay ahead, he could now formulate his problem as seeing "what happens when a kingdom gets organized." To this end he proposed to start with "one of the 'anarchist' groups" that spoke the Oturkpo dialect "and go on from there" (FEP:2/18/52). But in a subsequent paper to the Oxford anthropologists he turned back to linguistics, reading them "the riot act" for their failure to take language study seriously (with support from Louis Dumont, "a student of Lévi-Strauss"). Several days later he presented another paper, on the possibility of "giving some of my notions of exploitation a trial in Idoma," to a rather "mixed" reception, because "E.P. and his fair-haired boy Godfrey Lienhardt don't like such talk" (JMP:3/26/52). And toward the end of March Armstrong attended a meeting of the Royal Anthropological Institute at which Gladys Reichard, a visiting Boasian, presented a paper entitled "Working with American Indians," to which, on the strength of her study of the Navajo language, he got a dozen people to come. But instead she offered what he called "Tea-time Opinions about American Anthropologists" (among whom Ruth Benedict was "the saint"), attacking Redfield and his students for their failure to study "primitives" (or, as "you people [the British] call them, savages"). Prodded by Sally Chilvers (his "administrative mother at the Colonial Office"), Armstrong rose to insist that "the notion that one should go into the field knowing nothing of the tribe one was visiting nor of its neighbors was no part of Redfield's doctrine." Indeed, the phrase "you must have a problem" was "almost synonymous with the man" (JMP:RA/JM 3/26/52).

Armstrong's own sense of problem, however, was still in flux in late March, when he began working on a contribution to the *Peoples of the Niger-Benue Confluence* volume of Daryll Forde's Ethnographic Survey of Africa series. In the course of compiling information on the Igala and Idoma-speaking peoples he told Murra that he had discovered "less than a week ago" that their languages were "much closer to Yoruba than I had any idea," which "put another face on the ethnological origins of the kinship patterns in the Benue Valley." As a result, after a year in which "theory was on ice," he was still unsure of "fundamental problems of ethnological orientation" (DAP:RA/FE 3/27/52; JMP:RA/JM 3/26/52).

In this context of theoretical and ethnographic disarray Armstrong (by prior arrangement) defended his doctoral dissertation when Redfield was in England for four days on his way to Paris to lecture for Lévi-Strauss. As it turned out, neither Fortes nor Evans-Pritchard (both of whom were less than enthusiastic about the exploitation thesis) was able to attend, so at the last minute Evans-Pritchard (who was going on holiday with his family) arranged for Forde to take his place. The defense, held at a French restaurant over "a fine lunch," was "the best of all possible oral examinations," with Armstrong able to ponder answers to questions while sipping "reflectively on a vintage wine" (DAP:FE/RA

2/20/52, Ralph Tyler/FE 3/12/52, RA/RR 3/13/52, RA/FE 3/27/52; JMP:RA/JM 3/26/52). Forde led in the questioning, suggesting that "conquest," rather than being viewed "as a question internal to the particular state," might be treated in terms of "the necessity for resistance and reaction to external pressure." Picking up on one of Redfield's characteristic "you seem to be arguing" cues, Armstrong pursued the line that the "consideration of internal factors, though not complete in itself, was yet enough to account for the main features." After a brief consideration of "how the people were persuaded to accept exploitation," the "party broke up" with "one of Redfield's conclusive summaries": "In Africa the roads to the state have been many" (JMP:3/26/52).

Reflecting afterward on the exam, Armstrong analogized the opposition between Forde and Redfield to that between Trotsky, who argued that "developments external to the S[oviet] U[nion] were of decisive importance," and "Stalin's view" that "the nature and development of the internal relations was the really decisive factor." That his Communist Party experience was still very much a part of his thinking was further evident in his reaction to Bott's comments on "the Tavistock method of group analysis." In contrast to the therapy group, which to him seemed like "group psychic masturbation" with no purpose "outside the contemplation of itself," Armstrong thought that a "good CP branch should be able to do all the psycho-therapy the Tavistock method can manage" and at the same time tackle "the political problem squarely and actively" (JMP:3/26/52).

During April and May Armstrong labored on the Forde report, with a few days taken off learning to ski in the Austrian Alps and visiting Naples. Early in June he embarked on a freighter for Nigeria, continuing work on the Forde report during the three-week trip with the hope of finishing it in Ibadan before resuming fieldwork. On June 28 he wrote letters from Ibadan to each of his two mentors. He addressed Murra as a kind of elder brother to whom he could speak frankly about a range of anthropological, personal, and political issues—the latter from a Communist perspective. In contrast, Redfield was an Olympian figure, paternal rather than fraternal, who spoke from on high across a political divide and to whom he wrote in somewhat calculated and guarded terms but whose advice and assistance on matters relating to his anthropological career he sought in moments of professional crisis.

In writing to Murra Armstrong focused on interpretive issues in his Forde report, with which he had been grappling since his discovery, "along about April," that the Idoma and the Yoruba were "distant cousins" linguistically. This, in the context of historical research on the "depredations" of the Fulani expansion from the north, had thrown the "fantastic chieftainship puzzle" of the Idoma into "quite another perspective." As a solution he proposed the "plausible" hypothesis (more historical than developmental) that the Idoma, prior to the Fulani expansion southward, already had "clans" or "lands" in the pattern of the "petty, independent kingdoms or chieftaincies" seen in the eastern Yoruba districts and that when the Fulani expansion lost momentum with the end of the world slave trade, there was a fifty-year period prior to the entrance of the British in which these "petty chieftaincies, which had essentially been federations of groups of lineages for defensive purposes, evaporated into thin air" and the "inter-lineage quarrels and jealousies became more important" (JMP:6/28/52; cf. Armstrong 1955:96–98).

In writing to Redfield Armstrong dealt instead at considerable length with career issues he had mentioned briefly in writing to Murra. Just prior to his departure from England Fortes had introduced Armstrong to Alfred Métraux, an anthropologist attached to the United Nations Educational, Scientific, and Cultural Organization who "strongly nibbled" him for an eighteen-month job with the UNESCO mission on "mass literacy" in Nigeria. They wanted an "expert" to survey a group of local dialects and advise the government on "the suitability of various vernacular languages" for instructing children and adults and in selecting the orthography for each language chosen. The trouble was that Armstrong had "practically broke[n] his heart" over "this precise problem in Idoma last year." It all boiled down "to the fact that the people directly concerned—Government, missionaries and literate Africans—have a complete lack of respect for the size of the problem, for the languages, and for the people who speak them." It was "the absolutely literal truth" that they expected an "expert" to arrive in the evening and "the next morning to advise on the permanent orthography of a totally strange language." As a result, nobody, despite "all the hoopla," was really interested in developing an approach to mass literacy, which would take, as a start, "a minimum of a year's study" of each language in order to create "texts in the new system" that might then be "quietly introduced through the native markets so that quite a lot of people could become familiar with the [new] system before it ever came up for official consideration." Apprised of this prospect, Evans-Pritchard had advised Armstrong to accept the job, "write all the reports in London," and use the time and money to do "sensible anthropology—linguistics, if one likes" (DAP:RA/RR 6/28/52; JMP:RA/JM 6/28/52).

Thinking ahead "five years or so," Armstrong posed to Redfield a more general career problem. Having "always felt very strongly" the "moral obligations" imposed by the "thunderous situation of the modern world," he felt "a bit guilty" about staying too long "in a back-water like Nigeria." If he could do "something really effective about mass literacy for an important people here, like the Ibo or the Yoruba," that would be worth doing "for its own sake." But if the job was limited to "small groups that can never play much of a role in the world at large," then the only excuse for undertaking it would be "the possible theoretical importance" of his work. He was not, however, a linguist but simply a "social anthropologist with a strong interest in linguistics," and he did not presently

"control enough of linguistics" to make serious contributions to it "as a science." Furthermore, the UNESCO "business" would mean postponing indefi-
nitely "a project dear to my heart." Although for years he had "felt more or less
Marxistically inclined," this was not today a matter to be "played about with
light-heartedly," and he felt "substantially illiterate about the very things most
central" to his project. Having done no systematic reading or thinking about
economics since 1938, he lacked the basis "to give my hypothesis about exploitation a proper test in the field." And although he was "much enamoured of
dialectics," his work on "Society and Matter" (a copy of which he assumed Redfield must still have) was only the beginning of a serious study (DAP:6/28/52).
   In this context Armstrong felt he must decide whether to "run away from
the problem" and study "the Wahoozies of Dismal Swamp, Africa," or whether
he should undertake a "basic education in philosophy and science" so that he
could decide whether to pursue further the issues he had broached in "Society
and Matter." The first option, although the easiest, seemed "a form of [intellec-
tual] suicide." What he really wanted was to devote two years to serious reading
in dialectics, with "enough teaching to keep my hand in." To this end he had
already bought "the biggest Greek dictionary" he could find as well as the German editions of Kant and Hegel. He was not proposing "to postpone anthropology," which was "the only scientific discipline" in which he could aspire to
be "more than a dilettante." If there was "anything to dialectics," it could be
studied "as well in a society or a culture pattern as in an atom or in a plant." And
even if he simply went home to Cincinnati and did not emerge from his "co-
coon" until he felt intellectually prepared, he would probably then want to go
back to Nigeria to "test particular notions in the field." In the meantime, the
practical question he posed to Redfield toward the end of a three-page single-
spaced letter was: "Do you know of any payroll I could be on while doing such
a thing?" (DAP:6/28/52).
   Redfield's response was not encouraging. As Armstrong described the
UNESCO literacy enterprise, it seemed "doomed from the start." The "general
impression" Redfield got was that "you are pretty tired of intellectual isolation."
What Armstrong seemed really to want was to be where he "could talk about
general ideas, especially Marxian ones," to people who were also interested in
them, and this led to the general conclusion that he would "probably be hap-
pier" back in the United States. Although Redfield doubted that he could find
a payroll that would support two years' study of philosophy, a teaching job
somewhere seemed possible: "You have the competence, a doctorate, and unusual field experience, and if you tell us to, we can peddle these things among
the schools and colleges, [and] one of them will hire you," thereby providing
both a livelihood "and time left over to read Plato and Hegel." Redfield wondered, however, "what the ultimate function of your Marxian interest will be in
your life": "I can't tell whether it is something you have to get out of your sys-

tem or whether it is something that you will integrate wisely with your scientific work." In closing, Redfield turned to another option Armstrong had mentioned: a position with a field research unit such as the one Audrey Richards was organizing at Makerere. It was possible that the Carnegie Corporation might finance such a unit in Ibadan if Armstrong came back to the United States and tried to persuade them. And then, with a veiled (but still optimistic) reference to the rising tide of McCarthyism: "Here, I suppose, your Marxian interests would not make you, for the time being at least, a better salesman, but I don't think this is a real difficulty" (DAP:7/9/52).

Responding several weeks later, Murra was "not impressed" with the UNESCO job: those they sponsored "were the worst kind of eyewash, and white man's eyewash at that." But Armstrong's ideas on Idoma chieftainship and its relation to the Fulani and slavery were a "most exciting" combination of "historical and functional approaches." Better, then, to follow Evans-Pritchard's advice and stay in the field, since nobody was "doing any serious work and the Meads and Kluckhohns are winning by default." Offering a long report on the "first North American conference on African affairs," which he had just attended, Murra guessed that he himself had "reached that polarization where either I do science which is good and must be done, or I work for an African group—the rest is all sham and at our time, a delusion" (JMP:7/31/52).

Despite the apparent urgency of his appeal to his mentors, Armstrong did not write again until October. In the meantime he had returned to Agala, the hometown of his interpreter, a "bush village" a few miles southwest of Oturkpo. It was there, amidst the "throbbing life of an African village," which made it difficult to do "a piece of synthetic writing," that he finally managed to complete the Forde report (JMP:RA/JM 10/7/52). Based largely on the accounts of nineteenth-century travelers and the unpublished reports of district officers of the 1930s, it included a brief discussion of the Igala group near the Niger-Benue confluence, followed by a sixty-page treatment of the Idoma-speaking peoples farther to the east, each given its several paragraphs or pages. Two of these sections, however, were more substantial along lines reflecting the central themes of his letters to Eggan, Redfield, and Murra: "Whether or not in fact the Idoma had chiefs at all, their elaborate ideology on the subject not withstanding, remains a problem." The first section, on the social organization and political system of the Idoma generally, offered a brief historical elaboration of the hypothesis of Fulani expansion Armstrong had previously suggested to Murra. The other was a descriptive account of the Agala, the group among whom Armstrong had finally settled, in which the chieftainship was most highly developed and there were in fact two royal houses (Armstrong 1955:94–99, 118–22). In the event, this was the only general ethnographic account of the Idoma that Armstrong was ever to publish.

With the Forde report out of the way and the Idoma dictionary "on ice for the duration," Armstrong finally got down to intensive fieldwork at a single site, although he was still faced with the "embarras de richesses" and a "delicate problem of ethics." He had been admitted to "a whole flock of ceremonies that were hidden from me last year," on some of which he was "sworn to secrecy" lest they be revealed to the Idoma women (although in fact "the women do catch on, and there is a whole special ceremony for purifying them so they can have children again, when they do"). But since some Idoma were now literate, and any book about them would "get back here one way or another," Armstrong could think of no way of publishing these materials save perhaps in a technical journal with "the offending passages in Latin or Greek." In general, however, he felt "very much better about the whole show" than he had last year—"on top of the problem" rather than "half-drowned in it" (JMP:RA/JM 10/7/52).

Ten days later Armstrong wrote to Murra again, this time a "business letter" about career issues in the context of the impending presidential election in the United States. Although he planned to stay in the field for a few months longer, his passport was expiring in May 1953, and he wondered what the chances were of getting a new one "a) if Ike gets in b) if Steve[nson] gets in." He had also had a letter from Atlanta University urging him to resume his position there, and this raised the larger question of whether he wanted to play "in the Big League" or the Atlanta "Bush League," where he had felt "damn lonely, intellectually speaking," and where he had heard indirectly that he had been "brought peripherally into the C.P. blow-up" three years ago and "was pretty well finished there." But there was also the more general question, whether he wanted to be mainly "in the business of making anthropologists" or in "the research business." Quoting extensively from Redfield's July letter, he wondered if he "wanted to be peddled by RR" and whether Africa was "where I want to live." Things were a lot better this year than last (and he now had "a love to console me"), but unless his bodily chemistry changed, he doubted he could "again in this lifetime find the energy to spend two years in the bush." It was in this context that he had thought about "building a research institute" in Ibadan: "I would more or less be creating the only social setting within which I could conceivably live here." Finally, then, there were the questions, "How badly do I want to stay in the States?" and "Can I make a career there without having to do it on my knees?" (JMP:10/16/52).

Couching his response in the context of a grimly personal analysis of the political situation in the United States, Murra suggested that the big questions that Armstrong must answer were, "Do you want to come home? Can you live happily and effectively outside of the U.S.? Or do you need an American environment, no matter how repressive or punitive, to do your best?" This, because if Armstrong came back now, "the chances are you will never get out again in the foreseeable future." Passports were already difficult, and once the McCarran-Wood Act went into effect on December 25 they would be impossible without "denial or repudiation of the past, plus denunciation of others." Unlike some of his friends, who were pinning their hopes on Adlai Stevenson, Murra felt that Nixon, McCarran, Taft, and McCarthy had already set the tone of the election, and he did not see "where the forces to defeat them will come from." On the contrary, "the offensive against any progressive or liberal person" had just begun. If Armstrong decided to come home, he should not count on Atlanta University as a refuge: despite the "general indication of Negro militancy," Murra could not "see any support developing when one needs it." He doubted that Armstrong could expect a career possibility in the United Nations, where "some 45 Americans" had been fired in the last month alone. Nor did foundation support provide an option: Congress had already voted for a "full scale investigation" by the Cox Committee of foundations that benefited from federal funding, and Murra had seen the questionnaire that was being circulated to them, which included a large section on "what screening devices are you using to prevent subversives from getting grants." The big thing that Armstrong must decide, therefore, was "if you can or cannot live abroad for a long period to come" (JMP:10/26/52).

Murra himself seemed unsure. Despite the political repression, "some people will do best by coming or staying home," and Armstrong would have to decide if he was one of them. There might be academic positions in the United States where one could "hole up" (denominational institutions, or "fancy girls colleges" with "no liberal reputation"). On the other hand, given what Stalin had recently said about "contradictions within the western camp" being "as deep if not deeper" than those between East and West, one might be able to "make a stand" in Britain or Nigeria. And then again, while "a traditional career is pretty well out for our generation," one might "want to come home to put up a good fight, never mind anthropology or any other intellectual work." But "from all I know of you, no matter how much politics supplements it, [scholarly work] is still your preference as a way of life," and, if so, "you may be better off elsewhere." All of this said, Murra's most specific suggestion was that "if you decide to come home, let Redfield go to work peddling right away; he can do more for you if he applies himself than you can do for yourself" (JMP:10/26/52).

When Murra's letter reached Armstrong on November 8, the envelope had apparently been opened and resealed—an echo, he felt, of Nazi Germany. It was the same day he got the news of Eisenhower's election, which he took as a sign of imminent war: "The question was, how much war and in what forms" and whether the Republicans could "get away with it." Having a "sort of ex-MP's interest in prisons, big and small," he wondered about "rear exits that might exist" for a political refugee without a passport, whether to Puerto Rico, Canada, or Mexico. Nevertheless, he felt pulled to the United States by family ties, and, because "other things being equal, one can put up a better fight in a place one knows." So "just for the hell of it and also to make him feel

involved"—and because "I guess what I like most of all is the scholarly stuff"—
he would ask Redfield to "try and find me a place next year" (JMP:RA/JM
11/8/52).

It was in this context that Armstrong, four months after he received it, got
around to answering Redfield's letter of July 9. Having spent three months in
"the actual field," he now had "a fair fluency in the language," and he had "no
hesitation" in claiming "a deeper knowledge of Idoma than any other European
has of a coastal-type tone language." He now understood the lineage system:
"What looked last year like the *bellum omnium contra omnes* now has form and
predictability." He had finished his report for Forde, which helped him to synthesize a "bulky" and "diffuse" literature. And he was now equipped to focus on
"the development—and dissolution—of political institutions in a series of
closely related tribes with an astonishing range of culture types." Although one
could "easily spend a lifetime in the region," he thought his "bird's eye survey
should be worthwhile." Anticipating his return to the United States in the
spring, he told Redfield he felt ready to take a job "during the academic year
1953–54" (DAP:11/9/52).

In a short reply Redfield wondered whether "the designs for living you
suggested in your earlier letter are still in your mind" but promised that "we
shall certainly not hesitate to recommend you" (DAP:11/28/52). Responding
quickly, Armstrong answered Redfield's question: "Yes, though I would not insist on it." His "present feelings" had been strongly affected by a book review in
the *New Statesman* in which the writer, speaking of the Germans, "expressed irritation that they are 'always whoring after philosophy.'" That "barbed shaft"
had "struck home," and Armstrong decided that "unless I can do a bit better
than that, I had better stick to my last": "It is perhaps enough for a field worker
to be explicit about where he stands and leave till later heavy capital invest-
ments of time and energy into philosophical questions." Although he hoped
eventually to return to the Idoma, he thought he would do well "to have a
couple of years in some job where I could collect my thoughts, get my present
material organized and published, and get back into the mainstream of anthropological discussion" (DAP:12/15/52).

At the end of December Redfield forwarded Armstrong's letter, along with a
short memo, to Sherwood Washburn, then chair of the department at Chicago,
saying that "letters from Armstrong have shown in him progressive steadiness
and increasing disposition to work effectively" and, somewhat wishfully, that
the "Marxian and philosophical interests, once a little obsessive, have been
worked out of his system or solidly into his thinking." In this context Redfield
recommended that "we push him for a good job somewhere beginning next
Autumn probably" (DAP:RR/SW 12/29/52). A month later Armstrong was in
fact recommended, in slight preference to another Chicago candidate, for a position in the sociology department at Pennsylvania State College (now University) (DAP:Cole?/Mook 2/3/53).

In the meantime Armstrong continued his fieldwork in Agala, which was "seethingly alive" with dances, songs, masks, and fights. Writing to Murra late in January 1953, he reported that, "despite a stiff bout" with amoebic dysentery, he had finally made a "breakthrough into the center of Idoma culture." In addition to the "passage of time" and residence in the village (including Christmas and New Year's inside the family compound of his "best friend"), the key had been his "better command of language." He could now understand everything his neighbor Aji said and even converse with the paramount chief in the local dialect, albeit "a bit painfully." Although collecting texts was still a "slow business," like "chiseling the stuff out of granite," he had collected fifty pages, including a "very dramatic" text of the funeral inquest of the chief of the "red-light district of Oturkpo" that developed into a full-dress witchcraft trial. To have done this much in one of the "most difficult ethnological provinces in the world," where one dealt with a "really embittered particularism" of "sophisticated and intricate cultures" that changed every few miles, had done wonders for Armstrong's "self-esteem": given "tact and patience," he felt that there was "nothing I cannot find out" and was "pretty sure" that he "must come back again sometime" to do it (JMP:1/23/53).

For the immediate future, however, Armstrong decided to return to the United States. This, despite Murra's continuing grim picture of the job situation (including the firing of Jack Harris at the United Nations and of Gene Weltfish at Columbia) and his warning that "the investigation of all colleges and universities is just beginning: McCarthy & Jenner in the Senate and Velde in the house are heading the two committees and most [university] administrations have already collapsed and promised to cooperate" (JMP:JM/RA 2/23, 4/25/53; Price 2003:110–35, 154–63). Having declined the Atlanta job and having heard no "peep out of Redfield," Armstrong felt that the "most constructive thing" he could do, "careerwise," would be to "sit out next year," getting things into print, catching up with the literature, and "showing my face around," which, if all else failed, he could do from his family home in Cincinnati. And with that, on June 3 he embarked on the *Ile de France*, bringing with him his "best friend" from Agala, a young schoolteacher who had "a sharp eye for sociological fact," so he could "continue to work on the language" (JMP:5/3/53).

McCarthyist Apogee: The Federal Bureau of Investigation and the University of Chicago Department of Anthropology, 1953

On June 18, 1953, Armstrong wrote to Sol Tax from his parents' home in Cincinnati, reporting his return, "brimful of news from West Africa for all those who care to listen" and asking who was going to be around the department over the summer. On June 22 Tax, writing as associate dean of the Social Science Division, welcomed Armstrong back, indicating those in residence (Redfield,

Warner, and himself), those away (Washburn in Europe, Eggan in New Mexico), and those close by (Robert Braidwood, Donald Collier, Norman McQuown, and George Quimby) (DAP:6/18, 6/22/53). Armstrong also wrote to Redfield, saying that he had brought back his "Idoma assistant," who spoke a dialect different from the one he had studied intensively, and that he hoped to compare the assistant's district ("the closest thing to a 'kingdom'" in the Idoma Division) to the central Idoma districts. He also asked Redfield's advice on getting more material in shape for publication now that he had given a "final retouch in London" to his survey for Forde. He felt he had got "to the center of Idoma life this time," discovering "fundamental new things" until the day he left: as he was "literally moving his furniture out," a "high-ranking elder called me to his hut and offered to make me a witch." It was the "first real evidence" he had as to "whether there are conscious witches," but the gift was unfortunately forestalled when the village head was seen standing by, watching "very jealously." Armstrong also had a large body of linguistic material, including texts in Idoma and short reports on half a dozen other languages. Then, too, almost as an afterthought, he added that he wanted "to get around to revising my thesis for publication" (RRP:6/18/53).

As it happened, a meeting with Redfield was delayed, and in the meantime Redfield inquired whether Armstrong was writing a paper about Iturkpo, the largest center of the Idoma Division, which he was interested in for his work on the processes of urbanization.[4] He also asked Armstrong if he would be willing to meet with his daughter Lisa toward the end of September to serve as her informant on Iturkpo for "one chapter of her young people's book"—material that would "also serve my needs in some part" (RRP:7/22/53). Armstrong agreed to do so but reported also on a job possibility that had developed "with a fairly 'bush' denominational college at a salary I cannot scorn." Wondering "if somehow we might not do better than that" and suggesting perhaps Kenyon, or Antioch, or St. John's at Annapolis, he asked if Redfield might help: "I am [a] strange[r] to this business of job-seeking, and find it embarrassing." On the next day he wrote to Steward, asking if he knew of anybody "who needs a good Africanist or garden-variety social anthropologist" and would put in "a good word to him for me" (RRP:7/29/53; JSP:7/30/53).

Although there is a gap in the documentary record, it is clear that Redfield, who was to spend the fall term in Sweden, decided that Armstrong was the person who might fill in for him. Armstrong had once before taught one of Redfield's courses, had defended an intellectually challenging dissertation, had completed two years of fieldwork specifically lauded by the secretary of the British Colonial Social Science Research Council (DAP:Childers/RR 6/25/53),

---

4. Iturkpo is the Oturkpo of earlier letters and in postcolonial times is rendered Otukpo; similarly, Agala becomes Agila, and Ibo becomes Igbo.

and was interested in a wide range of anthropological, social scientific, and philosophical issues. More than that, he was admired and respected by his fellow students. True, there were some who knew him who, acknowledging his extensive knowledge and wide-ranging intellect, nevertheless felt in him more than a touch of intellectual arrogance. As one of them suggested, he liked to argue, and he was "quick to let you know that he was the authority" (PC).[5] But allowing for a bit of egoistic hyperbole, the general impression from informants who knew him is not inconsistent with his later remark to Redfield that he "never had difficulty attracting as many admiring disciples as I had time or inclination to entertain" (RRP:5/17/54). Although Redfield, who had served twelve years as dean of the Social Science Division, might well have assumed that the matter of his own temporary replacement was his to decide, later documents indicate that he consulted with Washburn (by cable) and with "other members of the department" (SSD:FE&ST/RT 9/9/53, SW/RT 9/17/53). On this basis he assured Armstrong that "his appointment would be forthcoming," and in response Armstrong sent a brief telegram on August 11, saying simply: "Many thanks stop I accept with pleasure" (RRP:8/11/53). A week later Redfield, who was leaving for Europe on August 27, replied briefly: "Good, I am glad you come. I shall leave to Tax or Washburn the formalities of your appointment," adding that "a little money" was "available to me to bring your Idoma here [from Cincinnati] should Lisa and you decide he is needed" (RRP:8/19/53).

Before those formalities could be processed, however, Armstrong's political past became an issue. That it did so at this time is not prima facie surprising. McCarthyism was approaching its apogee in September 1953, with particular emphasis on Communism in the universities (Patterson 1996:196–205; Schrecker 1986), and the University of Chicago, having previously that year been under attack, was bracing for another assault. In February several faculty members had been called to Washington to testify before the House Un-American Activities Committee; in early May the Illinois state senate passed two "Broyles Bills" similar to anti-Communist legislation vetoed by Governor Stevenson in 1951; in early June, at hearings in Chicago of the Jenner Senate Internal Security Subcommittee, eight employees of the university, four of them faculty members, refused to testify on Fifth Amendment grounds; in September internal administrative discussions were already under way as to how the university might effectively respond to the impending visit of the Reece Committee, which was investigating the tax-exempt status of philanthropic and educational institutions (MBT, vol. 43:5, 31, 99, 168; PPA:box 4, folder 1). During this period Redfield had been one of six members of a faculty committee appointed by Chancellor Lawrence Kimpton early in February to help

5. For an explanation of my handling of personal communications (PC), see "Oral and Written Informant Sources."

define the university's position regarding various degrees of faculty radical involvement and willingness to testify (PPA:box 2, folder 2, RR/LK 2/2/53). In
proceeding with the appointment, he must have assumed that Armstrong's
Marxist intellectual inclinations would not create a serious problem.

In late August, however, that assumption was proven incorrect when the FBI
informed Dean Tyler of the Social Science Division of Armstrong's Communist Party past. How the FBI found out about his impending appointment so
quickly is not clear, and Armstrong thought it "extraordinary" that they had intervened directly (RRP:RA/RR 10/5/53).[6] Be that as it may, he was called to
Chicago on September 3 to meet with Eggan and Tax, and it was in preparation
for this visit that he drafted a "brief statement of my intellectual and political
odessey [sic]" from his high school "brushes" with Italian Fascism, Roman
Catholicism, and Rochdale Consumer Cooperation, through his undergraduate study of Marxism, his prewar membership in the Communist Party, his postwar withdrawal, down to his "present position": that "my best contribution to
the hopes of mankind lies in my continued scientific work." While he could not
guarantee the results to anybody, he felt that his West African researches,
"apart from their value to anthropology as such," would "help Africa play an
increasing role in world affairs and . . . increase the self-respect of American
Negroes," thereby making a "real contribution to the growth of world democracy." In the present condition of military stalemate, war with Russia would be
an "act of madness" on the part of whichever side started it, and Armstrong

6. At a very late stage in the preparation of this essay I chanced to find evidence indicating that
Lloyd Warner may have played a role. Seeking FBI documents as illustrations, I came upon the one
reproduced in figure 4 as both typical (in the blacked-out passages) and specifically relevant (insofar as it referred to an event that figured in the adjoining text). It was only on the second reading
that the full significance hit home of the informant's statement that he had been very displeased to
have been assigned to the same cabin (as Armstrong) during the ocean voyage (FBI:SAC/director
10/20/50). Checking my file of Armstrong's correspondence for his account of the voyage on the
Cunard Parthia in the spring of 1950, I found his specific statement "I shared a cabin with Warner"
(11/28/77). While there is no direct evidence that Warner, three years later, was again the FBI's informant, the juxtaposition of these two documents suggests him as a likely candidate. It is perhaps
worth indicating that there is a certain adventitious character in my own access to these FBI materials. Inquiry to David Price, who over the years has managed to collect numerous such files relating to anthropologists (and has been helpful to me in many respects), indicated that he had not
come across material relating to Armstrong (cf. Price 2003 on the difficulties of obtaining full documentation under the Freedom of Information Act [FOIA]). Subsequently, however, thanks to
Jennifer Lewis, who had previously obtained Armstrong's file in connection with her own research,
I was able to consult his file, which was about two inches thick (nearly half of it collected by army
intelligence during his wartime service and later forwarded to the FBI). Unfortunately, the material I received contained no documentation specifically relating to the FBI intervention in 1953 (nor
any indication that information for this period was being withheld). One can only speculate as to
the nature of this hiatus, especially in view of Armstrong's statement, in a letter to Redfield, that
in 1944 "someone who saw it told me that their file on me was two feet thick" (RRP:10/30/53).

stood "fully ready to fight to protect the American people & nation from acts of madness on the part of the Russians or anyone else." In the meantime he proposed to "abstain from any political activity which by its provocative nature might endanger the conditions" for his scientific work. At the meeting itself, during which Dean Tyler was briefly also present, Eggan and Tax grilled Armstrong on the details of his memorandum: "We went into my past political activities and intellectual orientation—past and present—in utter detail." Armstrong later recalled that he left the meeting feeling that "the entire moral basis of social science in our Chicago *gemeinschaft*" had been destroyed and "walked down the Midway feeling that I had been raped; and I actually wept (it was the only time)" (GSP:RA/GS 4/24/78).

On September 9 Eggan and Tax forwarded to Dean Tyler "a recommendation by our department that Robert Armstrong be appointed an instructor for the coming academic year." In it they noted that the FBI intervention had made the appointment "controversial" and therefore "subject to approval by the Board of Trustees," and it was on this basis that Tax and Redfield (before he left) had agreed that Armstrong should be brought to Chicago "to ascertain the facts." After "exhaustive discussions" Eggan and Tax felt that "it is highly probable that Armstrong's loyalty to the United States is sincere, that his teaching in anthropology is not likely to suffer by reason of any of his political ideas, or that any students would be unfairly misled by him." Although they did not think of him as "a permanent member of the staff," he was "the best person available" to fill the immediate need of the department. As documentation, they reproduced a letter of recommendation by Redfield, "written earlier and for another purpose," praising Armstrong as "an established scholar and teacher" whose fieldwork met the high standards of contemporary British social anthropology. Accompanying their recommendation was a one-page typed statement by Armstrong in which he indicated that his Communist Party membership had lapsed in June 1948, "at which time I moved to another city" (in fact, to Puerto Rico), offered his combat service as evidence of his loyalty, and (in a penned addition) stated his willingness, if called before a "properly constituted government committee or board," to testify to "the statements made above" (SSD:FE&ST/RT 9/9/53, RA/ST 9/3/53).

Before the matter could be finally settled, however, an appointment form signed by the department chair had also to be forwarded, and on September 17 Washburn, by then back in Chicago, did so—but along with a memo indicating to Dean Tyler his serious reservations. When Redfield telegraphed him in early August, Washburn had suggested another student instead of Armstrong; but because he did not know "the present situation," he had assured Redfield he would "rely on your final decision," and, having done so, he had therefore signed the appointment form. However, he added that he had previously written to Redfield "asking for clarification" because he had "been told by one of our department that Armstrong was not to be trusted." No doubt preoccupied with his departure plans, Redfield did not reply. Failing the opportunity to "discuss this matter with those who made the decision," Washburn's "misgivings" remained (SSD:SW/RT 9/17/53).

Washburn's misgivings, along with the doubts of his unnamed colleague, were enough to kill Armstrong's chances. The next day Tyler returned the appointment form on the grounds that "the department is divided." Appointments likely to "involve public controversy" had to be taken up with the Board of Trustees, which was "willing to approve the appointment of faculty members who have the strong support of their departments as persons whose services are necessary, who have unique contributions to make to the University, and who are loyal even though they may be subject to public controversy and censure." But failing this "undivided support," Tyler felt "we cannot ask the Trustees to take action" (SSD:RT/SW 9/18/53). Three days later Washburn called Armstrong to tell him his appointment was not confirmed, followed by a short letter indicating that the department was "divided" in its opinion, "and the Dean's office was unwilling to push the matter under the circumstances" (GSP:SW/RA 9/21/53).

On September 25 Armstrong came again to Chicago for an interview with Washburn. It was not, he reported to Redfield, "a fortunate affair": he felt he was being "put on trial" by someone who knew little of his work and had not even looked at his dissertation but who nevertheless had "condemned" him for "intellectual arrogance" and for "deviousness." Regarding the first issue, Washburn had got "particularly excited" by Armstrong's apparently casual rejection of Catholicism in the political history, which, at Tax's suggestion, he had hurriedly prepared—a charge Armstrong countered in a letter to Eggan by citing his extensive readings in Catholic sources and a year-long college course in comparative religions (FEP:9/30/53). As to the charge of "deviousness," Armstrong insisted to Redfield that "from the beginning [I] neither hid nor advertized [sic] my political beliefs and affiliations," and he would have been perfectly willing to discuss them with Cole or Redfield if asked: "My fundamental criterion in these matters has always been that I am entirely willing to tell the whole truth to anyone who seems in fact interested in hearing the whole truth," not, however, to people who "seek for particular data in order to use them in such a way as to prevent the whole truth from being heard." He appreciated the courage Eggan, Tax, and Redfield had shown in "continuing to support an appointment that had been called into question over a political and philosophical position that [was] not [their] own." However, toward Washburn—whom he described to Murra as "a puritan who thinks he is a liberal but ain't"—Armstrong had a definite and lasting "feeling of grievance" (RRP:RA/RR 10/5/53; JMP:RA/JM 9/30/53).

Replying from Uppsala, Redfield attributed "the outcome of this affair" to

"the general state of American public feeling" and to the "unfortunate coinci-
dences of events in the Department—especially Dr. Washburn's return to the
position of central responsibility." But as much as he regretted it, he thought
Washburn "had the right and duty to withhold his approval" because "he did so
on a ground that is quite proper": "He had formed the judgment that you would
not be a reliable teacher." Although Redfield disagreed with Washburn, he
could not "from here and without knowledge of his line of thought, dispute it
with him." And while he himself found it "distasteful" to inquire into "a
scholar's political opinions" and had done so only when required to "as a result
of the information about you given to the Dean," he would have preferred that
Armstrong "had volunteered to us a statement of your connections with the
Communist Party." If Armstrong had done so, Redfield would still "have made
the recommendation": "But I would have felt better about you afterward." As
for the personal political history that Armstrong had written, Redfield preferred not to see it: "I do not like the writing of such documents." Granting that
Armstrong might feel "a little nervous" about the FBI's intervention, Redfield
encouraged him to accept the fact that they regarded him "as someone to be
watched": "Better you know it than you don't" (GSP:RR/RA 10/14/53).

Redfield insisted that his comments were not, "in any significant degree, a
qualification of my confidence in you," and Armstrong appreciated his "frank-
ness in telling me how you felt about my actions." He nevertheless felt called
upon to place his situation in a more realistic political context by recounting
the recent direct interference of the FBI in the election campaign for city council in Cincinnati, when an FBI report, "full of innuendo" about the city planning director, was published in the local newspapers, forcing his reformist political colleagues to denounce him retroactively without daring "to print a line
of criticism of the FBI." In such a political situation Armstrong felt he would
not have deserved Redfield's "thinking better" of him had he "volunteered a
statement of my former connections." Indeed, "such an act would have smacked
of servility and a lack of concern for the interests of certain of my friends and
former associates," including Redfield, who would have been placed in the
"same excruciating dilemma" that the Cincinnati city planning director's political colleagues had been. The "real shame" Armstrong felt was that "under
pressure" he had allowed himself to prepare two "signed statements" that "in
the hands of the FBI might have been used as evidence against close friends,"
whether or not "they were ever political associates."[7] Furthermore, it was not

7. Although neither statement contained names, other than those of world Communist leaders or the authors of Marxist books, Armstrong's acknowledgment of membership during certain
periods might possibly have been used to document the existence of a party group among fellow
students at the University of Chicago, as articles in the Chicago Maroon, Armstrong's correspondence with Murra, and informal oral evidence collected in the course of this research would suggest was in fact the case (cf. Coven 1992; Cohen 1993).

news to Armstrong that the FBI was watching him; they had been doing so since the early 1940s, when they "knocked me out of four different positions in the army," and again in 1950, when they tried to interfere with his Colonial Office appointment for fieldwork in Nigeria. What was new in the present situation was that "they have begun interfering with civilian employment." Armstrong had in fact discussed this with Dean Edward Levi of the Law School, who had "expressed his astonishment" that the FBI had taken the initiative but at the same time warned Armstrong that "as a University official connected with such cases" (a reference perhaps to his role as chair of the faculty committee on investigations) "he was in a position to find out why they so acted," and Armstrong should "not tell him anything that I wished kept confidential." In this context Armstrong offered Redfield a grim warning: "I believe that if the American universities do not resist this sort of political blackmail, they will soon wish they had!" (RRP:10/30, 11/10/53). In Armstrong's case the immediate effect of such "political blackmail" was his exile from the American university system.

McCarthyist Aftermath: Internal Academic Exile, 1954–1959

Redfield's wish that Armstrong had been more forthcoming about his Communist connections did not prevent his recommending him in response to an inquiry early in 1954 asking for candidates for a temporary appointment at Vassar College, for which Armstrong's close friend Murra was also being considered (RRP:Brown/RR 1/13/54). Although Redfield recommended Murra as an "exciting teacher who cares much about students and helps them to learn and to think," he indicated his choice would be Armstrong, who "had an excellent theoretical mind," had studied "in several social science fields," was "concerned with general education and inter-disciplinary work," and upon whose "judgment and good sense in dealing with students" Redfield had come to rely. However, there was "one circumstance about Armstrong that he has asked me to communicate to anyone who might consider him for employment": a "political attachment" in "earlier years" the "nature of which you will imagine" and that he would be "happy to discuss with you" (RRP:RR/Brown 1/18/54). When Vassar chose Murra (who had previously taught there), Armstrong was not dismayed: "It was 'his' job, and he needed it much worse than I do," since, unlike Armstrong, he had "no family to fall back on" (RRP:RA/RR 3/4/54).

Over the next several months there were "bubblings and mutterings from various directions" (JMP:RA/JM 2/12/54). But most did not develop, and those that did were forestalled at some point by the political issue, which Armstrong persisted in raising up front, even in the case of George Peter Murdock, whose political sympathies were strongly anti-Communist but who thanked Armstrong for laying his "political cards on the table" and "remained cordial"

5. Graduates of the Department of Anthropology at the Twenty-fifth Anniversary Reunion, November 1955. Armstrong is on the extreme left; next to him is St. Clair Drake (with crossed hands); then Sol Tax (with black-rimmed glasses); Fay-Cooper Cole (with white hair); and Fred Eggan (behind Cole's left shoulder, with shirt and tie). (Courtesy of the Special Collections Research Center, University of Chicago Library.)

(JMP:1/20, 4/20/54; cf. Price 2003:71–79). Writing to Eggan and to Redfield in March 1954, Armstrong reported that he had been proposed, "with strong backing from everyone who knew my work," for a position as senior anthropologist at the West African Institute for Social and Economic Research at Ibadan but had been turned down by the selection committee in London and told by a friend "who saw the correspondence" that it was "definitely the old political story." He had also been "told informally" that he was not among those selected for interview at Yale; had been informed by Atlanta University that there were "no openings at present"; had "heard nothing recently from New Brunswick"; and had received no answer in response to an inquiry to the University of Puerto Rico, which he felt might be related to the recent shooting attack by Puerto Rican nationalists in Congress and the tendency to blame things of this sort "on the left, no matter who does them" (FEP:RA/FE 3/15/54; RRP:RA/RR 3/4/54; JMP:4/20/54). In the face of these rejections Armstrong told Murra he was "very close to the conclusion that the practice for hire (in our generation) of the science of man and society is a hopeless dream." Living at home with his family in Cincinnati, where he worked in his father's business selling electrical equipment in the southern Ohio and Kentucky area, he decided that "if all else fails, why not use what we know about society to make a little money": "You take a lot less shit than you do in teaching, & it pays three times as well" (JMP:4/20/54).

During this period Armstrong continued to write on anthropological topics in his free time. There was an essay on "talking drums" in the Benue district in which he sought for the first time to link a "drum language" to a well-studied oral language "recorded in full phonemic orthography," with commentary on its sociological function (1954a; he was apparently unaware of Sapir's interest in this problem in the late 1920s [Darnell 1990:229–30]). A second essay, which he regarded as his most important early writing, was a re-presentation of "a highly dramatic event in the life of Oturkpo: the inquest into the death of a prominent politician, which developed into the witchcraft trial of a tribal elder." Published by Tax in the *American Anthropologist*, it included historical background, sociological identification of the "dramatis personae," a graphic representation of the mise-en-scène, and a complete text with extended commentary, in which Armstrong emphasized the lineage as a political rather than a kinship institution, an issue of "general theory" he felt American anthropologists had yet to appreciate (1954b; JMP:RA/JM 1/29/, 4/6/55; cf. Armstrong 1956). And there were others in process, including the (unpreserved) draft of a paper on "cultural patterns," in which he apparently pursued issues he had tried to deal with five years previously in "Society and Matter." Responding to criticism offered by Eggan, Armstrong agreed that he had not really defined pattern in "strictly material terms" and that he had only made "a couple of stabs in that direction to show the sort of definition I have in mind," suggesting that "a rigorously materialist definition of pattern would take me much farther into communication theory than I am yet able to go." Granting also that Eggan was correct in detecting a "personal equation" in his argument, he insisted that his own personal experiences were "perfectly good evidence" and that the main effect of the personal equation in this instance was to give "the passage in question" a "certain eloquence" that was absent when he discussed techniques of yam cultivation. If his response seemed "overly long and overly defensive," this reflected the fact that he got "rather lonesome writing like this in Cincinnati" and enjoyed "letting off steam" (FEP:RA/FE 2/26/54).

The theme of intellectual isolation was to be a recurrent one over the next several years. Writing to Redfield in early March 1954, Armstrong complained that "the thing that bothers me most is that lack of a clear work perspective makes it very difficult for me to plan my writing": "I keep postponing the really big job and concentrating instead on smaller things that seem more likely to 'sell'" (RRP:3/4/54). In response, Redfield wondered: "What, for you, is the 'really big job?' Do you feel like telling me?" (RRP:3/11/54). It was another two months before Armstrong answered, during which he had been "under a very considerable burden." His mother had died on April 8, and his father had been unable to attend the funeral due to coronary thrombosis and a duodenal ulcer, and Armstrong had taken on full responsibility for running his father's business. As he had done in Nigeria, Armstrong posed a series of life-choice options for the man whom, despite their political differences, he clearly thought of as his anthropological godfather. His own father's profitable business was there "for the taking" and would in fact provide "more time and resources for scientific work and writing than I would expect from academic work." What would be lacking, however, would be "local motivation or stimulation" for "hard, persistent, original work," which in Cincinnati would make him "different" and "unsociable" at best and "alarming" at worst. And it would take "great moral stamina" not to get absorbed in "the cheap excitement of the Business Roller-Coaster" while "dying an intellectual death, chocolate sundae in hand." But even if he tried, "for whom shall I work and write?" He was in the midst of "a severe crisis of morale on the question of audience." University faculties were already "scared" of him, and he doubted that "originality" was a "saleable commodity in academic quarters." If he wrote for students, what would he tell them to do, "considering my own experience"? As for posterity, would posterity "deserve my respect more than the present"? Lastly, he could write for himself, but it seemed too "expensive to entertain yourself with an activity that destroys or starves your social life" (RRP:5/17/54).

Turning then to "the really big job," Armstrong proceeded from "the more general to the more particular." What really interested him was "the workings of the human mind," as evidenced in systems of rationalizations for behavior, cultural patterns, phonemic systems, music, and worldviews. Whether manifest in "the opinions of a famous Idoma head-hunter or in those of a distinguished physical anthropologist," the "phenomenology of the mind" was the "connecting thread that binds together my somewhat diverse preoccupations." For the present, however, he hoped to "discover the Africans as people and to present them to the world" as "economic men," as "sentient people," as "thinking people," including "such matters as their world view and the relation between their languages and their thinking." Echoing (without reference) Franz Boas, Armstrong insisted that to do this required a "foundation in sound scholarship" in the "relevant African languages," including the collection and publication of "a lot of texts" relevant to "generalizations about African modes of thought and behavior"—the same sort of scholarship that was "well established in Chinese, Indian, ancient Greek and Egyptian studies" (cf. Boas 1905). The other "fundamental prerequisite" was "full and unreserved contact with Africans for long periods," without which they were likely to "hide the most important part of their culture" from the observer. In this context Armstrong's immediate "big job" was to get "my texts published and my dictionary brought fully into shape and published." In "odd moments" he would write various articles of "a more synthetic nature" and, if he had "time on my hands," improve and publish his thesis—and then "I must get back to Africa." Modeling himself on Marcel Griaule, Armstrong hoped to do "the kind of job in West African studies I have sketched above" and do it "rather better than he has done," but only if he could find a "sound financial basis for such a career." During "the next several months or year" he must decide how he would "spend the next twenty years or so." He could "no longer afford to be two or three years in Africa, out of touch with the day-to-day business of our profession, and then face the necessity of hunting again for a job." Although his father wanted him to take over the business, he hoped instead for "a really substantial alternative" and with this in mind turned to Redfield "for help in finding it" (RRP:5/17/54).

Over the longer run Armstrong's career can be seen as an attempt to pursue the ambitious Boasian agenda he sketched to Redfield. However, Redfield's response was hardly what Armstrong must have hoped for. After reading the letter "many times" Redfield encouraged Armstrong to take over his father's business as the means to achieve his broader goals. While it was clear that Armstrong "truly cared" about Africanist research as a means to "understanding the human mind," Redfield recalled many contributors to science and scholarship who did their research "without the classroom and the immediate presence of colleagues." As to audience, Armstrong should write "for me, and for hundreds who are interested in African peoples." Granting that it might be better for his scientific work if he "worked and wrote within an academic community," what Armstrong was asking for was not practical: "The positions now offered to young anthropologists" did not provide the assurances (continuity of employment, money for research) that Armstrong demanded. Better therefore to choose his father's business, "with the leisure it brings" (RRP:5/20/54).

Apparently disappointed by his anthropological godfather's advice, Armstrong did not respond for a month, when he reported that he had been formally offered a one-year appointment at Wayne State University in Detroit. While he felt that he enjoyed "the full confidence of the anthropological staff" and had been told that it was "unnecessary" for him to come to Detroit for the job interview, he had insisted, because "it would be very silly for me to leave my work at home without a clear political understanding." He was, however, "a bit apprehensive" because in the same phone conversation he had been asked to provide eight letters of reference. So he asked Redfield to write "a general character reference" that would help the administration "to look at me before they look at the stereotype" (RRP:6/19/54). When he phoned Redfield for some "last minute advice" prior to the interview, Redfield said that his own letter "had brought the matter out" and that Armstrong was "not bound to force information on them which they did not ask for." As a result, the interview was "a very coy game politically." Although Armstrong left thinking things had gone well, the chair called ten days later and "quite apologetically put the $64 question," saying the dean felt "the law requires it," to which Armstrong an-

swered "yes" (i.e., he admitted his former membership in the Communist
Party). Even then, the chair felt that "the thing could still be arranged," and
on July 12 Redfield, assuming that it had been, sent a brief note hoping that
Armstrong "would enjoy your work at Wayne" (JMP:RA/JM 7/16/54; RRP:RR/
RA 7/12/54). But by the end of the month the appointment fell through, despite letters of recommendation Armstrong had solicited from both Herskovits
and Steward (MHP:MH/E. Schuler 7/29/54; JSP:JS/ES 7/16/54), apparently
because "rumor" had reached Wayne that the Chicago department, confronted
with a similar situation, had withdrawn an appointment the previous year
(RRP:ES/RR 8/13/54). "Fed up with this sort of thing" and wondering how "social science, of all disciplines, can flourish in this atmosphere," Armstrong
resolved not to make "more applications for positions in this country," though
he would consider appointments that "came to him" without application on
his part, as had been the case in 1947 with Atlanta University (RRP:RA/RR
7/31/54).

   In the spring of 1955 it seemed that perhaps such a volunteered position
might materialize. Armstrong reported to Redfield that there had recently been
"correspondence and rumors" from Atlanta "about my going back there." Three
weeks later another possibility was broached in a letter from Steward, who had
left Columbia for a research professorship at the University of Illinois, where he
had been joined by Eric Wolf. Anticipating a second opening the following
year, Steward had suggested Armstrong as a "possible candidate" (JSP:JS/RA
4/20/55). By this time looking forward to "a chance to teach again," Armstrong
described to Steward his current work: a paper on recent African research provoked by his "accumulated irritations at the unreality of most of the papers
given at the Princeton and Chicago Africa conferences last year" (cf. JMP:RA/
JM 11/9/53); another intended to establish "a culture type, centering around
the lineage-corporations, which is common in Africa and which is still not too
well understood"; and a third on "the nature of the difference between society
and culture" (JSP:RA/JS 4/25/55). But although Redfield responded positively
to the Illinois department chair's request for an evaluation (RRP:RR/J. Hulett
5/9/55), it turned out that "all things considered, it would not be feasible" to
attempt Armstrong's appointment. The best Steward could offer was the possibility of inclusion in another large-scale research project for which he was seeking funding in the hope that "in three years the national climate would be im-
proved sufficiently to give you a better break" (JSP:5/11/55; cf. JMP:RA/JM
6/4/55).

   In August 1955 Armstrong's "better break" arrived quite suddenly when the
Atlanta University anthropologist Morris Siegel resigned and on the same day
Armstrong received a telegram offering him a five-year appointment as associate professor. He had already "had the political matter out" with the president,
the dean, and the department eighteen months before when he was still

6. Robert Redfield at his desk in 1956. (Courtesy of the Special Collections Research Center, University of Chicago Library.)

actively looking for academic employment, and Armstrong decided to take "the gamble" when his younger brother now agreed to quit his job in order to help in their father's business. He had not had the confirming letter in his hand for half an hour before he was reminded that "we live in a police state" by a telephone call from the FBI, ostensibly in regard to a government employee on whom they were running a security check. When two agents later came to his house (the first time in his life that the FBI had met him "face to face"), he gave the man "a clean bill of health"—although really, he suspected, they "were just giving me the once-over." Concluding that he must have "passed their exam," he anticipated "no further trouble" and looked forward to working on "my Idoma stuff" in an institution where there were usually "half a dozen African students." It was, he wrote to Murra, "a great relief to be back in anthropology" (FEP:RA/FE 8/26/55; RRP:RA/RR 8/26/55; JMP:RA/JM 9/8, 10/25/55).

After more than three years out of academia, Armstrong found that Atlanta looked much better than it had during his previous year there. Armstrong was reasonably well paid ($5,000 a year and $700 for summer school), had a relatively light teaching load ("only nine hours a week, of which six are graduate courses and all are anthropology"), as well as the expectation of tenure after five years. As he told Steward, "there was a lot of freedom" there, "both in the civil liberties sense and in the sense that the school is not puritanical." Furthermore, the university was now on the "main line" in that an "astonishing number of interesting visitors come through town," including recently the director of recruiting and training of the Gold Coast government. Armstrong himself was able to arrange for Roy Abraham, his African linguist friend (who regarded Armstrong as "his true successor"), to come to Atlanta for six months "to teach me Yoruba and other African languages" (JSP:RA/JS 5/2/56; JMP:RA/JM 5/5/56). And as the "Faculty Items" in the *Atlanta University Bulletin* testify, Armstrong was one of the more active faculty when it came to reporting local, regional, and national disciplinary or other activities, including his baritone supporting roles in *Manon* and *The Consul* at the Atlanta Academy Theatre (AUA:AUB [12/57]:21).

But there was a downside. The "race situation" made it "hard—though by no means impossible—to have a good social life" (although Armstrong also mentioned to Murra of "having had a love affair with a girl, believe it or not"). But what bothered Armstrong even more was that there was "nobody, black or white, who gives a tinker's damn about Africa, linguistics, theory, international politics"; he still felt like "a race horse in a small pasture" (JMP:5/5/56). When at the end of his first year back at Atlanta Steward broached again the possibility of Armstrong joining his three-year team project on "cross-cultural regularities," which the Ford Foundation had recently funded for $250,000, Armstrong responded immediately: "I guess that the next logical step is for you to make me a concrete offer," which he could use to request a leave of absence. In the meantime he was off to Harvard to join fourteen other social scientists and lawyers for a Social Science Research Council Training and Research Institute on Law and Social Relations, where the institute was "paying my summer salary" (JSP:RA/JS 5/2/56; cf. JMP:RA/JM 5/5/56).

It soon became evident, however, that Armstrong's anthropological interests had developed along lines that did not articulate well with Steward's scientistic comparativism. For Steward, ethnography was not an end in itself but a preliminary stage in a comparative and problem-oriented research agenda seeking to discover "whether certain acculturative factors, which seem potentially to operate throughout the world, do not combine in a limited number of ways to produce new cultural types." He was therefore doubtful about Armstrong's suggestion that Abraham might somehow be involved in the project and posed as a "direct question" whether Armstrong's "evident interest in language groups in West Africa really bears on our central problem" (JSP:6/30/36). By contrast, the comparative sociological concerns of Armstrong's doctoral dissertation were in fact receding into the background, and the more classically Boasian linguistic interests manifest in his field correspondence from Nigeria were coming more to the fore. Anxious to spin his linguistic interests into the orbit of Steward's global comparativism, Armstrong resisted the implication that they would distract from general comparative problems. He had only a "*minor* interest in language groups as such" but was primarily concerned with "using them as a means of communication with people." Insisting on his unusual competence in "West African tone languages," his "healthy respect" for the "subtlety and intricacy of African thought," and his "hundreds of personal contacts in Nigeria" and recalling the comparative approach of his doctoral dissertation, he felt that he could "do a first rate job with your problem in the West-African area": "First of all, and before everything else, my interest is in theory and problem." But at the age of thirty-nine he was experiencing "a difficulty elsewhere": he wanted more money than Steward was proposing, and in "a good West African phrase" urged Steward to consider whether "twice the job does not merit something like twice the salary" (JSP:7/26/56).

Although negotiations continued through the early fall, in the end Steward felt it would be "much wiser from the point of view of your future and the effective operation of the program if you continue your position in Atlanta" (JSP:11/15/56). Even before that, however, Armstrong, who had begun working intensively with Abraham, had himself decided that perhaps he did not "wholly understand the plan of the project," which he had read "only once, in [Steward's] office, 15 months ago" (JSP:9/26/56). And as he worked with Abraham—in what is in retrospect clearly one of the determinative experiences of his later career—he became "even more committed to a deep study of West Africa." The number of people who were "able and willing to learn West African tone languages and to use them in a human way to talk to real people in a field situation" was "very limited." As one of them, Armstrong felt he should better "see if somehow I cannot find money to do such a study," for which Atlanta had said they would be willing to give him a year and a half's leave (JSP:RA/JS 11/20/56; cf. Armstrong 1959a).

It was three more years, however, before Armstrong was able to escape the "limbo" of Atlanta. In the meantime he was pulled this way and that, professionally, as he pursued, somewhat opportunistically, various research and career possibilities that might enable him to enter the anthropological "big leagues." Writing to Murra early in March 1957, he reported that he had been "doing a lot of psychological fussing and fuming" since the meeting of the American Anthropological Association in Los Angeles, where he had given a paper in a panel on primitive law. His father had died shortly before, leaving him, on the one hand, "looking for a father image" and, on the other, half of an estate that was large enough that he could "retire right now" if he lived "very modestly" and "much better" if he moved to Europe. Or (with his previous summer seminar in mind) he might go to Harvard and take a law degree and combine anthropology and law. Or he might get his Atlanta job redefined as a "research job," as Major Abraham had suggested, but this would require him to "get over the feeling of being punished" by being there. Or perhaps something might develop from the two "nibbles" he got at the Los Angeles meetings, one from his friend Ira Reid, now at Haverford, and one from Berkeley. When neither of these came to anything, he wondered whether he should not rejoin the family business inherited by his brother, where he could make a "third more money for a third less work." But after checking out the Cincinnati situation he decided to stay at Atlanta and once again resolved to make "no further applications": he had done "nothing since 1953 but beg for jobs and grants," and he was "fed up to the gills." Even so, he made a trip to New Paltz, New York, to be interviewed for a job for which Murra had recommended him (JMP:3/3, 5/14, 6/1, 7/9/57).

Despite this professional indeterminacy Armstrong continued to pursue his Idoma interests along lines that were increasingly linguistic and textual rather than comparative sociological. In order to "help along" the nibble from Berkeley, Armstrong initiated a correspondence with Kroeber, whom he had encountered at the Philadelphia meetings of the International Congress of Anthropological and Ethnological Sciences in September 1956 (Armstrong 1956). Several months later Armstrong sent Kroeber a number of texts in two different Idoma dialects with the hope that Kroeber might advise him regarding their publication. In addition to several relating to legal disputes there were three written by "the Idoma school-teacher whom I brought back to Cincinnati," who had lived with Armstrong's family until he took the job at Atlanta. Two of them—a description of the life and death of an Agila boy and a "very frank discussion" of "love" by three Agila adolescent boys—were "so personal that it may be impossible to publish them." They had in fact been demanded back by his friend when the two exchanged "hot words about three years ago," but Armstrong thought that now his friend would very likely give permission. While he felt very strongly that "nothing should be done with them that would hurt or offend" his collaborator, he felt "just as strongly that they are absolutely unique historical and scientific documents, obtained at great cost to me, to the British Government, and to him," and since "they were written with my help and could not have come into existence in any other way[,] I think that they belong to neither of us, but to science" (AKP:RA/AK 2/2/57).[8]

That said, Armstrong told Kroeber that he already had fifty texts in the Oturkpo dialect and another forty in that of Agila that he wished to prepare for publication in a "really scholarly" manner modeled on that of "classics scholars." Taking advantage of the "grammatical foundation" laid by Major Abraham, he was working on a dictionary of the Oturkpo dialect and had a glossary of the Agila that would make possible a "full-scale grammatical and phonological comparison of the two," something that had "not been done for any Nigerian language." In contrast, his ethnographic work had given him only "spotty materials, rather like a collection of 'candid' snapshots." Although these would fit into a general ethnographic description at "key points," his fieldwork was "essentially incomplete": "Eighteen months is simply not enough for an African group." The "only unified book" he could write on the Idoma, although "scientific in some very important senses," would be "an essentially personal document" (AKP:2/2/57).

Apparently in response to a note from Kroeber encouraging him to reconsider his reluctance, Armstrong worked through his notes and texts and decided that he had "been so overwhelmingly impressed with what I don't have that it has been hard for me to think of using what I do have": "When it comes right down to it, I have a good deal of material." On this basis he outlined a "standard monograph" on the Idoma, ranging from ecology and history through language and thought, technology and economy, thence to various topics in social organization, and on to "life cycle" (including "relations between the sexes, and basic personality structure"), funerals, religion, "witchcraft, oracles and magic," "art, literature, music, dance, drums, etc.," winding up finally with "acculturation." To which Kroeber replied: "Well, you've outlined a good book. Now why not proceed to write it. Remember, nobody ever knows *everything* about *anything*" (AKP:RA/AK 3/15/57, with note by AK). But while Armstrong agreed to "get this book well under way" back in Cincinnati the next summer, he seemed more concerned with the publication of his texts, even "if it has to be done by main force": "I am just old fashioned enough that I think they ought to be in print, too" (AKP:RA/AK 5/14/57).

Although he did "a lot of work" on his Idoma materials at his home in Cincinnati throughout the summer of 1957, by that fall Armstrong's momentum had slackened. The "heart of the problem," he confided to Murra, was the

---

8. Fifteen months later, when Murra mentioned a festschrift in process for Paul Radin, Armstrong volunteered these texts, with the caution that they "must not be published in a place where the Idoma are apt to see them soon," and it would be better "if the translation were into German, since not even the missionaries in Idoma read German these days" (JMP:5/22/58). To the best of my knowledge, these texts (like those of several essays previously mentioned as in process in this period) have not been preserved.

need to "decide what big thing we really want to do with the second half of our lives"; until this was decided, "we will continue to drift, and no organization of our work or emotions will be possible." Although his own "short-term goal" was to get his "Idoma stuff written up," even that would "be much easier when I get the broad picture straight"—and as late as April 1958 he still had managed to do "precisely nothing" on his Idoma material (JMP:10/13/57, 4/23/58).

Exactly what was to be contained within the frame of that "broad picture" Armstrong did not specify. But there are hints in his correspondence that the problem of his relation to the Communist movement as embodied in the Soviet Union must have loomed in the background of his attempt to define the meaning of the second half of his own life. On February 25, 1956, Nikita Khrushchev, the first secretary of the Communist Party of the Soviet Union, delivered a "secret speech" on the "cult of personality" to the party's twentieth congress, the first since Stalin's death in 1953, in which he recounted the "extreme methods," "mass repressions," and "brutal acts of violation of Socialist legality" of Stalin's dictatorship (Khrushchev 1962). By May 5 the contents of the speech were widely known, and Armstrong, in writing to Murra, commented on "the intense debate going on over the meaning of the Russian business," a "spectacle" that he could not watch with "detachment" (cf. Howe and Coser 1962:490–93). Analogizing it by implication to similar events in the career of Ivan the Terrible, whose recently published correspondence with Prince A. M. Kurbsky he had been reading, Armstrong described the "grand monarch's" letters as "a unique piece of self-revelation," the "reverberations" of which "into more recent centuries are obvious and fascinating": "I am very anxious to have a couple of days with you in which to consider the state and prospects of the world—and of ourselves!" (JMP:5/5/56).[9]

While Murra's answer made no mention of the "Russian business," there is fragmentary evidence of Armstrong's continuing concern with the "broad picture." Writing to Steward in the aftermath of the Suez Crisis and the crushing by Soviet tanks of the Hungarian Revolution, he enclosed a letter (unpreserved in the Steward papers) he had written to the New York Times about "this damnable international crisis, which as you can perhaps imagine, has bothered me quite a lot" (JSP:11/20/56). And a year later, after contributing a paper on West Africa to a session entitled "Social Stratification and Evolutionary Theory" organized by Eleanor Leacock for the Chicago meeting of the American Anthropological Association, he commented on how "we have all become very

---

9. Kurbsky, a leading general and one-time favorite of Ivan IV, defected to the Polish-Lithuanian forces in Livonia in 1564 and over the next fifteen years wrote a series of five letters to Ivan in which he charged him with "laying waste" his own land and "destroying" his own subjects, "sparing not even suckling children," to which Ivan responded twice, once with a 170-page epistle attacking Kurbsky's "betrayal" and "treacheries" (Fennell 1955:245).

careful, qualified and qualifying Marxists": the "only real unifying thread was a sort of nostalgia for Marx which most of the participants shared and were careful to cover over with thick layers of subordinate clauses" (JMP:RA/JM 1/19, 4/28/58). All of which, considered in the context of later correspondence, is consistent with, if not confirmation of, a longer-run political and anthropological trajectory in which a political movement from Stalinism to liberalism was paralleled by an anthropological move from Marxist materialist approaches to comparative social organization toward a Boasian linguistic and textual particularism. The broader unifying framework was the study of mentalities and worldviews, and the practical anthropological goal was the solution of "the world's problems of race prejudice and cultural prejudice" (RRP:RA/RR 7/20/58).

By July 20, 1958, Armstrong seems finally to have made the decision that, insofar as it was given (or left) to him to choose, was to define the rest of his anthropological career. After a lapse of three years he turned again to Redfield, as he had on previous occasions when contemplating his future life course. He had just submitted a research proposal to the New World Foundation that he described as "merely one version of something I have been dreaming about ever since being in Africa: to do a really serious study of West African thought—or at least of the thought of one or two groups." To contextualize it Armstrong referred Redfield to his recent review of a "pioneer monograph of absolutely fundamental importance" by Marcel Griaule and Germaine Dieterlen on the "graphic signs" of the several Sudanese peoples (notably, the Dogon and the Bambara), which suggested that "these 'primitive' Africans," commonly assumed to be "incapable of abstract thought," were in fact "struggling with the philosophical problem of how something could proceed from nothing" (Armstrong 1957:139). In previously sending Murra a copy of the same review, Armstrong had felt it necessary to offer reassurance that he was not "getting spiritual on you" (JMP:RA/JM 10/5/57); in writing to Redfield, however, it became clear that he intended to make such a study his life work. His only criticism of the Griaule group was that they had been "spending more than twenty years on such a project before they get around to studying the languages involved," "an approach [that] does not deserve the name of science." Against this he posed to Redfield Major Abraham's most recent publication, the *Dictionary of Modern Yoruba*, which Armstrong was reviewing for the journal *Africa*. He spoke of it as a product of "incredible" labor that was at the same time "a work of peace," insofar as it contributed to "the development of understanding between peoples" (Armstrong 1959a:92). He and Abraham, he told Redfield, formed "a sort of mutual admiration society": "I regard him as a giant of African studies [and] he regards me as the only person alive who is both willing and able to either make use of this sort of book . . . or to go on to make further such studies." Previously, Armstrong had been "blocked emotionally and administratively" from taking on the job, but it now seemed to him that West Africa was "the epicenter of the world's problems of race prejudice and culture prejudice" and that a "basic part of the solution is the discovery and description of the real, very strange culture of this region" (RRP:7/20/58).

By way of further explication Armstrong commented on an essay Redfield had recently published in which he had imagined a meeting with a stranger to life on earth who interrogated him about the war that "is now cold and might get hot," which seemed to the stranger better called "mutual suicide." When Redfield replied "No" to the stranger's query whether he felt "more secure" now that "he" had the H-bomb, the stranger suggested that "young college people" might find a better way than threatening each other with "mutual destruction," seeking instead common interests "in keeping alive." This, because they were "more experienced" than Redfield, insofar as "they start knowing not only what you know but what you did." Following an exchange on the nature of progress, which Redfield "used to believe in" but seemed now to him like "going ahead and backward at one and the same time," the stranger asked, "Did you ever have a conference on the good life?" After proposing five agenda items (including the limits of population, the nature of growth, the definition of a good standard of living, "the right relation of man to the cosmos," and whether the "frontiers of human enterprise" were "always outward or sometimes inward?"), the stranger departed. Redfield was left alone in the sunset to ponder what he should have said in a message to young people regarding the similarities and differences between "we Americans" and the Russians, including notably the freedom that gave "us" the "larger share of power and the duty to extricate us all from the predicament" of ultimate mutual destruction, striving for the growth of "the human spirit . . . up to the last moment of possibility" (Redfield 1958).

Armstrong later recounted how, when he "made a flying tour of Europe" in the fall of 1958, at Oxford he informed Evans-Pritchard that Redfield was dying of leukemia, and "if you have anything to say to him, you had better do it quickly." After a "full minute" thinking, Evans-Pritchard had said simply, "He is a liberal of the *worst* sort" (GSP:RA/GS 4/24/78). In sharp contrast, Armstrong had previously told Redfield that he had read "Talk with a Stranger" several times and had since "read parts of it to my classes." It was so "beautifully written" that "it makes me want to cry"—not for anything it "says directly" but because it "comes drifting into an unresolved issue that affects me very personally, affects you, and, I believe, affects American social science": "It seems to me that our world is dying of intellectual cowardice and stupidity in key places." As his own contribution to the solution of this problem, Armstrong hoped to contribute to a dialogue with the Russians. He was not "intellectually afraid" of them, and he thought they could be "talked to," although he had "no confidence that my compatriots would understand it": "It is [a] world in which people would rather hit than discuss. And if they don't dare hit the enemy, then vulnerable folk in their own camp will do" (RRP:7/20/58).

But as Redfield had said, the main thing was "to survive—survive as a personality and intellectually, as well as physically." And for Armstrong this meant "going back into the field in 1959–60 [even] if I have to pay my own way," and he would have resigned, had not Atlanta University already given him permission. Although he had been made full professor and acting chair of his department, he felt as if he had been "now five years in exile," "in isolation from anyone who had the remotest idea" of what he was talking about. If he thought he was "doing good" at Atlanta, "it might be different," but he saw no reason to change "the judgment" he had formed back in 1948: that "a segregated *universitas* is a contradiction in terms"—a contradiction that, in both white colleges and black, "produces a continuous stream of pathological results, both in staff and students" (RRP:RA/RR 7/20/58).

Despite Armstrong's complaint to Redfield that he had "just about all I can take of being refused grants by foundations," including the rejections of applications that he made in 1957 to the Ford Foundation and to the Social Science Research Council, he did not, in the event, have to pay his own way back into the field (RRP:7/20/58; JMP:RA/JM 3/3, 11/2/57). Early in April 1959 he was able to report to Murra, who had just received a grant-in-aid from the Social Science Research Council for research in Peru, that the council had also awarded him a faculty fellowship for research in 1959–60 on "law and legal thinking in Nigeria." Armstrong hoped that "the Thaw" (the uneven and halting liberalization of the Soviet Union during the Khrushchev era) had perhaps "finally commenced here, too." Paradoxically, however, what had also "finally commenced" was the belated inclusion of Africa in the "area studies" programs, stimulated not by "thaw" but by continuing cold war tensions (Staniland 1991:25–31; cf. Rauch 1955; Berman 1983). Although as late as 1953 there was still only one university African studies center (at Northwestern, under the leadership of Herskovits), the movement toward self-government and eventual independence and the threat of Soviet influence in emerging "new nations" had by the later 1950s stimulated a growing governmental and foundation encouragement of initial stirrings within the academy (Gershenhorn 2004:169–200). In March 1957 this academic involvement was marked by a meeting of thirty-five scholars and specialists in New York City as an Ad Hoc Committee for the African Studies Association, to which, as Armstrong reported to Murra, he had been invited—"and they are paying the whole freight" (JMP:5/3/57; *African Studies Bulletin* 1[1]:3). Who, exactly, "they" were is not clear; but it is clear that Armstrong by this time was not without connections among the emerging elite of social scientific Africanists. Among these was Herskovits, the founding president of the African Studies Association who in 1954 had written on Armstrong's behalf to Wayne State (MHP:MH/E. Schuler 7/29/54) and may well have played a role when the Social Science Research Council (a year prior to establishing an African studies area committee) decided after all to support Armstrong's earlier proposal to study Yoruba language and law (SSRC

Annual Reports, 1958–59:71, 1959–60:18). Thus it was that in July 1959 the *Atlanta University Bulletin* was able to report that Dr. Robert G. Armstrong, professor of sociology and anthropology, had received "a grant of $6000 from the Social Science Research Council for the 1959–60 academic year" to study "the language and law of the Yoruba people of Western Nigeria" and that prior to his departure for Nigeria in October he was to spend "several weeks in London" consulting with Abraham, an "outstanding authority on African languages" (AUA:AUB [7/59]:22, [12/59]:20).

Armstrong and the Federal Bureau of Investigation, 1956–1959

A short time before he sailed for England Armstrong had his second face-to-face confrontation with the FBI, this time as the subject of investigation rather than as character witness on behalf of another. Over a period of months in 1956 and 1957 the Atlanta office had several times been authorized to "interview" him. However, each authorization was for only thirty days, and all of them had lapsed because the directives from J. Edgar Hoover specified that any interview must be carried on "when the subject is alone and off campus" (lest a conversation between whites attract attention in an all-Negro institution), which in Armstrong's case was impossible, since he lived in a dormitory on campus (FBI:6/12/56, 2/8, 3/27, 4/5/57). However, a year after the attempt to interview him had been abandoned, the case was reopened in March 1959 "in the light of current international tensions." By this time Armstrong had moved to a rooming house off campus, and after a further series of failed attempts a "surprise interview" was finally conducted by two agents on August 31, 1959 (FBI:3/5, 7/29, 9/3/59). In the course of the interrogation Armstrong admitted he had been a member of the Communist Party in the 1940s and that he was last active in 1948, when he "and some other Communist Party members" worked in the Progressive Party in Atlanta. Although he had been in contact with former comrades at Chicago in the early 1950s, he had never been asked to rejoin and would have refused had he been approached. He had always been loyal to the United States, and neither he nor any of his comrades had favored the violent overthrow of its government, nor was this, in his experience, the policy of the Communist Party. However, if he had not already left the party in 1948, he would have done so after Khrushchev's denunciation of Stalin in 1956. As supporting evidence he offered the agents a copy of the letter he had written to the *New York Times* in November 1956 (presumably, the one of which he sent Steward a copy at the time), the text of which was subsequently incorporated into his FBI file as a six-page single-spaced addendum to the report of the interview.

Entitled "Toward a Free World," Armstrong's letter was dated November 9,

1956, five days after Russian troops and tanks suppressed the Hungarian Revolution and twelve days after the beginning of the Suez Crisis, when Israel, supported by Britain and France, invaded Egypt in response to President Nasser's prior seizure of the Suez Canal and his earlier pan-Arabist threats against the existence of Israel (Patterson 1996:305–8). The letter opened with the suggestion that it would be a long time, after the action of the Russian "oriental despots," before "their professed love of peace" would ever again appear "sincere." Faced with "serious and widespread unrest," they would be "strongly tempted" to undertake "a military adventure, to divert people's minds from their domestic difficulties," and, unfortunately, the Middle East offered them "exciting possibilities." With this introduction Armstrong turned to the situation of countries like Egypt, facing an "excruciating problem of over-population based on a primitive type of hand agriculture" and unable to develop without outside aid. Since there was "no economic foundation for democracy," such societies were "almost inevitably governed by some sort of dictator," who, like Nasser, found it easy to divert his people's attention "to a hated symbol outside." At the same time, increasing awareness of "the contrasting and enviable status of Europeans" encouraged the peasants and the city poor to turn to "exaggerated nationalist movements" in order to "recapture some shreds of self-respect." Into this "dynamite factory" the Soviets were now moving, and if it was "obvious to us that Russia would treat Egypt as she treats Hungary," it was not obvious to an Egyptian.

Faced with this situation, the United States must in the first place "stand up to the Soviet Union," making clear that "we are ready to destroy her factories and armies" should she push beyond the "present line of military demarcation." But to take such a stand was only the beginning. In addition it would be necessary to embark on "an imaginative, positive program to give hope to the world at large": "The time has come to knock down the economic and ethnic barriers that have segregated great sections of mankind into impossible slums and that have prevented the full development of modern world industry." This would be accomplished by declaring, "through the United Nations," that "*the entire surface of the world is open and free to every human being*" to migrate "wherever he pleases" and to become a "full citizen of the country where he chooses to live." Freedom of personal movement, however, "must be accompanied by the removal of tariff barriers and the opening of the world to really free trade." Just as the repeal of the Corn Laws in England in the 1830s marked the beginning of a century of British industrial supremacy, the removal of such barriers would "inaugurate a true American century in which our pre-eminence would benefit the whole world." And if the competition of a "real world market" might require adjustments in the American economy, in the face of "Armageddon" their cost must be measured against the adjustments that "a third world war will force upon us." Finally, Armstrong's program "must be accompanied by really large-scale capital investment in the backward countries from European and American sources of capital" to "extend the benefits of capitalism to the whole world," in the process "turning the left flank of the Soviet Union" by requiring her to "open Siberia and Central Asia to large-scale settlement and development by her neighbors, the Chinese, Indians, and Arabs." If with "courage and vigor" we conceded "full human equality and full opportunity" to "our illiterate brothers," we might "enrich ourselves and the whole world in the process," bequeathing to "our children and grandchildren of the twenty-first century a civilization instead of a heap of rubble."

Four decades on, this remarkable text, written in early November 1956 and handed over to agents of the FBI on the last day of August 1959, begs reflection on a number of issues of motivation. Without venturing into the realm of depth psychology, one can suggest plausible motivational scenarios that may facilitate understanding of these two critical moments in Armstrong's life trajectory. Although the following comments are informed by and I think consistent with the evidence of available textual material and the testimony of informants who knew Armstrong, it must be acknowledged that they reflect also my own disillusionary experience of the events of 1956 and my own face-to-face encounters with the FBI in two "surprise interviews," the first on August 2, 1956, when I "refused to affirm or deny" membership in the Communist Party "or to furnish information concerning past Communist Party activities," and the second on December 19, 1961, when I was "polite to agents" but declined to discuss my "past activities or present sympathies." Although these experiences differed in outcome from Armstrong's, I would like to think that they have been the basis for empathic understanding rather than unreflective projection.[10]

From the time he joined the Communist Party in 1939 Armstrong's belief and action in the political world had been structured by a master narrative in which Marxism of the Soviet variety was intertwined with a vision of the Soviet role in the liberation of humanity and the achievement of a Communist utopia. When he left the Communist Party in 1948 it was not because of loss of faith in Marxism or the historical mission of the Soviet Union so much as a reflection of his dismay at the aridity of contemporary Marxist discussion in Soviet and American Communist discourse. The Khrushchev revelations early in 1956 were more profoundly disillusioning insofar as the Stalinist past of the Soviet Union was concerned, but they still left open the possibility of future reform and the eventual triumph of a more humane socialism in the Soviet Union. It was that flickering future promise that was finally crushed under the

---

10. The quotations are from the agents' reports in my own FBI file. In addition to the two face-to-face interviews, there was a third brief telephone interview in the fall of 1967, after I had turned in my draft card at a demonstration in Washington, in which I was quoted as saying that "I had nothing to say to the FBI about anything."

tracks of Soviet tanks in Budapest, thereby severing the last link between the ongoing processes of the historical world and the sequence of past, present, and future in the master narrative that since 1939 had provided the framework for Armstrong's belief and action as a political being.

Assuming that Armstrong's letter was motivated in part by his disillusionment, it still remains to suggest why that disillusionment should have been expressed in the context of policy proposals that would lead "toward a free world." One might assume that Armstrong's impulse to action in the world, although bereft of the master narrative that had long channeled it, retained its own autonomous motivating force. By nature he was a person with great confidence in the power of his intellect, often by some accounts displayed in personal interaction. As his reference to "Armageddon" suggests, early November 1956 was a moment in which he might well have felt called upon to take a public stand, and it would not be the first time he had done so by writing to a newspaper— in this case the one that more than any other addressed a national audience— nor would it be the last. Even so, the positive proposals he advanced—universal free migration, free trade at the risk of competition, and a kind of Marshall Plan for the underdeveloped world—seem in retrospect a utopian patchwork of nineteenth- and twentieth-century liberal assumptions, dramatically at odds with his long-held ideological orientation. Even granting a piecemeal consistency with certain universalistic and evolutionary tendencies in his prior thinking and perhaps also with its trajectory toward Boasian liberalism, his 1956 proposals seem to have a pragmatic situational aspect, as if, to avoid Armageddon, one had no recourse but to appeal to fundamental economic, political, and cultural-political assumptions of the American public.

To imagine why, almost three years later, Armstrong would have given his letter to the FBI is perhaps less problematic if one considers the immediate situation in which he did so. Responding to a knock on the door of his home to find himself unexpectedly confronted by two agents embodying the potent authority of what he regarded as the American secret police at a time when he was preparing to leave the country on a long-hoped-for overseas research trip, he might well have wished to convince them he was not a person whose freedom of movement they should in any way impede. In an effort to prove that he was no longer a security risk he might well have decided that, within the limits of conscience (and of his postdisillusionment ideological position), he would discuss in a general way his political evolution (though not the political commitments of other individuals). Recalling then his 1956 letter, he offered it to them as confirmatory evidence. And it was in fact taken as such: commenting on the text Armstrong had furnished "to show his present-day thinking on the rulers of the Soviet Union," the initial report of the interview noted that he had "deplored" the Soviet action in the Hungarian revolt as revealing "the Russians to be 'Oriental Despots.'" The report later sent on to J. Edgar Hoover suggested

STANDARD FORM NO. 64

Office Memorandum • UNITED STATES GOVERNMENT

TO : Director, FBI (100-39986)　　　　DATE: 9/4/59

FROM : SAC, Atlanta (100-4124)

SUBJECT: ROBERT GELSTON ARMSTRONG
　　　　　SM - C
　　　　　(OO: ATLANTA)

ALL INFORMATION CONTAINED
HEREIN IS UNCLASSIFIED
DATE 4-4-2000 BY [redacted]
　　　　　　91570

ReBulet to Atlanta dated 7/29/59.

The subject was interviewed by SAs [redacted] on 8/31/59, at his apartment, 592 Beckwith St., S. W., Atlanta, Ga. The following are the results of the interview with ARMSTRONG: _b7C_

A. The subject was only partially cooperative with regard to furnishing information on his own former Communist Party activities, and would not furnish any information regarding the activities of others.

B. The information furnished by the subject coincides substantially with that developed against him.

C. The subject admitted that he was a member of, and active in the Communist Party during the 1940's in Chicago, Ill. and Atlanta, Ga.

D. Subject would not be available as a potential witness since he does not care to make any statements about the Communist Party activities of others, and for this same reason he presents no potential as a Security Informant or Confidential Source.

E. No further contacts are contemplated with the subject since he is leaving the United States for a year. Consideration may be given to recontacting him after his return to the U. S. if it appears that he is in a position where he will have information of value to the Bureau.

REC- 99 100-27-1.2-5

2 - Bureau
2 - Atlanta (1 - 100-4124)
　　　　　　(1 - 100-5650) (COMMUNIST
　　　　　　　　　INDEX PROGRAM)　　29 SEP 8 1959

RRN:mel
(4)

7. First page of the summary report to J. Edgar Hoover of the interview by two special agents of the FBI on August 31, 1959. The second page (not reproduced here) included the recommendation that Armstrong be removed from the Communist Index of the Atlanta Office, and he was not recommended for the Security Index. (Courtesy of Jennifer Lewis, who obtained it under the Freedom of Information Act.)

that because "the subject was only partially cooperative" in regard to his own activities and was unwilling "to furnish any information" regarding others, he would not "be available as a potential witness" and presented "no potential as a Security Informant or Confidential Source." In view of his inactivity in the Communist Party for "over six years" he was not recommended for the Security Index and was also recommended for removal from the Communist Index until such time as he was again active or "in close association with Party members." In the meantime no further contacts were contemplated, since he was soon leaving the United States for a year—although "consideration may be given for re-contacting him after his return . . . if it appears that he is in a position where he will have information of value to the Bureau" (FBI:9/4, 9/10, 9/23/59).

By the time the final summary of his interrogation was placed in his FBI file on September 23, 1959, Armstrong, having in effect been declared free to move about the world, was already on his way to London and thence to Nigeria. Except for occasional short visits back to the United States, he was to live there for the rest of his life.[11]

The Émigré Anthropologist in Nigeria

Pecking away at the Mountain, 1959–1987

The nine years since Armstrong had discussed Nigeria's political future with Nnamdi Azikiwe in July 1951 were a tumultuous period in its history. The march of events picked up speed with each passing year, bouncing one way and another among the "convergence[s] of ethnic, regional and political cleavages . . . rooted in class action" as the political classes in each major region competed for power within the shifting constitutional framework that buttressed the waning power of a retreating British colonial administrative regime (Diamond 1988:45–63; Ige 1995:48–173; Falola 1999:81–93). In the aftermath of the constitutional revision of 1947 other political parties had emerged to compete with Azikiwe's National Council of Nigeria and the Cameroons (NCNC), which became the party of the Igbo in the eastern region. In the western region the rising party was the Action Group, dominated by the Yoruba; in the Hausa-Fulani emirates of the Muslim northern region, long favored by the British, the major party was the Northern People's Congress (NPC)—challenged, however, by the more radical Northern Elements Progressive Union

---

11. Save for two "Deleted Page Information Sheets," the text of Armstrong's 1956 letter is the last item in Armstrong's FBI file, as released under FOIA. Neither of the information sheets is dated; each indicates the withholding of only one page: the first, "in the interest of national defense or foreign policy," the second, lest it reveal the identity of a confidential informant.

(NEPU). Regional rivalry was already apparent at the 1950 constitutional conference, and in the regional elections of 1951 the three major parties, each powerful in its own area, were none of them able to command a national following. In March 1953, when the Action Group, with the backing of the NCNC and the NEPU, proposed self-government for Nigeria by 1956, the NPC resisted, fearing domination by the two southern regions. At another constitutional conference in London the British brokered an agreement by which the unitary state structure was scrapped in favor of limited tripartite regional self-government to be followed by national independence in 1960, with the northern region to have representation equal to that of the two southern states combined. By the time of the last constitutional conference in 1957 the numerous minority groups (together roughly one third of the population) were also demanding separate states within a confederation. But the British commission appointed to investigate the matter, fearful of "a general struggle for power in Nigeria" in which "any group with a corporate feeling" would become "the vehicle by which a politician reaches power," opposed the creation of any new states (Diamond 1988:54–55). In 1959, when general elections were held preparatory to independence, the NPC won a plurality; but the attempt of the Action Group to join forces with the NCNC in the formation of a government was unsuccessful, and instead the NCNC entered a coalition with the NPC. When national independence was celebrated on October 1, 1960, amidst an upsurge of optimistic enthusiasm, Azikiwe became governor general and Tafawa Balewa, the deputy leader of the NPC, prime minister. In the process, however, a great many issues "were swept under the carpet," including "ethnicity, minority complaints, violence, and growing corruption," as well as British manipulation of the decolonization process to protect their vital economic interests (Falola 1999:93; cf. Diamond 1988:90–92).

By the time Armstrong returned to Ibadan in October 1959 there had been changes as well at the University College. When it opened in February 1948 the college was housed in the derelict buildings of an abandoned military hospital in the bush north of the town. By 1953, when Armstrong returned to Chicago, the move had been largely accomplished to two dozen or so permanent buildings, including a library, assembly hall, classrooms, laboratories, offices, and student residential buildings (Mellanby 1958:65, 101; Ajayi and Tamuno 1973). By 1959 the original student body of 104 had grown to about 950, and the original senior staff of 12, of whom 10 were expatriates, had grown to 235, of whom 70 were Nigerians (Mellanby 1958:56; Olubummo and Ferguson 1960:94, 109). But despite substantial accomplishments, the college was from the beginning affected by regional and ethnic differences and was the subject of criticism from the major political groupings and in the popular press. Muslim students from the north, who in 1951 numbered only 10 in a student body of 338 (75 percent of whom were Protestant and another 20 percent

Roman Catholic), complained of persecution; Yoruba and Igbo students, who each made up a third of the enrollment, were sometimes at odds, on at least one occasion to the point of violence (Mellanby 1958:224–29; Abiri 1973; Adeleye 1973:89–92; Tamuno 1973). The main theme of early press criticism was the charge of racial discrimination, specifically, that Nigerian faculty were paid lower salaries than Europeans, who were eligible for expatriate travel allowances, and that these "inferior conditions" persisted until the eve of independence (Mellanby 1958:247; Olubummo and Ferguson 1960:109; Oloruntimehin 1973:102). In 1954 Azikiwe, describing the college as a "million-dollar baby," accused it of financial irresponsibility and failure to link its curricula to the "immediate needs of the country" (Okafor 1971:93). But the most systematic party critique was that of an Action Group Policy Paper in 1958, which called into question the exclusiveness of the residential system, the curricular priorities (including the lack of courses in anthropology and sociology), and the inadequacies of technical education as well as the general problem of "antinationalist bias," exemplified by the ethnic and regional imbalance, the pretense of academic autonomy, and the continuing predominance of expatriate faculty (Okafor 1971:94–97). Shortly after Armstrong's arrival, however, the last issue was significantly ameliorated by the appointment of his friend Kenneth Dike as the first Nigerian principal and, two years later, when the college was elevated to the status of the University of Ibadan, as its vice-chancellor or chief administrative officer (Adeleye 1973:72–73; Alagoa 1998).

During his first year back in Nigeria Armstrong was attached to the Nigerian Institute of Social and Economic Research at Ibadan, which after a period of decline in the later 1950s had been revived by an infusion of expatriate personnel and financial support (Mellanby 1958:215–18). Although his fellowship was for work on Yoruba language and law, Armstrong also spent time in Benue Province collecting materials for his Idoma dictionary. His major reported fellowship activity was an analysis, based on Abraham's *Dictionary of Modern Yoruba*, of the Idoma's traditional vigesimal numerical system, which reckoned the higher units by twenties (RAC:SSRC, box 17, folder 127, Nigerian Institute of Social and Economic Research *Annual Report*, 1959–60). Acknowledging this system as a "fascinating chapter" in "the development of human thought" and "evidence of a great deal of mathematical talent," Armstrong nevertheless felt that it created "serious obstacles" to Yoruba participation in the modern "mathematical" world—obstacles his proposed translation into the decimal system could overcome (Armstrong 1962a:5, 21–22).

By the end of his fellowship year Armstrong's self-redefinition as a linguistic anthropologist was formally marked by his appointment as the field director of the Ford Foundation–funded West African Languages Survey (Staniland 1991:29–30; cf. Magat 1979:34). Although he had not at this point published on any West African language, his linguistic interests would likely have become

known to Joseph Greenberg, the director of the project, if not through Abraham, then through Herskovits, who had directed Greenberg's doctoral dissertation on Hausa religion and who knew Armstrong, who also had the great advantage of being "on the spot" in Ibadan (Newman 1991; Silverstein 2002). In
July 1960 Armstrong reported to Murra that he had resigned from Atlanta University and would be spending "three weeks or so" in New York in September
"getting filled in" by Greenberg on West African languages before taking up his
new role, which included appointment as honorary research professor of linguistics at the University of Ibadan and the University of Ghana (the latter a
temporary appointment of administrative convenience). Although Armstrong
continued to publish occasionally on social anthropological topics relating to
his Idoma ethnography (e.g., 1961a, 1965b, 1966a), these appointments marked
a decisive turn to linguistic anthropology and to a different style of anthropological work. After reporting to Murra the good news that the Clarendon Press
had "finally agreed officially" to subsidize and print his Idoma dictionary, Armstrong announced that he had "sworn off" the "quicky, package-deal study that
is all finished and published in one year." Instead, he planned "just to keep pecking away at the mountain until some day there is a tunnel through it—not forgetting to enjoy life a bit on the way or between times" (JMP:7/8, 8/21/60).

In 1963, when Greenberg published his reclassification of all African languages into four distinct families, he thanked Armstrong as field director of the
West African Languages Survey for "numerous word lists" that had been collected (Greenberg 1963a). In that capacity Armstrong also played a leading
role in the several congresses on West African languages organized under the
auspices of the survey (Greenberg 1963b). And when, out of these early ventures, the *Journal of West African Languages* was inaugurated in 1965, followed
shortly thereafter by the West African Linguistic Society, Armstrong played a
major role in both. From 1964 to 1972 he was the most active member of the
editorial board of *JWAL*, the cover of which was regularly embellished with an
Idoma "talking drum" (see Armstrong 1954a), and for more than a decade he
was a member of the society's governing council (*JWAL* 1[1]:2–3; Bamgbose
1986; Boadi and Jungraithmayr 1989; Layiwola 1987; Williamson 1987, 1989).

Aside from these editorial and organizational activities, the bulk of Armstrong's publications in the early 1960s was also linguistic. In addition to word
lists and papers on grammatical topics, in particular, languages (Armstrong
1962d, 1964b, 1965a), these included several essays of a more general character in which the balance in his work between the universally human and the
culturally specific shifted noticeably. This shift is clearly evidenced by comparison with a paper commissioned for the Second World Congress of Negro Writers, which was held in Rome during the summer of 1959, prior to Armstrong's
departure from Atlanta University. Entitled "Le développement de l'unité culturelle en Afrique, au sud du Sahara."" (The Development of Cultural Unity in

Africa South of the Sahara), it is striking less for its Boasian orthodoxy than for its neo-evolutionary and even Marxist resonances. Armstrong began by offering a critique of "racial and color prejudice," suggesting that all races were "equally intelligent" and that linguists had found no evidence that any existing language could be called "primitive." But he was less concerned with defending cultural equipotentiality and variety than with urging a much larger-scale unity: because "the epoch of the small nation" had been superseded by that of "large super-states," the only way that Africa could hope to compete with Russia and America was to form "a truly modern state" that would encompass all of its 150 million black people. Similarly, in arguing the paramount importance of overcoming "cultural prejudice" (as opposed to that of race and color), he seemed less concerned with critiquing false "cultural symbols of European civilization" (such as proper table manners and clothing) than with arguing the inhibiting effect of certain African "cultural ideas, new and ancient" (including sorcery and animism), as "useless and superfluous baggage" in the attempt to achieve African unity. Insisting on the importance of European science, technology, erudition, and capital accumulation, he went so far as to suggest that the "cultural heterogeneity of Africa" was a result of "certain determinate economic processes" that were appropriate to "conditions of primitive agricultural technology" but were barriers to the entry of African peoples into a world market that would otherwise exploit them (Armstrong 1959b, my translation).

The shifting balance of the global and the local in Armstrong's anthropological orientation is evident in a paper he contributed to an international seminar on African history at the University of Dakar, Senegal, in December 1961. Partly, the shift was a reflection of his reimmersion in the ethnography and linguistics of specific local groups (the Idoma and, to a lesser extent, the Yoruba). As he had announced to Murra several months previously, it was "astonishing how wound up in localisms" he had become since his return to Nigeria (JMP:8/13/61); and in the Dakar paper itself he remarked on how "the worker in the field" struggled "to make some kind of sense of the ocean of data in which he is swimming" (Armstrong 1961c:133). Involved as he was in the work of Greenberg's linguistic survey, the kind of sense Armstrong sought was that of linguistic relations conceived in genetic (i.e., deep temporal) terms, and he was much attracted to the methods of "lexicostatistics" and "glottochronology" (the comparative study of basic vocabulary as a quantitative index to linguistic diversification over time), as developed by Morris Swadesh (another political exile during the McCarthy period), which had recently been summarized by Dell Hymes (1960, 1983; Armstrong 1961c:132–33). Although the method was controversial, Armstrong argued its utility in "accustoming us to the great time depths that I believe lie behind the present arrangements of languages" in West Africa. Societies there were "intensely local in their cultural orientation," and the linguistic situation indicated "great age and little movement" (Armstrong 1961c:128–29). Against the tendency of many scholars to assume that "the main events posited to explain the present relationship of [African] peoples took place only one or two thousand years ago," Armstrong suggested that the "rate of cognation in basic vocabulary" between Yoruba and Idoma suggested "well over 6,000 years of separation" (Armstrong 1962b:285, 1961c:132). What was at stake was in effect the same issue that had concerned Armstrong in his doctoral dissertation: whether major aspects of African culture were to be explained by recent intrusions of racially "superior" populations or whether they were evidences of native African cultural creativity over a longer period of time (1961c:127, where, however, he cited the later work of St. Clair Drake [1960]).

By the time Armstrong completed his term as field director of the West African Languages Survey, Dike, intent on giving "an authentic African character" to the University College of Ibadan (and regarding the Nigerian Institute of Social and Economic Research as "a millstone around his neck"), had negotiated a five-year grant from the Rockefeller Foundation for the establishment of an Institute of African Studies (IAS), in which Armstrong was from the beginning slated to become research professor of linguistics (Ajayi 1973:160–61; Mabogunje 1973; RAC:African Studies, box 1, folder 7, 3/25, 10/20, 10/25/61, 10/20/62). When he gave his inaugural lecture, "The Study of West African Languages," in February 1964, many of the themes developed in his earlier papers were revisited (Armstrong 1964a, cf. 1961b, 1961c, 1962c), this time, however, in the context of a review of the development of African linguistics, from its origins in the mid-nineteenth century up to Greenberg's critique of the presumed Hamitic status of Fula (the language of the Fulani). On the basis of a comparison of some eighty apparent cognates in five of the six subfamilies of Greenberg's Niger-Congo family, Armstrong suggested that there was an "underlying connection between Proto-Bantu and Proto-West Sudanic, and of Yoruba and Igbo to both," and beyond this "an immense antiquity of West African languages and therefore of West African culture" (1964a:21, 23). What was called for was the "study in depth" of as many West African languages as possible, not only as a sign of "respect for the peoples who speak the languages" but as a prerequisite to "the discovery of really deep African thought" (religious, philosophical, legal, poetic, and humorous), a problem that Griaule and Dieterlen had (to Armstrong's "astonishment") approached only through an interpreter (1964a:13–17).

There was, however, the question of who would carry on such studies and to what more immediate end. In his lecture Armstrong suggested, in terms consistent with Boas's approach to the study of languages, that because a speaker's native language was "much too close . . . for easy study," it would for a time have to be investigated by "foreigners" trained in linguistics, pending the moment when "Africans should become linguists in self-defense, so that any future 'linguistic' racists will not go unanswered" (1964a:14–15; cf. Stocking 1974a). In either case, the effect was to establish both a privileged position and a practical goal for the "professional linguist" in the increasingly charged political context of "language policy," an issue Armstrong addressed in two papers presented to conferences in the 1960s (1961b, 1966b).

Although there are substantial continuities of argument, the two papers differ significantly in their orienting situation. Written in late 1961, when the nation-founding optimism of the immediate postindependence period in Nigeria had not yet entirely faded in the face of reasserted ethnic and regional antagonisms, the first paper treated language policy in a global context as one of the "great paradoxes and dilemmas" faced by "modern Africans" in their relation to "what is going on in the rest of the world." On the one hand, the "serious business" of the world (industrial, technological, and scientific) was carried on in four languages: English, French, German, and Russian. On the other hand, Africa was "a very large continent" of "widely dispersed populations" speaking between one and two thousand different vernacular languages. None of them were "primitive"; each was learned in the context of the closest of human relations and "tightly bound up" with the "deepest emotions and most intimate memories." Each of them provided "the most complete model of a logical system" that most of their speakers would ever have and for each human group embodied and expressed its sense of its own "distinctiveness and individuality" and its concept of "the good, the true and the beautiful." The problem of maintaining individual and group self-respect and at the same time acquiring the linguistic competence necessary to participate in the modern world was to find some relationship between "vernacular" and "world" languages other than that of "dominance and suppression." The "only sound educational policy" was therefore simultaneous instruction in one of the world languages (in Africa, either English or French) and in the local vernacular, using instructional material developed for each vernacular based on systematic study by a "professional" linguist, undertaken in "decreasing order of their political and economic importance." Thus would science (in the form of linguistics) provide a solution to "the very problem which the growth of science and high technology" had created. The problematic if not utopian aspect of this scheme was manifest in a paradox Armstrong evidenced without marking: from the time the linguist started work it would be "perhaps five years" before teachers would be available who could instruct children in a given vernacular and "at least a generation" before the vernacular would be "well taught," a timetable oddly reminiscent of British colonial thinking in the preindependence period (Armstrong 1961b, cf. 1962c).

When Armstrong wrote his second paper on language policies five years later, Nigeria had just experienced a number of "signposts of disaster," including an October weekend "of severe violence and massacre" following "the general breakdown of law and order, and a series of murders in the East and North"

(Kirk-Greene 1971, 1:16, 2:476; cf. Diamond 1988; Ige 1995:241–89). The context was no longer that of emergent nations faced with rapid global change but that of impending civil war. Although Armstrong still insisted that language was the means by which people "become complete human beings," he now acknowledged that it was also an issue that "people kill each other over." Still giving priority to economic and social causes as against "any theory of linguistic causation," he nevertheless saw "a striking tendency for linguistic boundaries to coincide with boundaries of conflict." In this context the challenge was to find the "wise language policy" that could be "one of the levers available for improving a difficult political and social situation" (Armstrong 1966b:227–28). Unfortunately, there had been a widespread failure to deal with the "the innermost problem," which the conferees in 1961 had "hardly dared to spell out in print": "the fact that there is not a single West African country where a given language is spoken by more than a sizable minority of the population." Furthermore, despite a number of UNESCO conferences and pilot programs, "not even a beginning" had been made to prepare "the teachers and pedagogic materials that would be necessary for enforcing the use of an indigenous national language in any West African country." Indeed, no one had yet "really come to grips" with the organization of a "large-scale program" for the development of literacy (Armstrong 1966b:231–32).

Against this disappointing history of language policy Armstrong found cause for optimism in a substantial regional development of the institutions and personnel of "the science of linguistics" (in which of course he himself had played an important role). This "unprecedented mobilization of expert thought," including now "several West Africans with doctoral degrees in linguistics," was on the whole committed to the belief that "education should seize hold of and develop the ancient and widespread African habit of polyglottism" along lines similar to those he had advanced in 1961. Furthermore, there was by now general agreement among experts that "the complete development of a previously unwritten language for literacy purposes" would require both a "scientific" and a teaching grammar as well as literary texts, a bilingual dictionary, and the training of teachers—and that it would take "at least five years" for each vernacular language (Armstrong 1966b:230–34). What was most striking in Armstrong's agenda was the activity to which he was by this time devoting the major portion of his linguistic work: the collection of oral literature (Armstrong 1965c, 1968b, 1968c, 1969b, 1972b). At once the "test and source of scientific grammars and lexicons," it was "the capstone of the whole edifice of linguistic work." Indeed, the "worthy presentation" of traditional oral literature, in addition to being "fun instead of a deadly bore," was "what makes literacy in the respective language worth the trouble," inasmuch as it enabled the African student "to study the literature of Europe without acquiring an inferiority complex at the same time." In the traditional anthropological spirit of salvage ethnography

Armstrong insisted that "this generation has a supremely important opportunity" to make use of modern high-fidelity recording machines while "the great traditional artists" were "still singing and reciting" (1966b:235–36).

Unfortunately, the propagation of linguistic science and the preservation of oral tradition were not high on the agenda of Nigerian political groupings then involved in an increasingly violent competition for power. By the time Armstrong gave this paper the situation had become so tense that most of the Igbo staff members of the University of Ibadan had fled to the east, including Dike, who in addition to his role as vice-chancellor had also served as director of the IAS since its creation. Even before its formal founding in July 1962 Dike had mentioned Armstrong to the Rockefeller Foundation as a likely candidate for the directorship, and in January 1966 he was appointed deputy director (RAC:African Studies, box 1, folder 7, 10/25/61; AN 3[2]:5 [1966]). In July of that year Dike took formal leave from the university, and when he resigned as vice-chancellor in January 1967 (Oloruntimehin 1973:111–12) Armstrong became the effective head of the IAS. By the time the eastern region seceded to become the Republic of Biafra, followed by the outbreak of fighting between Biafran and federal forces in July 1967 (Kirk-Greene 1971, 2:476–77; Ige 1995), he had been formally appointed director. It was in this context that he made his most notable contributions to public political debate in Nigeria (Armstrong 1967a, 1967b, 1967c, 1969a).

The central theme of these writings was Armstrong's commitment to the "minority groups" of Nigeria (among them, the Idoma) as opposed to the three major ethnic groups. The first article, published in March 1967, prior to the Biafran secession, attacked the "moral category" of "bush," used by both Europeans and Nigerians to stigmatize groups presumed to be less "civilized," with the suggestion that the minorities, who did the bulk of "the real soldiering," were so regarded by the "clever city elites" of the major ethnic groups. In fact, Armstrong argued, the minorities together were "the largest single group in Nigeria." Possessed of a common language (English) and a "national leadership" (the officers of the Nigerian Army), they were "united in desiring a strong enough federal government" to provide a base for "their maneuverings with their dominant neighbors" (Armstrong 1967a). The second article was published on the eve of a decree by General Gowon (head of state since the coup of July 1966) subdividing the federal republic into twelve smaller states; it was shortly followed by the secession of Biafra. In this article Armstrong justified a "federal government" as a balance between the local autonomy that would give groups "physical and psychological security" and a central authority strong enough to keep them "from fighting each other" not only in order to prevent "outside powers from interfering" but also to develop a unified economic market and to foster "that feeling of oneness" and patriotism "indispensable to the effective organization of 55 million people in a dangerous world" (1967b).

The third article, written after the Biafran invasion of the midwest and the capture of Benin, was originally sent to the *New York Times* in August 1967 during one of Armstrong's occasional visits back to the United States. Although it was not published by the *Times*, Armstrong discussed it with "relevant officials" at the U.S. State Department on September 1 and on the same day presented it to a colloquium of the Nigerian Students Union in the Americas, after which it was published in the Lagos press by arrangement with the Nigerian embassy in Washington. Opposing outside intervention, Armstrong defended the policies of General Gowon (himself a member of one of the "minority groups") for his "great statesmanship in his relations with the heterogeneous groups who constitute the Federation," which had enabled the minorities, who constituted "over seventy percent of the fighting soldiers of the Army," to achieve an importance "they had never had before." He went on to suggest that, despite "the massacres" of September 1966, the generally negative attitude toward the Igbos "was not race prejudice as we have known it in the United States" and that it would "fall to manageable levels" if the Igbos would only cease their rebellion and join in the federal government that two generations of Nigerian nationalists had fought for "against great odds" (Armstrong 1967c:3–4, 6, 8, 13, 17).

The civil war in fact dragged on for another two years. Toward the end of it Armstrong, in preparation for "the making of a new constitution of Nigeria," reanalyzed the ethnic group proportions in the controversial census of 1952–53, which categorized some of the Yoruba and Hausa/Fulani as "borderline," in order to argue that the so-called minority groups were actually a slight majority of the total Nigerian population. Insisting that "the present Federal Military Government, in which the many sides of the country are duly represented, is the most democratic that Nigeria has ever had," he concluded in a characteristically optimistic hortatory mode: "We may therefore confidently hope that in the post-war period Nigeria will proceed in unity and good spirit to make the thousand adjustments that will be necessary in order to perfect and perpetuate her democracy" (Armstrong 1969a).[12]

Aside from his involvement during the civil war, Armstrong seems to have had little to say in print about public political issues during his years as IAS director (but cf. Armstrong 1980c). Although there were several essays of a more traditionally social anthropological character—on Idoma ideas of disease (Armstrong 1971a), Idoma kingship (1973b), and Idoma religion (1975)—and

---

12. The Biafran secession is one of several instances in this period when anthropologists took different sides on a major public issue (constitutional, legal, or, in this case, military), based in large part on the particular "my people" with whom they were ethnographically involved. Stanley Diamond, who did fieldwork in eastern Nigeria among the Anaguta (1967), was a vigorous supporter of the Biafran cause (1970; cf. Manners 1956; Rosen 1977).

two brief studies of the Yala language (1967d, 1968a), most of his anthropological energies were devoted to collecting Nigerian "oral literature" along even
broader lines than those he had sketched in 1966. As pursued by Armstrong,
oral literature (or "oral tradition") included narrative, poetic, and historical
literature as well as music, art, religion, and philosophy as manifested (or represented) in cultural performance—the full range, one might say (though
Armstrong did not), of European "humanist" culture. To undertake such a multi-
faceted study was an "enormous" project and an arduous and time-consuming
one for which a critical means of reproduction was the high-fidelity but un-
wieldy fifty-pound Nagra reel-to-reel tape recorder. The tapes thus collected
were, however, only the raw material and had then to be transcribed, translated,
and edited for publication, which was by no means guaranteed, given the production cost and limited market for the recordings. Armstrong compared the
task to the "treatment that we are accustomed to give to documents of ancient
or mediaeval European history" (1969c:13; cf. Boas 1905).

     Armstrong's fullest elaboration of the methods and goals of the study of oral
literature was offered in one of two papers he presented at the IXth International Congress of Anthropological and Ethnological Sciences, organized by
Sol Tax and held in Chicago over ten days in late August and early September
1973 (Stocking 2000:208–13). Attended by more than three thousand anthropologists from all over the world, the congress was an opportunity for Armstrong to re-present himself on a world stage to his American and Chicago professional colleagues, no longer as an émigré victim of McCarthyism but as an
anthropologist well established in his own local sphere—although the very size
of the gathering (not to mention the limited participation of the Chicago department) may have militated against any such attempt. Be that as it may, Armstrong's two papers, taken together, exemplify the two phases of his anthropological project (the early social organizational and the later linguistic), both in
the sequence and the dynamics of its development.

     The former, entitled "The Dynamics and Symbolism of Idoma Kingship,"
was a revisiting of the themes of his doctoral dissertation in the context of
twenty years of fieldwork in Nigeria. As Armstrong suggested, the "constitutional" arrangements of the small states of the Niger-Benue confluence were "of
great theoretical interest in the study of the evolution of human society from
one based on the relationships of kin-based associations or corporations to the
establishment of territorial states, in which citizenship comes from residence,
not from descent or kinship" (1973b:394). After offering examples from his dissertation, with references to Nadel, Fortes, and Evans-Pritchard as well as to
Gumplowicz and Henry Maine, Armstrong went on to consider "the structural
basis for Idoma kingship," specifically how, in the absence of a clearly defined
royal lineage among the competing corporate lineages, a king who was a member of one lineage could achieve "the necessary generality of interest to func-

tion as the chief officer of the whole, at once the ruler and servant of all." The Idoma answer to the problem of royal legitimacy involved first a rotation of the kingship among clans, supervised by the elders, followed by "an act of symbolic death" in which the new king's compound was sacked, leaving him dead to "his family and lineage attachments." Hidden away for a fourteen-day period of rituals, during which he lost all his personal belongings, his personal identity, and all the obligations he owed "to individuals and to his own family," he became instead "the general son of the land" (Armstrong 1973b:397–99).

In the opening sentence of his paper Armstrong suggested that his goal was to give "a brief *inside* view of the kingly office"—to "discover what the people really think about their king and how they relate him to their religion and cosmology"—as opposed to accepting a "remote, abstract, and administrative point of view" (1973b:393). He did so primarily on the basis of two oral sources, presented at some length: "a long tape-recorded interview with the now deceased king of Otukpo and his advisory council in 1952" and an "account of the death of a king and the installation of a new king dictated to me in Idoma by an elder in 1953" as well as on "personal experience" during many subsequent visits to Idoma (Armstrong 1973b:399, 400–401, 409). In short, he attempted to solve a problem posed by his early theoretical orientation in terms of methodological assumptions, evidentiary modes, and rhetorical styles more characteristic of the work in oral literature that had become the focus of his ethnography since his return to Nigeria.

A somewhat similar thrust is evident in the second paper, in which he considered at length the relation of linguistics to the study of oral literature. In addition to dealing in an "abstract" and value-neutral way with human "universals," linguistics had the "complementary and normative research goal" of "discovering and recording the peak phenomena of thought and speech in a great variety of societies," as embodied in their oral literature. Characteristically, a work of oral literature was a synthesis of various activities that "are different in kind": first, "the string of words" that composed it, but often also a musical form in which the words were embedded, or a dance, or "some kind of play involving masks," with a "special arrangement of performers and audience" in relation to "some shrine or altar," the whole being "related to other works of art." The publication of such a work was therefore inherently "multidimensional" (1973a:445–46). Armstrong suggested five such dimensions (1973a:447–51). First came the mastery of the work's language, including the way in which "surface structure and deep structure may be played against each other," the way in which rhythm and assonance function in place of meter and rhyme, the "elaborate word play" and the "elaborately structured parallelisms" so characteristic of West African verse (as well as of ancient biblical Hebrew poetry). The second dimension was the publication of "a faithful translation and a full annotation of both the original and the translated texts." The third was the publication of the "really good recordings" made possible by modern high-fidelity equipment. The fourth was "its visual aspect," in order to capture its relation to dance and the frequent use of masks. Finally, there was the placement of the text in its "full social, cultural, historical and, therefore, human contexts," offered, oddly for an ex-Marxist theorist, as an afterthought suggested by a colleague. On this basis, "traditional people" could now "speak directly into the permanent record, without their words being filtered and censored by interpreters, anthropologists and other intermediaries." In this process "linguistics reaches the ultimate expression of its value: the development of human communication on many levels and between all the peoples of the earth" (Armstrong 1973a:453–54).

For Armstrong, however, the goal was not simply the creation of an archive of cultural materials as they existed in the past and could be recaptured in written texts today. Later in his career he wrote a lengthy and generally laudatory review of a book entitled *African Art in Motion, Icon and Act* (Thompson 1974) in which he praised the author for insisting, as had others previously, on "the unity of arts in African performance" (Armstrong 1981b). Among a number of constructive suggestions, he commented on the author's failure fully to appreciate the complex relation of polyrhythms of dance and drum in what Armstrong recalled having previously spoken of as "talking dance," that is, dancing "to talking drums that the dancer understands" (Armstrong 1954b). Although Armstrong did not pursue the matter in the review, his work in general makes clear that performances of this sort, while they should be archived on film, were to be studied also for their regenerative cultural value in the present. To this end he was active in encouraging Nigerian artists who, in preserving traditional forms, creatively re-presented them.

As IAS director Armstrong's major priority was the collection and publication of oral literature, both traditional and contemporary, conceived in these broad aesthetically integrated and performative terms. The latter aspect of his project is abundantly evident in a brochure describing the institute published in 1974. Without acknowledged authorship but clearly in his voice, it spoke of the institute's aim "to reveal and preserve the finest parts of the tradition . . . and to encourage the imaginative development of new cultural forms and of new adaptations to modern life" (Armstrong 1974:1). In addition to more conventionally anthropological works among its nine major publication categories, the brochure listed "Bi-Lingual Literary Works," including two operas by contemporary Yoruba authors, recorded in performance and transcribed and translated by Armstrong with the help of two Yoruba assistants, as well as a poetic drama in Idoma and a music drama in Yoruba (1974:11–12). Included among "Nigerian Cultural Films" were not only the performance of various rituals but also "New Images: Art in a Changing Society" and "Culture in Transition" (Armstrong 1974:20–25). Under the heading "Ethnographic and Fine

Art Collections" the IAS was described as "a patron of modern art in Nigeria,"
its courtyard a venue for "traditional dances and performances of other kinds,"
including the display of contemporary sculpture (Armstrong 1974:4–6).

Armstrong's own research, however, was much more in the archival mode.
His annual report on his scholarly activities during his last year as director includes a long list of "researches completed since Spring, 1974," including twelve
Idoma texts (277 pages) "in fully linguistic writing [sic] with translations into
English and annotations, in fair copy, ready for publication"; two Idoma texts
of tape-recorded interviews (114 pages), "complete in typescript but not yet in
fair copy"; the translation of a document on Yoruba mining and smelting
(Adeniji 1977); and translations of three other Yoruba texts totaling 568 pages
in typescript but "still requiring editing"; as well as five recordings already produced and another five edited but not yet pressed, due to "production delays at
the new E.M.I. Pressing Plant in Ikeja" (IAS:*Annual Report* 1976–77).

Many of these ventures were to one degree or another collaborative efforts,
the extent of which Armstrong was quite scrupulous in noting. Thus, in the
case of a sixty-one-page interview with three elders on the Idoma concept of
law, he noted: "conducted by S. O. O. Amali [with] transcription, translation
and annotation by R. Armstrong, assisted by Oteikwu and Odumu Amali."
Such notations, of which there are a number, mark not only Armstrong's dependency on Nigerian cultural mediators but also his effort to involve and train
Nigerians in the work of cultural preservation and creative reproduction.

All of this depended, however, on establishing "very good relations with the
people involved" (Armstrong 1973a:445–51), and Armstrong's relations with
"his people" were in general excellent. A critical moment in their establishment seems to have come when, with the permission of the elders of Otukpo,
he recorded Idoma ancestral chants. Apparently, however, the consent of the
elders was not fully "informed," insofar as they had not realized that once the
chants were produced as records, "anyone" (including total strangers and
women) could listen to them. When "the truth dawned" there was "great consternation," and in order to "preserve his legitimacy" in the Otukpo community
Armstrong brought the entire stock of unsold records from Ibadan and in the
presence of the elders "smashed them one by one against a tree." Although this
incident is recorded here at third hand (as recalled by an informant who heard
it from Armstrong), its authenticity may perhaps be enhanced by the fact that
in 1969 a Rockefeller official, noting that Armstrong was "not overly sympathetic to the Ibos," explained this parenthetically by the fact that "he is an
Idoma 'chief,'" a status subsequently confirmed by the elaborate ritual of his funeral (RAC:RA/New York Times 9/27/67, annotation by KWT; see below).

Armstrong's chiefly title is said to have meant "spokesman" in appreciation
both of his linguistic work and his political support of the Idoma in the civil war
(PC). But as the title of his paper to the Chicago meetings ("Helping Africans

to Speak for Themselves: The Role of Linguistics") would suggest, his conception of his role was not without a certain tinge of postcolonial paternalist presumption—or so it would seem in retrospect (Armstrong 1973a). Be that as it
may, his situation as an *oyinbo* (expatriate) professor within what one contemporary expatriate sociological observer described as the "neo-colonial mandar-
inate" of a university founded upon the British Oxbridge model became problematic as Ibadan entered the later stages of "Nigerianization" (cf. Van den
Berghe 1973:18–19, 268). In addition to participating in the power politics of
the university, elite professors at Ibadan, both expatriate and Nigerian, exer-
cised a great deal of discretionary power within their respective domains; and
it is apparent from retrospective accounts that Armstrong, who was by disposition confident of his own judgments about action in the world, was not atypical
in this respect. Although he encouraged the research of the IAS's junior members, he conducted meetings in a manner recalled by one of them as somewhat
high-handed, without encouraging either participation in specific decisions or
general discussions of the program. He not only used IAS funds to provide the
infrastructures necessary for research, he also kept on its staff (despite the irritation of the university administration) several ethnic elders who lacked regular academic certification but who functioned as personal repositories of language and tradition and whose publications he facilitated (PC; Adeniji 1977;
Awujoola 1979). And there were instances where his presumption of budgetary prerogative seems to have provoked more serious irritation. Among these
was his support for the work of Suzanne Wenger, the artist-wife of the expatriate scholar Ulli Beier, a colleague of Armstrong at Ibadan who published extensively on Nigerian art and with whom Armstrong collaborated on the
preservation of Nigerian antiquities (Armstrong 1972a).

In 1960 Beier and Wenger had founded a cultural center at Ibadan called the
Mbari Club (Beier 1975; Ottenberg 1997:23; Kasfir 1999) and two years later a
second cultural center in Oshogbo, in Yoruba country fifty miles northeast of
Ibadan. After an epiphanal encounter with the high priest at a weekly ceremony
for the *orisha* (spirits or gods), Wenger undertook the creative reconstruction of
a decaying ritual site near Oshogbo. In the guise of the Àdùnní Olorisha she
filled the ceremonial grove with shrines to her own sculpted surrealist *orisha*
figures along with the creations of Yoruba artisans/artists who helped to realize
the ideas that first "took form" in "Àdùnní's head" (Wenger 1977:40). After she
and Beier separated and Wenger needed financial help to maintain the house
in Oshogbo, Armstrong managed to find funds to pay for the upkeep of the
house (which had previously served as a museum of popular Yoruba culture)
and to allow Wenger to continue living in it (PC). He also shepherded through
the Ibadan press *The Timeless Mind of the Sacred: Its New Manifestation in the
Osun Groves* (Wenger 1977). While his introduction suggested a certain dis-
tancing from Wenger's personalistic representation of Yoruba religious ideas,

8. The round building is Drapers Hall (named after its London City Company donors), the lecture theater of the Institute of African Studies. The main offices of the institute are in the large building looming behind. The monumental figures in the center foreground are by members of Suzanne Wenger's Oshogbo School. (Courtesy of the Institute of African Studies and LaRay Denzer.)

there were similarities between her re-creative project and his own, and he remained her close friend and advocate, eventually helping to edit an English translation of *Ein Leben mit den Göttern* (Armstrong 1983a). The association was not, however, one calculated to endear Armstrong to Yoruba academics, some of whom were inclined to question his control of their language and to dismiss Wenger as "one of the odd, but predictable, side-effects of colonialism, in search of a life untainted by the corruptions of the West" (Kasfir 1999:53).

Nor was this the only time that what were regarded as Armstrong's idiosyncratic intellectual and personal commitments irritated colleagues at Ibadan. In 1962 he had taken on as his field research assistant an Idoma high school student with literary aspirations, Samson Amali, who went on to study for an honors degree in English at Ibadan, in the course of which he produced several volumes of poetry. In 1970, in the journal *Ibadan*, Armstrong published a review of Amali's *Selected Poems* (1968), praising him as having "one foot firmly planted in the poetic and story-telling tradition of the Idoma" and the other "in the great stream of European and American poetry" (Armstrong 1970:93, 97). Quoting extensively from T. S. Eliot (on rejecting rhyme and regular meter), from Aristotle (on poetry as imitation of lived experience), and from Plato (on the ineffable manifestations of inspiration), Armstrong insisted that Amali's poems qualified as poetry in a mode similar to that of vers libre. He also indicated that he had collaborated in their production by occasionally suggesting topics and systematically helping to translate Amali's Idoma into English. Offering seven principles that should govern such collaboration (including the injunction: "The translating partner, no matter how senior he may be, must not attempt to change the original—on pain of excommunication and anathema"), he concluded by congratulating Amali for "cutting a new path in African literature" (Armstrong 1970:98).

A year later John McVeagh, a lecturer in the Ibadan English department, which had been a straggler in the "Nigerianization" of staff (Ajayi 1973:154), and perhaps by disciplinary tradition committed to an ethnocentrically canonical view of what poetry must be, published a slashing attack on Armstrong and Amali. Despite the fact that Amali was also McVeagh's student and Armstrong a person from whom he had "received favours which I remember with gratitude," McVeagh felt called upon to defend the very category of poetry, insisting that Amali was "not only not a good poet, he is not a poet at all, but a producer of nerveless claptrap," all by the "big confidence trick" of arranging it typographically to appear as poetry on the printed page. McVeagh responded with several confidence tricks of his own, rearranging the definitions of the words "gold," "white," and "drone" from the *Oxford English Dictionary* and concluding: "Perhaps I'll knock off a few more and publish a volume" (McVeagh 1971).

In rebuttal Armstrong described his own review as a "polite attempt" to defend Amali from the "formalistic, parochial identification of poetry with metered, rhymed verse which has been fashionable in European critical circles since the beginning of the nineteenth century" and to do this by deriving from within the broader Western tradition "a set of categories and attitudes appropriate to the understanding of African literature." When in 1965 he had read Amali's bilingual poem "The Grass House" to Robert Graves, "the well-known English poet," and they had discussed it for an hour, Graves had "reacted very strongly and positively" (Armstrong 1971b).[13] Not so, apparently, a number of Armstrong's Nigerian colleagues, who by one account "enjoyed this knockabout at Armstrong's expense . . . the more so since it was other *oyinbo* who were putting the boot in" (PC).

By 1973 there is evidence of significant dissatisfaction with Armstrong's role as IAS director. He had assumed that position in a moment of interethnic crisis, only months before the Rockefeller funding was to run out. In the absence

---

13. So too, after reading the Armstrong/McVeagh exchange, did Dell Hymes (a founding figure of the present-day study of "ethnopoetics"), who summarized his comments as "So I would say that (a) what Armstrong says and exemplifies about translation is good, and (b) Amali is an interesting poet" (PC:4/19/02; Hymes 2003). It may be of interest to note that Sapir had covered the same ground in his 1920s writings on the question of free verse (1921).

of funding from other external sources, he was immediately involved in the internal academic politics of the university in regard to budgetary matters and other issues. Armstrong was apparently fairly successful in obtaining funding within a constricted university budget as well as from outside sources. UNESCO and the Ford Foundation, along with the government of the Rivers State, provided support for a series of primary school readers in all that state's languages and major dialects (Armstrong 1974:8, 16–18); the government of the Benue-Plateau state supported Armstrong's Idoma research, which he carried on with the assistance of various members of the Amali family (IAS:RA reports). There were apparently some people associated with the IAS, however, who were troubled not only by the personalistic aspect of some expenditures but who felt that Armstrong had been too engaged "politically" in trying "to reap dividends" from his support of the federal government during the civil war (PC). In addition to issues of funding there was the matter of the special structural status of the IAS, in which little or no formal teaching was carried on, which had been a concern even during the Rockefeller period (RAC:RWJ interview, 4/23/64, JEB diary, 2/17–26/68). Armstrong, although research professor of linguistics, was not a member of the Linguistics Department, and other members of the IAS had only temporary appointments in departments.

A particularly problematic issue was the inclusion of archaeology in the IAS. In the original negotiations leading to its creation one of the primary motivations of Kenneth Dike, who was an historian by profession, had been to establish archaeology at Ibadan in order to supplement the inadequate written records of African history. Faced by traditionalist resistance to the creation of a separate department of archaeology, Dike settled for including a research professorship in archaeology within the new institute. The post was filled by Thurston Shaw, who in the late 1950s had carried on a major archaeological project at Igbo-Ukwu in eastern Nigeria (Shaw 1970, 1990:215; Ogundiran 2002). Although he and Armstrong had been good friends in the 1960s, their previous cordial relations deteriorated when Shaw in 1970 finally succeeded in getting archaeology established as a regular teaching department within the Faculty of Science. By Shaw's later recollection, Armstrong played a role that "felt like an attempt to strangle at birth" the new department, leading the vice-chancellor to intervene "to sort the dispute out" (PC). In this context it is worth noting that among the numerous references to the IAS in the history of the University of Ibadan published in 1973 there is not one mention of Armstrong, although Shaw's role in archaeology was specifically referred to on two occasions (Ajayi and Tamuno 1973:185–212). It seems likely that the 1974 brochure mentioned above (without acknowledged authorship but with a full-page photograph of Armstrong at his desk) may have been his response to this omission as well as the presentation of a research and publication program that reflected his priorities as director (Armstrong 1974:3).

9. Armstrong at his desk in his office in the Institute of African Studies (c. 1974), holding in his hand one of two small divination palm-nut cups called *agere Ifa* in Yoruba in front of a hanging by the Oshogbo School. The Picassoesque batik hanging on the wall is by Suzanne Wenger. (Courtesy of the Institute of African Studies and LaRay Denzer.)

By the time that brochure appeared Shaw was no longer listed among the staff, and instead not one but two research professorships, one in African art forms and the other in traditional African societies, religions, and thought systems, were noted as "vacant." Armstrong was thus alone atop a staff that, save for the "temporary cinematographer" and the "senior technician," was by then entirely Nigerian (Armstrong 1974:28). Given his identification with the Idoma, Armstrong was not a typical expatriate academic; however, his association with a minority "bush" group was not likely to strengthen his position in an institution that since the Biafran secession had been Yoruba dominated and to which the once powerful Igbo had recently returned. While there was a general recognition of the positive aspects of his role in the preservation and study of Nigerian languages and traditional cultures, there were some who felt that important areas of African studies were being neglected, and there was an accumulation of concerns about the structure of the institute and the style of Armstrong's administration. There were those who were disturbed by his "empire" building and even "murmurs" that he was "a CIA agent" (PC).

In 1974 these issues came to a head. Motivated by the feeling that it was an anomaly at that stage in Nigeria's development for the director of the institute to be an expatriate, a delegation went to the vice-chancellor, Oritsejolomi

Thomas, to ask that a Nigerian be appointed to the position (PC). Although Thomas at first defended Armstrong as a scholar of international reputation, the following year he did in fact appoint a Nigerian, Obaro Ikime. When Thomas was forced out during mass dismissals of governmental and academic staff by Gen. Murtala Mohammed, the leader of the anti-Gowon military coup of July 1975, Ikime returned to the history department, and Armstrong was called back as fill-in director. Within months, however, he was eased out when the new vice-chancellor needed to find a suitable position for S. O. Biobaku, a prominent historian and a supporter of Gen. Olusegun Obasanjo, another member of the military group who had assumed power after Mohammed's assassination early in 1976 and who over the next three years was instrumental in the military's moving toward the founding of the ill-fated second republic (PC; Ige 1995:385–87; Falola 1999:154, 161–77). When General Obasanjo (as a recently chosen "distinguished fellow" of the IAS) was invited to respond to a sharply critical paper given at a December 1979 seminar at Ibadan entitled "The Demise of the Rule of Law in Nigeria under the Military" and presented what he called "another point of view," Armstrong offered a brief commentary on the exchange. Granting that "no democratically-minded person likes a military government," he nevertheless defended its "mild-dictatorship" in the decade following the Biafra war as necessary to the preservation of the nation when "the alternative is the breakdown of all law whatsoever" (Armstrong 1980c:47).

Although Armstrong reached the formal retirement age of sixty at the end of the 1977 academic year, he continued on the Ibadan faculty in a series of one-year contract appointments. Free now of administrative responsibilities, he might have been expected to turn to the summation of the ethnographic and linguistic research he had done among the Idoma over the years, projects that might have established his enduring reputation among those Africanist anthropologists whose careers focused on a particular ethnic group. In the event, however, the publications of his last years were a rather diverse lot, including several revisitations of oral literary texts as well as occasional essays on various topics.

Notable among the former was his reconsideration of Duro Ladipo's opera *Oba Ko So* (The king did not hang), a product of the "development of serious African drama" during the early 1960s that Armstrong himself had encouraged. Written in 1963 "with the assistance" of Beier, it had later been recorded in performance by Armstrong and then transcribed, translated, and published in cooperation with the Yoruba elder A. L. Awujoola. Over the years, however, Armstrong had become aware of serious deficiencies in the translation, which he now sought to correct by a close textual reanalysis of the poetic rhetoric (with several critical asides on future Nobelist Wole Soyinka's readings)—this, however, to the end of reiterating a point Armstrong had made on a number of previous occasions: the tremendous job of scholarship (comparable to the study of the classical literature of Greece and Rome) still necessary if African thought was to be understood in its cultural and historical context (1978, cf. 1980a).

This sense of revisitation (occasionally verging on reiteration) is evident also in several occasional essays of a more social anthropological character. In 1975 Armstrong published a general essay entitled "African Religion and Cultural Renewal" in which he tried to "establish a useful perspective in the light of modern thought" to demonstrate that "the traditional religions of the preliterate Africans are deserving of respect and are of enormous interest in their own right" (1975:110). Readdressing issues and authors going back to his "Society and Matter" manuscript (subsequent scientific thought on the origin of the universe, Marx on religion "as the sigh of the distressed creature, the heart of a heartless world," Whitehead on what "the individual does with his own solitariness," Evans-Pritchard on divination and sacrifice), Armstrong suggested that African religions, "like all religions," were in a "state of turbulent shock as they confront modern life and modern science" and that "as a condition of African cultural renewal" their "serious practitioners" must be included in "economical [ecumenical?] dialogue with the established world religions" (1975:112, 113, 126, 130–31).

In 1979, at a UNESCO symposium, "Sociopolitical Aspects of the Palaver in Some African Countries," Armstrong was asked to frame the discussion by a consideration of "palaver" in more general terms as "open public debate" carried on until "the entire family or community reaches a general consensus." After a brief etymological/historical excursus on the word "palaver" he drew on his own experience among the Idoma of Otukpo in 1962, when he had been allowed to tape "the famous old lady singer Ediigwu," a sister of the king, performing a cycle of sacred funeral songs that were taboo if sung out of season and were in any case not for sale. After an hour or more of formalized debate among the elders, which Armstrong was permitted to record on his Nagra, it was agreed that he might record the cycle itself, with the justification that there had in fact been a death on the day before, and the payment required of him would not be for the songs but "for the goats and other things necessary" for "propitiation by each of the lineages" involved. The result was a "unique and priceless recording" not only of the cycle—published in New York in the Asch Mankind series and later re-pressed in Nigeria—but also of a community decision process that "must have happened thousands of times in the history of European contact with various West African communities." The dismissive (and racist) characterization of such performative events as "palaver" by early European slave traders was simply an expression of their "total incomprehension" of discussions that were actually enactments of "the constitutional structure of the communities they were dealing with" (Armstrong 1979:11, 22–23).[14]

---

14. Armstrong indicated that at this time (1962) the elders were already "aware of radios and gramophone records." How this might articulate with the previous account (undated and second-hand but offered by a reliable informant) of the smashing of unsold records to prevent them being

Armstrong's last publication, "The Etymology of the Word 'Ogun,'" was very much in the same revisitational mode. Written in 1984 for a volume on *Africa's Ogun: Old World and New*, edited by Sandra Barnes, one of several young American Africanists whose Nigerian research he facilitated, it did not appear in print until two years after his death. In it Armstrong argued that the Yoruba Ogun cult (which showed "amazing vitality among people directly concerned with modern technology") was an "amalgam and synthesis of originally separate cults" (1984:29) and that as one traveled east of the Niger the characteristic association with iron smelting became relatively less important than the symbolism of the hunter. Referring specifically to an Idoma text written, at his suggestion, by Ada Okau, a postgraduate student at Ibadan, Armstrong suggested that what was involved, symbolically, was the "resocialization of a dangerous hero" symbolized by the "washing of the killing from the face" of the successful hunter or warrior, usually by the blacksmith (another marginal social figure), lest the killing cause trouble at home (1984:31–32). Casting the argument into a long-term evolutionary frame, Armstrong proposed a sequence in which hunting reached back into the Lower Paleolithic, with war emerging in the Neolithic and the development of agricultural surpluses, and ironworking coming only at the end of the Neolithic (1984:34). As further evidence of the need to consider the "hunting aspects of Ogun" and to broaden "the search for his origins" Armstrong closed by presenting in full a poem of Samson Amali written when he was still a "sixth form schoolboy," which ended with the hunter

> Awaiting his game
> He had heard the voices
> Of spirits.
> Had met dangerous spirits
> He could talk
> With the animals
> He was the mystery man
> Of his land.
> (1984:37)

Aside from these revisitational textual and occasional essays, the largest single body of Armstrong's publications of his last decade dealt with particular languages and general linguistic issues. Although these writings, too, reiterate or echo earlier work, there was a significant shift in his research agenda once he

---

heard by women (see above) or with Armstrong's own account back in 1952 of being admitted to a "whole flock of ceremonies" forbidden to women (see above) is a problem for someone with closer ethnographic knowledge of the specifics of Idoma ritual theory and practice and their changes over time. Lacking such knowledge, I have included all three accounts both for their intrinsic interest and as exemplifications of three distinct moments in Armstrong's ethnographic interaction.

was free of his duties as IAS director. It was as if, realizing that the mountain at which he had been pecking away for almost twenty years had actually been thickened by the wealth of empirical material he had collected, he decided it was time to think more seriously about how to push the tunnel through. Evidence of such a shift is manifest in a major paper he contributed in October 1977 to the Twentieth German Orientalist Congress entitled "The Development of Fulani Studies—A Linguist's View." At first glance the paper clearly echoes Armstrong's critique (offered originally in his doctoral dissertation) of the notion that the Fulani were an intrusive racially "superior" group, and it depends heavily on "new work resulting directly or indirectly from the work of the West African Languages Survey" in the early 1960s (1977:78–79). Armstrong recalled, however, that he had initially accepted an interpretation deriving from Greenberg's linguistic work, which assumed the existence of two Fulani groups, but saw "the Black Tukulor group as original and the 'Berber-like' nomadic group as adventitious" (1977:16). However, at a conference in June 1977, "Directions for Research on Fulfulde and Fulani Culture," he was impressed by the strongly held view of Iya Abubakar, the vice-chancellor of Ahmadu Bello University, that there was really only one Fulb'e people who themselves saw "no boundaries between the Pastoral Fulb'e and any other Fulb'e group." Having decided "on reflection" that there was "a great deal to be said" for this view (1977:17, 78), Armstrong devoted the bulk of his October paper to a lexical comparison of Fulfulde with Kwa and the Benue-Congo languages, including proto-Bantu, to the end (summarily stated in the paper's abstract) of showing that there was "a very strong *prima facie* case" for the genetic affiliation of Fulfulde to the Niger-Congo family, at a point "between five and ten thousand years ago, or before the desiccation of the Sahara was complete" (1977:448).

In 1980 Armstrong spent several months at the University of Marburg, where he lectured in German and carried on further research with Hermann Jungraithmayr, the editor of the journal in which his 1977 essay was published. By December 1981 there is evidence to suggest he had undertaken a general reconsideration of his linguistic project. Unsure of his future in Nigeria when his last annual contract expired, he made several attempts to seek employment in the United States, including an initiative to the University of California at San Diego, the home institution of David Laitin, another of the American academic researchers whose work he had facilitated. The application, he told Laitin, had given him an occasion for stating "the main thrust of my somewhat multifarious research interests," which he felt now began "to make a lot of sense of what has been a vast collection of stray facts" (DLP:12/22/81).

Enclosed to Laitin was a copy of a document Armstrong had sent along with his letter of application: "The Idomoid Languages: An Anthropological Linguistic Study." Based on his "more than thirty years in the area," it was an attempt to make what had been peripheral (the Idoma and related groups near the confluence of the Niger and Benue rivers) central to "the understanding of ancient tropical African culture" and indeed to see "Africa from a broad tropically centered perspective." Although Armstrong listed a number of situational and archaeological bases for this "working hypothesis" (which he might be "the first anthropologist to suggest"), he based it "most importantly" on the linguistic evidence: the "line of Idomoid languages" that formed the "easternmost interface" between the Kwa (or Guinea Coast) languages and the Benue-Congo languages (including Bantu but not the "click languages" of southern Africa), which extended eastward "fan-wise all the way across Africa to the Indian Ocean." In this context Armstrong cited several of his most recent linguistic publications as steps toward the establishment of his hypothesis: his use of "the technique of 'mass comparison' of a small group of languages" to establish the relationship of seven Idoma or Idomoid languages (1981c) and his lexicostatistical study of fifty languages as a tentative attempt to establish that the Idomoid languages were "a distinct group" (1980b, cf. 1981a) as well as further confirmatory studies being carried on with Jungraithmayr. The "next step" would be to "try to set up sound correspondences" and to pursue "grammatical comparisons on the basis of data already collected" and then, having "proved the genetic relationship of this vast group of languages," to attempt to divide them into "families, sub-families, and sub-sub-families" (Armstrong 1981c).

Viewed in the colder light of retrospect, the proposal document itself seems rather casually pastiched together, with quotations from Wittgenstein and Thomas Kuhn on the problem of defining "natural families," references to the long-delayed completion of Armstrong's Idoma dictionary and his collection of Idoma texts, and a laundry-list conclusion on "the meaning and importance of such studies," including several reiterative references to the study of "African logic," "African mind," and "African mental capacity." Perhaps not surprisingly, early in 1982 it received a polite brush-off from the assistant vice-chancellor for academic personnel at San Diego (DLP:M. Javet/RA 1/21/82).

In the letter he sent Laitin Armstrong was more open about "the inner point" of his proposal: in contrast to "most attempts to see Africa as a whole" by starting from some point on the periphery and working "more or less gradually towards the center," he decided to start from "the black center of Africa." It was not, he granted, an entirely new position: "Some such point of view" was "already expressed" in his doctoral dissertation. Furthermore, making the Niger-Benue confluence the originating center was "just a good guess." He suggested, however, that "we will never get the perspective right unless we make a beginning" (DLP:12/22/81). After twenty years of pecking away at the thickening mountain, he made several further attempts to drive the tunnel forward toward the light on the other side.

In March 1982 Armstrong was "madly trying" to finish a paper for the West African Languages Conference that would "sum up thirty years of work on the

Idomoid languages." Progress on its preparation for publication was slowed, however, by several severe health problems, the treatment of which required a trip to London. For nine weeks he was "in and out of hospitals," undergoing diagnostic tests and "quite a lot of surgery," including an orchidectomy (surgical removal of the testicles) for prostate cancer and a quadruple bypass to remove the "clutter" in his coronary arteries. During "all this fun," including five weeks of recuperation, he somehow was able to finish a lengthy article entitled "The Idomoid Languages of the Benue and Cross River Valleys" (CSP:RA/CS 3/25, 11/9/82).

Published in April 1983, with "special funds to include the substantial data that Professor Armstrong has collected" (*JWAL* 13[3]:2, the article attempted "to go beyond lexico-statistics" to present "a series of sound correspondences" among the Idomoid languages, which, as a group, followed "the widespread Eastern Kwa pattern," forming the "easternmost interface between the Kwa and the Benue-Congo languages to the east" (Armstrong 1983b:91). As evidence, Armstrong offered a brief list of Idomoid vowel correspondences, followed by a much longer "hypothetical" presentation of "Proto-Idomoid Word Stems" based on a comparison of 129 words in 11 Idomoid languages with words from a number of groups to the east previously studied by other scholars, including Proto-Benue-Congo, Proto–West Sudanic, and Proto-Bantu (1983b:97–100, 100–124). A second major evidential section was devoted to a "synoptic view" of what was known about the phonologies of each of the seven dialects of Idoma and the four related languages of the Idoma group, all but two of them based on material collected by Armstrong himself (1983b:125–40). The "reliability" of the phonologies was admittedly "variable." At one extreme there was material collected in three hours in 1951; at the other there was the material from Otukpo, which included "a large 2-way dictionary that is still on card files," backed up "by hundreds of pages of texts written by Mr. Isaac Ochinyabo and Mr. (now Dr.) Samson O. O. Amali and many others," much of it transcribed from tape-recorded chants, songs, stories, and interviews (Armstrong 1983b:125, 131). Armstrong was modest in his general statements, acknowledging that the stems of Proto-Idomoid might be regarded as "pseudo-reconstructions" and treating the whole effort as only a beginning, offered "as a useful framework for further work" (1983b:141).

Although his final contract at the University of Ibadan had been extended for three months to cover the period (and the expenses) of his medical trip to London, by the time this article appeared Armstrong had no regular employment, without which he was not legally permitted to remain in Nigeria. None of the various American postretirement possibilities he had been pursuing having materialized, he decided to accept an appointment as visiting professor of linguistics at the University of Nigeria, Nsukka. While there he wrote a short piece arguing that there was a system of ten vowels in Proto-Kwa that was manifest in a number of Niger-Congo languages (Armstrong 1985a:107). By early 1985 he had also drafted what was to be his last treatment of the Idomoid languages of Nigeria.

Rather than a summation, what Armstrong drafted was a continuation of the 1983 paper. After a review of the earlier scholarship, in which Abraham was credited with "the first really linguistic study of Idoma" (cf. Armstrong 1967e), Armstrong offered a classification of the Idomoid languages. Although their dispersion, their "very considerable formal differences," and the fact that they "have no strong political-economic center" had concealed their genetic unity until recently, Armstrong's tree diagram (first published in Berlin in 1980) suggested the sequence of their branching relationships in terms of Swadesh counts of "percentages of probable cognation in the basic vocabulary" (1985b:9). From that point on the paper was a painstakingly detailed comparative analysis first of the languages' morphophonology and then of their syntax, with side glances to English, French, German, Russian, Spanish, Yoruba, and Igbo.[15] The paper culminated in a brief critique of Noam Chomsky from the perspective of the method of Armstrong's own study, which, by beginning "with actually recorded sentences or speech-acts," provided "a criterion of truth, since we know that the sentences exist and have been uttered by someone at least once." His approach was, in short, a "deep reverse of setting up a conjectural, a priori 'deep structure' and then by transformations and deletions hoping to arrive at a plausible 'surface structure'" (Armstrong 1985b:51–52). And with that claim the typescript broke off, never to see the light of publication.

Living and Dying in Style, 1959–1987

There are, of course, many anthropologists whose published writings bear only a tip-of-the-iceberg relationship to the ethnographic material they have collected; indeed, the same might be even more true of the profession as a whole, if one were to include all those whose initiatory field experience was never realized in significant publication. There are many reasons for this, including, in Armstrong's case, the several lost years of the 1950s and the time given to what, despite the delegation of 1974, may be retrospectively viewed as a foundational role during the decade in which he served as IAS director. Even so, he managed to publish a considerable body of anthropological work, as reflected in a bibliography of close to one hundred items—a research effort that, if it did not include a systematic ethnographic monograph, nevertheless provided a rich body of material about Idoma (and to a lesser extent Yoruba) society and culture not

15. In reviewing a penultimate version of this manuscript, Kay Williamson noted that I had offered no specific reference to Armstrong's Igbo studies, referring me to his edition of Abraham's unfinished Igbo-English dictionary (as discussed in Williamson 1992).

only in the form of journal articles but also in texts, translations, and recordings, many of them coauthored with Nigerian collaborators. These genres are less bibliographically conventional but nevertheless time-consuming to produce.[16]

On the other hand, one cannot help being struck by the disjunction between Armstrong's grandiose early ambitions and the more modest achievements of his postdoctoral career. Without minimizing the situational factors that contributed to this retreat from ambition, one is tempted to suggest also a psychological aspect in terms of a temperamental disinclination or disability to traverse the often difficult path from conception to creation. Perhaps Armstrong experienced a dawning fear that the grasp of his abilities (or possibilities) would not match the reach of his ambitions—and a consequent reassessment of his lifestyle priorities in favor of a more relaxed and less driven mode of existing in the world. Recalling Armstrong's comment to Murra in 1960 forswearing the "package-deal study that is all finished and published in one year" and his intention instead to keep "pecking away at the mountain until some day there is a tunnel through it" while "not forgetting to enjoy life a bit on the way or between times," one is inclined to give some weight to the force of conscious choice implied in that last phrase (JMP:7/8/60). For if Armstrong did not write a major ethnographic monograph on the Idoma or complete his long-promised Idoma dictionary, it is the case that he managed to find (or to create) for himself in Nigeria a life that he obviously enjoyed "along the way."

Armstrong did not "go native" in any storybook anthropological sense. It was not his style to take up long-term residence in a village; rather, the primary residential situation of the life he established for himself in Nigeria was that of a member of the academic elite at the University of Ibadan (Van den Berghe 1973). He was, in some respects, less formal than other professors, both expatriate and Nigerian, especially in his later years; one informant recalls him as "totally oblivious to fashion with his faded Hawaiian shirts and baggy pants or Bermuda shorts, shuffling along in an old pair of sandals" (PC). But as research professor and as IAS director he was provided with, and obviously enjoyed, many perquisites.

Like others of his status he lived within the gated university community in a spacious tile-roofed single-story bungalow surrounded by a garden, with separate servants' quarters behind. There was a large living room area lined with bookshelves with a baby grand piano in one corner and room for dancing.

16. "Close to one hundred" not only because the variety of materials makes exact counting difficult but also due to the accretional way in which Armstrong's bibliography has been reconstructed: first, from a vita he sent me in 1978, with additions from one he sent to David Laitin in 1979, others from a manuscript report to the Institute of African Studies of his research activities in the early 1970s obtained for me by Laray Denzer, and still others from Constance Sutton in 2002, as well as several which I came across in my research. While I have drawn on materials from all of these categories, I have not attempted to synthesize them in a single Armstrong bibliography.

Across from the front entrance was the dining area, down two steps and separated only by a low divider of cupboards and bookshelves on which was displayed Armstrong's collection of *ibeji* (carved Yoruba twin figures). Parallel to the divider was a large dining table, one end of which functioned as his worktable, with his file of Idoma dictionary card slips and a typewriter adapted with linguistic characters. Behind his place at the head of the table on the left was the kitchen; to the right at the other end was a corridor lined with pieces of Wenger's statuary, extending past two guest rooms and a bathroom, on to Armstrong's own bedroom and bath occupying one end of the bungalow.[17]

To assist his living there were always Nigerian servants who performed the daily tasks of cleaning, cooking, and serving the meals; some of these servants brought their families. There was a longtime majordomo who cooked for the household and who sometimes threatened to leave when he and Armstrong got into an argument. And there were several young men, protégés who stayed for years and who drove Armstrong's car and helped around the house. Armstrong encouraged and supported these young men's education, in several cases even through graduate school.

Within this domestic sphere Armstrong was a generous host to occasional houseguests, including a series of younger American scholars embarking on research in Nigeria and, for extended periods, two of the institute's Yoruba elders, Pa Adeniji and Prince Awujoola. There were frequent dinners, with Armstrong leading discussion around the table, making storytellers proud of their abilities by his hearty laugh. By one account, talk would often revolve "around the use of a particular Idoma or Yoruba phrase, which Armstrong would sing (generally with a native speaker at the table), and then providing a scholarly exegesis on its meaning" (PC). And in addition to what one participant called the "intellectual salon" around the dinner table in the bungalow, others recall Friday nights out, when Armstrong would take friends to a favorite Lebanese restaurant in Ibadan—which may have contributed to his growing portliness over the years.

Armstrong's life in Ibadan was further enriched by music, which had been an avocation since his year in Atlanta, when he sang baritone in several operatic performances. Early on, he remarked that singing was for him the therapeutic equivalent of psychoanalysis, and he continued to sing in local productions in Ibadan: Gilbert and Sullivan, Menotti's *Amal and the Night Visitors*, Handel's *Messiah*, and as the Commandant in Mozart's *Don Giovanni*. An active member of the Ibadan Music Circle, he served as its president in 1980. But the most striking evidence of his musical passion was perhaps the piano—a prized possession, despite the fact that the man who tuned it had to travel a hundred miles

17. The information on Armstrong's domestic situation in this and the following four paragraphs comes from personal communications from several different informants.

from Enugu, only to have it soon go out of tune again in the Ibadan humidity. Its initial arrival, however, was a memorable moment, celebrated by a musical evening in the bungalow, his friends gathered to enjoy live jazz, classical music, and "high life."

Armstrong was able to maintain his convivial lifestyle in Ibadan during the series of one-year contracts he held there after his formal retirement in 1977. But when these contracts ended at the time of his health crisis of 1982 and he was forced to seek other employment after the frustration of his attempts to return to the United States, it was no longer possible for him to enjoy the privileged life of the Ibadan professoriate. There are in fact hints here and there that his last several years were rather lonely and unhappy ones. In the fall of 1985, at the end of a second year at Nsukka, he retreated to Otukpo, where he found refuge in a small house owned by the Methodist Mission, which provided him also with an honorary appointment as advisor on Bible translation in order to satisfy the legal requirements of his continuing residence in Nigeria. With the assistance of Idowu Ajibola, his foster son who in 1975 had been brought to Ibadan as a six-year-old orphan by Armstrong's collaborator, Yoruba Prince Awujoola, Armstrong somehow was able to cram into three rooms his library and his baby grand piano. For the next few months he continued to work on his grammar and dictionary of Idoma, typing his collection of three-by-five-inch slips into a newly acquired computer—until one morning he spilled orange juice on it and it ceased to function, symbolically putting the quietus on a project begun more than three decades before. During his last months Armstrong's health continued to deteriorate, until on April 29, 1987, he died "on the palms" of his foster son.[18]

Armstrong's funeral was delayed for a month, during which three interested groups negotiated over the planning. According to the Methodist bishop, Armstrong had in his last months returned to the religion of his childhood, and one report would have it that he in fact gave several sermons; from this point of view he should have a Christian burial. Given his chiefly status as *ode'ejo*, however, the council of Idoma chiefs were strongly in favor of a traditional Idoma ceremony, including the inquest that had been the subject of one of Armstrong's earliest articles (1954b). Finally, there was the Amali family, whom Armstrong regarded as his "family in Nigeria," led by Samson Amali, who with Armstrong's support had completed a doctorate at the University of Wisconsin (Amali

18. A belated attempt to investigate the significance of this phrase with a local Yoruba informant suggested that in the moments of impending death a close relative lifted the head of the dying person on his own palms to enable the dying one to see those present and them to hear his last words; a second Yoruba informant, contacted by LaRay Denzer, suggested that it meant simply "to die peacefully," the hands serving as a pillow (PC). According to Shamsudeen (Samson) Amali, he and Armstrong were still working on the Idoma dictionary at the time of Armstrong's death, and Professor Amali is "continuing the work" even to this day (PC).

1985). By the time of Armstrong's death Amali was senior lecturer in theater arts at the University of Jos in northern Nigeria and by Armstrong's will the inheritor of all his possessions in Nigeria, including the piano, the computer, and his research materials (PC:KW). By mid-May, however, a compromise funeral plan had been arrived at, and Amali, as "Chief Mourner" and head of "Professor R. G. Armstrong's Burial Committee," was able to write to Bolanle Awe, then IAS director, informing her that the funeral would take place on May 29 and 30, when "Professor Armstrong [would] be given full Idoma traditional and Christian burial rites," according to the "tentative program" he enclosed (IAS:Amali/Awe 5/18/87).

The funeral, which was attended by a delegation of eight from the institute, seems by several accounts to have followed fairly closely the tentative program (IAS:Awe/vice-chancellor 6/5/87). At nine o'clock on the morning of May 29 the corpse was to have been taken from the University of Nigeria Teaching Hospital at Enugu, where it had been kept for the month since Armstrong's death, and thence driven fifty miles northwest to the Department of Languages and Linguistics at the University of Nigeria, Nsukka, where a commemorative program had been arranged by the department. From there the funeral party proceeded another seventy miles northeast to Otukpo, where they were received by the Och'Idoma and the council of traditional chiefs, and the IAS delegation presented a Yoruba dirge in Armstrong's memory. However, by Idoma tradition, the Och'Idoma refused to view the body, because (as Armstrong had noted in his article on Idoma kingship) the king's assumption of office was "an act of symbolic death," and one of the taboos of his status prohibited him from setting eyes upon a corpse (1973b:398, 400). After lying in state in front of the Och'Idoma's palace for three hours, during which traditional dances were performed, the coffin was taken to the Methodist Church for a Christian service and then carried to Upu Otukpo, the village in which Armstrong had done much of his fieldwork. The day ended with an all-night wake at the Amali family compound, during which there were performances by a dozen or more Idoma and Tiv musical groups—paid for, as were the bulk of the funeral expenses, by the Amali family (PC:KW).

As the corpse lay in state on the morning of the second day, there were speeches by dignitaries and representatives of institutions, including the Universities of Ibadan, Jos, and Nsukka, a number of governmental representatives, and the Otukpo and Idoma traditional councils. After the speeches (some twenty in the tentative program), the traditional inquest to determine the agent that might have caused Armstrong's death was held in a shaded grove, with visitors under canopies at the edge of the central area, within which the coffin rested, surrounded by members of the Amali family (PC:KW). As was not unusual, the inquest was adjourned without a final verdict (Armstrong 1954b), followed by several hours more of traditional dancing. The coffin was then

10 and 11. The two images reproduced here of Armstrong's funeral events are scanned from photographs taken in 1987 by the late Kay Williamson: the upper one is of the dancing at the Amali compound; the lower one is the traditional Idoma inquest prior to the burial on the second day. (Courtesy of Kay Williamson.)

carried in procession to the grave, a small house for the dead of the sort that Armstrong had described in his essay on kingship (1973b:401–2). There Samson Amali, in place of the scheduled "graveside oration," simply chanted a single mournful triplet: "Professor Robert Armstrong, Professor Robert Armstrong, Professor Robert Armstrong" (PC:KW). And with that the émigré anthropologist and Idoma *ode'ejo* was laid to rest in the Nigerian earth.

Unfinished Business Fifty Years On

Counterfactual Possibilities, Subtextual Themes

Having recounted a series of episodes in the narrative of Armstrong's life, the question remains: what larger meaning(s) can one give to what might otherwise seem simply a patchwork of biographical moments? The parenthetic plural is not without significance but reflects my experience in the writing of this extended essay. Over a decade ago, when I began preliminary work, I was somewhat naively inclined to think of it as a study of victimization in the McCarthy period, in which I was doubly implicated, as a potential victim who had somehow "walked between the raindrops" and as a member of the department from which Armstrong had been excluded in 1953. Inspired by his phrase ("unfinished business"), I envisioned a kind of belated moral reparation, the finishing of a shameful business by making it publicly known. However, over the years of intermittent research and writing I have come to see the matter as rather more complex.

In part this reflected a retrospective tendency (that grew stronger with my own aging) to contemplate the ways in which my scholarly life was at points entangled both with events in the "outside" world and within a more personal experiential realm. This autobiographical perspective was in turn manifest in an increasing interest in the lives of anthropologists, considered not simply as professional beings but in the wholeness of their human experience. In this context I was led to a reconceptualization of what I thought of as my "terminal project": "Anthropology Yesterday: From the Science of Man in World Crisis to the Reinvention of Anthropology, 1945–1972." Rather than a single thematically integrated study, it would be a series of biographical essays, each separately publishable should mortality intervene but which if viewed together (like a set of transparent overlays) might suggest a pattern-in-depth of interrelated themes (Stocking 2000, 2004a). Although Armstrong was not originally among the anthropologists I had in mind, it later dawned on me that, as a victim of McCarthyism, he would fit rather well—despite (or perhaps because of) his being relatively unknown—as a complement to Clyde Kluckhohn, a major figure who played an active role as an advisor to the U.S. government during the early cold war period (Stocking in process).

As research proceeded, however, I realized that the "unfinished business" of an Armstrong essay was a more ambitious project than I had originally thought. I became aware of bodies of source material (including informant recollections and archival materials) that both enriched and complicated the narrative. This was especially the case with Armstrong's years in Nigeria, which at first I had thought of primarily as a form of political exile, to be treated perhaps as a coda to the main story but which in fact amounted to more than half his professional life. Since I could not travel to Nigeria and had little prior knowledge of its peoples or its history, I was heavily dependent on published sources and on letters (air- or e-mail) to people previously unknown to me who, sometimes after months, kindly took the time to respond to my inquiries (see "Oral and Written Informant Sources"). While this mode of research echoed both the methodological problems of the midcentury "study of culture at a distance" and the ethical issues of postreflexive ethnography, it greatly enriched my understanding. In the process, however, the narrative grew longer and the meanings that I would derive from it more complex: beneath and beyond its mosaic of narrative moments there were not only subtextual themes that might be drawn to the surface but also counterfactual possibilities that might highlight changes and continuities in Armstrong's career, each provoking retrospective reflections from a fin-de-siècle/postmillennial viewpoint on the "unfinished business" of his life. While none of these can be explored here in detail, what follows is an attempt to sketch some of them within constraints of time, distance, method, and ethics.

Of the subtextual themes, the least explicit is perhaps Armstrong's homosexuality, of which I first became aware when one informant suggested that it might have been a factor in the withdrawal of his appointment at Chicago in 1953.[19] Although this piqued my interest as perhaps evidence of a linkage between different modes of professional exclusion during the McCarthy period, there seemed at first nothing to confirm it in contemporary texts. And while several other informants were in varying degrees suspecting or aware of his homosexuality, others were not—as might be expected in a period when emerging from the closet, except in a few communities of the like-minded, was to take a substantial personal risk, roughly equivalent to announcing one's membership in the Communist Party. Indeed, it was only in post–gay liberation retrospect that it dawned on me that several of my comrades of the 1940s and 1950s might have been "gay"—a term that, to most heterosexuals in that period, still

---

19. As in the case of others in this period and since, the term "bisexuality" might be used if one were to encompass all of the manifestations of sexuality in Armstrong's life, including the "affair with a girl" that he mentioned to Murra in 1956 and the suggestion of one informant that in his early years at Ibadan he had taken a Nigerian wife. However, the fact that he added "believe it or not" in his note to Murra would suggest that his primary sexual identity was what would now be called "gay."

had no specifically sexual reference (Duberman 1991; Werth 2001; Shand-Tucci 2003).

There is some evidence to suggest that Armstrong's homosexuality became an issue during the Puerto Rico project. Reminiscing in 1983, he recalled that another member of the Steward team had become involved in the urban "gay scene" and that "he himself was not entirely innocent." But although by one informant's account his relationship with the son of the alcalde may have been a factor in his abandoning fieldwork in Caguas, in 1983 Armstrong recalled that his "job problems" had "little to do with his 'personal life'" (L-PP:8/4/83). This seems to have been the case in Nigeria, where the cultural atmosphere in regard to matters sexual during the later colonial and early postcolonial period was in important respects much freer than it then was in the United States. In Ibadan personal behavior did not in general have professional consequences, and alternative lifestyles were not uncommon. Male homosexual behavior per se did not carry an ostracizing moral taint, nor did it define a lifelong personal identity. Rather, it was usually characteristic of a particular life phase or of certain life situations (including, no doubt, the "colonial situation") prior or complementary to heterosexual marriage—and not in a way that permanently determined either one's self-perception or one's social standing. More generally in Nigeria, a man's status was established primarily by his family position, and while it was validated by children, within a wider extended family framework there were various ways to acquire them, including not only heterosexual intercourse but also fosterage. By contrast with the constraints and dangers in their home countries, such a sexual world could seem very attractive to expatriate homosexuals, of whom Armstrong was by no means the only one. The testimony of various expatriate and Nigerian informants suggests that his inclinations (which became more evidently manifest over the years) were fairly well known and for the most part seem not to have compromised his professional life. Although his homosexuality is not obviously manifest in his anthropology, it seems quite likely that it was a factor in his decision to settle permanently in the sexually more relaxed environment of Nigeria after he returned there in 1959 and in his "enjoying life a bit along the way" during the quarter century to follow.

The counterfactual question suggests itself, however, whether Armstrong's life might have been different had the FBI *not* intervened in his appointment at Chicago or had Washburn *not* indicated his opposition to it.[20] The case of

---

20. I have not attempted to investigate the role of Washburn in the way that I might have if he, rather than Armstrong, were the subject of this essay. Focusing on Armstrong, there is convincing evidence that Washburn played a critical role in the withdrawal of his appointment, that Armstrong was aware of this, and that he felt unjustly treated—and also that Redfield offered a more sympathetic explanation of Washburn's role, which Washburn later professed not to remember. If the essay were about Washburn, other sources would certainly have been consulted and alternative motivations and understandings perhaps suggested.

another young academic called before the Jenner Subcommittee the preceding June casts a glancing light on what Armstrong's life situation might have become. Among those who had refused to testify was a chemist named Ralph Spitzer, who (along with my then father-in-law, Horace Davis) had been summoned to Chicago from Missouri, where both men had been teaching at the University of Kansas City (Davis and Davis n.d.:227). By coincidence, Spitzer, prior to his appearance before the subcommittee, had been offered in writing a three-year appointment at the University of Chicago, despite the fact that in 1950 he was dismissed on political grounds from the faculty of Oregon State University. On August 20, 1953, F. C. Ward, the dean of the college, sent a memorandum to Chancellor Lawrence Kimpton reporting that, after receiving two statements from Spitzer and interviewing him the preceding week, he could "recommend favorable action on his appointment with a good conscience as to his extra-academic as well as his strictly academic fitness." Ward had been convinced by Spitzer's statement "in writing" that he had "never been a Communist" as well as by his "willingness" not only to have the statement published by the university "in case of bad publicity" but also to postpone his appointment for one year to avoid "the ruckus" that it "would probably stir up at this time." On this basis, Ward recommended that the trustees approve the appointment at their September meeting (PPA:FCW/LAK 8/20/53). A year later, Spitzer's appointment as of October 1, 1954, and his resignation on the same day were recorded in the university's personnel files, Spitzer having by that time decided to pursue medical studies in Canada, where he was for many years a member of the faculty at the University of British Columbia.

Armstrong's case, which was almost contemporaneous with Spitzer's, differed in several respects. Unlike Spitzer, Armstrong *had* been a member of the Communist Party; but also unlike Spitzer, he had *not* refused to testify before an investigative committee, nor was he (then or later) called upon to do so. On the other hand, like Spitzer he *did* provide written statements to university representatives about his radical past—in his case with assurances as to his future willingness to fight for his country in a war against the Soviet Union. Since the foremost concern of university administrators was apparently to avoid any possible "ruckus," and since Armstrong was the chosen temporary fill-in for a former long-term dean of the Social Science Division (and member of the special university committee on anti-Communist investigations), it seems probable that, had Washburn not objected, the appointment would have gone through. It seems unlikely, however, that it would have led to a permanent position. The man who took Armstrong's place (without knowledge of his case) stayed only until the end of the academic year (PC), and the regular appointments made during this period were in the more "scientific" aspects of anthropology (physical anthropology and archaeology), save for two in the specific areas of Redfield's research interest—India and Mexico (Stocking 1979). On the other hand, it seems probable that, absent the need voluntarily to unburden himself regarding the failure of the Chicago appointment, Armstrong might have obtained one of the positions he unsuccessfully applied for in its aftermath: at Yale, Wayne, Rutgers, or the University of Illinois. Whether such an appointment, if permanent, would have affected the direction of his life and work might have depended on whether he subsequently received leave to return to Nigeria and on when this occurred. If he had not been there in 1959 as "man on the spot" for Greenberg's linguistic survey, it is unlikely that he would have received the adjunct appointment as research professor of linguistics at Ibadan.

On this basis, it is possible that Armstrong's career might have followed a more conventional pattern, with bouts of fieldwork in West Africa interspersed between stretches of teaching and writing in the United States. One can imagine the realization of unfinished or unpreserved papers of the 1950s, when the isolating and dispiriting conditions of his internal academic exile may well have blocked his creativity. From there one can imagine the realization of Armstrong's hopes for a career in the anthropological "big leagues," including perhaps participation in the radical anthropological politics of the 1960s.

This imaginative exercise in counterfactual history, with all its tentative "likely's," "not unlikely's," and "perhaps's," is not intended to resolve all "might have been's." Rather, it is to use them to explore certain general themes in the life that Armstrong actually led. The most striking theme is his abandonment of explicit Marxist analysis. This must be understood not only in terms of the withdrawal of Armstrong's appointment at Chicago but also in terms of the character of his Marxism and his relationship to the Communist Party. Armstrong had originally been attracted to Marxism during the Great Depression, when he was an economics major at Miami University and Marxism seemed to provide a framework for understanding the contemporary "crisis of capitalism." From the time he joined the Communist Party in 1939 (including his inactive period during military service), he seems to have had no qualms about following shifts in the party line, including the defense of the Nazi-Soviet pact of August 1939, the commitment to the war effort after the invasion of the Soviet Union in June 1941, the abrupt shift of attitude toward Earl Browder between the Teheran summit in 1944 and the Duclos letter in 1945, and activity in the Progressive Party in 1948. Although by Armstrong's account his party membership lapsed (never to be renewed) when he went to Puerto Rico in the fall of 1948, his observations on the current European political situation, along with his consideration of the Shirokov volume as a course text (sanitized by the deletion of "Marxist" from its title), suggest that his Marxism at that point remained within the framework of Communist Party orthodoxy—and it seems clear that it continued to do so on into the 1950s.

It is in this context that one must consider the Marxism of Armstrong's early anthropological writings. It is worth noting again his emphasis on the "productive activity of mankind" (in contrast to the "reproductive") as the most powerful of the forces "constantly producing mutual changes" within the "dynamic, interacting whole" of Cheyenne society, although this idea is not explicitly manifest in his master's thesis on the Cheyenne. And while the two statements of his dissertation topic after his return from the war in the fall of 1946 did not refer specifically to Marx, they pursued variants of the same concern: the first proposal was offered with minimal elaboration as a test of his master's thesis hypothesis of the importance of changes in economy and technology; the second was recast as a comparative study of the sexual division of labor and forms of descent as a further test of the relationship of "economic process" and "political process" as components of a totalizing "social process." If Armstrong later complained of the obsolescence of Marxist thought since Lenin and of the "religious" attitude of "active communists" toward Russia and the Communist movement, his effort in 1949 and 1950 to develop a more intellectually satisfying approach to "Society and Matter" was not a repudiation of the Marxist-Leninist tradition but an attempt to integrate it with philosophical and scientific writings of the sort he had encountered during his years in the heady intellectual atmosphere of the University of Chicago.

With the abortion of that overly ambitious venture, which was not well received either by his comrades or his academic mentors, Armstrong resumed his dissertation project, now recast (with an eye to current discussions in the Soviet Union) as a comparative study of "state formation." Based on an explicitly Marxist hypothesis conceived in an implicitly evolutionary framework, it attempted to correlate aspects of social structure and forms of capital accumulation with the degree of "exploitation" in each of six recently studied African societies. Struggling along the way to resolve empirical discrepancies by appeal to the notion of "contradiction," Armstrong was able this time to carry his Marxist project through to completion, and while he was aware of serious weaknesses in his argument, he expected to continue his study of exploitation and related problems for "years to come." Four years after his departure ("as friends") from the Communist Party Armstrong indicated to Redfield that he was still interested in studying the "sort of issues" he had explored in "Society and Matter" (DAP:6/28/52).

That he did not do so can be viewed simply as an adaptive move in a hostile environment. In both of his early Marxist efforts Armstrong had gone farther out on a Marxist limb than other radical anthropologists, a number of whom employed Marxist categories or wrote in loosely "Marxish" terms without specific reference to Marx (cf. Vincent 1990:228–29, 239–40). Even Stanley Diamond's library dissertation at Columbia on state formation in Dahomey (one of Armstrong's six groups), which dealt with the "emergence" and "maturity" of "class systems," referred to Marx and Engels only once in a prefatory list of Western political theorists whom Diamond had "spent many rich hours" reading; within the text itself, the writers frequently cited (other than historical sources) were all figures in the modern anthropological tradition, including Maine, Tylor, and Herskovits (Diamond 1951:ii, 124–26). The comments of Armstrong's academic mentors regarding the more explicitly Marxist aspects of his argument must have raised serious doubts about the advisability of pursuing that line further—doubts that would have been much more sharply felt after his Communist Party membership had cost him a job in the fall of 1953. He might well have concluded that he had to choose between Marxist commitment and an academic career in anthropology.

But there is more to be said about Armstrong's abandonment of Marxism than the impact of McCarthyism. To this end it is worth comparing his Marxism to that of the group of returning veterans beginning graduate work in anthropology at Columbia in the fall of 1946 who formed a small study group that was later christened ("only half ironically") the Mundial Upheaval Society (MUS). When three of the core members (Mintz, Manners, and Wolf) went off to Puerto Rico early in 1948 as members of the Steward team, the group apparently suspended its fortnightly meetings until it was "reactivated" in the fall of 1949 after their return from the field. Although the Mundialists differed on what they considered "essential reading" and apparently did not formally "read Marx," they discussed books in a broader Marxist tradition, including Karl Wittfogel's *Wirtschaft und Gesellschaft Chinas* (1931), Paul Sweezy's *Theory of Capitalist Development* (1942), and C. L. R. James's *Black Jacobins* (1938). During the group's post–Puerto Rico revival, when the members were writing their dissertations, they read papers deriving from their own work, including a "critique of Redfield's folk-urban continuum" by Mintz. Despite serious disagreements over such basic issues as "different evolutionary models; mechanical versus dialectical materialism; whether anthropology was part of the sciences or humanities; and Marxist visions of the future," their "lively" discussions were never so "heated" as to impede the "exchange of ideas." This, despite their varying political commitments, which ranged from Stalinist to ex-Communist to Trotskyist to romantic anarchist (Wolf 2001:4–5; Mintz 1994).

Ultimately divisive issues were, in short, bracketed in the interest of fruitful discussion of the work at hand. Although there is no hint of the influence of the Columbia sociologist Robert Merton (1949), the Mundialists seem to have been more concerned with the "middle range" of a generalized Marxist approach, insofar as it would, on the one hand, facilitate a critique of and provide an alternative to current anthropological theories (notably, the Benedictian/Meadian study of culture and personality and the Redfieldian approach to culture change) and, on the other, suggest problems and concepts that would enrich the interpretation of their particular ethnographic material. Such a "middle-range" Marxist approach, not specifically labeled as such, may have been adaptive during the 1950s, when direct mention of the names of Marx and

Engels was the equivalent of waving a red flag before the bulls of McCarthyism, in contrast to the later 1960s, when more explicitly Marxist analyses were on the verge of becoming, if not strictly mainstream, then relevant discursive currents within mainstream anthropology. In the interim, the more flexibly middle-range Marxist discussions of the Mundialists, unentangled in the orthodoxy of Stalinist Communism, may also have shielded them from the disillusioning impact of the Khrushchev revelations and the suppression of the Hungarian rebellion.

By contrast, for Armstrong (who in 1952 could still extol the therapeutic virtues of discussion in a "good Communist Party branch" and who had shown a strong propensity for treating theory at the grandest level) the events of 1956 seem to have had a more profoundly disillusioning effect, both politically and ideologically. It is significant that in the process of reorienting himself he turned again (in the aftermath of the death of his own father) to Redfield. In contrast to Steward and Leslie White, whose influence on 1950s neo-evolutionary and Marxish anthropology is well known, Redfield's influence during that decade has perhaps been underappreciated (cf. Kerns 2003; Peace 2004; Wilcox 2004). Intellectual agendas, however, are set not only by the ideas they advance but by the alternatives they reject, and it is no accident that several early papers of Mundialists critically engaged Redfield's folk-urban continuum (Mintz 1953; Wolf 1955). In the aftermath of his disillusion Armstrong also reengaged Redfield but in very different terms: on the one hand, anthropologically, in terms resonant of Redfield's interest in "world view," and, on the other hand, politically, in terms of a liberal emphasis on intercultural tolerance.

When I was well along in the writing of this paper, it was suggested to me that one route intellectually out of the Communist Party was the shift from "large-scale Marxist preoccupations to liberal particularism" (PC:SM), and to a considerable extent that holds true in the case of Armstrong as in my own.[21] However, for Armstrong it was a turn not simply to more particularistic ethnographic concerns but also to an alternative solution of the problem of totalization that was foreshadowed in Armstrong's work prior to his political disillusionment and that perhaps reflected aspects of his underlying intellectual

---

21. At the time the comment seemed apt in my own case, in which "the disillusion of the Khrushchev revelations eventuated in a mix of [historical] particularism, [ambivalent] relativism, [political] hopelessness, and comradely nostalgia—I never became anti-[Communist], and remained respectful of my own and my comrades' motivation, however ultimately misguided" (PC:GS/SM 1/9/02). Although empathic retroprojection has, I hope, facilitated my interpretation of Armstrong, there are some qualifications to be made. In Armstrong's case the nostalgia (manifest in conversation with a radically minded friend in the 1980s and in snatches of interpretation in several of his later essays) seems in its expression to have been more intellectual than comradely, the loss of hope more tempered by congenital optimism, the relativism less troubled by ambivalence, and the particularism manifest in relation to ethnic groups rather than historical individuals.

character. It could be argued, for instance, that there was a "fit" between his army cryptographic work and his deeply rooted musical interests, on the one hand, and an interest in the meaning patterns of particular cultures and the sound patterns of particular languages, on the other. Be that as it may, there are aspects of his early anthropological efforts, both theoretical and ethnographic, that suggest a tension between metahistorical or large-scale social theoretical concerns and ethnographic particularism, in which a move to totalization was made in mentalistic cultural terms. In his master's thesis the "pursuit of relevant data" was carried on not only in terms of the ethnographer's "principal ideas" but also in terms of his "emotional reactions" to the "intrinsically lovable" in Cheyenne "character" and to the "cohesiveness" of their "folk community" (Armstrong 1942:1–9, 126–29). From this point of view, Armstrong's difficulty in defining the "socio-cultural phenomenon" of Caguas, his abandonment of "Society and Matter" at just the point where he planned to treat the concepts of "culture" and "society," and the challenges he faced in his early Nigerian fieldwork all point to more general problems: on the one hand, how to relate his rather grandiose "dialectical" concerns to the frustrating phenomenal rich-ness of the ethnographic material he encountered in the field and, on the other, how to understand that ethnographic richness in its culturally specific totality. The latter tension was evident in his correspondence with Murra in the oppo-sition between a comparative study of "the range of political structures in one ethnic group" and a more "intensive study" of the "soul of a people." Murra, fa-voring the former, refused to see them in opposition; Armstrong, over time, clearly chose the latter.

Although the more direct intellectual influence on Armstrong may well have been Redfield's, his shift may be placed in a broader disciplinary perspec-tive in terms of two options classically formulated by Boas in "The Study of Geography": on the one hand, the physicist's search for general laws and, on the other, the cosmographer's "loving penetration" and affective apprehension of phenomena. Manifest throughout the history of anthropology, both approaches have been "available" for different anthropologists in different personal, polit-ical, and historical contexts through various channels other than direct cita-tion of Boas, who was himself in this instance speaking typologically of episte-mological and methodological possibilities that did not depend on specific intellectual influences but on the temperamental predisposition of the investi-gator (cf. Boas 1887; Stocking 1989:279–80, 339–40). Be all this as it may, it is the case that Armstrong's rather diverse anthropological interests had become more focused by the later 1950s, when it seems clear that their main thrust was toward the investigation of human mental productions, as embodied in cultural performances or texts that might be collected or elicited by the ethnographer, as well as in the study of language, all of these in their ethnographic particu-larity and totalizing cultural specificity but with the assumption they were susceptible also of transcultural and universally human generalization in a liberal democratic mode. Although Armstrong seems to have arrived at this position without specific reference to Boas's work, his intellectual trajectory may be described archetypically (and as such oversimplified) as carrying him from Marx to Boas.

Influence, Resonance, Re-presentation

Given this trajectory in Armstrong's career, what can we say about the impact of his anthropological oeuvre in terms of its longer-term influence (or resonance) during his lifetime and since his death?[22] Judged by various criteria, Armstrong left relatively few traces in the history of anthropology. In the early stages of this study it seemed that, save for a few members of his student cohort at Chicago, he was little remembered even by Africanist anthropologists in this country and likely to be confused with another Nigerianist, Robert Plant Armstrong, who received his Ph.D. at Northwestern in 1957. Seeking what might be a more rigorous measure, I turned to the *Web of Science* for citations of Armstrong's work between 1956 and 2001 along with those of five other anthropologists whose careers touched his in the early years. All five anthropologists were cited at least three times as often as Armstrong (86 citations): Stanley Diamond, who completed a library dissertation on the Dahomey "proto-state" a

22. After reading the antepenultimate version of this essay Dell Hymes objected to my treatment of Armstrong's influence on the grounds that "success in a life" was not to be measured simply by "a long bibliography" or the number of its citations (with which I agree) and that such life-success might also be evidenced in Armstrong's funeral ritual (which I had gone to some trouble to re-present, with this very idea in mind). Another colleague has wondered why I bothered to "waste" so much historiographical effort on a figure who had neither influence in the past nor relevance in the present. Granting that "influence" is difficult to define, demonstrate, or trace, there nevertheless seem to me good historiographical reasons for considering it (and the related problem of "resonance")—not least insofar as doing so may cast light on general tendencies in the history of anthropology, both during and since the period being studied. The present attempt complements previous ruminations on the topic in two other components of the larger project of which this essay is intended to be a part: an essay on Sol Tax (Stocking 2000:245–56) and another on A. Irving Hallowell (Stocking 2004a: 237–53; cf. the reflections in Stocking 1987:169–72). Without attempting here to articulate present comments with prior ones, my hope is that some additional aspects of the influence problem may be evident in the pages that follow, by example if not by systematic explication. And since much of my motivation in the case of Armstrong has been personal (I hope self-reflexively), I should perhaps add that I am well aware that my interest in Armstrong's influence (or lack thereof) and in the general topic reflects aspects of my own personality (in which achievement anxiety is very strong), of my professional situation (as an established but marginal member of an elite anthropology department), of my intellectual history (which has recurrently focused on the tension between historicism and presentism), and of my career phase (as a late septuagenarian scholar whose own anthropological oeuvre is now virtually complete and open to critique, neglect, and other intergenerational forces of the "influence" process) (Stocking n.d.; cf. Castañeda 2003).

year prior to Armstrong's more ambitious one on six African cases and who later worked among the Anaguta of east-central Nigeria (c. 280); Robin Horton, who worked among the Kalabari of southeastern Nigeria and who was Armstrong's IAS colleague before going on to teach first at the University of Ife and then at the University of Nigeria in Port Harcourt (c. 350); Paul Bohannan, who worked among the neighboring Tiv while Armstrong was doing his early fieldwork among the Idoma (435); and two of the "Columbia gang" on the Steward Puerto Rico project, Eric Wolf (402) and Sidney Mintz (433).[23]

Acknowledging the assumptional and empirical vagaries of citation analysis, one may nevertheless use these results as reference points in considering the problem of Armstrong's influence. The vast majority of the citations of his works were of publications that appeared before 1970 (76 of 86 citations), and this is even more the case among his most cited works, only five of which continued to be cited into the 1990s. The most frequently cited was his contribution to *Peoples of the Niger-Benue Confluence*, a volume in Forde's Ethnographic Survey of Africa series (Armstrong 1955), which remains to this day a reference point for anthropological discussions of groups that have not since been the subject of intensive fieldwork (Kolapo 1999). Next came one of the only two of Armstrong's works that were reviewed in a major anthropological journal, his inaugural lecture at Ibadan, "The Study of West African Languages," which (although the review had been on several points quite critical) continued to be cited for almost twenty years after its first publication (1964a; Wolff 1965; Uzukwu 1982). The third, "The Use of Linguistic and Ethnographic Data in the Study of Idoma and Yoruba History," was one of Armstrong's early publications on the uses of glottochronology in historical reconstruction (1961b, 1961c; Bondarenko and Roese 1999). The fourth, "A West African Inquest," was Armstrong's most important publication from his early Idoma fieldwork and his only one in the *American Anthropologist* (1954b; Ogede 1995). The last was his early publication, "Yoruba Numerals," which was favorably reviewed in the same journal (1962a; Wolff 1963; Gerdes 1994). His later work, during and after the period when he was IAS director, was little cited—with the notable

<hr>

23. I am grateful for the assistance of Ellen Bryan of the Regenstein Library reference service in searching the *Web of Science*. When it became evident that there were few if any citations to his work among the many Armstrongs in the *Science Citation Index* or among the "Armstrong R" entries in the *Social Science Citation Index* and the *Arts and Humanities Citation Index*, the search was limited to "Armstrong RG" in the latter two sources. The figures for Robert Plant Armstrong, Stanley Diamond, and Robin Horton are approximations arrived at after scanning to eliminate others with the same name and first initials. A search of the "author index" of the *Annual Review of Anthropology* from 1972 (when it separated from the *Biennial Review*, in which there was no such index) until 1999 (after which it ceased to be included) produced similar results: only two references to Robert G. Armstrong during the 27-year period, in contrast to Stanley Diamond (19 citations in 12 years of the 27), Robin Horton (23 citations in 13 years), Paul Bohannan (33 citations in 15 years), Sidney Mintz (45 citations in 17 years), and Eric Wolf (125 citations in 25 years).

exception of a richly textual study of Idoma "theological" thought based on earlier fieldwork in which he argued that "the earliest systematic religious and cosmological ideas" of ancient Africa were "no primitive beginning" but rather "the end points of millennia of intellectual activity and development," fully deserving of "a big place in the general history of human ideas" (Armstrong 1982:14; Lawal 1995).

These results fit the trajectory evident in the prior narrative account of Armstrong's career, which moved from an early global aspiration for universal anthropological meaning to a later local ethnographic and linguistic preoccupation, with a brief gesture at the end toward comparative significance. This pattern may be contrasted with the citation indicators of the five anthropologists previously mentioned in terms of differences in their publication or career patterns. The closest in this respect is Horton, whose citations include no major monograph on the Kalabari; Horton, however, was a frequent contributor to Africa, and several of his essays, eventually collected in a volume on *Patterns of Thought in Africa and the West* (1993), became long-standing reference points in a debate about "primitive" mentality that has been central to anthropology since the later nineteenth century. In the case of Bohannan, there are not only a number of longer works on the Tiv (e.g., 1957) but various books on more general anthropological topics, including a textbook in social anthropology (1963). Diamond's Nigerian ethnography represents only a portion of his anthropological oeuvre and in his later career was overshadowed by his work on "the idea of primitivism" (1974) and other more politically oriented writings reflecting his participation in "the reinvention of anthropology" in the aftermath of the crisis of the 1960s (1979; cf. Hymes 1972). Similarly, the work of both Mintz and Wolf, although richly ethnographic, began in the 1960s to engage larger world-historical projects from a Marxist point of view (Mintz et al. 1984; Mintz 1985; Wolf 1969, 1999). In short, the careers of all five moved from the locally ethnographic toward larger issues in the history of debate within the discipline or in the relation of its traditional subject matter to broader historical processes, including especially the expansion of European colonial power over non-European "others" (Wolf 1964, 1982). With the exception of Horton, a British anthropologist who "stayed on" in Nigeria, they all were able, after passing through the political minefields of the 1950s, to establish themselves in important academic institutions in the United States. Three of them (Diamond, Mintz, and Wolf) went on to play significant roles in the "critique" and "reinvention" movement of the later 1960s and early 1970s, thence to become elder statesmen of radical anthropology as it moved from the margins to the mainstream of academic anthropology in the 1980s and 1990s. But if they were critics of the "world system" of European domination, they nevertheless enjoyed the benefits of participation in what has been called the "academic world system" of anthropology (Kuwayama 2003, 2004).

Within this hegemonic anthropological system American (specifically U.S.) anthropology, although initially sharing intellectual dominance with the British and the French, was increasingly influential intellectually and was in fact preponderant institutionally and demographically (i.e., numerically). The gap between Armstrong's citational rate and that of his anthropological alters may be considered in this context. Had Armstrong remained in the United States, it is possible that his career pattern might have paralleled that of the "Columbia gang." With the fading of McCarthyism and the expansion of academic opportunities in the early 1960s he might have established a position from which to turn again to larger-scale anthropological issues in the tumultuously radical atmosphere of the later 1960s. Instead, save for occasional visits to the United States, he remained in Ibadan, an ocean away from the center of the academic world system of anthropology, and was less likely to participate in the critical tendencies that eventuated in a call for its "reinvention." His political impulses were expressed rather in the defense of the Nigerian republic against the Biafran secession and in a more traditional Boasian defense of the Idoma as deserving a "big place in the history of human ideas." By the same token, his anthropological impulses were expressed in the collection of Idoma texts and the construction of an Idoma dictionary, neither of them activities likely to win him citations in the *Web of Science*. Just as the Idoma (a minority people within a Third World nation) were doubly marginal to the European world system, so Idoma texts and an Idoma dictionary were doubly marginal to the world system of academic anthropology.

Viewed from the center of that system, Armstrong's influence in Nigeria is not so easily tracked. Over the years, as the *Web of Science* included more Third World–oriented sources, the proportion of citations of Armstrong's work by Nigerian (or, in several instances, other African) writers increased, from six of twenty-seven in the 1970s to ten of fourteen in the 1990s. Keeping in mind the delegation of 1974 and the larger postcolonial nationalist impulse it represented, one might hypothesize an early suppression of short-term historical memory, followed by hints of recovery as local Nigerian scholarship became more solidly established. In this context it is worth noting that in a 1976 symposium on mother-tongue education in West Africa, a topic central to Armstrong's interest, he was cited only once, and then incidentally (Bamgbose 1976:15; cf. Williamson 1985; Adeniran 1987; Bamgbose 1991:54; Bamgbose et al. 1992). Beyond that, I can only add that none of the citational material I collected would justify the recuperation of Armstrong as an important local influence. Insofar as such numbers can be given interpretive weight, the changing proportion of citations by site seems stronger as an index of declining influence at the center than of resurging influence at the periphery.

If so, this may have bearing on the general problem of influence in anthropology. Long-prevailing disciplinary dogma would have it that fieldwork-based ethnographic knowledge is foundational to modern anthropology and that as such it gives anthropology a special status among humanistic disciplines. It has even been argued by some to be of more long-lasting significance than the fads and fashions of anthropological theory (e.g., Murdock 1972). In contrast to this widespread assumption, it might be suggested that with a few exceptions the publication of ethnographic (or linguistic) material per se is unlikely to establish or sustain a reputation in mainstream academic anthropology. While a few major figures in the early phases of the modern academic discipline—Boas, Malinowski, Evans-Pritchard, among others—are remembered for their ethnographic contributions, it is in large part because their pathbreaking ethnographic work was accomplished at a time when the fields unplowed by academic ethnographers were many and academic ethnographers were few, and that in this context they created masses of ethnographic material that continue to provide grist for the mills of theoretical interpretation and debate.

Closer to the ethnographic and disciplinary present, it might be argued that what beefed up the citation rates of Armstrong's anthropological alters was not their ethnographic work but their more generalizing larger works (or, in the case of Horton, several theoretically significant articles). Although several of Armstrong's later linguistic articles aspired to a certain theoretical significance, there was little or nothing in his published work that systematically addressed the "big questions" that had originally motivated his anthropology (1950a, 1950b). Furthermore, the "big book" that in fact preoccupied him, the dictionary of Idoma (a genre little likely to have been frequently cited in the *Web of Science*), remained incomplete at the time of his death and does so still.

Armstrong's disappearance from disciplinary view is a more complex historical problem than the problematic evidence of citation analysis suggests.[24] It

24. After reading a penultimate draft of this essay Kay Williamson, who was extremely helpful as an informant and interlocutor, offered a marginal query: "Were you looking at citations by anthropologists? Linguists such as I do refer to some of his works." While linguistic journals are covered to some extent in the *Web of Science*, it seems likely that they get short shrift (along with local publications in "peripheral" areas). Another linguist, Larry Hyman (whom Williamson had recommended I contact), quoted to me a passage from his own keynote address at the Fourth World Congress of African Linguistics at Rutgers in June 2003:

Why describe African languages? The loss of a language, African or otherwise, is a serious event which is compounded by everything that we failed to do in terms of documentation. Least of our failures may be our inability to know what it might have told us about Language in general. Once in 1970 when I visited Robert Armstrong, then director of the Institute of African Studies in Ibadan, I walked in on a session where he and his assistants were transcribing some mega-recitations of Idoma chants, which had been laboriously recorded over a period of weeks with a single reciter. When I expressed my fascination, Armstrong replied, "Imagine all of the Iliads and Odysseys that are walking around out there," succinctly characterizing the importance and vastness of the situation. Even if a language is not itself en-

may also be understood in terms of his political victimization and exile, the complexities of his particular ethnographic-cum-colonial situation, his commitment to the IAS, and his dedication to the subdiscipline of linguistic anthropology—as well as his early death relative to his citational alters. It may reflect as well aspects of the larger discipline of anthropology (the reach of which exceeds the grasp of all but the greatest of its devotees) and of the larger world of scholarship, where many are called but few are chosen, and the half-life of citational immortality may be over well before the physical life of the scholar. But whatever interpretive balance is struck between such contextual factors, it seems evident that, after decades of "pecking away at the mountain," the light that Armstrong found at the end of the tunnel was neither so bright nor so far-reaching as he might once have hoped.

Perhaps, however, a shift in the modality of metaphor from light to sound may help to justify the historiographical effort here devoted to a figure whose historical significance estimated in terms of "influence" seems to have been limited. The question could then be asked, What in the career and work of Robert Gelston Armstrong might today be called "resonant" in the sense of "reinforcement or prolongation of a sound" by its "reflection or sympathetic vibration" with the sounds of contemporary anthropology, leaving aside the question of putative influence, direct or indirect (as well as that of originally innovative or derivative quality—a variant, one notes, of the traditional anthropological question of "independent invention" versus "diffusion")? And in the new modality, one could also ask, What in Armstrong's work might in the present *sound* familiar but on closer listening emit pulses of audible dissonance, in the etymological sense of sound "apart"—discordant or incongruous sounds that call into question an initial impression or expectation of similarity? In terms of the dualisms of previous historiographical discussion, "resonance" is perhaps more suggestive of "presentism" and "dissonance" of "historicism." Methodologically, however, the two terms may be seen to mediate the opposition insofar as they suggest an ear open to the full range of sounds to be heard in the surviving evidence from a particular historical past rather than an ear

---

dangered, certain aspects of the culture may be. So, we are sensitized to the urgent need to get out there, even if many of us don't drop everything and go and do it. . . . You hear people contrast "theory" and "data," as in "some people are more interested in the data than in theory," or "we have enough data, what we need is more theory." There's a sense in which Robert Armstrong's actual tape recordings of the Idoma chants are data, but both the transcription and the description require an analysis of considerable sophistication.

Although Hyman went on to suggest that fifteen years later he had cited information about the Idoma language he had gotten from Armstrong in his *Theory of Phonological Weight* (1985:49–51), what is striking in the passage quoted is the enduring strength of the tradition of "salvage" ethnography in the field of linguistic anthropology.

cocked to catch only those that harmonize with the themes of a present interpretive score.[25]

A young radical enculturated into the more flexible and variegated Marxism
of the later twentieth century, anticipating a resonantly precursory Marxist
voice in the era of McCarthyism and taken aback by seemingly dissonant tones
in "Society and Matter," with its dependence on Soviet philosophers of the
Stalinist era, might be inclined to dismiss as historiographical static what from
Armstrong's standpoint was at the very least resonant if not generative discourse. Without some adjustment of their historiographical hearing aids, more
present-minded auditors are not likely either to hear Armstrong's historical
voice in context or to sort out resonances more relevant to the anthropological
discourse of the present. With these cautions in mind, let us turn from homosexuality (about which he did not specifically speak) and from Marxism (about
which he spoke in a different dialect before lapsing into silence) to topics of
greater centrality in the main body of his published anthropological writings.
Keeping an ear open for the dissonances that make possible a contextual historical understanding, we may perhaps hear resonances of themes in contemporary anthropology: the critique of racism, Afrocentrism, and "humanism"
versus "scientism" in anthropology.

In the course of research on Armstrong's influence it was suggested to me by
a friend who had known him that I should keep in mind his positive historical
role in critiquing racist assumptions. There is no doubt that, despite residual (or
neo-) evolutionary assumptions evident especially in his early anthropology,
Armstrong held generally "progressive" views on race and race relations. But
the extent to which these views were original to him and as such influential
among anthropologists is another matter. When he arrived at the University of
Chicago in the fall of 1939, the anthropological groundwork for the critique of
racial assumption had long since been laid by Boas (Stocking 1968:133–234).
And while efforts by Boas in the early 1930s to mobilize scientists against Nazi
racism had met resistance among more conservative scientists (including anthropologists), at the end of December 1938 the American Anthropological
Association unanimously approved a resolution foreshadowing major points of
the UNESCO statements on race of 1949 and 1951 (Barkan 1988:201–3). The
fact that the resolution was presented (although not authored) by Fay-Cooper

25. On "resonance" see also Stocking 2000:254–56. When my then long-time editor at the
University of Wisconsin Press, Betty Steinberg, first read a draft of that passage, she resisted the
term "resonance" on the ground that in its common sense of "echoing" it could only work in one
temporal direction, from past to present, since (chrono)logically, one could not find in the past
echoes of the present, because it had not yet happened, which is a rather more rigorous historicism
than I then intended. At the time, she reluctantly allowed me to have my authorial way, which has
since led me to this further historiographical whimsy—yet another step in the evolution of my
views on presentism and historicism (Stocking 1965, 1999; cf. Di Brizio 1995; Dias 2003).

Cole was consistent with prevailing sentiments of the Chicago department, especially among the graduate student cohort on the ground when Armstrong arrived the following September. While there is no doubt that such progressive views on race were important motivating factors in his subsequent anthropology, he is not unique in this respect; the same could be said of other progressive or radically inclined anthropologists of his generation. In short, if Armstrong's views are appropriately to be reemphasized today, it is not because they have been directly influential but because they seem resonant today in an historical moment when a reassertion of biological determinism in the public realm threatens an antiracialist consensus that by and large has prevailed within anthropology for most of the last half century (Lieberman et al. 2003; cf. Caspari 2003; Cartmill and Brown 2003).

A second tendency in contemporary anthropology (or at its margins) where the issue of influence or resonance might be addressed is that of Afrocentrism. That one of Armstrong's early articles was commissioned for the Second World Congress of Negro Writers and published in an early volume of *Presence Africaine* (1959b) suggests a possible relationship that would seem at first to be confirmed by an index citation to "Armstrong, R." in a recent edited volume, *The Afrocentric Paradigm* (Mazama 2003:284). But in the text of that article, by a leading spokesman of the movement, the reference, although favorable, is in fact to Robert Plant Armstrong (Asante 2003:39, 52), whose mentor, Herskovits, is one of the small number of non-African or non–African American figures included in the various listings of precursory or "pre-Afrocentric" figures in this and other volumes on the topic (Asante 1999:113; cf. Gray 2001). Surprisingly, those lists seem not to include Boas, whose Atlanta University commencement address, "The Negro's Past," was explicitly acknowledged as a formative influence by W. E. B. Du Bois, a frequently listed precursor (Boas 1906, cf. 1904; Williams 1996:74). That Armstrong should not have made the list, however, is no surprise, given the citational trajectory of influence outlined above. On the other hand, insofar as an insistence on the self-generated cultural creativity of African peoples is a foundational tenet of "the Afrocentric idea" (as opposed to the more problematic claims of Africa as "the cradle of human civilization and therefore culture"; see Dove 2003:166, with reference to Cheikh Anta Diop; cf. Lefkowitz 1996), then the inclusion of Armstrong might be justified, if not as influential, then as resonant, on the basis of his critique of the Hamitic hypothesis and his persistent insistence on the "subtlety and intricacy of African thought."

However, one cannot include Armstrong without acknowledging significant dissonances. These dissonances are especially evident in relation to the problems of cultural and epistemological diversity or unity: on the one hand, the unity of African culture as against the diversity of African cultures; on the other, the unity or plurality of ways of knowing the world. Regarding the issue

of cultural diversity: while there are passages in Armstrong that suggest a commitment to African unity, either as a cultural category or as a political goal, his
primary professional activity was in studying the diversity of African cultures in
their ethnographic and linguistic specificity and in their historical relationships. Regarding the issue of epistemological diversity: while Armstrong actively encouraged the training and increasing participation of African students
in linguistic and anthropological work and insisted on a certain cultural rela-
tivity as essential to that inquiry, he did not regard "the idea of scientific neu-
trality and universality as untenable" (Mazama 2003:7). If sound anthropological knowledge was for him a means to cultural and political liberation, it was
at the same time part of a progressively accumulating universal body of knowledge that was in a general sense "scientific."

    This underlying universalist scientific commitment (cast sometimes in evo-
lutionary terms) remained to the end an aspect of Armstrong's anthropology.
Nevertheless, there is also discernible, over the course of his years in Nigeria, a
more "humanistic" approach to anthropological inquiry, especially in regard to
issues of ethnographic method. It is here that resonances of contemporary concerns are perhaps most audible. In arguing the importance of "acoustic" (or
instrumental) phonetics as a supplement to "articulatory" (or observational)
phonetics in the reconstruction of a tenth vowel in the proto-Kwa language,
Armstrong did not hesitate also to introduce a "scientific-artistic anecdote"
about a Yoruba dental student (later to be his own dentist in Ibadan) trying unsuccessfully to correct the pronunciation of a friend of Armstrong who was unable to hear the difference between *kpé* and *gbé*: "I had been studying singing
intensively in New York, and it was obvious to me that Aremu's vocalization of
[e] had the beautifully musically rounded, resonant, Italianate *bel canto* quality
that I was spending good money trying to acquire" (1985a:108). So also, in discussing the basis of belief in the power of sacrifice (a question that "leaves most
scientists cold"), Armstrong suggested the "not very fashionable name of 'em-
pathy'" to characterize the "participatory" basis of sacrificial ritual, insisting
that a "satisfactory answer" would depend on "a great deal of first-rate, depth-
interviewing in vernacular languages" (1975:130). And in exploring the question of the seniority of Earth to God in West African theology he drew on texts
recorded and translated with the help of several named Nigerian coworkers in
the course of interviews over a period of twenty years, including one with the
king of Otukpo and his royal council ("of which I am a member"), in the course
of which competing views of seniority were argued (Armstrong 1982:8–9).
Manifest in these passages and elsewhere in Armstrong's work are a number of
methodological markers of contemporary "humanistic" anthropology (empa-
thy, reflexivity, dialogicality, textuality, literariness), none of them unique to it
but each of them often used to set it off from more "scientistic" tendencies in
the discipline (*Anthropology and Humanism Quarterly*, passim). In Armstrong,

however, the clarity of these resonances is blurred a bit by dissonance, insofar as they are manifest not as alternatives to a more scientific approach but as pre-conditions or supplements, still sometimes cast in neo-evolutionary terms, as in his last published essay, where Samson Amali's poem "The Hunter" was offered as supporting evidence for an interpretation of the origin of the Ogun cult in a cultural evolutionary framework (1984).

Despite such dissonances, it seems clear in retrospect that the thrust of Arm-strong's anthropology was from science to humanism and that in his later work, which constitutes the larger (although least cited) portion of his oeuvre, the humanist tendency is clearly the predominant one.[26] Insofar as intellectual an-cestors are chosen retrospectively by virtue of their perceived resonance rather than their traceable influence (as indeed they often are, and not without justi-fication), then Armstrong, though unread today, is perhaps a candidate for in-clusion as a collateral member of a humanist lineage that can be traced back to Boas—although Boas, in terms of the defining polarity, was himself an intel-lectual hybrid (Stocking 1986:197). There is no citational evidence that Arm-strong was strongly influenced by Boas, and the Boasian resonances in his work could of course be "independent inventions" in response to his own ethno-graphic experience or perhaps "diffusions" from some other mentoring source. However, there is at least one indirect connection, inasmuch as Armstrong was a student of Cole, who obtained a doctorate under Boas, and Armstrong's ref-erences to Sapir suggest another. But whatever their source, the Boasian reso-nances in his work are numerous and strong enough to suggest that, although not himself an influential figure, Armstrong might appropriately be co-opted retrospectively as a precursor of contemporary neo-Boasianism, one center of which has been the department from which he was excluded in 1953 (cf. Bashkow et al. 2004).

Other ears than mine may catch in Armstrong's work snatches of resonances different from those just noted. After reading the penultimate draft of this es-say, Constance Sutton, who knew Armstrong (as well as others mentioned in this essay) and who was extremely helpful as an informant/interlocutor, noted four ideas in Armstrong's "early work/theorizing" that were "now accepted, but were not then characteristic ways of thinking about society and culture." First, he anticipated the "processual" approach in anthropology by seeing society as a "dynamic, interacting whole," the parts "constantly producing mutual changes," and the same could be said for his early attention to the notion of

---

26. The polarity between the humanistic and the scientific impulses/tendencies, like most po-larities, is perhaps better regarded as heuristic than as hypostatic, as a help in understanding com-plex intellectual phenomena rather than as a postulation of opposing essences. In the world of ac-tual discourse, where they function as identity markers for both actors and their antagonists as well as for historians, the boundaries between the two tendencies can be sharpened as well as blurred.

"contradictions" (i.e., conflicting elements in a social or cultural system). Second, in his master's thesis on the Cheyenne he picked up the issue of cultural retention despite enforced acculturation, which today is the dominant theme of anthropologists writing about the global/local relationship and about how past traditions continue to inform the present. Third, she pointed to his depiction of Caguas as a nexus of contradictory relationships within a town with a strong local feeling based on common residence but many of whose residents traveled outside the town to make a living:

> I wish I had read that when I encountered the village I studied in the late 1950s and was struggling how to write this up in my doctoral dissertation. Of course it was only a nexus of "contradictory" relationships if you implicitly assumed that "community" meant people who lived a "womb to tomb" existence with the same set of relationships—which was implicitly the earlier model anthropologists had of people they studied. Today having a strong local feeling (identity) while moving around the world is something anthropologists have been documenting all over the place as they study transnational migrations.

Finally, Sutton suggested that Armstrong's interest "in the inverse relationship between kinship and statehood . . . was revisited in the late 70s and 80s by feminist anthropologists who examined in considerable detail the shifts that occurred in kin/gender relations as societies became more politically centralized in Peru, Polynesia, and West Africa" (PC:10/1/03). It is worth noting, however, that Sutton's reactions were elicited by materials presented in this essay from Armstrong's early career (his master's thesis and his doctoral dissertation) and that she did not recall his having discussed them during the years she knew him. He seems not to have developed them systematically himself, unless perhaps in unpublished papers that have not survived in the sources I consulted (such as the one on "cultural patterns" he sent to Fred Eggan in 1955 that I was unable to find in the Eggan manuscripts). It is perhaps worth noting, however, that when he visited me in Chicago in 1978 he did say, "We need a new paradigm. It should focus on the Third World. It will not be self-reflexive but multi-reflexive"—but by that time his own early paradigmatic efforts had long been abandoned. Even so, if such resonances were to vibrate in the minds of other readers, they might perhaps become instances of Armstrong's rediscovered or retroprojected precursory influence.[27]

Generalizing, one might suggest that the boundary between "resonance" and

27. At a late point in the completion of this essay Herb Lewis recalled to me having been "impressed" by a paper that Armstrong gave in 1955 at the Boston meeting of the AAA entitled "State Formation in Africa": "It is my recollection that he argued against the British Africanist pallid sense of the state as a peace-maintaining organization with a balance of reciprocities, etc.—sort of the John Beattie view articulated a little later. Instead, he said (I think) there is no real circle of reciprocity but these states were really exploitative, rulers over people" (PC:8/5/05).

"influence" is always historically renegotiable, insofar as present-day anthropologists may read the work of past writers with whom they may or may not have prior connection, selecting from the body of their writings ideas (however fragmentary or elaborated) that resonate with their own, and on that basis discover them as intellectual ancestors, either as sources of intellectual legitimacy or as food for serious anthropological thinking. In such a case, retrospectively chosen ancestors can indeed be said to have present influence, regardless of their historically verifiable lineal or collateral connections. (Cf. Pouillon 1980:39: "Tradition for us, too, is a 'retroprojection': We choose what we say we are determined by; we present ourselves as the heirs of those we have made our predecessors.")

Having suggested that possibility, there is one more question of resonance to be considered, the one with which this essay began: Armstrong as victim of cold war McCarthyism. When an earlier, much shorter version of this paper was presented to a group of colleagues interested in the history of the human sciences, one of the questions raised in discussion (although not so phrased) was "Cui bono?": For whose benefit, that is, who stands to gain from this? To what purpose, that is, what utility is this? The questioner (Saul Thomas, a student of mine who had done extensive research on another early cold war anthropologist—and whom I here paraphrase) was worried that in the current political environment, when "the war on terrorism" poses a serious threat to fundamental civil liberties, some of the things I said about Armstrong might give aid and comfort to present enemies—this by obscuring the more general historical processes driving McCarthyism and by implicating Armstrong in his own fate (e.g., by recounting episodes in which he might be regarded as cooperating, albeit reluctantly, with his inquisitors). Somewhat taken aback at the time, I recall affirming my awareness of more general historical processes, my commitment to civil liberties, and my discomfort at the thought of giving aid and comfort to their enemies. Granting the force of these issues and the timeliness and legitimacy of pursuing them, I would at the same time insist once again on both the historiographic and moral legitimacy of my own project, which emphasizes the experience and the consciousness of the actor who is the primary focus of my attention, as best as I can reconstruct them.

Rather than trying to rewrite the wrong of Armstrong's victimization, as I was originally inclined to do, I have tried instead to re-present him not simply as victim but in the complex fullness of his human being. Beyond that, however, I have tried to re-present him as in significant ways "representative" of American anthropology in the middle years of the twentieth century. For if he was not an anthropological "star" of the first magnitude, Armstrong's life experience as an anthropologist may nevertheless cast light, either by reflection or refraction, on a number of the tendencies and tensions in American anthropology in a period when it was undergoing significant changes. Among others,

these include the entry into new and challenging areas of ethnographic research and the opening up of new and problematic sources of funding; the accompanying changes in fieldwork styles and sensibilities; the interaction of
British social and American cultural anthropology; the accommodations of the
functional and historical approaches; the evolving critique of race and the persistence of evolutionary thinking; the delayed emergence and attempted repression of Marxist viewpoints; the opposition between psychological and materialist interpretations; as well as such enduring and recurring tensions in
anthropology as those between universalism and cultural relativism and between science and humanism. These tendencies and tensions were manifest, on
the one hand, in Armstrong's wide-ranging eclectic intellectual style and, on
the other, in the shifts in emphasis in his anthropological point of view over the
course of his career. And they were manifest also in his interactions with particular anthropologists (notably, Murra and Redfield) and in his marginal relationship to important intellectual affinity groups within anthropology: on the
one hand, through Murra to the radical materialist group sheltered by Julian
Steward at Columbia, where links were extended also to students of Leslie
White; on the other hand, through Redfield to a looser but recognizable liberal
idealist group variously interested in culture and personality (Mead), values
(Kluckhohn), and civilizations (Redfield). In both cases his relationship was
"marginal" because in neither case did Armstrong become seriously involved in
the group's organized anthropological projects.

Armstrong's marginality, of course, may be viewed in the context of other
processes at work in American anthropology and in American culture generally in the postwar period—processes that ran counter to the contemporary
and retrospective self- and public images of the discipline as not simply de-
fenders of but as open to otherness. To a greater extent than has perhaps been
generally appreciated, midcentury anthropology was dominated—ideologically, institutionally, and demographically—by native-born white Protestant
liberal male academics. In different ways and to varying degrees, members of
other sociocultural categories (women, radicals, homosexuals, Africans and
Native Americans, even Catholics and Jews) were either excluded, or under-
represented, or kept at the margins, or impelled to deny or repress aspects of
their own identities. Although the articulation of these various exclusionary
processes is beyond the scope of this essay, it is certainly relevant to Armstrong's
disciplinary marginality that he belonged to two of these groups and had close
academic connections with a third. As an accused Communist exiled from
American academia at the height of the McCarthy period, a closeted homosexual before gay liberation, and an internal academic refugee in an African American University, Armstrong's career of marginalization took an unexpected turn
from exile to expatriation, and for two decades he enjoyed the relatively privileged life of research professor on the faculty of a major Nigerian university, finally to be buried with chiefly honors among "his people."

Re-presented here in terms of its complex and contradictory fullness, Armstrong's life history as an anthropologist is perhaps not easily considered as "representative" in a systematic comparative sense. Even so, one may hope that it can provide useful empirical grist for the mills of historians of differing interpretive inclinations, including those for whom the critical question of meaning is "cui bono?" in the postmillennial historical world. And if my own interpretive mill has not finally resolved what Armstrong called the "unfinished business" of his exclusion from the anthropology department at the University of Chicago in 1953, it may at least offer a kind of posthumous reparation by writing for him a place in the historiography of twentieth-century anthropology in the United States and in Nigeria—and at the University of Chicago.

Acknowledgments

In the years during which I worked on this essay my efforts were supported by grants and fellowships from the Lichtstern Fund of the Department of Anthropology of the University of Chicago, the Wenner-Gren Foundation for Anthropological Research, the Dibner Institute for the History of Science and Technology, and the Andrew W. Mellon Foundation Emeritus Fellowship program. Over that period I accumulated many scholarly and personal debts. To those whose names I may have forgotten or misplaced I must offer anonymous and apologetic thanks. To several others mentioned in the text (including Fred Eggan, Sol Tax, Sherwood Washburn, and Kay Williamson) I can only offer thanks posthumously. In the course of my research there were many archivists who made possible consultation of unpublished sources, including, among others, Monica Blank of the Rockefeller Archives Center; Mike Morris of the Institute of Social and Cultural Anthropology, Oxford; Cathy Mundale of the Robert Woodruff Library, Atlanta University; and William Roberts of the Bancroft Library, University of California–Berkeley. I would like especially to thank Dan Meyer and the staff of the Special Collections Center of the Regenstein Library, where a number of collections contain materials relating to Armstrong's Chicago years, and Jake Homiak and the staff of the National Anthropological Archives, where the papers of John Murra include correspondence with Armstrong over more than a quarter of a century. I am also indebted to Jennifer Lewis, who made available to me her copy of Armstrong's FBI file, and to LaRay Denzer, who did research on my behalf at the Institute of African Studies, University of Ibadan, as well as to the staff of the institute, who facilitated her inquiries. And once again, my deep appreciation to all those listed under "Oral and Written Informant Sources" who greatly enriched my understanding of Armstrong and particularly of his Nigerian years. Of these I would like especially to thank J. F. Ade. Ajayi, Idowu Ajibola, Bolanle Awe, Ayo Bamgbose, Sidney Kasfir, David Laitin, Sidney Mintz, and Thurston Shaw as well as Constance Sutton and the late Kay Williamson, who in addition to contributing as informants carefully read and helpfully commented on the penultimate draft. Others who read part or all of various drafts include Greg Beckett, Dell Hymes, Sidney Mintz, James Redfield, and Robert Richards, and especially Richard Handler, who in the course of a careful editing read the essay several times and provided a home for it in print. Among students who have been lively participants in courses in which

Armstrong was discussed I would particularly like to thank Marina Alcalde, Aaron Ansell, Tom Guthrie, and David Madden as well as Bernard Dubbeld, Kevin Caffrey, Byron Hamann, Tal Liron, and Saul Thomas, who also served as research assistants during the period when I was actively writing. Helpful comments were offered also by members of the History of the Human Sciences Workshop of the Morris Fishbein Center for the History of Science and Medicine. Others who assisted in various ways include Ira Bashkow, Roger Blench, Matti Bunzl, Raymond Fogelson, Raymond Smith, and Kevin Yelvington. I should also mention Drs. Philip Dobrin, Bruce Gewertz, and Ashesh Jani, who saw me through a major health crisis in 2002–3. And, as always, there is my wife, Carol Bowman Stocking, who continues not only to tolerate but in many and varied ways to facilitate my research while pursuing her own as a sociologist on issues in clinical medical ethics and geriatrics, specialties appropriate to the care she devoted to me during my health crisis and its aftermath.

References Cited

To indicate their place in the development of his thought, all items by Armstrong are listed by date of first publication or (when publication was delayed) by the date of their completion or public presentation; in both instances, the date of the edition actually consulted or of the actual publication is indicated in brackets within the entry.

AA   American Anthropologist
AJS   American Journal of Sociology
AN   African Notes
AUB   Atlanta University Bulletin
HAN   History of Anthropology Newsletter
HOA   History of Anthropology
IASOP   Occasional Publications, Institute of African Studies, University of Ibadan
JWAL   Journal of West African Languages
RAL   Research in African Literatures

For other acronyms see "Manuscript Sources."

Abiri, J. 1973. The Making of the University of Ibadan, 1957–62. In Ajayi and Tamuno 1973:49–68.

Adeleye, R. 1973. The Independent University, 1962–68. In Ajayi and Tamuno 1973:69–98.

Adeniji, D. 1977. Ise Irin Wiwa ati Sisun [Traditional Yoruba Iron Mining and Smelting]. Ed. and trans. R. Armstrong. Ibadan.

Adeniran, A. 1987. Language Planning and Practice in Africa: The Need for Political Intervention. AN 10(1):1–7.

Ajayi, A. 1973. Postgraduate Studies and Staff Development. In Ajayi and Tamuno 1973:151–67.

Ajayi, A., and T. Tamuno, eds. 1973. The University of Ibadan: A History of the First Twenty-five Years. Ibadan.

Alagoa, E. J., ed. 1998. *Diké Remembered: African Reflections on History. Diké Memorial Lectures 1985–1995.* Port Harcourt, Nigeria.

Amali, S. O. O. 1968. *Selected Poems.* Privately printed. Ibadan.

———. 1985. An Ancient Nigerian Drama: The Idoma Inquest: A Bilingual Presentation in Idoma and English Together with Odgwudegwu: An Original Bilingual Play in Idoma and English. *Studien zu Kulturkunde* 71. Frankfurt.

Armstrong, R. 1942. The Acculturation of the Cheyenne and Arapaho Indians of Oklahoma. Master's thesis, University of Oklahoma (copy preserved in the Institute of Social and Cultural Anthropology, Oxford).

———. 1949. Intergroup Relations in Puerto Rico. *Phylon* 10:220–25.

———. 1950a. Society and Matter.Ms., DAP.

———. 1950b [1952]. State Formation in Negro Africa. Ph.D. dissertation, University of Chicago.

———. 1953. To the Faculty of Anthropology. Ms., political autobiography, in the author's possession.

———. 1954a. Talking Drums in the Benue–Cross River Region of Nigeria. *Phylon* 15:355–63.

———. 1954b. A West African Inquest. *AA* 56:1051–75.

———. 1955. The Igala [and] the Idoma-Speaking Peoples. In *Peoples of the Niger-Benue Confluence.* Ethnographic Survey of Africa series, D. Forde, gen. ed., Part 10:77–90, 91–155. London.

———. 1956 [1959]. The Idoma Court of Lineages. In *Proceedings of the IVth International Congress of Anthropological and Ethnological Sciences,* 390–95. Philadelphia.

———. 1957. Review of M. Griaule and G. Dierterlen, *Signes graphiques soudanais. Man* 8:138–40.

———. 1959a. Review of R. C. Abraham, *Dictionary of Modern Yoruba. Africa* 29:92–94.

———. 1959b. Le développement de l'unité culturelle en Afrique, au sud du Sahara. *Présence Africaine* 24/25:316–20 (translations by the author).

———. 1961a. The Religion of the Idoma. *Ibadan* 13:5–9.

———. 1961b [1963]. Vernacular Languages and Cultures in Modern Africa. In *Language in Africa.* Ed. John Spencer, 64–72. Cambridge, Eng..

———. 1961c [1963]. The Use of Linguistic and Ethnographic Data in the Study of Idoma and Yoruba History. In *The Historian in Tropical Africa: Studies Presented and Discussed at the Fourth International African Seminar at the University of Dakar, Senegal.* Ed. J. Vansina et al., 127–39. London.

———. 1962a. *Yoruba Numerals. Nigerian Social and Economic Studies* 1. London.

———. 1962b. Glottochronology and African Linguistics. *Journal of African History* 3:283–90.

———. 1962c [1964]. The Role of Linguistics in African Studies. Paper presented at the First International Congress of Africanists. *Phylon* 25:135–45.

———. 1962d [1963]. The Verb in Idoma. In *Actes du second colloque international de linguistique négro-africaine,* 127–57. Dakar.

———. 1964a. *The Study of West African Languages: An Inaugural Lecture.* Ibadan.

———. 1964b. Notes on Etulo. *JWAL* 1(2):57–60.

———. 1965a. Comparative Word Lists of Two Dialects of Yoruba with Igala. *JWAL* 2(2):51–78.

238   GEORGE W. STOCKING, JR.

———. 1965b. Intestate Succession among the Idoma. In *Studies in the Law of Succession in Nigeria*. Ed. J. Derrett, 212–29. Oxford.

———. 1965c. *Oka Ko So*. Transcription and translation of the Yoruba text of selections from the opera by Duro Ladipo. *IASOP* 3.

———. 1966a. Prolegomena to the Study of the Idoma Concept of God. *AN* 4(1): 11–17.

———. 1966b [1968]. Language Policies and Language Practices in West Africa. In *Language Problems of Developing Nations*. Ed. J. Fishman et al., 227–36. New York.

———. 1967a. Nigeria, 1965–67: Release from Old Prejudices. *Nigerian Opinion* 3(3): 171–73.

———. 1967b. The Nigerian Federation. *Nigerian Opinion* 3(5/6):201–2.

———. 1967c. *The Issues at Stake—Nigeria, 1967*. Ibadan.

———. 1967d. Yala (Ikom) Notes and Pronoun Paradigms. *Research Notes* (Department of Linguistics, University of Ibadan) 1:25–30.

———. 1967e. Foreword to the second (posthumous) edition, R. C. Abraham, *The Idoma Language. Idoma Word Lists. Idoma Chrestomathy. Idoma Proverbs*, 3. London.

———. 1968a. Yala (Ikom): A Terraced-Level Language with Three Tones. *JWAL* 5: 49–58.

———. 1968b. *Oka Ko So*. Transcription and translation of the complete Yoruba text of the opera by Duro Ladipo (with R. Awujoola and V. Olayemi). *IASOP* 10.

———. 1968c. *The Palmwine Drinkard*. Transcription and translation of the complete Yoruba text of the opera by Koa Ogunmola (with R. Awujoola and V. Olayemi). *IASOP* 12.

———. 1969a. Estimating Ethnic Group Proportions from the Population Census of Nigeria, 1952–53. *Nigerian Opinion* 5:415–19.

———. 1969b. The Collection of Oral Tradition in Africa. *AN* 5(2):12–16.

———. 1969c. Traditional Dirge of Lt. Col. Adekunle Fajiuji's Funeral. *AN* 5(2):63.

———. 1970. Selected Poems (a review of Amali 1968). *Ibadan* 28:93–98.

———. 1971a. Idoma Traditional Attitudes towards Disease. In *The Traditional Background to Medical Practices in Nigeria*, 1–5. OP 25.

———. 1971b. A Brief Rejoinder to McVeagh. *Ibadan* 29:100.

———. 1972a. A Statement on the Purchase and Sale of Antiquities. In *Nigerian Antiquities: Report of a Symposium Held at the I.A.S.* (special number of *AN*, 95–96).

———, ed. 1972b. *Bilingual Literary Works*. Institute of African Studies, Ibadan.

———. 1973a [1979]. Helping Africans to Speak for Themselves: The Role of Linguistics. In *Language and Society: Anthropological Issues*. Ed. W. McCormack and S. Wurm, 445–59. The Hague.

———. 1973b [1980]. The Dynamics and Symbolism of Idoma Kingship. In *West African Cultural Dynamics*. Ed. B. Schwartz and R. Dumett, 393–411. The Hague.

———. 1974. *University of Ibadan: Institute of African Studies* (brochure).

———. 1975. African Religion and Cultural Renewal. *Orita: Ibadan Journal of Religious Studies* 9(2):109–23.

———. 1977 [1978]. The Development of Fulani Studies—A Linguist's View. In *Struktur und Wandel afrikanischer Sprachen*. Ed. H. Jungraithmayr, 7–89. Berlin.

———. 1978. Traditional Poetry in Ladipo's Opera *Oba Ko So*. *RAL* 9:363–81.

———. 1979. The Public Meeting as a Means of Participation in Political and Social

Activities in Africa. In *Sociopolitical Aspects of the Palaver in Some African Countries*, 11–26. Paris.

———. 1980a. Amos Tutuola and Kola Ogunmola: A Comparison of Two Versions of *The Palmwine Drinkard*. *Callaloo* 8/10:165–74.

———. 1980b [1981]. The Idomoid Language Sub-Family of the Eastern Kwa Border-land. A Progress Report. *Marburger Studien zur Afrika- und Asienkunde* 28:5–23.

———. 1980c. Comment on the "Rule of Law." In *The Demise of the Rule of Law in Nige-ria under the Military: Two Points of View*. Ed. S. O. Biobaku, 46–48. Ibadan.

———. 1981a. The Consonant System of Akpa. In *Kiabara, Journal of the Humanities* (Port Harcourt), 26–56.

———. 1981b. Review of Thompson 1974. *RAL* 12:527–36.

———. 1981c. The Idomoid Languages: An Anthropological Linguistic Study. Ms., DLP.

———. 1982. Is Earth Senior to God? An Old West African Theological Controversy. *AN* 9:7–14.

———. 1983a. Editor's Note. In Wenger and Chesi 1983:44.

———. 1983b. The Idomoid Languages of the Benue and Cross River Valleys. *JWAL* 13(1):91–149.

———. 1984 [1989]. The Etymology of the Word "Ogun." In *Africa's Ogun: Old World and New*. Ed. S. Barnes, 29–37. Bloomington, IN.

———. 1985a. The Tenth Vowel in Proto-Kwa. *JWAL* 15(1):104–10.

———. 1985b. The Idomoid Languages of Nigeria. Ms. in the possession of Constance Sutton.

Asante, M. 1999. *The Painful Demise of Eurocentrism: An Afrocentric Response to Critics*. Trenton, NJ.

———. 2003. The Afrocentric Idea. In Mazama 2003:37–53.

Awujoola, R. 1979. The Iron Worker's Prayer (Yoruba text transcribed and translated by R. Armstrong and Awujoola). *AN* 8:29–35.

Bamgbose, A., ed. 1976. *Mother Tongue Education: The West African Experience*. Paris.

———. 1986. The West African Linguistic Society, 1965–1986. *JWAL* 16(1):3–4.

———. 1991. *Language and Nation: The Language Question in Sub-Saharan Africa*. Edin-burgh.

Bamgbose, A., et al., eds. 1992. *Implementation Strategies for the Language Provisions of the National Policy on Education*. Abuja.

Barkan, E. 1988. Mobilizing Scientists against Nazi Racism, 1933–1939. *HOA* 5:180–205.

Bashkow, I., et al., eds. 2004. A New Boasian Anthropology: Theory for the 21st Century. *AA* 106(3):433–94.

Beier, U. 1975. *The Return of the Gods: The Sacred Art of Susanne Wenger*. Cambridge, Eng.

Berman, E. 1983. *The Influence of the Carnegie, Ford, and Rockefeller Foundations on American Foreign Policy: The Ideology of Philanthropy*. Albany, NY.

Boadi, L., and H. Jungraithmayr. 1989. In Memoriam, Robert G. Armstrong. *Frankfurter afrikanistische Blätter* 1:4–5.

Boas, F. 1887. The Study of Geography. *HOA* 8:9–16.

———. 1904. What the Negro Has Done in Africa. *Ethical Record* 5:106–9.

———. 1905. The Documentary Function of the Text. In Stocking 1974b:122–23.

———. 1906 [1945]. The Negro's Past. In *Race and Democratic Society*, 61–69. New York.

Bohannan, P. 1957. *Justice and Judgment among the Tiv*. London.

———. 1963. *Social Anthropology*. New York.

Bondarenko, D., and P. Roese. 1999. Benin Prehistory: The Origin and Settling down of the Edo. *Anthropos* 94:542–52.

Bowditch, E. 1819. *Mission from Cape Coast to Ashantee*. London.

Browder, E. 1944. *Teheran: Our Path in War and Peace*. New York.

Busia, K. 1947. The Position of the Chief in the Modern Political System of Ashanti. Ph.D. dissertation, Oxford University.

Cartmill, M., and K. Brown. 2003. Surveying the Race Concept: A Reply to Lieberman, Kirk and Littlefield 2003. *AA* 105:114–15.

Caspari, R. 2003. From Types to Populations: A Century of Race, Physical Anthropology and the American Anthropological Association. *AA* 105:65–76.

Castañeda, Q. 2003. Stocking's Historiography of Influence: The Story of Boas, Gamio and Redfield at the Crossroad to Light. *Critique of Anthropology* 23:235–63.

Castro, V., et al., eds. 2000. *Nispa Ninchis/Decimos Diciendo: Conversaciones con John Murra*. Lima.

Coon, C. 1948. *A Reader in General Anthropology*. New York.

Cohen, R. 1993. *When the Old Left Was Young: Student Radicals and America's First Mass Student Movement, 1929–1941*. New York.

Coven, R. 1992. Red Maroons. *Chicago History* 21:20–38.

Darnell, R. 1990. *Edward Sapir: Linguist, Anthropologist, Humanist*. Berkeley, CA.

Davis, M. R., and H. B. Davis. N.d. *Liberalism Is Not Enough*. Privately printed.

Diamond, L. 1988. *Class, Ethnicity and Democracy in Nigeria: The Failure of the First Republic*. Syracuse, NY.

Diamond, Si. 1992. *Compromised Campus: The Collaboration of Universities with the Intelligence Community, 1945–1955*. New York.

Diamond, St. 1951. Dahomey: A Proto-State in West Africa. Ph.D. dissertation, Columbia University.

———. 1967. The Anaguta of Nigeria: Suburban Primitives. In *Three African Tribes in Transition*. Ed. J. Steward, 361–505. Champaign, IL.

———. 1970. Who Killed Biafra? *New York Review of Books*, February 27:17–27.

———. 1974. *In Search of the Primitive: A Critique of Civilization*. New York.

———, ed. 1979. *Toward a Marxist Anthropology: Problems and Perspectives*. New York.

Dias, N. 2003. Review of Stocking 2001. *L'Homme* 166:254–58.

Di Brizio, M. 1995. "Présentisme" et "historicisme" dans l'historiographie de G. W. Stocking. *Gradhiva* 18:77–89.

Dove, N. 2003. Defining African Womanist Theory. In Mazama 2003:165–84.

Drake, S. C. 1960. The Responsibility of Men of Culture for Destroying the "Hamitic Myth." *Présence Africaine* 24/25:228–43.

Duberman, M. 1991. *Cures: A Gay Man's Odyssey*. New York.

Evans-Pritchard, E. 1948a. *The Divine Kingship of the Shilluk of the Nilotic Sudan*. Cambridge, Eng.

———. 1948b [1962]. Social Anthropology. In *Social Anthropology and Other Essays*. New York.

———. 1956. Preface. In *Taboo*. By F. Steiner, 11–13. London.

Falola, T. 1999. *The History of Nigeria*. Westport, CT.

Fennell, J. 1955. *The Correspondence between Prince A. M. Kurbsky and Tsar Ivan IV of Russia, 1564–1579*. Cambridge, Eng.

Fortes, M., and E. Evans-Pritchard, eds. 1940. *African Political Systems*. London.

Foster, W. 1951. *Outline Political History of the Americas*. New York.

Gerdes, P. 1994. On Mathematics in the History of Sub-Saharan Africa. *History of Mathematics* 21:345–76.

Gershenhorn, J. 2004. *Melville J. Herskovits and the Racial Politics of Knowledge*. Lincoln, NE.

Gray, C. 2001. *Afrocentric Thought and Praxis: An Intellectual History*. Trenton, NJ.

Greenberg, J. 1963a. *The Languages of Africa*. Bloomington, IN.

———. 1963b. West African Languages Congress. *African Studies Bulletin* 6(3):30–31.

Grossman, V. [S. Wechsler]. 2003. *Crossing the River: A Memoir of the American Left, the Cold War, and Life in East Germany*. Amherst, MA.

Heidbreder, E. 1935. *Seven Psychologies*. New York.

Herskovits, M., and F. Herskovits. 1938. *Dahomey, an Ancient West African Kingdom*. New York.

Hofmayr, W. 1925. *Die Schilluk*. Vienna.

Hooton, E. 1946. *Up from the Ape*. Rev. ed. New York.

Horton, R. 1993. *Patterns of Thought in Africa and the West: Magic, Religion, and Science*. Cambridge, Eng.

Howe, I., and L. Coser. 1962. *The American Communist Party: A Critical History*. New York.

Hyman, L. 1985. *A Theory of Phonological Weight*. Dordrecht.

Hymes, D. 1960. Lexicostatistics So Far. *Current Anthropology* 1:3–44.

———, ed. 1972. *Reinventing Anthropology*. New York.

———. 1983. Morris Swadesh: From the First Yale School to World Prehistory. In *Essays in the History of Linguistic Anthropology*, 273–330. Amsterdam.

———. 2003. *Now I Know Only So Far: Essays in Ethnopoetics*. Lincoln, NE.

Ige, B. 1995. *People, Politics and Politicians of Nigeria (1940–1979)*. Ibadan.

James, C. L. R. 1938. *The Black Jacobins: Toussaint L'Ouverture and the San Domingo Revolution*. London.

Kasfir, S. 1999. *Contemporary African Art*. London.

Kerns, V. 2003. *Scenes from the High Desert: Julian Steward's Life and Theory*. Urbana, IL.

Khrushchev, N. 1956 [1962]. The Crimes of the Stalin Era; Special Report to the 20th Congress of the Communist Party of the Soviet Union.

Kirk-Greene, A. 1971. *Crisis and Conflict in Nigeria: A Documentary Sourcebook, 1966–69*. 2 vols. London.

Kolapo, F. 1999. Post-Abolition Niger River Commerce and the Nineteenth-Century Igala Political Crisis. *African Economic History* 27:45–67.

Krige, E., and J. Krige. 1943. *The Realm of a Rain Queen: A Study of the Pattern of Lovedu Society*. London.

Kroeber, T. 1970. *Alfred Kroeber: A Personal Configuration*. Berkeley, CA.

Kuwayama, T. 2003. "Natives" as Dialogic Partners: Some Thoughts on Native Anthropology. *Anthropology Today* 19(1):8–13.

———. 2004. The World System of Anthropology. In *The Making of Anthropology in East and Southeast Asia*. Ed. S. Yamashita et al. New York.

Lauria-Perricelli, A. 1989. A Study in Historical and Critical Anthropology: The Making of *The People of Puerto Rico*. Ph.D. dissertation, Columbia University.

Lawal, B. 1995. A-Ya-Gbo-A-Ya-to + Metal-Sculpture which Is an Emblem of Membership in the Ogboni Society: New Perspectives on Edan-Ogboni. *African Arts* 28:36.

Layiwola, D. 1987. Obituary. Robert G. Armstrong, 1917–1987. *AN* 11:vii–viii.

Lefkowitz, M. 1996. *Not out of Africa: How Afrocentrism Became an Excuse to Teach Myth as History*. New York.

Lieberman, L., et al. 2003. Perishing Paradigm: Race—1931–99. *AA* 105:110–13.

Linton, R. 1936. *The Study of Man: An Introduction*. New York.

Mabogunje, A. 1973. The Humanities and Social Sciences. In Ajayi and Tamnuno 1973:168–90.

Madden, D. 1999. Culture, Personality, and the Philosophy of Social Science among Chicago-Area Anthropologists in the 1930s: A History of the Social Science Research Council's Sub-Committee on Acculturation. Seminar paper, GSP.

Magat, R. 1979. *The Ford Foundation at Work: Philanthropic Choices, Methods, and Styles*. New York.

Manners, R. 1956. The Land Claims Cases: Anthropologists in Conflict. *Ethnohistory* 3:72–81.

Mazama, A., ed. 2003. *The Afrocentric Paradigm*. Trenton, NJ.

McVeagh, J. 1971. Poetry and Mr. Amali. *Ibadan* 29:93–97.

Mead, M. 1939. *From the South Seas: Studies of Adolescence and Sex in Primitive Societies*. New York.

Mellanby, K. 1958. *The Birth of Nigeria's University*. London.

Melville, H. 1847. *Omoo: A Narrative of Adventures in the South Seas*. New York.

Merton, R. 1949. *Social Theory and Social Structure*. Glencoe, IL.

Mintz, S. 1953. The Folk-Urban Continuum and the Rural Proletarian Community. *AJS* 59:136–43.

———. 1985. *Sweetness and Power: The Place of Sugar in Modern History*. New York.

———. 1994. An Impartial History of the Mundial Upheaval Society. *AnthroWatch* 2(3):19–20.

———, et al. 1984. *On Marxist Perspectives in Anthropology: Esssays in Honor of Harry Hoijer*. Malibu, CA.

Mohammed, A. M. 1995. The Background of 1st October 1960: The Source Material from European Companies. In *Inside Nigerian History, 1950–1970: Events, Issues and Sources*. Ed. Y. B. Usman and G. A. Kwanashie, 282–91. Ibadan.

Murdock, G. P. 1972. Anthropology's Mythology. *Proceedings of the Royal Anthropological Institute for 1971*.

Murdock, G. P., et al. 1950. *Outline of Cultural Materials*. New Haven, CT.

Murphy, R. 1981. Julian Steward. In *Totems and Teachers: Perspectives on the History of Anthropology*. Ed. S. Silverman, 171–208. New York.

Nadel, S. 1942. *A Black Byzantium: The Kingdom of Nupe in Nigeria*. Oxford.

Newman, P. 1991. An Interview with Joseph Greenberg. *Current Anthropology* 32:453–66.

Ogede, O. 1995. Context, Form and Poetic Expression in Igede Funeral Dirges. *Africa* 65:79–96.

Ogundiran, A. 2002. Archaeology, Historiographic Traditions, and Institutional Discourse of Development. In *Nigeria in the Twentieth Century*. Ed. T. Falola, 13–36. Durham, NC.

Okafor, N. 1971. *The Development of Universities in Nigeria*. London.

Oloruntimehin, B. 1973. The University in the Era of the Civil War and Reconstruction. In Ajayi and Tamuno 1973:99–126.

Olubummo, A., and J. Ferguson. 1960. *The Emergent University*. London.

Ottenberg, S. 1997. *New Traditions from Nigeria: Seven Artists of the Nsukka Group*. Washington, D.C.

Patterson, J. 1996. *Grand Expectations: The United States, 1945–1974*. New York.

Peace, W. 2004. *Leslie White: Evolution and Revolution in Anthropology*. Lincoln, NE.

Pouillon, J. 1980. Anthropological Traditions: Their Uses and Misuses. In *Anthropology: Ancestors and Heirs*. Ed. S. Diamond, 35–52. The Hague.

Price, D. 2003. *Threatening Anthropology: McCarthyism and the FBI's Surveillance of Activist Anthropologists*. Durham, NC.

Radcliffe-Brown, A. 1937 [1956]. *A Natural Science of Society*. Chicago.

Rattray, R. 1923. *Ashanti*. Oxford.

———. 1927. *Religion and Art in Ashanti*. Oxford.

Rauch, J. 1955. Area Programs and African Studies. *Journal of Negro Education* 24: 409–25.

Redfield, R. 1941. *The Folk Culture of Yucatan*. Chicago.

———. 1958. Talk with a Stranger. In *The Social Uses of Social Science: The Papers of Robert Redfield*, 2:270–83. Chicago.

Redfield, R., et al. 1936. Memorandum for the Study of Acculturation. *AA* 28:149–52.

Rosen, L. 1977. The Anthropologist as Expert Witness. *AA* 79:555–78.

Sapir, E. 1921. The Musical Foundations of Verse. *Journal of English and Germanic Philology* 20:213–28.

———. 1924. Culture, Genuine and Spurious. *AJS* 29:401–29.

Schrecker, E. 1986. *No Ivory Tower: McCarthyism and the Universities*. New York.

Seligman, C. 1939. *The Races of Africa*. London.

Shain, R. 1988. The Black and the White: The Use of Dualities in Etulo Historical Thought. *Journal of Religions in Africa* 18:237–54.

Shand-Tucci, D. 2003. *The Scarlet Letter: Harvard, Homosexuality, and the Shaping of American Culture*. New York.

Shaw, T. 1970. *Igbo-Ukwu: An Account of Archaeological Discoveries in Eastern Nigeria*. 2 vols. Evanston, IL.

———. 1990. A Personal Memoir. In *A History of African Archaeology*. Ed. P. Robertshaw, 205–20. London.

Shirokov, M. 1938. *A Textbook of Marxist Philosophy*. London.

Silverstein, M. 2002. Joseph Harold Greenberg (1915–2001). *AA* 104:630–33.

Staniland, M. 1991. *American Intellectuals and African Universities, 1955–1970*. New Haven, CT.

Steward, J. 1949. South American Cultures: An Interpretative Summary. *Bulletin of the Bureau of American Ethnology* 143, vol. 5:669–772.

———. 1950. *Area Research: Theory and Practice*. SSRC Bulletin 66. New York.

Steward, J., et al. 1956. *The People of Puerto Rico: A Study in Social Anthropology*. Urbana, IL.

Stocking, G. 1965. On the Limits of "Presentism" and "Historicism" in the Historiography of the Behavioral Sciences. In Stocking 1968:1–12.

———. 1968. *Race, Culture, and Evolution: Essays in the History of Anthropology.* New York.

———. 1974a. The Boas Plan for the Study of American Indian Languages. In Stocking 1992:60–91.

———. 1974b. *The Shaping of American Anthropology: A Franz Boas Reader.* New York.

———. 1976. Ideas and Institutions in American Anthropology: Thoughts Toward a History of the Interwar Years. In Stocking 1992:114–77.

———. 1979. *Anthropology at Chicago: Tradition, Discipline, Department.* Chicago.

———. 1986. Franz Boas and the History of Humanistic Anthropology. In Stocking 2002b:63–75.

———. 1987. *Victorian Anthropology.* New York.

———. 1989. The Ethnographic Sensibility of the 1920s and the Dualism of the Anthropological Tradition. In Stocking 1992:276–342.

———. 1991. "Included in This Classification": Notes toward an Archeology of Ethnographic Classification. *HAN* 18(1):3-11.

———. 1992. *The Ethnographer's Magic and Other Essays in the History of Anthropology.* Madison, WI.

———. 1995. *After Tylor: British Social Anthropology, 1888–1951.* Madison, WI.

———. 1999. Presentism and Historicism Once Again: The History of British Anthropology as Intellectual and Personal History. *Journal of Victorian Culture* 4(2):328–35.

———. 2000. "Do Good, Young Man": Sol Tax and the World Mission of Liberal Democratic Anthropology. *HOA* 9:171–264.

———. 2002a. British Colonialists, Ibo Traders and Idoma Democrats: A Marxist Anthropologist enters "the Field" in Nigeria, 1950–51. *HAN* 29(2):3–11.

———. 2002b. *Delimiting Anthropology: Occasional Essays and Reflections.* Madison, WI.

———. 2002c. Reading the Palimpsest of Inquiry: *Notes and Queries* and the History of British Social Anthropology. In Stocking 2002b:164–206.

———. 2002d. Society, Matter, and Human Nature: Robert Gelston Armstrong and Marxist Anthropology at the University of Chicago, 1950. *HAN* 29(1):3–10.

———. 2004a. A. I. Hallowell's Boasian Evolutionism: Human Ir/rationality in Cross-Cultural, Evolutionary and Personal Context. *HOA* 10:196–260.

———. 2004b. Antropologia em Chicago: A fundação de um departamento independente, 1923–1929. Trans. P. Dentzien. In *Antropologias, Histórias, Experiências.* Ed. F. Peixoto, H. Pontes, and L. Schwarcz, 15–59. Belo Horizonte, Brazil.

———. In process. An untitled essay on Clyde Kluckhohn, so far covering the period 1905 to 1945.

———. N.d. Glimpses into my own Black Box. Unpublished essay, subject to revision.

Strachey, J. 1933. *The Coming Struggle for Power.* New York.

———. 1935. *The Nature of Capitalist Crisis.* New York.

Sweezy, P. 1942. *Theory of Capitalist Development: Marxist Principles of Political Economy.* New York.

Tamuno, T. 1973. The Formative Years, 1947–56. In Ajayi and Tamuno 1973:22–48.

Thompson, R. 1974. *African Art in Motion, Icon and Act.* Los Angeles.

Uzukwu, E. 1982. Igbo World and Ultimate Reality and Meaning. *Ultimate Real Meaning* 5:188–209.

Van den Berghe, P. 1973. *Power and Privilege at an African University.* Cambridge, MA.

Vincent, J. 1990. *Anthropology and Politics: Visions, Traditions, and Trends*. Tucson, AZ.

Warner, M. 1988. *W. Lloyd Warner: Social Anthropologist*. New York.

Wenger, S. 1977. *The Timeless Mind of the Sacred: Its New Manifestation in the Osun Groves*. Ibadan.

Wenger, S., and G. Chesi. 1983. *A Life with the Gods in Their Yoruba Homeland*. Wörgl, Austria.

Werth, B. 2001. *The Scarlet Professor: Newton Arvin: A Literary Life Shattered by Scandal*. New York.

Whyte, L. L. 1948. *The Next Development in Man*. New York.

———. 1963. *Focus and Diversions*. New York.

Wilcox, C. 2004. *Robert Redfield and the Development of American Anthropology*. Lanham, MD.

Williams, V. 1996. *Rethinking Race: Franz Boas and His Contemporaries*. Lexington, KY.

Williamson, K., ed. 1985. *West African Languages in Education*. Vienna.

———. 1987. Professor Robert G. Armstrong. *JWAL* 17(2):4–5.

———. 1989. Robert Gelston Armstrong, 1917–87. *Africa* 59:518.

———. 1992. R. C. Abraham and D. Alagoma: Their Contribution to Igbo Studies. In *Papers in Honor of R. C. Abraham (1890–1963)*. Ed. P. Jaggar. *African Languages and Cultures* Supplement 1:131–40.

Wittfogel, K. A. 1931. *Wirtschaft und Gesellschaft Chinas: Versuch der wissenschaftlichen Analyse einer grossen asiatischen Agrargesellschaft*. Leipzig.

Wolf, E. 1955. Types of Latin American Peasantry. *AA* 57:452–71.

———. 1964. *Anthropology*. Englewood Cliffs, NJ.

———. 1969. *Peasant Wars of the Twentieth Century*. New York.

———. 1978. Remarks on *The People of Puerto Rico*. In Wolf 2001:49–62.

———. 1982. *Europe and the People without History*. Berkeley. CA.

———. 1999. *Envisioning Power: Ideologies of Dominance and Crisis*. Berkeley, CA.

———. 2001. *Pathways of Power: Building an Anthropology of the Modern World*. Berkeley, CA.

Wolff, H. 1963. Review of Armstrong 1962a. *AA* 65:1194–95.

———. 1965. Review of Armstrong 1964a. *AA* 67:1598.

Manuscript Sources

This paper is based to a great extent on manuscript materials in a number of archives, identified in the parenthetic citations by the following abbreviations.

AKP   Alfred Kroeber Papers. Bancroft Library, University of California, Berkeley.

AUA   Atlanta University Archives. Letters in the Rufus Clement Presidential Records and copies of the *Atlanta University Bulletin*.

CSP   Constance Sutton Papers. Materials in the possession of Constance Sutton, Department of Anthropology, New York University.

DAP   Department of Anthropology Papers, Robert Armstrong file. Special Collections Research Center, Regenstein Library, University of Chicago.

DLP   David Laitin Papers. Letters in the possession of David Laitin, Department of Political Science, Stanford University.

FBI Federal Bureau of Investigation, Robert Gelston Armstrong file. Obtained under the Freedom of Information Act by Jennifer Lewis, copy in the possession of the author.

FEP Fred Eggan Papers. Special Collections Research Center, Regenstein Library, University of Chicago.

GSP George Stocking Papers. Letters and other materials sent to the author by Armstrong in 1977–78.

IAS Institute of African Studies. Copies of materials obtained by LaRay Denzer.

JMP John Murra Papers. National Anthropological Archives, Smithsonian Institution.

JSP Julian Steward Papers. University Archives, University of Illinois, Urbana-Champaign.

L-PP Lauria-Perricelli Papers. Copies of Armstrong field notes provided by Antonio Lauria-Perricelli.

MBT Minutes of the Board of Trustees. Special Collections Research Center, Regenstein Library, University of Chicago.

MHP Melville Herskovits Papers, Northwestern University Archives.

PPA Presidents' Papers Addenda. Special Collections Research Center, Regenstein Library, University of Chicago.

RAC Rockefeller Archive Center, North Tarrytown, NY. Rockefeller Foundation Collection Record Group. 1.2 Projects. Series 497. Nigeria Access, box 1. University College, Ibadan. African Studies; Social Science Research Council, Accession 2. Series 1. Committee Projects, Subseries 3. African Studies, box 17, folders 126–27.

RLP Robert Lowie Papers. Bancroft Library, University of California, Berkeley.

RRC Russian Research Center Papers. Harvard University Archives.

RRP Robert Redfield Papers. Special Collections Research Center, Regenstein Library, University of Chicago.

SSD Social Science Division Papers. Special Collections Research Center, Regenstein Library, University of Chicago.

Oral and Written Informant Sources

Although this essay is based largely on research in published or manuscript sources of a conventional intellectual historical sort, I have also collected information by conversation or correspondence with a number of people who knew Armstrong or the situations of his life and who were kind enough to respond to my oral or written queries. Because several of them for one reason or another preferred not to be named as the providers of particular bits of information, and others were not reachable when the publication process began, I have chosen to treat them all as anonymously as possible, without specific citation. Except in the case of several with whom I engaged in extended correspondence, or who provided me with manuscript materials, or who offered comments upon reading all or portions of the manuscript, they will simply be indicated by PC, for "personal communication." However, to give readers some indication of the importance of this contribution to my research, I list here in alphabetical order all of those who provided information or opinion, without regard to its extent, topic, or role in my interpretation: Ruth Adams, Robert McCormick Adams, J. F. Ade. Ajayi, Idowu Ajibola, Shamsudeen O. O. Amali, Andrew Apter, David Apter, Bolanle Awe, Akande Azeez, Ayo Bamgbose, Chris Bankole, Sandra Barnes, Frederick Barth, Paul Bohannan, Edward Bruner, Manuela Carneiro da Cunha, Alice Chandler, LaRay Denzer, Ira Harrison, Sidney Kasfir, David Laitin, Antonio Lauria-Perricelli, Herbert Lewis, Jennifer Lewis, Peter Lloyd, Sidney Mintz, John Murra, Simon Ottenberg, Pat Oyelola, Lisa Redfield Peattie, J. D. Y. Peel, David Price, David Sapir, Thurston Shaw, Ralph Spitzer, Janet Stanley, Constance Sutton, Pierre van den Berghe, Murray Wax, and Kay Williamson. This essay would not have been possible in its present form without their assistance, for which I am very grateful. None of them, however, should be held in any way responsible for errors of fact or distortions of interpretation that may have been introduced in the long course of its composition.

KROEBER AND THE CALIFORNIA CLAIMS

Historical Particularism and
Cultural Ecology in Court

ARTHUR J. RAY

In 1946 the U.S. Congress established the Indian Claims Commission (ICC) to address the grievances Indian tribes held against the U.S. government. The commission culminated a sixteen-year political battle over an idea nearly a half-century old (Rosenthal 1990:47–94). Anthropologists played leading roles as experts who supported or opposed Indian claims. Although it was not the first time these professionals became embroiled in legal/political issues concerning Indians, their participation in the ICC process had a greater impact on the discipline and the claims process than did earlier encounters for a number of reasons. Most notably, the commission operated for over thirty years, and during that time opposing sides spent unprecedented sums on new research into Indian history. Also, the nature of the claims encouraged experts to adopt an interdisciplinary and multisourced methodology, known as ethnohistory, which was a relatively new approach. Commission hearings became a forum where ethnohistorical experts supporting Indian plaintiffs or the government defendant offered opposing theories about Indian culture and history to advance their client's cases. Often, new research and theoretical models challenged traditional understandings of Indian history.

Of the hundreds of cases heard, the California Indian claims were among the

---

Arthur J. Ray, History Department, University of British Columbia, is author of *Indians in the Fur Trade* and *I Have Lived Here since the World Began*. Currently, he is studying aboriginal and treaty rights claims research in Australia, Canada, New Zealand, and the United States. Elected a fellow of the Royal Society of Canada in 2002, he is co-editor of *Canadian Historical Review*.

most important. The cast of experts who appeared for the opposing sides reads like a Who's Who of mid- and late-twentieth-century American anthropology. A. L. Kroeber was the most notable of them. Many of his former students who had achieved prominence in the field by the time of the hearings either helped or opposed him. In this respect, the California Indian claims were largely an affair of the "Berkeley school of anthropology," which Kroeber had created over the previous half-century. Reflecting the times, Indian input was minimal. As one of the early participants in ICC cases observed, since lawyers and commissioners were more comfortable dealing with anthropologists than with Indians, anthropologists became, in effect, surrogate Indians within the judicial system (Lurie 1985:370).

Much was at stake for Kroeber. As the leading witness for the Indians, his understanding of their history was centrally at issue. His perspective was challenged by some of his best students, Harold Driver, Ralph Beals, and Julian Steward. Significantly, their challenge came at a time when North American anthropology was moving away from the historical particularistic approach initiated by Boas and sustained by Kroeber, both of whom shied away from metanarratives about cultural processes. The younger anthropologists, in contrast, mobilized a scientific comparative method to develop theories of cultural change. Driver and Steward favored these newer approaches and employed them for the government's defense. In particular, Steward's focus on culture-environment relationships put him at odds with the culture-area approach Kroeber promoted.

Given these circumstances, the California Indian claims raise two important questions. How did Berkeley anthropologists deal with their scholarly differences in the adversarial atmosphere generated by litigation? In other words, how did the event shape the discourse that took place? Also, what impact did the expert witnesses' participation have on the subsequent direction of ethnohistorical research in North America? I will address these issues by considering (1) the historical memory of Kroeber's involvement, (2) the nature of the claims litigation process, (3) Kroeber and the culture-area approach in support of Indian plaintiffs, (4) the cultural ecology for the defense, and (5) the experts, lawyers, cross-examination, and rebuttal. Throughout, my focus will be on Kroeber's participation in the California Indian claims.

Remembering "the Beard"

In the halls of the anthropology department and in the library of the University of California–Berkeley, photographs of a bearded Kroeber gaze down at faculty and students. Many of his former students fondly remembered him as "the beard." Two book-length biographies have been written about him, one by

Steward (1973) and the other by his wife, Theodora (1970). Although the two biographers are nearly silent about his participation in the California claims, Steward devoting only three sentences to it and Theodora seven paragraphs, they leave a clear impression that Kroeber was skeptical of the process and participated in it only reluctantly. Steward, for example, in his terse comment on Kroeber as an expert witness said that his former teacher "had always avoided governmental matters, and it seems to me that his participation on this occasion was rather half-hearted" (1973:16).

As told in Theodora's affectionate and protective story of her husband's life, officials from the Bureau of Indian Affairs initially asked Kroeber if he would join other "Indian specialists," government officials, and Indians at a "round table" to discuss the possibility of reaching an agreement about the California claims without having to resort to litigation (Kroeber 1970:221). This never happened. Instead, the claims were brought before the commission. Once the process began, her husband learned just how bitterly the Justice Department intended to fight against the Indians, and "this put a different face on Kroeber's own role and his moral and professional responsibility. He was retained directly by the law firm representing the California Indians, which in turn paid what looked at the time to be a reasonable fee with some expense monies for preparation of maps and the like" (Kroeber 1970:222). In fact, Kroeber's contract was lucrative for the time but also ethically problematic, as it provided an incentive to be on the winning side: in addition to expenses, he received a signing bonus of $500, then $50 a day for his services, and an additional $50 a day (for all the days he had worked) if the claimants were successful. Note that the government paid $50 a day whether or not it won a case, so government experts did not have quite the same vested interest in the outcome of a case as the Indians' experts did (RHP).

According to Theodora Kroeber, her husband was the "decisive voice and conscience in a no-holds-barred legal battle," but outside the hearings Kroeber "was at pains to maintain good relations with his colleagues and former pupils who were giving evidence, some for the government, some for the Indians. So far as I know no friendships were blasted by the hearings; the Berlin Wall of that court was not between the scientists of opposing sides but between the world of science on the one side and the world of litigation on the other" (Kroeber 1970:222). She concludes that her husband's "participation in the case was altogether aberrant and unsatisfactory." It was also professionally "expensive": it "interfered with his writing and research for five crucial years, from January 1952 to June 1956" (Kroeber 1970:222–23).

Steward's and Theodora's reminiscences imply that Kroeber, unlike the other experts, remained detached from a battle that raged for five years. Other biographers do not mention the event, thereby leaving the impression it had been inconsequential to him (Rowe 1962; Beals 1968; Harris 1968). This is improbable. Although Congress originally intended that the ICC would provide a nonadversarial setting for airing and settling Indian grievances against the U.S. government, the commissioners and lawyers who took part looked to the Court of Claims for their precedents, partly because it had been the primary venue for Indian claims before 1946 and decisions of the ICC could be appealed to it. This meant that the commission adopted most of the procedures used by courts, with the result that the California claims battle lasted almost ten years. All too often, intense and protracted adversarial struggles such as this foster an us-against-them mentality and a strong desire to be on the winning team. The extent to which an expert witness becomes ensnared in this kind of thinking depends partly on the extent of the expert's involvement at different stages of the process. To evaluate Kroeber's response to the pressures of the event it is important to begin by outlining how the litigation process in North America normally unfolds from the perspective of the participation of expert witnesses.

Witness Participation in Claims Litigation

Figure 1 is a five-stage model of litigation based, in part, on my experience as an expert witness in several claims trials (Ray 2006). In Stage 1 an aboriginal group decides to challenge some aspect of the colonial legacy that affects them adversely by having their legal counsel file a statement of claim before a commission or court. The lawyers normally work closely with their aboriginal clients to prepare a statement that takes into account current legal theories about the rights in question, the case law, and their understanding of the relevant historical issues. Often the statement of claim is amended several times before the trial or hearing commences. Usually, the ethnohistorical experts who will become involved in the litigation do not have input at this stage. Most often they are selected after the statement of claim has been filed. These pretrial statements are important for the expert witness, however, because they identify and frame the key historical question(s), thereby giving direction to the research agenda and establishing the polarities of the dispute.

---

1. Stages of Witness Participation in Claims Litigation

Stage 1	Preparation and filing of statement of claim or pleadings
Stage 2	Selection of experts and preparation of written reports
Stage 3	Preparation for oral testimony
Stage 4	Presentation of oral testimony: evidence-in-chief, cross-examination, redirect, and rebuttal
Stage 5	Posttrial/posthearing phase: publication of claims research in academic venues

Stage 2 begins when the plaintiffs and the defendant select experts to pre-pare reports that will serve as the basis for their evidence-in-chief. These re-ports are prepared in consultation with the lawyers who have retained the ex-perts. The extent to which the Native community is involved at this stage varies. If oral history evidence is an important component of an expert's report, close contact is necessary. Ethnohistorians who use other lines of evidence may choose to minimize contact in order to avoid being vulnerable to charges of be-ing an advocate instead of an independent expert. Normally, the witnesses the government hires to help prepare its defense do not have access to the aborigi-nal community because they are members of the adversary's team. The extent to which a team of experts works independently or jointly in the preparation of its submissions depends on the lawyers' assessments of the advantages and dis-advantages of collaborative efforts in an adversarial regime. Having a highly in-teractive team facilitates the productive exchange of ideas and increases the chances of presenting a harmonious set of reports and oral testimony. On the other hand, a highly collective approach jeopardizes the independence of each expert and makes the team's effort vulnerable at its weakest point (the "house of cards" fear).

Stage 3 involves the preparation for the presentation of the expert's oral evidence-in-chief. When preparing for this event the lawyers work closely with their expert to select the evidence to be highlighted at trial or in hearings. They take a number of factors into account in preparing the list of questions their ex-pert will answer in this evidence-in-chief. The plaintiffs' expert and legal coun-sel have to pay particular attention to (1) the defendant's reply to the statement of claim, (2) the expert reports that were filed in support of the defendant, and (3) issues that may have been raised by the testimony of any preceding wit-nesses. The defendant's experts, who appear after the plaintiffs have presented their case, address the statement of claim and the written and oral submissions of the opposing witnesses. Significantly, once the trial or hearing phase begins, issues often arise that had not been anticipated at the outset because each case develops a dynamic of its own as it unfolds. The extent to which lawyers inter-act with their experts at this pretestimony stage varies. Sometimes close con-tact takes place when the goal is to present a tightly scripted testimony. When, on the other hand, the object is to pose a few broad questions and let the expert run with them, contact may be minimal.

Stage 4 begins with the oral testimony of the plaintiffs' experts followed by that of the defendant's experts. Once the expert completes the evidence-in-chief, opposing counsel tests it in cross-examination. The goal of the cross-examiner is to challenge those aspects of the testimony that are harmful to the client's case, which may include challenging the expertise of the witness and/or taking the opportunity to advance the client's perspective. Significantly, lawyers often ask their experts to help them prepare for the cross-examination of the opposing attorney's experts. Sometimes experts become deeply involved in this groundwork.

Occasionally, Stage 4 ends with redirect testimony, when lawyers ask their witnesses to address issues that have arisen as a result of cross-examination. Also, after the defendant has finished presenting expert witnesses, the plaintiffs, who bear the burden of proof, may opt to have their own experts give rebuttal testimony, which is also subject to cross-examination. This happened in the California Indian claims. Usually, the participation of experts ends with the conclusion of Stage 4, but sometimes after the hearings the experts help the attorneys file proposed findings of fact before the court or tribunal. This posttrial (or posthearing) phase can be considered Stage 5, in which experts often publish aspects of their reports and/or write about their experience. Sometimes this publication may occur before the trial or hearing is completed, but lawyers generally discourage this.

Kroeber and the Culture-Area Approach in Support of the Indian Plaintiffs

Given Kroeber's stature, both the Indians and the government wanted him to serve as their leading expert. By the summer of 1952 both parties had approached him. This was well after various California Indian groups had banded together as two separate legal entities and filed claims. (One, the Indians of California [IOC], filed a petition on March 24, 1949, and the other, the Council of California Indians [CCI], submitted an amended petition a month later, on April 28.) His first contract offer came from the Justice Department, whose legal team was led by attorney Ralph Barney. Over the next four years Kroeber would have many encounters with Barney, for whom he developed an intense dislike. The government's offer was presented by Acting Assistant Attorney General Ralph Luttrell in August 1952. Luttrell wrote Kroeber informing him that

> claims have been filed against the Government by "the Indians of California": who allege that they represent all of the Indians (or their descendants) who were living in what is now the State of California in 1852. These plaintiffs claim that at the time of the Treaty of Guadalupe Hidalgo of July 4, 1848, when the United States gained the territory from Mexico, they "owned and had immemorial possession of and were entitled to the sole use, occupation and possession, in the accustomed Indian manner," of all the lands in California except those granted by Spain or Mexico. (AKP:RL/AK 8/6/52)

Here the assistant attorney general was paraphrasing the IOC statement of claim (Ross 1976:6); he continued: "From our study—gained largely from your published writings on the situation as it existed in California—we understand that each tribe, or band or group of Indians living in California claimed the right to use and occupy a definite area of land to the exclusion of all other groups. What we are interested in determining is what land each of the tribes, bands or specific groups *actually used and occupied* as distinguished from the area each claimed" (emphasis in original). Luttrell informed Kroeber that he "was to name his fee for research services." In addition, the government would pay him $50 a day for any time he spent in court as well as any other expenses, including those for research assistants, "at the rate of $1.50 per hour" (AKP:RL/AK 8/6/52).

Vacationing when Luttrell's letter arrived, Kroeber was interesting in the Justice Department's proposal and drafted a reply by the end of August (AKP: AK/RL 8/28/52). He stated that the basic research question the government proposed was a challenging one for ethnologists to address:

> Land "actually used and occupied" by native groups is going to be ~~difficult~~ **hard** to define because it slides off in a gradient.[1] A ~~village~~ **settled** site with houses ~~on it~~ is certainly both occupied and used. But the watershed ridge that bounds the valley ~~claimed~~of this group might ~~only~~**never even** [be] visited ~~only rarely~~**except** in pursuit of a wounded deer, or ~~most often~~**perhaps chiefly** at a gap through which a trail ran to the next valley ~~having~~ **harboring** a distinct but friendly group. In between these **extremes were all** transitions of utilization: frequent, limited but seasonally regular (with and without ~~occupation~~ [a double strikeout here; the second is not readable]; occasional; rare; practically none.

After citing a number of illustrative examples, Kroeber posed a crucial question:

> Now how are ~~you~~we going to interpret that sort of situation—multiplied 500 times for as many autonomous groups **in varying local environments**—in terms of "actually used and occupied"? It would ~~take~~ **require** an army of assistants and cartographers, for example, ~~and~~ wouldn't be more than **a mass of** endless ~~detail & and mening ?? data ??~~ detail, contestable at point after point as to non use.

Kroeber then proposed an approach that could help the government achieve its goal of "pulling claims down from billions to millions":

> Isn't there some way of generalizing the ~~picture, say having~~ evidence? Say to try to establish the average ~~of~~proportion of a valley land given (1) over to permanent residence, (2) to frequent but occasional use, (3) to seasonally ~~limited~~ **brief** but ~~important~~ **significant** use on account of food products, (4) to local or sedentary use, (5) to negligible use: and there aim at the same ~~for~~ category percentages for (6) hill and brush land; and again for mountains, bare plains, and deserts. That **would be** something I could make a stab at ~~and are~~ **estimating** and at substantiating with ~~typical~~ examples ~~with~~—mostly already described or mapped. It would

---

1. Strikeouts are in original draft; bold letters indicate insertions Kroeber made to his initial draft.

make **a whole lot more** sense to me; and perhaps to you also, but—how about the court?

This exchange of letters highlighted the issues that would become central to the California claims cases as they unfolded and to most other ICC cases and, generally, land claims cases in North America to the present day.

The Justice Department did not respond immediately to Kroeber's proposal. So, in frustration, he drafted a second letter to Luttrell in late September that he did not send for another month. In it he stated that he had concluded the government was not interested in his ideas and did not want to engage his services. Therefore, he considered that their negotiations were finished, and he expected the government to treat them as having been confidential (AKP:AK/RL 9/21/52). At last, in December 1952, the new assistant attorney general sent Kroeber an apology and a reassurance that the government was interested in his proposal:

> We regret that your letter of August 26th has not been answered. The propositions set forth there have been the subject of a number of conferences within the Department and the legal implications of the position you suggest the Government take on aboriginal land use have been explored. The *Indians of California* case has been a matter of deep concern to everyone in the Department who has been working on it. We have come to the conclusion that the approach outlined in your letter might well serve as a basis for a just and effective presentation of the facts involved. We wish to express our thanks for so generously giving us the benefit of your wisdom and experience in this matter.
>
> Mr. Barney and Dr. Jones have made plans to talk with you in California in January. . . . We understand that you have made no commitments, and will make none to the Indians' attorneys until after Mr. Barney and Dr. Jones talk with you personally. It is our hope that some definite arrangement can be made at that time in regard to your appearance as a witness so that the case may be expedited. (AKP:James McInerney/AK 12/11/52)

The Justice Department had dallied too long, however. On December 12 Kroeber had agreed to work for the plaintiffs' attorneys, and he signed a contract with them three days later (RHP).

It is not clear why Kroeber decided to work for the plaintiffs. It seems likely that his underlying sympathy for the Indians was a key factor that made him receptive to their pleadings, as he himself suggested in a letter to Barney:

> As I told you, I have been under considerable local pressure since returning here. Especially my old friends among the Indians, I found, would not have understood if I had been even nominally "against" them.
>
> I want my testimony to be as fair to the government as to the Indians, and while my function will be only to supply information as to ownership, occupancy, and

use, I very much hope an equitable and reasonable settlement will be reached. While I do not know the answer, I am sure it can be found. (AKP:AK/RB 12/19/52)

This letter suggests Kroeber expected the hearings to be a fact-finding affair. This was not to be. He had committed himself to a complex process about which he had little understanding.

California Indian groups had filed two sorts of claims. One category involved those who had lost their tribal affiliations after Euro-American contact. Most California Indians had suffered this fate, including those who had joined together as the IOC and the CCI. Both legal entities claimed the right to petition on behalf of all the Indians of the state for compensation for the loss of the lands their ancestors held in 1848. The ICC identified the IOC's claim as Docket 31 and that of the rival CCI as Docket 37. The IOC and the CCI retained influential Washington-based law firms specializing in Indian litigation. Each sought to have the competing claim dismissed. Eventually, the commission grew weary of this legal bickering and merged the two dockets. The other category of claim involved Indians who had maintained their tribal affiliations. Their claims, of which there were several, concerned specific tracts of land. Kroeber entered the fray in December 1952 and three months later convinced his colleague, archaeologist Robert Heizer, to join his team (RHP; Heizer's contract is dated 3/10/53). Heizer was the foremost authority on California archaeology. Subsequently, historian of Hispanic America Donald Cutter, historical demographer Sherburne Cook, and anthropologist Omer Stewart became team members. Stewart, who had been an undergraduate under Steward before pursuing a doctoral degree with Kroeber and who appeared as an expert for Indian claimants in opposition to Steward in other ICC cases before and after the California Indian claims, served as Kroeber's understudy in case his health failed.

Kroeber and Heizer contracted to provide testimony and exhibits that included but were not limited to descriptions of "the way of life of the Indians of California before the coming of the white man, the various territories inhabited by the several tribes of Indians, and the nature of their Aboriginal occupancy, the thrust of the white man into California and the destructive impact of this invasion upon the way of life of the Indians and their dispossession from their ancestral lands" (AKP:Memorandum, 1/24/55). Kroeber agreed to work closely with attorney Reginald Foster, who was a member of the CCI's legal team, to draft an outline of the proposed testimony before the commission. According to the initial agreement, another member of the plaintiffs' team, attorney Walton "Wally" Hamilton, would travel to the West Coast to help Kroeber make final preparations for the hearings. Subsequently, Kroeber developed a close personal and professional relationship with Hamilton.[2]

2. The firm of Wilkinson, Cragun and Barker represented the IOC. Francis Goodwin was associated with this firm and corresponded extensively with Kroeber. The firm of Arnold, Fortas and

Kroeber began work immediately. The CCI was anxious to have him make his presentation on their behalf as soon as possible, given his age (he was seventy-six when he signed his contract) and uncertain health (he had previously suffered a heart attack). By the end of January 1953 Kroeber had drafted a ten thousand–word preliminary statement about Indian ownership of California land. He continued revising this statement until May 1954, when he submitted his "Basic Report on California Indian Land Holdings" (a copy of which defense attorney Barney demanded in order to prepare his cross-examination of Kroeber [AKP:WH/AK 5/12/54]).

In the opening sections of his statement Kroeber discussed the documentary sources and ethnographic authorities he had used. He maintained that the observations of early white explorers, travelers, missionaries, and ethnographers were largely objective because "their motivation, usually, was not in any sense political, nor was it gainful. Rather it was dictated by sheer intellectual curiosity." Drawing a distinction between observations that members of European nationalities made about their neighbors—observations grounded in a long history of conflict and rivalry—and those they made about people living in other parts of the world, Kroeber argued that anthropologists' descriptions of Indians were "relatively impartial" because of the gulf between their culture and those of their primitive subjects (1954:20).

At the core of his report Kroeber defined the "land-owning group." He stressed that in California these groups tended to be smaller than those found in most other areas of the United States. Thus he found the terms *tribe* and *band* inappropriate, since the former connoted a corporate group larger and more complex than was characteristic of California Indian societies, while the latter normally was applied to nomadic hunters having ill-defined territories. He proposed, therefore, *tribelet*, defining it as a group of fewer than five hundred people who were politically independent and owned land collectively. This was his most innovative contribution to the hearings. Indeed, while preparing for the hearings he drafted an article on the tribelet for a special issue of the new journal *Ethnohistory*, devoted to questions that ICC research posed for anthropologists (Kroeber 1955).

Following his discussion of the sociopolitical dimension of California Indian society, Kroeber turned to the kinds of evidence that would prove that Indians occupied the land and had concepts of ownership. First, he noted that Indians used land primarily for obtaining food, but they also used it for "travel, recreation, exploitation of mineral resources, and the like." "There is no question,"

Porter acted for the CCI. Shortly after signing on Kroeber received a letter from Glen Wilkinson asking him to be a witness for the Klamath, Modoc, and Yahooskin bands of Snake River Indians for their loss of territory. Kroeber declined, saying he'd signed an exclusive contract with the CCI. Wilkinson approached him again in the spring of 1953 and asked him to join the IOC group (AKP:GW/AK 1/8/53, AK/GW 1/25/53, WH/AK 4/1/53).

he declared, "but that the concept of ownership of certain defined tracts by the community or tribelet was quite definite among the California Indians, and that ordinarily the claims of each community were recognized by adjoining communities" (Kroeber 1954:47–48). Acknowledging instances of overlapping territories and disputes about boundaries, he nonetheless argued, "each community owned, wholly in and by itself and by inherent right, a certain tract of land. This was a universal *a priori* assumed by all California Indians." This notion that the political map of precontact America was static and divided into bounded territories occupied by autonomous groups was well established in American anthropology, going back at least to the pioneering work of James Mooney (1861–1921). Kroeber had mapped the distribution of California Indians this way nearly thirty years earlier in his classic handbook (1925).

Second, Kroeber stated that Indian groups resented unauthorized incursions into their territory, which demonstrated that they had a notion of "trespass." And third, he noted that peaceful crossing of territories normally took place by "invitation." Kroeber noted that California Indians commonly invited neighbors into their territories to take part in ceremonies or rituals when they had food surpluses to share. Kroeber's fourth and fifth lines of evidence concerned key features of Indian territories, namely, that they were permanent (static) and had defined limits. Regarding permanence, he noted that, where sufficient information existed, it was clear that the tracts of land Native groups held had remained largely unchanged for long periods of time. Most disruptions followed the onset of Euro-American settlement. Regarding territorial boundaries, Kroeber declared that "community or tribelet" landholdings had definite boundaries, though these were unmarked, since "technologically, the California Indians were too retarded to have put up continuous boundary indications such as fences; nor could they well have maintained them; nor was there need for them—there was no livestock to keep out nor planted gardens to protect" (1954:50–51).

Finally, Kroeber discussed private property. He noted that in some parts of the state individuals or families privately owned land "or its potentialities and usufructs." Still, "this condition did not obliterate the right of the community, but was clearly an added feature, something that had developed out of and on top of community ownership" (Kroeber 1954:54). He noted that the most extreme case for private ownership was in the northwestern part of the state among the Yurok and their neighbors, where "hunting, fishing, and gathering rights definitely were property, and could be bought and sold, or ceded in a settlement or marriage contract." Kroeber added: "It is significant that even among these groups it was only certain fishing places, or groves of oaks, and so on that were privately owned or claimed. They were, so to speak, spots carved out of the common public domain" (1954:55).

In early 1954, while he was still working on his report, he began helping to plan strategies for the hearings, which the commission had scheduled for the summer. Kroeber's correspondence with Hamilton and various other records that he kept during this period make it clear that all aspects of his participation were carefully scripted. It was during this time that Kroeber drafted "The Indians of California: Plan of Proof," which apparently was intended to be a general guide for the presentation of ethnohistorical data to the commission. In this plan he warned against making cultural generalizations: "There must be great caution—or even avoidance—of imposing from our culture and our law—or even those which fit the Eastern Algonquins, the Sioux, the Cuyamas or the Apaches upon the communities of California. . . . [T]he inquirer must be on his guard not to be shocked at the discovery that 'ownership' and 'occupancy'—like other aspects of their culture—present a bewildering miscellany among the Indians of California." After providing several pages of general questions that would have to be addressed concerning issues of cultural unity and diversity, political organization, the differential impact of Euro-American contact, and the varied ways California Indians made a living, Kroeber devoted a short closing section to "Land, and Its Occupancy," where he noted: "Here, even more than elsewhere, it is imperative that the facts be made to tell their own story, that the picture be induced from the concretions of Indian life." It was necessary, he continued, to consider whether Indians had words in their languages for "land," "property," and "ownership." Kroeber suspected they did not but subsequently changed his mind about the issue (AKP:undated plan, reel 153, 381–95, cf. RH/AK 2/4/54).

Although Kroeber and his team consulted thousands of published and unpublished sources, they drew most heavily on two. One was Kroeber's *Handbook of the Indians of California* (1925), and the other was a map of tribal areas he prepared. Kroeber worked particularly hard on the map, which involved revising the map that had appeared in his handbook, one that had been based mostly on linguistic data. Variants of Kroeber's map, referred to as Exhibits ALK 1–3, became the center of attention in all the California claims cases.

In May 1954, as the hearings loomed, Hamilton asked Kroeber for some last-minute advice about what should be included in the Indians' opening statement. Kroeber's reply outlined a methodology that has come to be known as the "direct historical approach":

> There should be a brief section on [the] character of *original* evidence on Indian occupation, how it ultimately rests on observation and especially on *information given* [in] statements made by natives, on how these are located in concrete detail but have to be . . . consolidated by the inquirer ("ethnologist"), and how such evidence being directed at pre-American conditions reaches back into the past *before 1850* and ties up with the documentary-historic reports [of] explorers & travelers, and with the archaeologists' discoveries. I think the unbroken continuity with the aboriginal past is the thing to emphasize here; also that the ethnologist

is a good deal like a judge eliciting ~~the true~~ facts ~~by~~ directed by unbounded questioning. I will write this. (AKP:AK/WH 5/17/54, emphasis in original)

Kroeber also stressed to Hamilton that some crucial anthropological terminology would have to be explained to the commission:

> There are some ~~other~~ words we anthropologists use in a special sense. . . . "Extinct" to us means a language, or culture is gone [not] that the people who spoke or lived it left no descendants; but the desc. may have become American. . . . "Unoccupied" land means without settlements, not "unused"; "Unclaimed" means swamps etc. occasionally visited or traversed, but without heavy subsistence . . . etc. Driver will collect such statements for Barney; and we ought to have an answer ready—perhaps say it first. (AKP:AK/WH 5/17/54)

Thus was Kroeber building an ethnohistorical argument that was the antithesis of the one he previously had proposed to the Justice Department, which had modeled a notion of the "gradient" stretching from settled village sites to the "watershed ridge" that separated one group's territory from that of its neighbor (AKP:AK/RL 8/28/52).

Kroeber and his team of experts, with the exception of Omer Stewart, had no prior experience as expert witnesses. To address this problem, Kroeber arranged to have Stewart conduct a seminar on his experience of testifying before the commission for Shoshone groups in the Great Basin cases (AKP:AK/WH 5/17/54). The seminar took place in Berkeley on March 5, 1954. Kroeber described it immediately afterward in a letter to Foster: "[The seminar] was extremely useful. Heizer and I went over the ground with him yesterday, and today he talked to the four of us—Cutter and Cook included—and answered questions. We agree that we have a new view of what will be needed in the way of testimony: especially preparation of a full series of specific exhibits" (AKP: AK/RF 3/6/54). As the hearings loomed Kroeber and Hamilton produced numerous drafts of questions for his evidence-in-chief and that of other team members. On the eve of his testimony Kroeber informed Hamilton that "my main concern is that my prepared Outline of Questioning be given over-all coherence so that the general order is preserved and I do not lose my place" (AKP:AK/WH 6/20/54).

By all accounts Kroeber performed brilliantly. The hearing took place in the Moot Court of the University of California–Berkeley law faculty in accordance with his wishes (AKP:AK/RF 4/24/54). Stewart, who was present, reported:

> Kroeber spoke or submitted to cross-examination for three hours a day for ten days. It was a masterful performance by a gifted scientist and talented, energetic scholar. Because of timing and emphasis, change of pace, and dozens of other practices which kept the interest of the Commissioners and others in the court room, Kroeber was an exceptionally impressive witness. The fifteen main points covered included a definition of anthropology, an explanation of ethnological

procedures, an evaluation of ethnogeography and demography, a characterization of California Indian political-territorial groups, an exposition on land use for food and other purposes, etc. (Stewart 1961:185)

Members of the CCI legal team also were pleased. They thought Kroeber had been their strongest witness (AKP:Thurman Arnold/AK 7/15/54). And Hamilton was particularly impressed, as an expansive letter to Kroeber suggests:

The proceeding at Berkeley was one of the events of a lifetime which stands sharply out. Never before have I taken part in an engagement in which anthropology, history and the law were so closely fused. The whole affair in the omnivorous indices of the law would be set down under the heading of administrative procedure, but that only indicates how little legal tags tell about the thing they are meant to describe. The words are silent in respect to the clash of cultures, each of which is a tangle in itself which touched off the whole affair. (AKP:WH/AK 12/30/54)

Contrary to what Steward and Theodora have said, Kroeber seems to have enjoyed the experience; writing to one of the Indians' lawyers, Thurman Arnold, who had missed the hearings to tell him how they were going, Kroeber reported:

They've had Cutter, Mareno, and Cook on since, and expect to end with Barrett today, but I have only hearsay on them all.

Hammy is a good general, and Reg [Reginald Foster] a dignified master of ceremonies and commissariat.

My wife probably was more troubled about my part than she let on and now admits she's glad it's over; but I rather had fun out of it. And [Commissioner Edgar] Witt and [Commissioner William] Holt certainly act as if they believe we had built up a real case.

Barney treated me with respect, and Hammy led off a most brilliant redirect, which stimulated Reg, [Francis] Goodwin, and Livey to fire in some pat questions, and so they ended me in a bit of a clamor on the afternoon of the eighth day.

The next morning I came down with laryngitis and have been wholly out of circulation since, good timing anyway. (AKP:AK/TA 7/7/54)

Cultural Ecology for the Defense

Until this time Kroeber seems to have had a largely dispassionate involvement in the claims process. But as his role changed during the hearings, the work became emotionally more difficult for him. He had begun as an authoritative presenter of interpretations and supporting evidence. As the hearings wore on, however, Kroeber found himself vigorously challenged by his students, who offered a new interpretation of California ethnohistory that departed from his classic culture-area work.

When the plaintiffs' witnesses concluded their testimony, the commission adjourned for over a year (an unusual procedure) before it reconvened in the autumn of 1955 to hear the defendant's evidence. Kroeber's correspondence reveals that, as the renewal of hearings approached, he became anxious that his friend Hamilton might not take part. Congress had not yet appropriated the additional funds the lawyers needed to carry on and, also, Hamilton was ill. Kroeber's concern about this issue prompted him to write to Arnold:

> In our respective ways, your firm and the anthropological experts in Berkeley are in the same position of having extended credit that now looks dubious.
>
> Hammy writes that it is unlikely that he will come for the June 27 hearing. He has not answered my inquiry as to who will conduct the case in his place.
>
> If your firm is withdrawing from, or curtailing your participation in case 37, I should much appreciate being advised of the fact. . . .
>
> Personally I feel that in view of the investment you have already made, it would be wise not to withdraw Hammy as captain and strategist of counsel while the hearings are actually on. I think that his non-appearance would be construed as an admission of defeat—writing off of a loss. (AKP:AK/TA 6/29/55)

At the beginning of June 1955 he wrote Hamilton directly to apply some moral pressure:

> I am exceedingly sorry that you are presumably not coming out for the June 27 [they did not begin until the autumn] hearings both because I shall miss you, and because of case 31-37.
>
> The moral effect of Arnold, Fortas & Porter not participating will be unfavorable on Indian clients, on the public, possibly on the commissioners.
>
> If you are presumably loaded with other work, three days of Arnold's presence at the opening would help lift morale mightily.
>
> We are certainly a bit waterlogged, and we may be a sinking ship, but we are not sunk yet.
>
> In fact, I'm betting we're going to make port and deliver cargo.
>
> Perhaps not. But if it turns out right, wouldn't A, F. & G feel just a bit sheepish at having pulled out when the going got thick? (AKP:AK/WH 6/3/55)

In the course of his correspondence regarding Hamilton's participation, Kroeber also made it clear that there were other members of the plaintiffs' legal team that he disliked; he did not want to work with them (in particular, Goodwin; AKP:AK/RF 6/23/55, AK/TA 7/12/55). In the event, the crisis over Hamilton's participation soon passed, to Kroeber's relief. At the end of June he wrote Arnold to tell him how pleased he was that Hammy was not going to be replaced by Goodwin. In a revealing gesture he signed his letter "'V' for victory, Alfred," a closing he used in his correspondence with other members of the legal team in July and August (AKP:AK/TA 6/29/55, AK/WH 7/20/55, AK/RF 8/1/55).

   While the issue about who would lead the cross-examination of the government's experts was being sorted out, the plaintiffs' team of lawyers and experts planned their approach to this next aspect of the case. It was understood from the outset that Kroeber would play a central role in formulating questions to be posed to the government's experts. But, thinking it risky for the team to rely solely on him, Kroeber warned Foster:

> I do not want the responsibility and load of being the only anthropological expert advising your battery of lawyers on cross-examination and rebuttal. Nor would it be wise for you to rely wholly on my health and strength. Barney has sewed up most of the Californianists. I think Omer [Stewart] has the local ethnological knowledge, shrewdness, and experience in court; and I can work with him. Can you and Hammy work with him? I am suggesting him as expert in 37, not 31. (AKP:AK/RF 6/23/55)

It was Hamilton who pursued this topic with Kroeber. Hamilton agreed that it was out of the question for Kroeber to carry the whole burden. He wanted both Stewart and Heizer to join Kroeber at the hearings and listen to the government's expert testimony:

> For listening and for strategy I personally prefer Bob Heizer to Omer Stewart. If, however, we find it necessary to put on witnesses in rebuttal, I would be inclined to pick Omer over Bob. This is not because Omer would have more to say, but because he would carry to the witness chair a good deal more self-assurance and would stand up a little better under fire. Here, as I think Bob himself will admit, his modesty carries with it a bit of liability, and Dr. Omer's self-assurance, which at times is a trial to all of us, may well prove to be an asset. (AKP:WH/AK 8/4/55)

Thus was Hamilton thinking beyond the cross-examination phase and considering the role that personalities play in courtroom theatrics. In the end, the legal team adopted Hamilton's three-man team approach but opted to use Heizer in rebuttal instead of Stewart.

Meanwhile, Barney had not revealed the government's defense strategy, even though the resumption of the hearings was now scheduled for early September. Kroeber, of course, was in the best position to anticipate it, as he did in a letter to Hamilton:

> I have no idea what line Barney will take, not even whether positive or negative. So far he has only denigrated and picked [acting as a cross-examiner]. I do not know what constructive thesis they could develop.
>
> He told me he would have Beals, Driver, Ermine [Wheeler-]Voegelin,[3] Julian Steward, [William Duncan] Strong, [Abraham] Halpern, [Walter] Goldschmidt. I know them all, of course and all their work that has ~~reference~~ relevance to California, and can sense to what kind of cross-examination some of them would be

---

3. Wheeler-Voegelin headed the Great Lakes and Ohio Valley Ethnohistorical Survey at Indiana University. It was funded by the Justice Department to support its defense against ICC claims (see Tanner 1991).

particularly vulnerable; but I am far from sure whether such tactics would be of value. . . .

I expect he will not forego his inclination to argue from lesser utilization of cer-tain portions of ~~their~~ territories to a lesser ownership of them. My way of meeting that would be by emphasizing territoriality as a basic fact of the life of *all* popula-tions in human history, and going on down to most birds and mammals and many fishes and insects: California Indian usages only exemplify an inescapable prin-ciple. (AKP:AK/WH 7/25/55, emphasis in original)

When the hearings resumed, Barney's witness list was as impressive as he had told Kroeber it would be. As Kroeber feared, Beals's team had chosen a path that was nearly identical to the one he had originally proposed to the Justice Department. Beals repackaged it as the "ecological theory" of California Indian history. He acknowledged being influenced by Ralph Linton, who in 1936 had proposed thinking of hunter-gatherer peoples' territories as having two compo-nents: an intensively exploited "home range" and a less-frequented "extended range" (Linton 1936; cf. Rigsby 1997:21). More important, one of Beals's key team members was Julian Steward, whose earlier work (1936, 1938) had estab-lished him as a leading cultural ecologist. Significantly, Steward made some of his most important theoretical advances in cultural ecology between 1952 and 1955, when he was deeply involved in the Shoshonean and California claims. Recently, anthropologists Bruce Rigsby (1997:24–27) and Sheree Ronaasen, Richard Clemmer, and Mary Rudden (1999:171–72) have argued that Stew-ard's effort to promote the government's case strongly influenced his thinking about cultural ecology. His approach involved focusing on the "culture core" to explain culture change. He was particularly interested in developing a multi-lineal cultural evolutionary model. Steward envisioned the culture core as be-ing the constellation of cultural traits and practices that were associated with a people's exploitation of their specific environment, or home range (1955b:30–42). He theorized that concepts of property and territoriality, of particular rel-evance to Indian claims, emerged at certain stages of technological and politi-cal development. In the Great Basin cases (Northern Paiute and Shoshone) he argued that the claimants' society had not advanced far enough for a system of landownership and tenure to emerge.

Under Beals's direction the Justice Department's team of ethnohistorical ex-perts applied emergent cultural ecological theories to California Indians. They grouped the state's Indians into different categories according to the kinds of fundamental cultural ecological adaptations they had made (RBP). In effect, they used culture cores to define the home ranges, or nuclear areas, of California Indian groups. These areas were determined by calculating the total amount of each group's territory needed for its primary subsistence. In essence, the nuclear areas were the spatial manifestations of the culture cores. For most ecological types the core area comprised a small fraction of a tribelet's homeland. The Justice Department argued that these core areas were the only lands the California Indians had effectively occupied before 1848. The Beals model further envisioned that land-use intensity diminished away from the home range toward an ill-defined outer margin. This meant that there were likely "no-man's-lands" and areas of overlap on the outer edges of tribal territories. The Beals model presented a dynamic geopolitical map that differed from Kroeber's static one. It served the government's purpose, since extant American case law and the ICC act indicated that Indian groups were eligible for compensation only if their ancestors had communally owned and occupied a distinct area to the exclusion of outsiders.[4]

In addition to advancing their ecological theory, Beals and his fellow experts argued that massive depopulation had taken place after contact, leaving large areas of the state effectively unoccupied when the United States gained control. Also, they contended, mostly through the testimony of Goldschmidt, that private ownership was a feature of northwestern California Indians, who depended on salmon. Such a notion, if accepted, threatened to undermine the legitimacy of the communal title claim, which was the only type eligible for compensation.

Experts, Lawyers, Cross-Examination, and Rebuttal

Beals gave each member of his team primary responsibility for a particular area of research. He distilled a 260-page report from the 4,000 pages of manuscript he received. In the end, the Justice Department did not submit the report to the commission. According to Beals, Barney decided "to use it as a basis for extended direct examination of the consultants and me on the witness stand. . . . He was thus able to ignore sections of the report that he thought might weaken the government defense or that might be vulnerable on cross-examination, particularly if wrenched out of context" (Beals 1985:148).

Beals found testifying to be extremely unpleasant: "Barney called me as his first anthropological witness. Putting the information he wanted to appear into the record was a slow process lasting, in my case, about three days, a tedious but

4. This line of defense against Indian claims before the ICC was not new. The Justice Department presented a similar, albeit less sophisticated, argument to the ICC in January 1952 to counter the Coeur d'Alene claim (Ross 1976). In that case, their expert divided tribal territories into three categories: nuclear areas (settlement sites), intermediate areas (adjacent to settlements and continually used for subsistence), and outlying areas (used only occasionally). It should be noted here that Steward employed a different strategy against the Northern Shoshone. In this case he argued that the claimants' ancestors had not developed a sufficiently complex society to facilitate the development of notions of landownership. Also, the resources that Northern Shoshone relied upon were too meager (Ronaasen et al. 1999:176–78).

relatively calm and rational proceeding." During Beals's evidence-in-chief
Barney had him explain the ecological theory (often referred to as ecological
anthropology) that underpinned the more detailed regional studies the other
government experts would present. According to Beals, the cross-examination
that followed "was a shock, a brutal attempt at intimidation attacking my accuracy and credibility. . . . The lawyer hectored, shouted, bullied, shook his
thick forefinger under my nose until I was almost overcome by a desire to snap
at it with my teeth. . . . The experience was gruelling and emotionally and
physically exhausting. I was outraged and felt degraded" (1985:149). The other
government witnesses also were subjected to a withering cross-examination.
Driver, who had played a leading role in helping the government's lawyers
cross-examine Kroeber, was subjected to particularly harsh questioning. He was
the statistician of the group who had helped develop the formulas the government's experts used to calculate the land-use intensities. The cross-examiners
demonstrated that the scheme, which seemed to be based on precise scientific
calculations, was, in fact, an educated guess.

It is notable that Beals, in common with his other team members, blamed the
plaintiffs' lawyers for his wrenching experience on the witness stand. He said
that members of his and Kroeber's teams of experts remained on friendly terms
throughout the hearings, dining together daily, albeit being careful not to discuss the case. Beals reported that on one occasion Kroeber got so upset by the
plaintiffs' lawyers' cross-examination of the government witnesses that he
threatened to withdraw from the proceedings (1985:151). This view appears to
confirm Theodora's memory of events. What Beals seems to have been unaware
of was the extent to which Kroeber, and Heizer and Stewart also, were involved
behind the scenes. Kroeber's papers make it clear, for instance, that he played a
major role in developing the cross-examination strategy and edited various
drafts of the proposed lists of questions. In addition, he provided questions for
the lawyers based on the unfolding testimony of individual witnesses.

Regarding the latter activity, Kroeber's papers contain a file marked "Notes
for examination [of Beals, Ralph]," which shows how meticulously Kroeber carried out his task as coinquisitor. For example, he prepared notes instructing the
cross-examining lawyer, Donald Gormley, how to respond to Beals's answer to
a question about whether Indians used mountain uplands. If Beals replied no or
gave a qualified affirmative answer, Gormley was to take him to seven exhibits
that demonstrated upland usage. Kroeber also had tactics to deal with any mis-
takes he thought Beals made. For example, Beals had testified there were no
deer in the Central Valley before European contact. Kroeber cites contrary evidence for the lawyer. Recalling the case years later, Beals thought he'd done
well under cross-examination, only being tripped up once concerning this particular issue (1985:149).

When the defendant rested its case, Heizer and Kroeber returned to the stand in rebuttal. Kroeber's preparation for this stage of the hearings and his rebuttal testimony indicate that he was willing to assail the government's defense team because they had challenged his anthropological understanding of California Indians. He also believed that the Beals approach did not take into account the totality of cultural-environmental relationships the way his culture-area approach did. Furthermore, Kroeber thought the Beals approach tended to substitute theory for essential cultural and environmental detail. His attitude is made clear in the answers Kroeber proposed to make to a series of questions that Goodwin intended to ask him when he appeared in rebuttal. In response to a proposed two-part question that asked what the ecological approach showed and why it should have been used, Kroeber sketched out a three-point reply he intended to make:

(1) Novelty. Seems to upset Powers-Powell-Merriam-Kroeber standard ethnic classifications, thus confuses interpretation; (2) Allows singling out a part of a habitat which is within one life-zone or ecologic type, as being typical or important, and minimizing or discarding the rest . . . ; (3) End by denying or belittling most of area actually used. Is unrealistic—far from actual situation. User likely to drift from fact into hypothesis by selection—by artificial tearing apart of actual situation. (AKP:"Rebuttal Testimony," 511–22)

Kroeber's appearance in rebuttal gave Barney one last chance to spar with him through cross-examination. Regarding the issue of equating intensity of land use with effective "use and occupancy," Kroeber chose not to deny the government's assertion that the Indians could have made their livelihood from small portions of their traditional territories. Instead, he pointed out that that was true of primitive and advanced societies alike around the world, citing Japan and modern California as examples (NAR:3305–6). The defendant's perspective, Kroeber argued, overlooked the nonutilitarian aspects of land use. Barney then asked him how the Indians used the land other than for making a livelihood from it. Kroeber replied, "Well, he got a lot of intangibles, like the view and feeling happy and . . . secure which are important things in life. He got freedom to travel [and] . . . to live his life his way. He may have gone on a mountain top to get supernatural power which he believe[d] in, which is the same thing as the Christian belief in God" (NAR:3335). Barney asked Kroeber if he meant to imply by this statement that "what we ought to pay the Indian for is the loss of his native culture?" Kroeber replied, "We ought to pay him for his native possessory rights which he felt he had and which were violated from his point of view." Barney persisted, inquiring if possessory rights were supposed to include nonutilitarian uses of the land. Kroeber used this opportunity to elaborate his perspective:

That is included among other things. If your point is actual use for food and shelter and clothing and so on and the rest doesn't matter I don't think—you have got to have your food and you have got to have sleep and shelter but that isn't the whole of life to an Indian any more than it is to us. I see it always as a larger whole in which the subsistence is basic and they pyramid up into the sunshine and supernatural. (NAR:3336)

Regarding the depopulation issue, Kroeber noted there was no scholarly consensus on the extent of depopulation in different parts of the state (NAR:3311). The issue was irrelevant in any event, Kroeber contended: the diminution of local Indian populations did not necessarily lead groups to reduce the size of the territories they exploited and claimed as their own. Rather, they simply harvested fewer resources from these traditional territories (NAR:3346–48). Regarding the issue of private ownership in northwestern California, Kroeber (and Heizer) maintained that individual and family ownership was subordinate to the group's collective title.

Barney, of course, held an ace in his hand that he waited until the end to play. His team of experts resented the fact that the plaintiffs' lawyers had "ridiculed the ecological approach" they employed (Beals 1985:149). Barney therefore produced the letter Kroeber had written to Luttrell three years earlier and made Kroeber read it to the commission (NAR:box 3041). Beals recalled this episode with relish:

> I was delighted when defendant's lawyer, Ralph Barney, produced a letter Kroeber had written before he agreed to help the plaintiffs and was still seriously considering undertaking work for the government. In this letter, Kroeber outlined almost exactly the same ecologic approach we had developed. Faced with this letter (and about as discomfited as I ever saw Kroeber), under cross-examination he admitted the validity of the ecological position and conclusions derived from it. (1985:149)

As Beals indicates, Kroeber was embarrassed by Barney's action. No doubt he was angry as well, since, as noted earlier, he had expected the government to treat their earlier negotiations as confidential. This probably explains why he seems to have developed a loathing for Barney afterward. For example, even before the hearings concluded the two sides had begun drafting their proposed findings of fact. The experts helped the lawyers with these tasks and assisted them in crafting replies to their opponents' findings after they had been filed before the commission. In March 1959, four years after the hearings, the plaintiffs' lawyers sent Kroeber a copy of Barney's supplemental proposed findings and asked him to critique it. Kroeber did so in three installments. When sending the last one in mid-April, he appended a note saying: "I have gone after Barney hard as regards accuracy and evidence, and I hope without bickering, but I pulled no punches. He proves to be pretty despicable, without regard to truth and only contempt for honesty" (AKP:AK/Robert Barker 4/14/59).

Fact and Theory in Court

Kroeber and his students' involvement in the California Indian claims suggests a number of general issues associated with the participation of ethnohistorical experts in litigation. We have seen that Kroeber and his students became entangled in the litigation process shortly after the claims were filed (Stage 2). They approached the research and writing of their reports (Stage 3) in much the same ways they would have for academic purposes. During the process of testifying, especially when being cross-examined and presenting rebuttal testimony (Stage 4), the opposing sides became committed to the interpretation of California Indian history they advanced in support of their clients. As Beals admitted, "The entire research staff over time became unconsciously biased toward the defendant's needs. In the adversary relationship, the government became 'our' side. This attitude became much more overt once the hearings actually began, reinforced in part by the behavior of one of the lawyers for the plaintiffs" (1985:147–48). Kroeber, on the other hand, blamed the government's lead lawyer, Ralph Barney. Blaming the lawyers on the opposite side in this way, the anthropologists used them as scapegoats to avoid openly expressing any hostilities they might have felt toward one another. We have seen, however, that the experts helped in the detailed planning of the cross-examinations and fed the lawyers the questions that highlighted the weaknesses of opposing colleagues' testimony. In other words, by hiding behind the lawyers these experts tried to avoid testing old friendships and collegial relations.

In this respect, the California hearings were not unique when compared to other ICC cases. By the mid-1950s such cases were generating professional and personal tensions among the ethnohistorians who were participating as expert witnesses. These tensions were dividing forensic anthropologists into two camps, those who worked for the Indians and those who worked for the government. The first group believed they had a moral and professional obligation to work for Indians (Ray 2006). Those who worked for the government, on the other hand, tended to believe their primary responsibility was to provide objective scientific information when asked to do so. Anthropologists became so concerned about this division that they devoted panels to it at two national meetings, one in Detroit in 1954 and one at Bloomington in 1955. Sol Tax, editor of the *American Anthropologist,* chaired the second symposium, which took place at a joint meeting of the American Ethnological Society and the Central States Anthropological Society. Many prominent anthropologists and archaeologists attended, including several of the experts who were engaged in the California claims (Driver, Steward, Strong, and Wheeler-Voegelin).

In his opening remarks, Tax explained why he had become so worried about the problem:

As editor of the *American Anthropologist* I received a paper on one side of this issue. Then I received several letters saying "Don't you dare publish it." That is why I wanted to have this meeting here. It is better to get out any bad blood rather than leave these things unsaid. Anthropologists have got themselves in a position where they are impugning the motives of other anthropologists. Anthropology is in a bad position right now. The bickering and accusations that result from claims cases threaten the whole profession, especially when it is all kept underground. (AKP:5/5/55)

Tax worried that the inability of expert witnesses to be detached professionals cast doubt on their credibility as social scientists. But he also worried that anthropological knowledge could be used to override the needs and wishes of the Indians (Stocking 2000:193–97). Both issues remain salient today (cf. Rigsby 1995).

Similar to other ICC cases, the California claims also starkly demonstrated the extent to which the statements of claims and the legal objectives of the plaintiffs and defendants established the polarities of the debate that took place between the opposing experts. Leading off the Bloomington symposium, Tax summarized this problem as it related to ICC cases more generally:

The basic land issue seems to be the contiguous boundary theory vs. the vague nuclear territory theory. The Contiguous Boundary Theory draws tribal distribution maps as though there were boundaries. The other theory says that there was a territory which was used, which may overlap, or between which there may have been interstices.

The government likes the second view better because it saves them money. The Indians like the first view best. The plaintiff tries to prove continuous boundaries. . . .

Since the burden of proof is on the plaintiff, they have to prove boundaries. The government doesn't have to. Thus the United States has the advantage of our ignorance. The anthropologist functions well if he doesn't know on the government side, but the tribal anthropologist *has* to know. Thus the government anthropologist can be holier-than-thou, and ask: "How do you know? Were you there?" (AKP:5/5/55)

This problem is still with us (cf. Ray 2003). The plaintiffs bear the burden of proof, which means that it is often sufficient for the defendant's witnesses merely to raise doubts. At any point in time there is a sufficient diversity of theoretical perspectives to do this. These perspectives also serve to identify what are considered "data" and to provide a scheme for interpreting it. As Steward put it at the time of the California Indian claims:

In a scientific and literal sense, virtually no evidence presented in these cases can properly be called "primary evidence," "first-hand knowledge," or an "eyewitness account." It is therefore ridiculous to proclaim: "the facts speak for themselves." . . . In using this secondary, or predigested evidence, both from the Indian informant and the historical source, the anthropologist redigests it according to his own point of view. He himself becomes "evidence" in that his testimony is based to an incalculable extent upon his theory (explicit or implicit), his experiences among the people, his travels over the territory, his reading of the historic documents and his broader knowledge of primitive people. (1955a:300–301)

Commenting on this issue over thirty years later and in relation to the Canadian context, ethnologist Edward Rogers observed: "Although academics have traditionally debated their views through the medium of publication in scholarly journals, the issues are no longer the innocent disagreements that once occurred in these journals, although they may at times be equally vitriolic" (1986:211).

In the instance of Kroeber and his students it is clear that the California claims exposed an emergent cleavage within the "Berkeley school." As a Boasian particularist Kroeber disdained the adoption of positivist methodologies and organized his evidence in terms of historically given culture (and especially linguistic) areas and the autonomous groups that lived within them. In contrast, Driver and Steward, who were on the opposing defendant's team of experts, were interested in developing theories about culture change based on cross-cultural comparisons. The "ecological theory" of California Indians they helped Beals develop reflected this different outlook. The Beals team challenged the relevance of a linguistic-based approach to land-tenure issues. As an alternative they presented to the commission what was, in essence, a comparative ecological study of five hundred different Indian groups generalized into six ecotypes that were based on subsistence land use. Kroeber objected to the use of this approach before the ICC because its main purpose was to whittle down the scope of Indian claims by ignoring nonsubsistence activities. Furthermore, he questioned the validity of most of the land-use intensity calculations, which, he thought, imparted a false sense of scientific precision. More generally, Kroeber recognized that Beals's ecological approach presented a perspective on California Indian history that differed from the one he had spent a lifetime developing. Beals, on the other hand, was proud of his team's accomplishment for this very reason. He understood that their model was innovative. This was why Beals was pleased when his report, which Barney had withheld from the commission for strategic reasons, was published in 1974 (Beals and Hester 1974). Significantly, even Kroeber's teammate, Heizer, who also assailed the ecological model before the commission, subsequently adopted it in a book he coauthored in 1980 (Heizer and Elsasser 1980).

In the end the commission found Kroeber to be the most convincing witness. In these hearings, as in those of most other claims, commissioners opted for more traditional cultural anthropological perspectives and questioned the utilitarian outlook offered by cultural ecologists. Based on this older anthropological outlook, the commissioners concluded that California Indian claimants collectively had been illegally dispossessed of 64,435,000 acres of land. (This included other groups who had not been involved in Dockets 31 and 37; see Stewart 1978:708.) Rather than engaging in further litigation about the evaluation of these lands, lawyers representing the claimants persuaded their clients to opt for a negotiated settlement. After protracted discussions with the Justice Department, in 1963 the lawyers representing the Indians obtained a settlement of $29.1 million, which, before the lawyers' fees of slightly more than $2.6 million were deducted, amounted to a mere forty-five cents an acre.

Acknowledgments

I would like to acknowledge the financial assistance of the Canada Council Killam Fellowship Program and the Social Sciences and Humanities Research Council of the Canada Research Grant Program, which have made this research possible. I would like to express my appreciation to the staffs at the Bancroft Library, University of California–Berkeley, and at the National Anthropological Archives, Smithsonian Institution, Suitland, Maryland, for their cheerful and generous help. I would also like to thank Dr. Dianne Newell, History Department, University of British Columbia, and Dr. Bruce Rigsby, professor emeritus, Department of Anthropology and Sociology, University of Queensland, for their comments and suggestions.

References Cited

Beals, R. 1968. Alfred L. Kroeber. *International Encyclopedia of the Social Sciences*, 8:454–63.
———. 1985. The Anthropologist as Expert Witness: Illustrations from the California Indian Land Claims Case. In Sutton 1985:139–55.
Beals, R., and J. Hester. 1974. *Indian Land-Use and Occupancy in California*. 3 vols. New York.
Harris, M. 1968. *The Rise of Anthropological Theory*. London.
Heizer, R., and A. B. Elsasser. 1980. *The Natural World of the California Indians*. Berkeley, CA.
Kroeber, A. L. 1925. *Handbook of the Indians of California*. Washington, D.C.
———. 1954 [1974]. Basic Report on California Land Holdings. In *Indian Land Use and Occupancy in California*. Ed. R. Beals, 9–68. New York.
———. 1955. Nature of the Land-Holding Group. *Ethnohistory* 2:303–14.
Kroeber, T. 1970. *Alfred Kroeber: A Personal Configuration*. Berkeley, CA.
Linton, R. 1936. *The Study of Man*. New York.
Lurie, N. 1985. Epilogue. In Sutton 1985:363–82.
Ray, A. 2003. Native History on Trial: Confessions of an Expert Witness. *Canadian Historical Review* 84:253–73.

———. 2006. Anthropology, History and Aboriginal Rights: Politics and the Rise of Ethnohistory in North America. In *Pedagogies of the Global: Knowledge in the Human Interest*. Ed. A. Dirlik. Chicago.

Rigsby, B. 1995. Anthropologists, Land Claims and Objectivity: Some Canadian and Australian Cases. In *Native Title: Emerging Issues for Research, Policy and Practice*. Ed. J. Finlayson and D. E. Smith, 23–38. Canberra.

———. 1997. Anthropologists, Indian Title and the Indian Claims Commission: The California and Great Basin Cases. In *Fighting Over Country*. Ed. J. Finlayson and D. E. Smith, 15–45. Canberra.

Rogers, E. 1986. Epilogue. *Anthropologica* 28:203–16.

Ronaasen, S., et al. 1999. Rethinking Cultural Ecology, Multilinear Evolution, and Expert Witnesses: Julian Steward and the Indian Claims Commission Proceedings. In *Julian Steward and the Great Basin*. Ed. R. Clemmer et al., 170–202. Salt Lake City.

Rosenthal, H. D. 1990. *Their Day in Court: A History of the Indian Claims Commission*. New York.

Ross, N. A., ed. 1976. *Expert Testimony before the Indian Claims Commission* (microform). New York.

Rowe, J. H. 1962. Alfred Louis Kroeber. *American Antiquity* 27:395–415.

Steward, J. 1936. Economic and Social Basis of Primitive Bands. In *Essays in Anthropology Presented to A. L. Kroeber in Celebration of His Sixtieth Birthday, June 11, 1936*. Ed. R. Lowie, 331–50. Berkeley, CA.

———. 1938. *Basin-Plateau Aboriginal Groups*. Bulletin no. 120, Bureau of American Ethnology. Washington, D.C.

———. 1955a. Theory and Application in Social Science. *Ethnohistory* 2:292–302.

———. 1955b. *Theory of Culture Change*. Urbana, IL.

———. 1973. *Alfred Kroeber*. New York.

Stewart, O. 1961. Kroeber and the Indian Claims Commission Cases. *Kroeber Anthropological Society Papers* 25:181–90.

———. 1978. Litigation and Its Effects. In *Smithsonian Institution Handbook of North American Indians*, vol. 8: *California*. Washington, D.C.

Stocking, G. W. 2000. "Do Good, Young Man": Sol Tax and the World Mission of Liberal Democratic Anthropology. *History of Anthropology* 9:171–264.

Sutton, I., ed. 1985. *Irredeemable America: The Indians' Estate and Land Claims*. Albuquerque, NM.

Tanner, A. 1986. The New Hunting Territory Debate. *Anthropologica* 28:19–36.

Tanner, H. H. 1991. Erminie Wheeler-Voegelin (1903–1988), Founder of the American Society for Ethnohistory. *Ethnohistory* 31:58–72.

Manuscript Sources

AKP   Alfred Kroeber Papers. Bancroft Library, University of California–Berkeley. Those pertaining to Indian land claims are found in Series 4: Indian Land Claims, 1904–62, BANC Film 2049.

NAR   National Archives and Records Administration, Washington, D.C., Indian Claims Commission Transcripts of Testimony.

RBP   Ralph Beals Papers. National Anthropological Archives, Smithsonian Institu-
        tion, Suitland, MD. Box 30, file labeled "Dept. of Justice: Research Plans, Corr.
        A Research Program related to the Claims Brought Against the United States
        Government by the Indians of California."
RHP   Robert Heizer Papers. Bancroft Library, University of California–Berkeley.
        BANC Film 2106.

Index

Abraham, Major Roy, 142, 146, 169–70, 174, 207
Abubakar, Iya, 204
Adler, Felix, 80
African Studies Association, 176
Afrocentrism, 229
Ahmadu Bello University, 204
Ajibola, Idowu, 210
Albizu Campos, Pedro, 118
Amali, Samson, 197–98, 203, 206, 210–13, 231
Andaman Homes, 44, 47, 51, 53, 57
Andrade, Manuel, 105
Anthropological Survey of India, 42
Anthropology and penology, 43–46
Arapaho Indians, 107–9
Armstrong, Robert G.: at Atlanta University, 114–17, 167–69, 176, 185; and Cold War politics, 172–73, 177–82; and the Communist Party, 103, 105–7, 111–12, 121, 129–30, 141–42, 148, 158–62, 167, 177–82, 216–20; dialectical materialism of, 121–29, 134, 150, 218, 220; doctoral thesis on African state formation, 112–14, 116–17, 132–40, 147–48, 192–93; early education, 102–4; and E. Evans-Pritchard, 129–32, 134, 140, 147, 149, 175; and the FBI, 129–30, 158, 161, 168–69, 177–82; fieldwork in Nigeria, 144–46, 151–55, 220; funeral of, 210–13; graduate studies at the University of Chicago, 104–9; homosexuality of, 215–16; influence of, 222–35; and the Institute of African Studies, 190, 194–95, 198–201; masters thesis on Cheyenne and Arapaho, 107–9, 220, 232; military service, 109–12; and John Murra, 105–6, 114n, 117–21, 146–49, 151–53, 162, 220, 234; Puerto Rico research of, 117–21, 126, 215, 220, 232; rapport with African colleagues, 195–96, 202n; and Robert Redfield, 105, 107, 112, 114, 118, 126, 129, 132, 140–41, 147–

51, 154, 156, 159–62, 164–67, 174–76, 220, 234; and the study of oral literature, 192–94, 201, 226n; study of West African languages, 149, 155, 170–72, 184–90, 195, 203–7, 230
Armstrong, Robert P., 222, 229
Arnold, Thurman, 261
Atlanta University, 114–17, 120, 152–53, 163
Azikiwe, Nnamdi, 144, 182–84

Balewa, Tafawa, 183
Barnes, Albert, 90–91, 93
Barnes, Sandra, 203
Barney, Ralph, 253, 255, 257, 260, 261, 263, 267–69, 271
Battle of Aberdeen, 49
Beals, Ralph, 249, 263–69, 271
Beier, Ulli, 196, 201
Benedict, Ruth, 87, 88, 93, 94, 147
Biafra, 190–91
Bildung, 79–81
Bingham, Ernestine, 105, 145
Boas, Franz: and aesthetic style, 86–88; and cultural diffusion, 81–88, 93–94; and the culture concept, 70–75, 82, 94; and W. E. B. DuBois, 69, 77–81, 88–90, 229; and the Harlem Renaissance, 69–71, 88–91; and Zora Neale Hurston, 69; *Mind of Primitive Man*, 86, 93; and race, 75–79, 228; mentioned, 231
Bodin, Jean, 13, 19, 27
Bohanan, Paul, 223–24
Boorde, Andrew, 26–27
Bose, Netaji Subhas Chandra, 42
Bott, Elizabeth, 146, 148
Bourdieu, Pierre, 33
Bourne, Randolph, 70
British Colonial Social Science Research Council, 117, 120, 156
British Museum, 44, 52
Browder, Earl, 110–11, 217

—